MARKETING

For All the Marbles Every day

2018 Edition

People and events shaping the continuing evolution of marketing practice

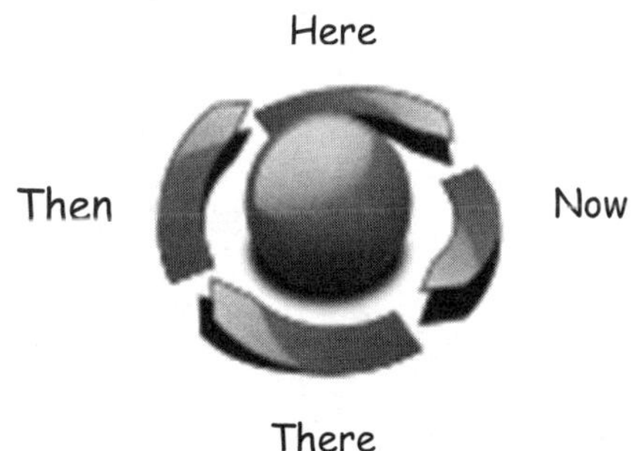

Charles L. Martin, Ph.D.
Wichita State University
Charles.Martin@wichita.edu

CIBER Publications: Derby, KS USA
www.MarketingMarbles.com

Library of Congress Cataloging-in-Publication Data

Martin, Charles L.

Marketing For All the Marbles Every Day / Charles L. Martin – 2018 edition

p. cm.

Includes index.

ISBN: 978-0-9981227-2-4 (hardback)

ISBN: 978-0-9981227-3-1 (softback)

To… Marilyn.

From marketing fame to marketing flame!

For 28+ years, she has always been marbleous,

and has always been there for me.

Thank you SHPCDFLOMLAOWAB !

Contents

Welcome Students!

Overview of *Marketing FAME*, rationale for the unique content and format, quotations from students who have read *Marketing FAME*, and a few suggestions to extract the most value from reading the book.

Day by day planner and content

Daily planner includes ample space to note objectives, reminders, hourly appointments and dead-lines for the day. **Content** includes 743 stories of influential people and events shaping marketing practice -- each organized by a key day of the year associated with the people and events. One or more stories are included for every day of the year.

Index

A detailed alphabetized list with more than 11,000 entries – representing 754 individuals, 594 organizations and brands, 423 holidays, events and occasions, 49 U.S.states, 102 countries, and a countless number of topics and concepts found in this year's edition of *Marketing FAME*.

About the author

A brief biographical sketch of the author, Dr. Charles L. Martin, the Full Professor of Marketing in the W. Frank Barton School of Business at Wichita State University in south central Kansas, USA. Contact information is included.

Welcome Students!

Welcome to the 2018 edition of the annual book series, ***Marketing For All the Marbles Every day*** – or ***Marketing FAME,*** for short. This is a different kind of business book that combines unique content with a unique calendar format to create a reading experience like no other – one that challenges you to think about business, marketing and your career in fresh, new ways. Gratefully, *Marketing FAME* resonates with the overwhelming majority of college students who read it. If you're like them, you'll find the reading experience informative, interesting, occasionally humorous, and definitely worthwhile. Read some of their comments in the accompanying boxes.

Because of the book's unique content and format, this "Welcome" section describes some of the ways *Marketing FAME* differs from traditional business textbooks and makes a few suggestions to help you extract the most value from it. If you're an instructor, feel free to contact us for ideas and suggestions to help you use *Marketing FAME* in your courses.

"This was by far my favorite text to read because of the ability to create additional thought in almost every section. I really liked [*Marketing FAME*] because of the nature of the text. It didn't seem like a textbook and included many real-world examples, which is the type of content that I prefer to read." – Jacob, senior sports management student

"*Marketing FAME*… was without a doubt the most interesting 'textbook' that I have had in college." – Marie B., senior business student

"I really enjoyed reading the *FAME* book and I did learn a lot from it. I was able to see marketing in a different light and for that I am thankful!" – Marina, senior marketing major

743 stand-alone stories

To begin, this year's edition of *Marketing FAME* consists of 743 short, concisely-written sections or entries we'll call "stories" – averaging about 160 words. Because the stories are short and to the point, key take-away points are readily apparent. And the book can be read quickly in small daily doses, as time permits.

Marketing FAME
2018 Edition

Contains **743** stories, representing…

- **754** individuals
- **594** organizations & brands
- **423** holidays, events, and occasions
- **49** U.S. states
- **102** countries
- **A countless number of topics**

Each story stands on its own, so to speak, so you don't have to read them in the same order they appear in *Marketing FAME*. You can read them in any order you or your instructors prefer. The detailed index includes more than 11,000 entries, so there's a good chance it will lead you to the specific concepts, topics, companies, events, or people that interest you.

However, it's a good idea to read many of the stories near the calendar date on which they are presented. Doing so will help sensitize you to the numerous windows of marketing opportunity that open wide during some periods of the year, but may be closed at other times. For example, in early January, read the stories that correspond to the pages for January 1 and January 2 regarding New Year's resolutions. By reading these stories early in the year, you'll be more likely to notice and learn from the marketing efforts that pop up in your community and in your favorite media at that time of year – timely advertisements and promotions that tap into consumers' interests in setting personal goals in early January. Similarly, by reading about "March madness" a few weeks later (March 15), you'll have a heightened sense of awareness of some of the business and marketing implications that arise during that annual period of high interest in college basketball. New Year's resolutions and "March madness" are only two examples; dozens of other specific holidays, occasions, and calendar-linked events are discussed throughout the year, and hundreds of others are noted.

Even if you first read the stories out of sequence, using the appointment block (to the left of each day's stories) to manage your own day-to-day affairs will serve as a daily reminder to revisit the stories of the day and think about the windows of marketing opportunity that may be open for that day or period of the year.

> "I liked the non-continuity of [*Marketing FAME*]. Textbooks are topic 1 is pages 1-30, etc. *FAME* was unpredictable and exciting to read."
> – Andrew, MBA student

> *Marketing FAME* "gives ideas of the different methods of marketing that students can use. It's interesting to see not only businesspeople, but non-businesspeople perform marketing in different ways and all be successful. Seeing the different industries' approaches to marketing gives a well-rounded perspective of how students can use and consider using marketing in their careers. Overall, *Marketing FAME* is very insightful."
> – Jessica B., MBA student

> "I liked the humor and entertaining stories to illustrate concepts." – Nathan, MBA student

Invitation to think critically

> "I think the quotations were awesome. I even wrote some of them and shared them with my friends while I was reading it." – Lena, MBA student

The 743 stories are about people and events that have contributed to the evolution of business and marketing practice. Many include thought-provoking direct quotes that represent the featured person's perspective, but not necessarily the only perspective or the most commonly-shared perspective; other opinions may be found elsewhere in *Marketing FAME*.

> "[I like the] thought-provoking questions. I also like how there are many subjective questions that gives the reader something to think about."
> – Stuart R., MBA student

Multiple points of view from businesspeople as well as non-businesspeople are included to show variability in thought about important issues and how "conventional" wisdom is not always universally embraced. Accompanying many of the more debatable perspectives are explicit invitations for you to "Agree or Disagree?" For example, two separate stories quoting business leaders on July 9 first challenge you to consider whether marketers place too much reliance on price, and then to entertain the possibility that sales contest winners should be rewarded with merchandise prizes rather than cash prizes. These are two examples of the dozens of opportunities you will have to "Agree or Disagree?" throughout the edition. Further, numerous other discussion questions are raised throughout the year. Be prepared, as your instructors may wish to discuss these and other issues in class.

> "It is interesting to read such a variety of topics and ideas in one book. I was unfamiliar with many of the names and their stories – some inspirational and some cautionary." – Jennifer P., MBA student

> "Very unique and interesting to read. It was a nice change from your standard textbook."
> – Kara, senior marketing major

> "Interesting reading with a lot of useful information that was presented in a concise, thought-provoking manner." – Ragadeesh, MBA student

Marketing and more

As you read, and hopefully savor and digest *Marketing FAME*, you'll notice the inclusion of a wide variety of issues pertaining to topics you'd expect to find in a "marketing" book. Examples include branding, buyer behavior, pricing, promotion, advertising, distribution, customer service, marketing research, personal selling, publicity, retailing, international trade, and so on. Again, explore the detailed index in the back of the book to see what other marketing topics are included.

> "The information available in *Marketing FAME* can definitely be utilized in our marketing jobs."
> – Akhilesh, MBA student

But *Marketing FAME*'s content is not restricted solely to mainstream marketing topics. Also included are stories and perspectives that address more general career-boosting topics such as leadership, decision-making, problem-solving, technology, human relations, innovation, ethics, teamwork and quality, to name a few. Regardless of where your career path leads – marketing or otherwise – you should find these topics to be highly-relevant.

> *Marketing FAME* "provides numerous challenges and intellectual questions urging the reader to consider multiple points of view."
> – Shawn, MBA student

Emotional distinction

Marketing FAME's story format is not only unique, but advantageous in that it facilitates communication to *both* your head and your heart. That is, dozens of stories nudge you to read beyond the key descriptive details of "information" to consider the emotional context of the stories as well. How do consumers *feel* about various holidays and occasions? What do entrepreneurs *feel* when they encounter setbacks or risk all of their savings to start or grow their companies? Don't be surprised if you feel inspired or motivated by some stories, angered by some and saddened by others.

> "I liked the humanization of marketing." – John E., MBA student

For <u>all</u> of us !

As a future marketing professional, it may be difficult for you to *truly* understand what many holidays and occasions mean to your customers and prospective customers if you don't make an effort to experience these important days emotionally. And as a future business decision-maker, it's okay -- even desirable -- if you find yourself empathizing with people featured in the stories or vicariously experiencing emotions of hopeful anticipation or anxiety, elation or disappointment, compassion or callousness, that challenge them and add to the complexity of business decisions. Go ahead and laugh, cry, or pound your fist as you see fit. The emotions will broaden your understanding of the stories and the story-makers, etch them in your memory, and help prepare you for the range of emotions you'll surely encounter throughout your career.

"To see something whether it be a story, quote or just a small reminder every day like the ones in the book would be [to] put a positive start to your day… Not many book/calendars are like this one, with inspirational quotes and stories."
– Anonymous undergraduate student in an introductory marketing course

Now and then

Many of the 743 stories are about present-day people and events that sculpt the practice of marketing. Many others represent contributions of yesteryear that shaped the direction of marketing's evolution and, more often than not, continue to resonate with today's marketing professionals. In other words, *Marketing FAME* includes a mix of both past and present – a blend that's essential to understanding marketing today, how the field has evolved throughout history, and how its future may unfold.

"Enjoyed the historical stories. Best way to avoid future failure is by studying the past." – William, MBA student

"*Marketing FAME* did a great job helping me realize how marketing is an ever-changing field. I'll never be bored in this field." – Anastasia, MBA student

Of course, *Marketing FAME*'s inclusion of many topics' historical backgrounds enables you to learn from the experience and wisdom of past generations – lessons that continue to be relevant today. Further, understanding the history behind an occasion, event, idea or practice offers three other benefits that you might not have considered. First, your effectiveness as a marketer developing tie-in promotions to celebrate or otherwise observe occasions and historical events or people will be limited if you know little about the occasions, events or people. Stanley Marcus, former President and CEO of Neiman-Marcus, the Texas-based department store chain, once observed how employees with liberal arts backgrounds grounded in history tended to be more effective than business school graduates in terms of creating in-store displays to commemorate holidays and events. All too often, Marcus lamented, employees from business schools simply did not understand the occasions as well.

Marketing FAME "did a great job at combining current events and marketing related perspectives." – Courtney, senior marketing major

"Historical and present-day quotes are inspiring, and it's interesting to know how the marketing terms were developed… It is more interesting to read [*Marketing FAME*] compared to a traditional marketing textbook because it includes actual stories, variety of data, and events." – Eri, undergraduate marketing major

Second, the historical perspectives challenge you to understand the dynamic and ever-changing nature of the business world. To be successful in most careers, you must embrace and participate in the evolution. More specifically, several stories show how common business practices that we may take for granted today did not exist until someone dreamed, developed and implemented them. For example, it is commonplace today for retail stores to use coat-hangers to display clothing items and save labor, but that wasn't the case before the coat-hanger was invented and adopted by retailers. Previously, retail clerks spent a large portion of their day folding, unfolding and refolding clothes. Accordingly, this aspect of *Marketing FAME* is intended to help you exercise your innovation muscles by implicitly prompting you to contemplate questions such as: "What's next?" and "What practices can ***I*** pioneer that may be commonplace in the future?"

"*Marketing FAME* certainly did put things in a down-to-earth context by reasoning that all things have not been done the same way forever, and important people had to lead others into thinking differently about marketing. Textbooks often show only what perspectives are in the current times, not how to look past the current marketing structures." – Layton, MBA student

Third, familiarizing yourself with the past equips you with valuable conversation fodder to help you build rapport and otherwise interact with clients, coworkers and acquaintances. Rather than getting the conversation marble rolling by asking others well-worn questions about how they like the weather these days, for example, try "Do you know what happened (or who was born) 100 years ago today?" or "That reminds me of what Jack Welch said back in the 1990s…"

> "In business you are going to have to talk to people that you have never met before, and to know interesting things like this will help in breaking the ice and make the conversations interesting."
> – Reginald, senior marketing major

Further, if you're a traditional-age college student who is conversant about the past, you're well-positioned to interact with older generations of businesspeople and consumers whose firsthand experiences with episodes of history may have a profound impact on their present-day perspectives and preferences. Being familiar with at least a couple of generations of history will help you to connect and empathize with others, and it can help you to avoid the stigma of being poorly educated, insensitive or inexperienced – perhaps unfair evaluations of businesspeople not familiar with history, but criticisms that exist nonetheless.

Here and there

Marketing FAME is geographically inclusive as well. You may find some featured people and events familiar because they are geographically close to home. They may represent brands that you use or stores where you shop. When you read about marketing practices at McDonald's or Wal-Mart, for example, it may be easy and interesting for you to visit these companies' local stores after class to verify the practices firsthand.

> "The marketing info from around the world is very relevant and helps see how marketing works on an international scale." – Sommer, MBA student

Other stories reach out to you from faraway places. As advances in technology, communications and logistics link the world, marketers must be prepared to look beyond their backyards and broaden their national and international perspectives. Accordingly, stories for this year's edition come from 49 U.S. states and 102 countries.

> **Tip for American college students**
> As you read *Marketing FAME*, you may find it helpful to periodically remind yourself that less than five percent of the world's population lives in the United States.

Calendar-led marketing and buyer behavior

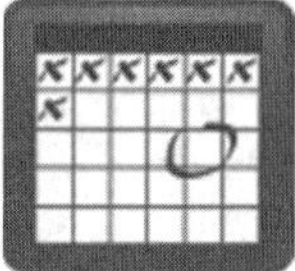

Quite likely you've already thumbed through enough pages of *Marketing FAME* to see that its content is organized like no other book you've been assigned to read in college. It's calendrically organized, featuring one or more people or events that sometimes coincidentally and sometimes not-so-coincidentally correspond to the day of the year they are discussed. This type of organization is intended to sensitize you to the importance of calendrical timing in the marketplace.

> "I really enjoyed reading the *FAME* [stories]. They were fun and educational… [and] were very relevant to marketing students to open up possible marketing opportunities that we didn't realize were there." – Kameron, undergraduate marketing minor

"What's the marketing relevance of calendrical timing?" you might ask. In part, it's attributed to the predictably periodic calendrical timing of seasonal changes, most holidays, and periods when buyers have the need, money and time to shop. These and other considerations mean that buyers' behaviors and marketers' actions are frequently calendar-led, i.e., they are greatly influenced by the date on the calendar. Thus, many marketing initiatives are more appropriate or likely to be more effective during some times of the year than during others. As an example, consider that American retailers who shelve chocolate Santas and heavy winter outerwear in November and December may benefit from their timing decisions by tallying high sales numbers during these two months, whereas those who shelve the same merchandise six months later may suffer the fate of poor calendrical timing and sell few of these items during that period. Therefore, *Marketing FAME*'s calendrical form of organization is a useful way to remind budding marketing professionals, such as yourself, to think about what calendrical periods mean to buyers and organizations, and thus when to do what, or what to do when.

> "The calendar format is nice and more interesting than themed chapters. The number of stories and the length of stories is just right." – Debra, MBA student

> **Read more to learn more**
>
> Beyond *Marketing FAME*, read the following articles by Charles L. Martin to learn more about calendar-led marketing, calendar-led buyer behavior and calendars as marketing tools. They can be found on the resource website, www.MarketingMarbles.com
>
> - "Calendars: Influential and widely used marketing planning tools," *Journal of Brand Strategy*, 5(2), 2016, pp. 1-14.
> - "How nature, culture and legal calendars influence the calendrical timing of consumer behavior," *Journal of Customer Behavior*, 15(4), 2016, pp. 337-368.
> - Calendar-led marketing: Strategic synchronization of timing," *The Marketing Review*, 17 (1) Spring 2017, pp. 73-86.

Even when there's no obvious calendrical significance of an individual's birthday or an event's anniversary, each daily dose of information implies a marketing opportunity to celebrate or otherwise commemorate the date and occasion nonetheless.

As an example, November 17, 2018 is the 184th birth date anniversary of Nancy Green, the original model and spokesperson for the Aunt Jemima brand of pancake mix. The *Marketing FAME* story for that date summarizes Green's role and contributions, and then articulates a couple of universal marketing lessons regarding convenience and sampling that stem from the story. Beyond these generally applicable take-aways, however, the brand's manager might seize the opportunity to celebrate Green's birthday and thus promote the heritage of the brand. Further, restaurants might promote the date with special Aunt Jemima recipes developed for the celebratory occasion. Or, more generally, organizations could celebrate the date by saluting Green as a successful and inspirational African-American woman. The marketing possibilities are endless, but they begin with knowledge of what birthdays, occasions or events fall on the specific date.

Although not every day represents the same mix of potential marketing opportunities for every organization, every day does represent one or more opportunities for some organizations whose marketers are willing to seize them. So, as you read *Marketing FAME*, think about how each day is unique and how each day's stories might possibly link with your organization, or with its values, brands or customers. An endless number of opportunities are waiting for *you* to discover them.

> "I liked that [*Marketing FAME*'s] organization was based on the calendar year, as marketing can change at different times of year." – Logan, MBA student

> "I feel I got to know a lot of important quotes and practical marketing rules from the book, which we normally don't read in [traditional textbooks]."
> -- Nandita, senior non-business major

More than 15 minutes

The American pop artist Andy Warhol once implied what reality television is confirming, i.e., we're all destined for 15 minutes of fame. Of course, it's doubtful that Warhol was thinking specifically about marketing, because you'll need much more than 15 minutes to fully benefit from *Marketing FAME*.

Still, 15 minutes may be ample time to achieve fame-status communication. That is, after reading *Marketing FAME*, please share your evaluation with the marbleous team. In a 15-minute email, let us know what you enjoyed or didn't enjoy about *Marketing FAME*, how future editions can be improved, and what your most and least favorite stories are. If you have an idea for a great story that should be included in future editions, let us know that too. Contact us through the contact page at the series' website, www.MarketingMarbles.com, or contact me directly at Wichita State University, Charles.Martin@wichita.edu

Thank you and happy reading!

Charles L. Martin, Ph.D.

"The information… actually stayed around in my head, and I have had conversations about what I have learned in those pages of *Marketing FAME* with others. In other words, I was able to comment in conversations that I previously would not have been able to speak to." – Sonya, MBA student

"Excellent, well done – it helps students taking marketing courses to relate classroom knowledge with real life marketing happenings/events. A more panoramic view." – Ajaiyeoba, MBA student

Marbles masquerading as nuts?

"[I liked] the shortness of the stories; I have the attention span of a squirrel so short bursts of interesting info are good." – Michael R., MBA student

Don't forget to visit our
official website this year,
www.MarketingMarbles.com
It has lots of extra cool
stuff to help you be a
marbleous marketer.

January 1, 2018
Monday
New Year's Day

Objectives & reminders

Appointments

Early morning

---
8 a.m.

---
9 a.m.

---
10 a.m.

---
11 a.m.

Noon

---
1 p.m.

---
2 p.m.

---
3 p.m.

---
4 p.m.

---
5 p.m.

---
6 p.m.

Later evening

Happy New Year!

About three-fourths of the world's consumers celebrate New Year's Eve and/or New Year's Day – more than any other holiday of the year. For many of these consumers, new aspirations and resolutions accompany the beginning of a new year.

In the U.S., New Year's resolutions most frequently pertain to health and fitness, career, personal growth and interests, personal finance, time management, family and relationships, education, home improvement and real estate, and recreation and leisure. So, it's a great period for marketers in these categories to show how they can help consumers follow-through on their resolutions.

> **Key principle of calendar-led marketing: Strike when the iron is hot**
> Marketing activities such as advertising and promotion tend to be most effective when buyers are already predisposed to act.

In the U.S., New Year's Day is a holiday for federal workers. As such, most government offices are closed, including post offices; mail is not delivered. Like most of the dozen or so days designated as federal holidays, state and local governments, banks, and many businesses follow the fed's lead and also are closed on January 1.

> **Convoluted statistical analysis**
> "Now, there are more overweight people in America than average-weight people. So overweight people are now average. Which means you've met your New Year's resolution." -- Jay Leno, American comedian and former talk show host

---

January 1st first

On January 1, 1928, the first air-conditioned high-rise building opened -- the Milam Building, in San Antonio, Texas. The 21-story building had been specially designed for air conditioning. As the adoption of air conditioning grew in the U.S. during the decades that followed, so grew the population and economic prosperity of the hot southern states.

January 2, 2018
Tuesday
Heroes' Day (Haiti)

Objectives & reminders

____

____

____

Appointments

Early morning

8 a.m.

9 a.m.

10 a.m.

11 a.m.

Noon

1 p.m.

2 p.m.

3 p.m.

4 p.m.

5 p.m.

6 p.m.

Later evening

New Year's resolutions are for businesspeople too…

Routine planning helps prevent businesspeople from losing their marbles. Accordingly, Susan Ward, author of *Your Guide to Small Business*, recommends that small business operators commit to the New Year's resolution of making business planning a weekly event. She observes:

> "Planning is vital if you want a healthy, growing business. Business planning lets you take stock of what worked and what didn't work, and helps you set new directions or adjust old goals. So why do it just once a year or once a quarter? Set aside time each week to review, adjust, and look forward -- or even better, make business planning a part of each day. Not only will this help you avoid costly mistakes and stay on track, but you'll feel more focused and relaxed."

____

…and for college students

Ileana Brito and Jessica Calleja of jobpostings.net recommend eleven New Year's resolutions for college students to consider:

1. "Learn something new.
2. Join a networking group.
3. Put time for you on your calendar.
4. Set realistic goals.
5. Drop what's not working for you and move on.
6. Get organized.
7. Spend more time with family.
8. Focus on the positive.
9. Get 8 hours of sleep.
10. Be kinder to your body.
11. Get into shape."

____

Product differentiation

One of the most well-known and certainly the most unique insurance firms in the world was founded on January 2, 1688 – Lloyd's of London. Over the years the firm has differentiated itself from the competition by insuring what other firms don't. In the process, their unique insurance policies have helped Lloyd's generate landslides of publicity. Consider how other firms in other industries might be able to appeal to a unique niche in the market by offering goods and services that would-be competitors don't.

January 3, 2018
Wednesday
Religious Affairs Day (Indonesia)

Objectives & reminders

___

___

___

Appointments

Early morning

8 a.m.

9 a.m.

10 a.m.

11 a.m.

Noon

1 p.m.

2 p.m.

3 p.m.

4 p.m.

5 p.m.

6 p.m.

Later evening

Straw first

Marvin C. Stone patented the wax drinking straw on January 3, 1888. Early prototypes involved strips of paper wound around a pencil, then glued together. To prevent the paper straws from getting too soggy in liquid, Stone soon began using paraffin-coated Manila paper. By 1905, the popularity of the paper straw prompted Stone to invent a machine to produce them.

Paper straws remained popular until the 1960s when plastic straws began to dominate the market. Today, beverage marketers and straw manufacturers know that by varying the width of straws they can influence the rate and amount of drink consumed, i.e., consumers drink more from thicker straws than from thinner ones.

New use of drinking straws "discovered"
One hundred and ten years after Stone's innovation of the paper straw, three-year-old Brandon Martin became what he believed to be the first to discover an alternative use for straws. The young boy realized that straws are not necessarily for sucking liquid. Rather, he "discovered" that by blowing air through a straw and into a beverage he could transform the liquid delivery device into a bubble-making machine!

Of course, Brandon Martin wasn't the first three-year-old to make this discovery, but like millions of children since1888, he *thought* he was. Because his parents did not tell him that his discovery was not a first, Brandon's bubbles were not burst and he continued to explore the world around him -- considering creative and alternative uses of tools and tackling tasks in innovative ways.

Today, consider how often employees' bubbles of innovation are burst when supervisors or co-workers note that an idea has already been considered, tried, or dismissed. No one wants to hear "everybody knows that."

Because people tend to be more excited about their own discoveries than about those of others, innovation-oriented organizations have no problem with multiple "discoveries" of the same innovation.

January 4, 2018
Thursday
World Braille Day

Objectives & reminders

Appointments

Early morning

---
8 a.m.

---
9 a.m.

---
10 a.m.

---
11 a.m.

Noon

---
1 p.m.

---
2 p.m.

---
3 p.m.

---
4 p.m.

---
5 p.m.

---
6 p.m.

Later evening

Flexibility, always

"I am a man of fixed and unbending principles, the first of which is to be flexible at all times." – Everett M. Dirksen, U.S. Senator (Illinois), born in Pekin, Illinois on January 4, 1896

Happy birthday: Louis Braille

Born in Coupvray, France on January 4, 1809, Braille's left eye was injured when he was only three. The accident led to an infection in both eyes, then to blindness. While attending the Royal Institution for Blind Youth (Paris), 12-year-old Braille began inventing a raised-dot or bump system of letters to enable the blind to read more easily than they could with previously developed systems for the blind. At age 15, his initial system involving combinations of six dots was complete. By the time he was 20, Braille published the first book using the "Braille" system. Today, the Braille system is used throughout the world -- not only in books for the blind, but also in brochures and restaurant menus, and on signs.

Visually impaired Americans

Based on the 2015 National Health Interview Survey, about 23.7 million American adults say they "have trouble" seeing (even when wearing glasses or contact lenses) or that they cannot see at all. As the Baby-Boom generation grows older, expect the number of visually impaired adults to double. As a marketer, consider what you might be able to do to reach and serve these consumers. As an employer, consider what you might be able to do to assist these workers.

Important observation: Advertising is important

"[Advertising is] the most important aspect of the mass media. It *is* the point. Advertising supports more than 60 percent of magazine and newspaper production and almost 100 percent of the electronic media." – Jean Kilbourne, social theorist and frequent critic of advertising, born in Junction City, Kansas on January 4, 1943. This quotation is from Chapter 1 in her book, *Deadly Persuasion: Why Women and Girls Must Fight the Addictive Power of Advertising.*

January 5, 2018
Friday
Eve of Epiphany

Objectives & reminders

___

___

___

Appointments

Early morning

8 a.m.

9 a.m.

10 a.m.

11 a.m.

Noon

1 p.m.

2 p.m.

3 p.m.

4 p.m.

5 p.m.

6 p.m.

Later evening

Christmas tradition (& market) continues

Christmas is celebrated by some people on January 5 and 6, with January 5 being the eve of Epiphany. In some countries (e.g., Spain and Italy), children traditionally do not receive gifts until January 5. In Italy, legend has it that an elderly woman -- Befana -- descends down the chimney during the night and leaves presents for children. In Spain, children first fill their shoes with barley and straw for the magi's animals, then hope that the wise man -- Balthazar -- will leave gifts.

___

Happy birthday: William Hughes Cunningham

Born in Detroit, Michigan on January 5, 1944, Cunningham earned three degrees from Michigan State University (including a Ph.D.), but has spent most of his professional career in Texas, where he joined the faculty at the University of Texas (Austin) as an Assistant Professor of Marketing in 1971. Cunningham advanced rapidly, becoming Dean of U.T.'s College of Business in 1983, President of the University in 1985, and Chancellor of the U.T. System in 1992.

Along his career path, Cunningham somehow found the time to write or co-write a dozen marketing and business books, including *Effective Selling* (1977), *Marketing: A Managerial Approach* (1987), *Introduction to Business* (1988), and *Business in a Changing World* (1992), among others.

Avoid this mistake

"One common mistake made by many salespeople is waiting too long to close the sale. As soon as the customer gives any indication that it is time to close the sale, the salesperson must do so. Some salespeople find it difficult to ask for the sale, and... they just keep on selling. At some point, they run a real risk of losing the sale because they mention product or service features that either confuse the buyer or make the buyer rethink the purchase decision."
-- William H. Cunningham

January 6, 2018
Saturday
Epiphany

Objectives & reminders

___

___

___

Appointments

___

Early morning

___

8 a.m.

___

9 a.m.

___

10 a.m.

___

11 a.m.

___

Noon

___

1 p.m.

___

2 p.m.

___

3 p.m.

___

4 p.m.

___

5 p.m.

___

6 p.m.

___

Later evening

___

Happy birthday: Louis L. Holtz

Born in Follansbee, West Virginia on January 6, 1937, "Lou" Holtz coached college football for more than 40 years, at William and Mary, North Carolina State, University of Arkansas, University of Minnesota, Notre Dame, and University of South Carolina.

Holtz developed a reputation for inspiring his players, but was also a stern disciplinarian. As the quotes in the accompanying boxes show, much of his philosophy of football also applies to business.

Lou Holtz' business & career insights

Competition
"You might not be able to out-think, out-market or out-spend your competition, but you can out-work them."

Excellence
"If you don't demand that your people maintain high performances to remain on your team, why should they be proud of the association?"

Unlucky breaks
"The man who complains about the way the ball bounces is likely the one who dropped it."

Self-promotion
"If you burn your neighbor's house down, it doesn't make your house look any better."

Self-discipline
"Without self-discipline, success is impossible. Period."

___

Integrity is fundamental: Agree or… agree?

"If you don't have integrity, you have nothing. You can't buy it. You can have all the money in the world, but if you are not a moral and ethical person, you really have nothing. You only have one thing to sell in life, and that's yourself." – Henry R. Kravis, financier who co-founded the investment banking firm of Kohlberg Kravis Roberts & Co., born in Tulsa, Oklahoma on January 6, 1944

January 7, 2018
Sunday
Orthodox Christmas Day

Objectives & reminders

___

___

___

Appointments

Early morning

8 a.m.

9 a.m.

10 a.m.

11 a.m.

Noon

1 p.m.

2 p.m.

3 p.m.

4 p.m.

5 p.m.

6 p.m.

Later evening

Service as a moving target

The findings of an Accenture web-based survey of 3,352 consumers in Australia, Brazil, Canada, China, France, the United Kingdom and the United States were released on January 7, 2008.

Among other service-related findings, the study found that 52 percent of the respondents said that their expectations for better service had increased over the past five years. The inflation of consumer expectations appears to be most pronounced in the emerging economy of China as 93 percent of Chinese respondents said that they had higher service expectations than they did five years earlier. Another startling finding is the 47 percent of respondents worldwide who asserted that their expectations were met only "sometimes," "rarely" or "never."

Given these findings, companies should not become complacent when it comes to service. Service levels that might have been good enough to satisfy customers in the past may not be good enough today.

> **Applicable for service firms too?**
> "No matter how far a person can go, the horizon is still way beyond you." – Zora Neale Hurston, American writer, born in Notasulga, Alabama on January 7, 1891

So, what would make for a more satisfying customer service experience? One suggestion was offered by 43 percent of the respondents: "the ability to resolve an issue with a single call rather than speaking with multiple service representatives."

Mistakes as breakthrough innovations

Great ideas and great brands are not always engineered or otherwise planned. Sometimes they occur by accident. For example, in January 1878, Procter & Gamble began production of a high-quality affordable soap called "White Soap." Shortly thereafter a workman unintentionally left the soap-mixing equipment running while he went to lunch. This error caused air to be whipped into the soap which caused it to float.

Within weeks the company received several letters requesting more of the soap that floats. The company honored the requests, changed the soap's name to "Ivory," and began promoting the floating feat. Today, Ivory is one of the oldest and most-recognized brands in the world.

January 8, 2018
Monday
Coming of Age Day (Japan)

Objectives & reminders

______

______

______

Appointments

Early morning

8 a.m.

9 a.m.

10 a.m.

11 a.m.

Noon

1 p.m.

2 p.m.

3 p.m.

4 p.m.

5 p.m.

6 p.m.

Later evening

Happy birthday: Thomas J. Watson, Jr.

Born in Dayton, Ohio on January 8, 1914, Watson grew up in the shadow of his father -- the legendary Thomas J. Watson who had built a small tabulating company into one of the largest and most respected firms in the world -- International Business Machines (IBM). Nothing about Junior's interests or academic performance in high school and college suggested that he would follow in his father's footsteps. Indeed, the younger Watson was a poor student who was more interested in partying than in a career.

It wasn't until after serving in World War II as a pilot that 32-year-old Watson, Jr. took an interest in seriously working for IBM. But, when he did so, he brought with him enthusiasm and a sense of urgency that propelled the company into the digital electronic computer age and win the respect of his colleagues. Six years later, Junior became company president (1952), then four years after that, chairman (1956).

After his retirement from IBM in 1971, Watson, Jr. was asked what his great vision for the company was twenty years earlier. He confessed that he originally had no such vision or plan. Rather, he explained that his driving motivation was simply a desire not to embarrass or disappoint his father.

Timing market opportunities

"There's a fine line between eccentrics and geniuses. If you're a little ahead of your time, you're an eccentric, and if you're too late, you're a failure, but if you hit it right on the head, you're a genius." -- Thomas J. Watson, Jr.

Genius

Watson, Jr. must have been a genius. He "bet the company" on IMB's System 360 mainframe computer in 1964, and won.

Yes, but go fishing with someone else

"I never hesitated to promote someone I didn't like... I looked for those sharp, scratchy, harsh, almost unpleasant guys who see and tell you about things as they really are. If you can get enough of them around you, and have patience enough to hear them out, there is no limit to where you can go." -- Thomas J. Watson, Jr.

January 9, 2018
Tuesday

Martyrs' Day (Panama)

Objectives & reminders

____

____

____

Appointments

Early morning

8 a.m.

9 a.m.

10 a.m.

11 a.m.

Noon

1 p.m.

2 p.m.

3 p.m.

4 p.m.

5 p.m.

6 p.m.

Later evening

Happy birthday: Richard M. Nixon

Born in Yorba Linda, California on January 9, 1913, Nixon went on to become the 37th president of the United States (1969-1974).

While Nixon is remembered as the only U.S. President to resign the presidency (in the aftermath of the Watergate scandal), he also did a great deal to resume diplomatic relations with the Soviet Union and China which paved the way for businesses to enter these huge markets.

Leadership
"If an individual wants to be a leader and isn't controversial, that means he never stood for anything." -- Richard M. Nixon

My-way-or-the-highway leadership: Agree or disagree?

"I hope with all my heart that you will serve under me... but if there are things you do not like about engaging in business with me, by all means take this opportunity to resign." – Iwasaki Yataro, founder of Mitsubishi (one of the world's first big business organizations), born in Aki, Japan on January 9, 1835

Work for the fun of it

"The superstition that all our hours of work are a minus quantity in the happiness of life, and all the hours of idleness are plus ones, is a most ludicrous and pernicious doctrine, and its greatest support comes from our not taking sufficient trouble, not making a real effort, to make work as near pleasure as it can be." – Arthur Balfour, British steel-making industrialist, born in East Lothian, Scotland on January 9, 1873

Marketing dreams

"I dreamed that I went shopping in my Maidenform bra." – advertising slogan developed for The Maidenform Company in 1949. The provocative campaign lasted for more than 20 years and included women "dreaming" of doing several everyday things wearing only their Maidenform undergarments – without embarrassment. The company was founded in the early 1920s by Ida Rosenthal who was born in Rakaw, Belarus on January 9, 1886.

January 10, 2018
Wednesday
Majority Rule Day (Bahamas)

Objectives & reminders

____

____

____

Appointments

Early morning

8 a.m.

9 a.m.

10 a.m.

11 a.m.

Noon

1 p.m.

2 p.m.

3 p.m.

4 p.m.

5 p.m.

6 p.m.

Later evening

Happy birthday: Roy Edward Disney

Born in Los Angeles, California on January 10, 1930, Roy Edward Disney was the son of businessman Roy Oliver Disney and nephew of the entertainment and amusement park legend, Walt Disney. He began his 58 years of employment with the family business -- The Walt Disney Company -- after graduating from college in 1951. He worked his way up the corporate ladder to become Vice Chairman.

> **What's important?**
> "When your values are clear to you, making decisions becomes easier." -- Roy E. Disney

Business organizations' birthdays on January 10

1870 Standard Oil was incorporated by oil magnate John D. Rockefeller and his colleagues. Standard Oil became the first major oil company in the United States.

1900 National Civic Federation was formed in Chicago. The organization sought to promote improved labor-management relations by involving businesspeople, labor leaders and the general public.

1910 The company that became Hallmark Cards was founded by Joyce Hall. Today, the Kansas City, Missouri firm produces hundreds of greeting card designs for dozens of occasions. Since 1910, astute marketers have used greeting cards to stay in contact with customers and keep their products and companies top-of-mind.

Binoculars not always a good idea

"We can often become so focused on our dreams and goals that we lose sight of the responsibilities right in front of us." – John Maxwell, leading authority on leading, on page 52 in his book, *The 360 Degree Leader: Developing Your Influence from Anywhere in the Organization*, published on January 10, 2006

January 11, 2018
Thursday

Lagami Biraki (Japan)

Objectives & reminders

______

______

______

Appointments

Early morning

8 a.m.

9 a.m.

10 a.m.

11 a.m.

Noon

1 p.m.

2 p.m.

3 p.m.

4 p.m.

5 p.m.

6 p.m.

Later evening

Advertising comes of Age

Advertising Age, which dubbed itself as "the national newspaper of advertising," debuted with its first issue on January 11, 1930. The weekly publication was priced at 3 cents per copy, but subscribers could have the entire year for one dollar. Today, *Advertising Age* continues to be published, although its price has increased.

One story in the first issue of *Advertising Age* covered speeches made by food experts at a gathering of food manufacturers in New York City. In the article, Dr. Louise Stanley, chief of the Bureau of Home Economics of the Department of Agriculture, explained that, "[h]abit, palatability, economy and convenience are the four factors which most influence food choice by the consumer."

Limits to food marketing: Agree or disagree?

"Food does not lend itself to high-pressure salesmanship. We have had doughnut weeks and other kinds of weeks, but it must be remembered that the total amount of food to be eaten cannot be increased. The capacity of the stomach is limited." -- Louise Stanley, 1930

Islamic mosque in the United States

On January 11, 1949, the cornerstone was laid for one of the first Islamic mosques in the U.S. -- on Connecticut Avenue in Washington, D.C. The mosque was part of a larger Islamic Center and was built to serve all American Muslims. The Center included a library, classrooms, museum, and a large auditorium. By 2016, the number of American Muslims had grown to 3.3 million (about 1 percent of the population), according to Pew Forum estimates.

Not-invented-here syndrome

"Men often oppose a thing merely because they have had no agency in planning it, or because it may have been planned by those whom they dislike."
– Alexander Hamilton, American statesman and financier whose picture is on the U.S. $10-bill, born in the British West Indies on January 11, 1755

January 12, 2018
Friday
National Youth Day (India)

Objectives & reminders

____

____

____

Appointments

Early morning

8 a.m.

9 a.m.

10 a.m.

11 a.m.

Noon

1 p.m.

2 p.m.

3 p.m.

4 p.m.

5 p.m.

6 p.m.

Later evening

Happy birthday: Mary L.C. Guinan

Born in Waco, Texas on January 12, 1884, Guinan was first an actress, but then launched a unique marketing career as a night club greeter and hostess in New York City in the mid-1920s. She managed the social atmosphere of the night club to ensure positive customer experiences, but she also found that customers spent more money if they were welcomed, humored with jokes, and otherwise recognized. Her charm, personality and humor set examples for customers to follow.

Other customers as service providers

In many service and retail businesses, customers come into contact with other customers more frequently than with employees. Often the quality of the service experience is shaped -- either positively or negatively -- by the behavior or presence of other customers.

Customer-contact sports?

Why are some seating sections at spectator sporting events designated for "home" fans while others are intended for "visitors"?

Today, marketers of service businesses often borrow from Guinan's knack for understanding and enhancing customers' experiences in service environments. For example, guests waiting to ride the train that encircles DisneyWorld are treated to jokes and trivia by the train's host. The monologue puts customers in the "Disney mood" and makes the wait more palatable. Once on the train, guests participate in a sing-along of Disney tunes.

Help wanted: CXO

At the 2003 U.K. Services Marketing workshop in Liverpool, England, researchers Chris Voss and Aleda Roth proposed that service businesses appoint a "Chief Experience Officer" (CXO). Like Guinan, CXOs could help define and manage the social experience for customers by setting an example and facilitating interaction between customers. Further, CXOs might include managing other aspects of the physical environment too, such as lighting, colors, sounds, smells, arrangement of furniture and merchandise, employee attire, and so on – everything that potentially contributes to the *total* customer experience.

January 13, 2018
Saturday
Korean-American Day

Objectives & reminders

___

___

___

Appointments

Early morning

8 a.m.

9 a.m.

10 a.m.

11 a.m.

Noon

1 p.m.

2 p.m.

3 p.m.

4 p.m.

5 p.m.

6 p.m.

Later evening

Happy birthday: Horatio Alger, Jr.

Born in Revere, Massachusetts on January 13, 1832, Alger studied to be a minister and longed to be a poet. But he found his life's calling in the 1860s as the "greatest salesman of the American Dream" when he wrote his first of 134 dime novels, called *Ragged Dick* (1867).

The main character in *Ragged Dick*, like those in most of his novels, was a downtrodden boy with a disadvantaged background whose courage, determination and strong work ethic propelled him to a successful life. Alger's rags-to-riches books were enormously popular and encouraging, particularly to young boys.

> **Learning machine**
> "No period of my life has been one of such unmixed happiness as the four years which have been spent within college walls" -- Horatio Alger

In 1947 the Horatio Alger Award was established to recognize rags-to-riches success stories of hard work and perseverance, and to inspire young people. The list of honorees includes dozens of notable business legends, including William P. Lear, Wally Amos, Bernard Marcus, James Cash Penney, Oprah Winfrey, Conrad Hilton, Ray Kroc, and Mary Kay Ash. In 2017, the Award was bestowed upon 11 more recipients, including Roger S. Penske, Marcia G. Taylor, John H. Scully, Mellody Hobson and John Elway. Their inspirational success stories may be found here: https://www.horatioalger.org/2017-honorees/

Speaking of stick-to-it-ness

Another believer in the American dream was Ray Stanton Avery, who was born exactly 75 years after Horatio Alger's birth -- on January 13, 1907. Avery, the inventor of self-adhesive labels, founded Kum Kleen Products in 1935 to produce and market them. The following year, the name of the company was changed to Avery Products, now Avery Dennison Corporation.

> **Commitment!**
> Be like a self-adhesive address label on a mailed envelope: stick to it until you get there.

January 14, 2018
Sunday
Orthodox New Year

Objectives & reminders

Appointments

Early morning

---

8 a.m.

---

9 a.m.

---

10 a.m.

---

11 a.m.

Noon

---

1 p.m.

---

2 p.m.

---

3 p.m.

---

4 p.m.

---

5 p.m.

---

6 p.m.

Later evening

Calendar-led marketer recognized

On January 14, 2008, the finalists for the prestigious Marketing Campaign of the Year accolade were announced by the World Retail Congress. Department store retailer J.C. Penney was among the six finalists for its "Every Day Matters" campaign. Not to be out calendar marketed, competitor Ross stores soon followed with a new slogan and campaign of its own, "It's a Brand New Day."

Happy birthday: David Wesson

Born in Brooklyn, New York on January 14, 1861, Wesson was an American chemist who, in the early 1900s, figured out how to purify and then hydrogenate cottonseed oil for cooking purposes. He founded the Southern Oil Company to capitalize on his innovation. Thanks to Wesson, the first vegetable oil used in the United States was cottonseed oil. Although the ingredients have changed, today the Wesson Oil brand continues – one of ConAgra Foods' brands, manufactured in Memphis, Tennessee.

Is he mistaken? ☺

"We're all proud of making little mistakes. It gives us the feeling we don't make any big ones." – Andy Rooney, former journalist and observer of human behavior, born in Albany, New York on January 14, 1919

Float this publicity idea

In San Francisco, on January 14, 1988, Gary Sussman transformed a 6,000-pound bar of Ivory soap into a statue as part of a celebration of the area's 1849 gold rush. Because soap-carving is not an everyday occurrence, the statue successfully generated publicity for both the Forty-Niner event as well as for the Ivory brand. The size of the statue also contributed to its novelty and therefore its publicity potency.

Evaporation leadership

"Constant kindness can accomplish much. As the sun makes the ice melt, kindness causes misunderstandings, mistrust and hostility to evaporate." – Albert Schweitzer, German theologian, physician, musician, moralist, and winner of the Nobel Peace prize (1952). Schweitzer was born in what is now Haut-Rhin, France on January 14, 1875.

January 15, 2018
Monday
Martin Luther King, Jr. Day

Objectives & reminders

____

____

____

Appointments

Early morning

8 a.m.

9 a.m.

10 a.m.

11 a.m.

Noon

1 p.m.

2 p.m.

3 p.m.

4 p.m.

5 p.m.

6 p.m.

Later evening

Happy birthday: Martin Luther King, Jr.

Born in Atlanta, Georgia on January 15, 1929, Reverend and Dr. King was a prominent civil rights leader who advocated nonviolent protests to achieve equal rights. Tragically, he was assassinated in 1968. In 1986, his birthday was recognized as a Federal holiday in the United States, now celebrated annually on the third Monday in January – today.

Character metric
"The ultimate measure of a man is not where he stands in moments of comfort, but where he stands in times of challenge and controversy."
– Martin Luther King, Jr.

Research tool is born

Wikipedia, the online community encyclopedia, was born on January 15, 2001. That's when Jimmy Wales, Wikipedia's founder, posted the first entry. Since then thousands of people with topic-specific information have posted what they know on literally millions of additional topics that are continually revised – including thousands of entries pertaining to business and marketing subjects. Although Wikipedia is sometimes criticized for including inaccurate information, it is often a good "first source" for researchers interested in an unfamiliar topic.

If you're not already familiar with Wikipedia, explore the website at www.wikipedia.org.

How Wikipedia is changing the world
"I think Wikipedia had a big impact on how people think about collaboration and knowledge, as well as the thinking about how to design security into social systems. We emphasized accountability and transparency over gate-keeping. It was a philosophical change to leave things open, to make sure things can be fixed easily and you can see who did what, rather than pre-vetting contributors at the start."
– Jimmy Wales

January 16, 2018
Tuesday
Teachers' Day (Thailand)

Objectives & reminders

____

____

____

Appointments

Early morning

8 a.m.

9 a.m.

10 a.m.

11 a.m.

Noon

1 p.m.

2 p.m.

3 p.m.

4 p.m.

5 p.m.

6 p.m.

Later evening

From whiskey a no-no, to Whiskey A-Go-Go

Prohibition began in the United States on January 16, 1920. For the 13 years that followed, the 18th amendment to the U.S. Constitution prohibited Americans from legally buying or selling alcoholic beverages. Although the ban reduced the overall consumption of alcohol, it certainly did not eliminate it. Rather, much of the demand remained and sellers resorted to numerous illegal means to fill it.

Exactly 43 years after Prohibition began, on January 16, 1963, Los Angeles' first "go-go" club opened, Whiskey-A-Go-Go. Soon go-go clubs were opening throughout the country. Whiskey-A-Go-Go and its imitators featured recorded music. For lower- and middle-income consumers, the go-go clubs (later known as "disco" clubs) represented an economical alternative to clubs that offered live music.

In 1977, discos became a national sensation, largely attributed to the release of the disco movie starring John Travolta, *Saturday Night Fever*. Twenty-million copies of the movie's soundtrack were sold.

Can holiday planning be too early?

"Watched a man setting up a Valentine's Day display in a store window. It's the middle of January, but the merchants need to get a jump on love, I guess. Don't get me wrong -- merchants are fine folks. They give us choices and keep us informed on the important holidays. How would you know it was Halloween or Valentine's Day or Mother's Day early enough to do something about it, if merchants didn't stay on the job?" -- Robert Fulghum, in his best-selling book, *All I Really Need To Know I Learned in Kindergarten*, p. 34

Statistics to help answer the question

Ninety percent of surveyed consumers who purchased one or more Valentine's Day gifts reported doing so within one week of the occasion. In another survey conducted "only days before Father's Day," 53 percent of gift-givers had not yet decided what gift to purchase for Dad. Christmas shoppers, in contrast, often buy one or more gifts months before Christmas Day.

January 17, 2018
Wednesday
Benjamin Franklin Day

Objectives & reminders

___

___

___

Appointments

Early morning

8 a.m.

9 a.m.

10 a.m.

11 a.m.

Noon

1 p.m.

2 p.m.

3 p.m.

4 p.m.

5 p.m.

6 p.m.

Later evening

Japanese tragedy

A devastating earthquake killed 5,372 people, injured 33,000 people, and destroyed more than 151,000 buildings in the port city of Kobe, Japan on January 17, 1995. The 20-second quake measured 7.2 on the Richter scale.

Thousands of Japanese businesses were affected by the earthquake. In addition to the $200 billion in direct damages, another $50 billion in losses were attributed to the quake's interruption of business activities. Here are a few examples:

- The online system for 140 branches of Sakura Bank crashed.
- Telecommunication lines for Hanshin Bank were rendered useless.
- Most workers for manufacturers like Mitsubishi could not commute to their jobs; highways and railways to and in Kobe were either destroyed or access blocked.
- Manufacturers such as Matsuchita Electric could not ship product due to the chaos in the transportation system; all international shipping from Kobe ports ceased.
- Food could not be delivered to supermarkets normally. Instead, 7-11 convenience stores chartered seven helicopters to deliver box lunches to the earthquake-affected area.

As tragic as the Kobe earthquake was, experts acknowledge the likelihood of even more devastating earthquakes in Japan's future. Depending upon the severity and epicenters of future Japanese quakes, the economic effect of such disasters may be felt not only in Japan, but also in the United States and elsewhere around the globe as Japan cashes in its worldwide investments to rebuild its quake-damaged country.

Prepared for a crisis?

Although it can be discouraging and even depressing to dwell on the possibility of future crises, acknowledging the possibilities and preparing for them is essential for the survival of people and businesses. Although many crises cannot be prevented, some are preventable, and crisis management plans may be able to lessen the impact of those that cannot be prevented.

January 18, 2018
Thursday
International Religion Day

Objectives & reminders

______

______

______

Appointments

Early morning

8 a.m.

9 a.m.

10 a.m.

11 a.m.

Noon

1 p.m.

2 p.m.

3 p.m.

4 p.m.

5 p.m.

6 p.m.

Later evening

Happy birthday: Shirley Polykoff

Born in Brooklyn, New York on January 18, 1908, Polykoff began her career as a secretary who later became an advertising copywriter. Unfortunately she was fired as a copywriter after misspelling several names in the first ad she wrote.

Polykoff eventually went to work for the ad agency Foote, Cone & Belding (FCB) in the mid-1950s where she was soon assigned to the Clairol (hair coloring) account. At the time, only about seven percent of American women colored their hair. To encourage women to color their hair, Polykoff wrote and orchestrated one of the most effective ad campaigns of all time that featured the memorable and risqué line, "Does she... or doesn't she?... Only her hairdresser knows for sure." Within six years, Clairol was pleased that 50 percent of American women colored their hair.

Did she or didn't she...
Only her husband knew for sure

While working at FCB, Shirley Polykoff eventually became the highest paid employee at the ad agency. However, before her husband died in 1961, she refused to be paid more than $25,000 a year, because she believed that a wife's earnings should never exceed those of her husband. After his death, Ms. Polykoff's compensation quadrupled within a decade.

Listening can go too far: Agree or disagree?

"It's useful to put an ear to the ground, but there's nothing more debilitating than trying to put both of them there." – Paul John Keating, 24th Prime Minister of Australia (1991-1996), born in Bankstown, Australia on January 18, 1944

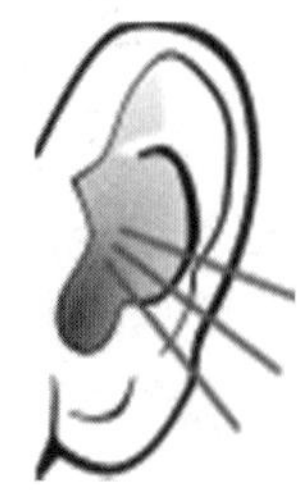

Time for a change? Go with the odds

"An individual is more apt to change, perhaps, than all the world around him." -- Daniel Webster, lawyer, and U.S. Secretary of State (early 1840s and early 1850s), born in Salisbury, New Hampshire on January 18, 1782

January 19, 2018
Friday
Popcorn Day

Objectives & reminders

____

____

____

Appointments

Early morning

8 a.m.

9 a.m.

10 a.m.

11 a.m.

Noon

1 p.m.

2 p.m.

3 p.m.

4 p.m.

5 p.m.

6 p.m.

Later evening

Happy 100th birthday: John H. Johnson

Born in the tiny town of Arkansas City, Arkansas on January 19, 1918, Johnson moved to Chicago to attend high school, because there were no high schools for blacks in Arkansas City.

After high school, Johnson began his career at the age of 18 -- as a part-time assistant to the editor of an employee publication in an insurance company. One of his job tasks involved what we might describe today as exploratory market research. That is, Johnson's boss asked him to find and summarize magazine articles about the black community -- blacks' interests, lifestyles, challenges, and so on.

Johnson collected quite a lot of articles and learned a great deal about the black community in that first job, but found that there were no magazines in the U.S. targeted directly to African-Americans. So, with the help of his mother who backed a $500 loan and the loan of the insurance company's mailing list, he launched Johnson Publishing Company and published *Negro Digest* at the age of 24 (1942). Three years later, *Negro Digest* evolved into *Ebony* magazine.

In the years that followed, Johnson's company published other magazines (e.g., *Tan, Hue, Jet* and *Ebony Man*) and diversified into a traveling fashion show (Ebony Fashion Show) and five mail order companies. Today, Johnson Publishing is among the largest African-American-owned publishers in the United States.

Pushing and pulling to succeed

Although Johnson sold 3,000 initial subscriptions to *Negro Digest*, newsstand distributors were not interested in carrying the magazine because they didn't believe it would sell. Johnson's efforts to convince them -- a *push* strategy -- failed.

Undaunted, Johnson resorted to a *pull* strategy by asking friends to visit newsstands and specifically ask to buy a copy. Some newsstand operators responded positively by asking their distributors for the magazine. After these first newsstands began carrying the magazine, Johnson paid his friends to make sure that the first several issues sold out, which aroused further interest among the distributors and garnered even wider distribution.

January 20, 2018
Saturday

National Skiing Day

Objectives & reminders

___

___

___

Appointments

Early morning

8 a.m.

9 a.m.

10 a.m.

11 a.m.

Noon

1 p.m.

2 p.m.

3 p.m.

4 p.m.

5 p.m.

6 p.m.

Later evening

National Skiing Day

U.S. President Ronald Reagan first proclaimed January 20 to be National Skiing Day in 1989. According to Reagan:

> "[T]he practicality and pleasure of skiing are worth celebrating by all of us, and that is the reason for this National Skiing Day. Skiing is advantageous to many of us for the jobs and income it generates. It also proves useful for residents of isolated areas; rescue teams; and Armed Forces units. Additionally, national and international sports groups, including Special Olympics International, recognize the athletic and therapeutic benefits of skiing for handicapped people and include it in their regular programs. Skiing is now one of our most popular winter sports."

For marketers, skiers represent both a direct market (e.g., ski equipment, apparel, lift tickets, etc.) and an indirect one (e.g., lodging, food, transportation). Recent estimates suggest that 12-15 million Americans call themselves skiers. For the 2015-16 ski season, they collectively accounted for 52.8 million skier visits – including all forms of skiing (i.e., downhill, Alpine, snowboarding, cross country, and freeski). American skiers also spent about $4.7 billion that year on skiing equipment, apparel, accessories and rentals.

Demographically, American skiers are more likely to be male than female by about a 3:2 margin, depending on the type of skiing. In terms of age, the 25-34 age group accounts for the most skiers across all types of skiing -- about 28%, on average -- followed by 35-44 (17%) and 18-24 (15%) age groups. Skiing activity tends to be highest in the Rocky Mountain region, in terms of the number of annual skier visits (22.3 million), followed by the Pacific (11.7), Northeast (9.3), Midwest (5.5) and Southeast (4.0) regions.

Data interpretation and application: Invitation to discuss

How could President Reagan's comments and the above ski market data be used to market products and services not directly related to skiing – products such as laundry detergent, automobiles and soft drinks? Be specific.

January 21, 2018
Sunday

National Hugging Day

Objectives & reminders

____

____

____

Appointments

Early morning

8 a.m.

9 a.m.

10 a.m.

11 a.m.

Noon

1 p.m.

2 p.m.

3 p.m.

4 p.m.

5 p.m.

6 p.m.

Later evening

Good day to think about expectations

Happy birthday: Reuben Mark

Born in Jersey City, New Jersey on January 21, 1939, Mark began his business career with Colgate-Palmolive Co. at age 24. Early in his career at C-P, he gained valuable international experience by working as a salesman for company divisions in Venezuela, Canada and the Far East. In 1984, Mark was appointed as the company's CEO, then as chairman in 1986 – roles he played for the next 22+ years.

Exceeding expectations

In terms of career advice, Mark points out the importance of workers trying to do more than what's expected. He suggests always asking yourself, "How can I make it better than expected?" He recalls his early days as a salesman when he paid his own way to attend an important sales meeting because the personnel manager had told him there were no company funds budgeted for him to attend. Mark made a positive impression at the meeting when he met a high level executive who had learned that Mark had paid for the trip himself. The impression helped Mark move up the corporate ladder.

Salespeople as expectation managers

"Real [customer] satisfaction... is determined... during the sales interview, the time at which a customer can either come to understand fully what the product is going to do for him or what it will not. After he has purchased, satisfaction consists in seeing these expectations fulfilled. A salesman is, in effect, the manager of his customer's expectations. By what he says, he can introduce valid or false expectations into the customer's mind. By what he does not say – in explanation or as an inquiry to test the customer's understanding – he can allow misconceptions to continue and to bring disillusionment after purchase." – Robert R. Blake and Jane S. Mouton, *Guideposts for Effective Salesmanship* (1970), p. 207. Born on January 21, 1918, Blake was a business consultant who wrote or co-authored 45 books and more than 200 articles, many of which considered managers' and workers' orientation toward their jobs – especially in terms of individuals' concern for productivity versus their concern for people (often couched in terms of Blake and Mouton's Managerial Grid Model).

January 22, 2018
Monday
Unhappy Day

Objectives & reminders

____

____

____

Appointments

Early morning

8 a.m.

9 a.m.

10 a.m.

11 a.m.

Noon

1 p.m.

2 p.m.

3 p.m.

4 p.m.

5 p.m.

6 p.m.

Later evening

Cheer up!

According to health psychologist Cliff Arnall (then at the University of Cardiff, Wales), Monday of the last full week in January – today – may be the most unhappy, depressing day of the year in Britain, most of the United States, and elsewhere in the Northern Hemisphere. Further, this week may be the most depressing week of the year.

Arnall's research combined a number of variables to enable him to reach this unhappy conclusion. For example, by late January the joyous Christmas season is history, but Christmas credit card bills are very much a present-day reality. The shortened number of daylight hours and the cold weather also conspire to dampen spirits at this time of year. For many people, the misery is compounded by facing the fact that they've already broken their New Year's resolutions.

To combat the late January blues, psychologists suggest several possibilities. Exercise is one. Breaking one's routine and doing something unusual is another. Not surprisingly, travel agents offer their own psychological prescription this week – travel. It seems that travel agents book a disproportionate number of trips this time of year as blues-weary consumers are open to the idea of heading south to escape inclement weather.

Time for exercise

"Exercise releases hormones that give us a sense of well-being, and it should be seen as an antidote to feeling down or blue." -- Leslie Godwin, "life transition coach"

At work, a few extra pats-on-the-back may be in order this week. And, of course, throwing a party for workers is always a good idea, because there's always something to celebrate, even in late January.

Further, the week provides an endless number of opportunities to do something special for customers -- ranging from simple gestures such as buying customers a cup of coffee or making a few "thank you" phone calls, to more ambitious efforts such as launching a new promotion or event.

Feeling normal

"Knowing that it's normal to feel down at this time of year can be a real help." -- Nancy A. Ferguson, licensed social worker

January 23, 2018
Tuesday
National Handwriting Day

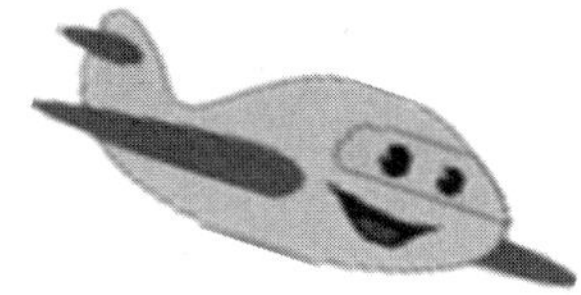

Objectives & reminders

____

____

____

Appointments

Early morning

8 a.m.

9 a.m.

10 a.m.

11 a.m.

Noon

1 p.m.

2 p.m.

3 p.m.

4 p.m.

5 p.m.

6 p.m.

Later evening

Happy birthday: Gerald M. Goldhaber

Born in Brookline, Massachusetts on January 23, 1944, Goldhaber was a communications professor at the State University of New York in Buffalo. He now heads Goldhaber Research Associates in Williamsville, New York. He has authored or coauthored numerous communications-related books, including *The Handbook of Organizational Communication.*

Goldhaber's recipe for success -- and for living -- is to strive for excellence: "I have always believed that the search for excellence should govern the lives of all people. There is virtually nothing that a human being cannot achieve if he or she lives in accordance with this standard and possesses a strong sense of morality and a good sense of humor."

Common leadership quality: Give credit to those led

"The people of Southwest Airlines are not only exceptional but unmatched in the understanding of their minds; the goodness of their hearts; and the joy of their spirits. Their vision, and their dedication to making that vision an ongoing reality, have engendered a magnificent family that has enjoyed bringing the freedom and pleasure of flight to most of America and now, by example, to much of the world. Southwest has enjoyed a great 25 years and, if our People always remember how they did it, they will always be able to do it." – Herbert D. Kelleher, then chairman, president and CEO of Southwest Airlines, in a letter to shareholders on January 23, 1997

Reputation matters

On January 23, 1930, Procter & Gamble extended its "99.44 percent pure" Ivory Soap brand with the invention of Ivory Snow. The powdered soap sold well, and continues to be a formidable brand today.

However, several years after the introduction of Ivory Snow, a picture of model and "actress" Marilyn Chambers was portrayed on millions of boxes of Ivory Snow – until it was learned that Chambers also had appeared in a series of XXX-rated movies. Apparently not wanting consumers to associate Ivory Snow with anything that might be less than "99.44 percent pure," P&G discontinued the use of Chambers' picture.

January 24, 2018
Wednesday
Compliment Day

Objectives & reminders

____

____

____

Appointments

Early morning

8 a.m.

9 a.m.

10 a.m.

11 a.m.

Noon

1 p.m.

2 p.m.

3 p.m.

4 p.m.

5 p.m.

6 p.m.

Later evening

A competitive world

Late January 1927 was an exciting period for the automobile industry in the U.S. as automakers proudly rolled out their new models at the Grand Central Palace in Manhattan, New York. Interested buyers and a curious press attended the show to see the wide variety of makes and models available for 1927. Almost all makes were present at the exhibition, with the notable exception of Ford.

Intense competition in the industry, however, coupled with the Great Depression of the 1930s, conspired to force most of the automakers out of business within a few short years.

The list of 1927 U.S. automakers present at the Manhattan exhibition – below – was published in the January 24, 1927, issue of *Time* magazine. The added dates in parentheses indicate the years when most models were phased out.

> Auburn (1936), Buick, Cadillac, Chandler (1928), Chevrolet, Chrysler, Davis (1928), Diana (1928), Dodge, Duesenberg (1937), Du Pont (1932), Elcar (1931), Erskine (1930), Essex (1932), Flint (1927), Franklin (1934), Gardner (1931), Hudson (1957), Hupmobile (1941), Jordan (1932), Kissel (1931), Lincoln, Locomobile (1930), McFarland (1928), Marmon (1933), Mood (1931), Nash (1957), Oakland (1931), Oldsmobile (2004), Packard (1958), Paige (1928), Peerless (1932), Pierce-Arrow (1938), Pontiac (2010), Reo (1936), Rickenbacker (1927), Star (1931), Stearns-Knight (1930), Studebaker (1966), Stutz (1934), Velie (1929), Whippet (1931), Wills-Sainte Claire (1927), Willys-Knight (1933)

Shake-out history lesson

It's not unusual for relatively new and rapidly growing industries to attract numerous (too many?) competitors. But when market growth slows and/or when some companies gain a competitive advantage in the marketplace, a shake-out period usually follows; some competitors leave the industry while others merge.

January 25, 2018
Thursday

Tatiana Day
(Russia, Ukraine, Belarus, Moldova)

Objectives & reminders

____

____

____

Appointments

Early morning

8 a.m.

9 a.m.

10 a.m.

11 a.m.

Noon

1 p.m.

2 p.m.

3 p.m.

4 p.m.

5 p.m.

6 p.m.

Later evening

BET launched

A new cable television option emerged on January 25, 1980, with the debut of Black Entertainment Television (BET) -- a channel designed to target African-American consumers. Initially, BET included only a few hours of programming weekly, including primarily older movies and music videos. Over the years, however, the programming mix has expanded greatly and diversified -- while the audience has grown to 18.15 million viewers weekly (spring 2016 data). In 2001 BET was sold to Viacom for $3 billion, which made BET's founder and CEO, Robert L. Johnson, the first African-American billionaire in the United States.

What it takes

"As an entrepreneur… you have to have an ability to engage people to believe in you, while being lucky enough to be in the right place at the right time." -- Robert L. Johnson

---

Wealth effect bet

Many investors experienced a *wealth effect* on January 25, 2017, when the Dow Jones Industrial Average (DJIA) reached record highs. On that day, the DJIA (a stock market index of 30 large U.S. firms) broke through the 20,000 barrier for the first time -- reaching 20,082 during the day and closing the day at 20,068. It had been almost 18 years earlier when the DJIA first broke the 10,000 mark.

Like other round numbers surpassed on the DJIA's upward climb over the years, 20,000 was significant in that it generated considerable media attention and some euphoria about the upward trend and its possible continuation – prompting many investors to contemplate the increased value of their investment portfolios and how they might spend some of their new financial gains.

Known as the *wealth effect*, investors' heightened sense of prosperity driven by climbs in the stock market as well as appreciation in home prices, is of particular interest to marketers of consumer durables and luxury products. When consumers feel wealthy, they're more likely to consider purchasing items they previously considered unaffordable. So, astute marketers in several product categories track the progress of the stock market and step-up marketing efforts when the stock market climbs sharply or reaches round-number milestones like 20,000.

January 26, 2018
Friday

International Customs Day
Australia Day

Objectives & reminders

___

___

___

Appointments

Early morning

8 a.m.

9 a.m.

10 a.m.

11 a.m.

Noon

1 p.m.

2 p.m.

3 p.m.

4 p.m.

5 p.m.

6 p.m.

Later evening

1,000-plus patents!

On January 26, 1900, O.H. Duell, the Commissioner of Patents for the U.S. Patent Office, circulated an open letter in an effort to identify "colored" inventors in the country. His goal was to help prepare a "Negro Exhibit" at the upcoming Paris Exposition. Numerous replies were received, leading to the identification of more than 1,000 fully-documented patents owned by black Americans. The patents represented a range of inventions including household items, electrical devices, mechanical appliances, and chemical compounds.

Era's prolific black inventors

1. Elijah McCoy -- received more than 50 patents, including one for the "lubricating cup" used to oil machinery in operation. The lubricating device was so highly regarded that users differentiated it from imitators by referring to it as "the real McCoy." (read more on May 2)
2. Granville T. Woods -- received more than 35 patents for various electrical devices.
3. Jan E. Matzeliger -- invented a machine used in the manufacture of shoes. The machine revolutionized the industry.
4. Garrett A. Morgan -- invented a gas mask (later used in World War I) and an automatic traffic light, among other things.

___

Multi-color innovation

U.S. Patent #3,167,440 was issued to Noah W. and Joseph S. McVicker on January 26, 1965, for the Play-Doh brand modeling compound. Since Play-Doh's creation nine years before the McVickers' patent, more than three billion cans have been sold. Although the original Play-Doh was positioned for younger children, recent reformulations of the compound have enabled the owner (now Hasbro) to reposition the brand to include older children too.

Modeling insight

"Life is what you make of it, sort of like Play-Doh." – Anonymous

January 27, 2018 Saturday

International Holocaust Remembrance Day

Objectives & reminders

____

____

____

Appointments

Early morning

8 a.m.

9 a.m.

10 a.m.

11 a.m.

Noon

1 p.m.

2 p.m.

3 p.m.

4 p.m.

5 p.m.

6 p.m.

Later evening

Strike!

The economy of Pittsburgh, Pennsylvania was devastated on January 27, 1946, when tens of thousands of steelworkers began a strike that lasted 19 days. The strike was finally settled when workers and their employers agreed to an 18½- cent-per-hour pay increase.

Today, communities recognize the potential downside of basing the economy on only one or a few industries or companies. A strike, plant closing, act of terrorism, sudden drop in demand, or natural disaster could cause a ripple effect throughout the community.

Not only does the primary business or industry suffer, but supporting businesses in the community are likely to suffer as well as their customers find themselves out of work or afraid of soon being so. Not surprisingly, consumer spending tends to drop when unemployment or the fear of unemployment grips a community.

Fortunately, the negative impacts tend to be lessened when a community's economy is diversified -- a factor to consider before committing substantial resources to enter a geographic market. Today, Pittsburgh's economy is considerably less dependent on the steel industry than it was in 1946.

Strikes as a strike's silver lining?

Although the long-term effects of strikes can be devastating, there can be short-term advantages for businesses that think creatively and take action.

As an example, when airplane manufacturing employees in Wichita, Kansas went on strike during the mid-1990s, a local bowling center -- Fireside Lanes -- recognized that unemployed aircraft workers would have some extra time available until the strike was settled. So, the bowling center developed a series of promotions and price-deals to entice the striking aircraft workers to spend their free time bowling. Marketers of other entertainment activities and time-consuming services could develop similar promotions to tap the strike market.

January 28, 2018
Sunday
Data Privacy/Protection Day

Objectives & reminders

___

___

___

Appointments

Early morning

8 a.m.

9 a.m.

10 a.m.

11 a.m.

Noon

1 p.m.

2 p.m.

3 p.m.

4 p.m.

5 p.m.

6 p.m.

Later evening

Principle CEO appointed!

Robert Bartels was the first marketing scholar to attempt to identify and articulate the principles of marketing -- in his doctoral dissertation and the classic article that followed (see "Marketing Principles" in the October 1944 issue of the *Journal of Marketing*).

But Bartels isn't the only business thinker with an interest in codifying the "principle" building blocks of business. Take William H. Swanson, for example. On what would have been Bartels' 91st birthday -- January 28, 2004 -- Swanson became the CEO, President and Chairman of Raytheon Company, the aerospace conglomerate.

Not wanting his managers to have to wade through millions of words of management philosophy, Swanson collapsed his years of managerial experience into a series of principle-like statements to share with managers. The collection was published by Raytheon in a 76-page booklet called *Swanson's Unwritten Rules of Management.* Most of Swanson's "rules" are widely applicable throughout an organization -- regardless of one's job title.

Swanson rules

R1	"You remember one-third of what you read, one-half of what people tell you, but 100 percent of what you feel."
R2	"Have fun at what you do. It will be reflected in your work. No one likes a grump except another grump!"
R3	"If you are not criticized, you may not be doing much."
R4	"A person who is nice to you but rude to the waiter -- or to others -- is not a nice person."

___

Listening is more than hearing

"Real listening is a willingness to let the other person change you." – Alan Alda, American Emmy Award-winning actor, perhaps best remembered for his role as Captain "Hawkeye" Pierce in the hit television series M*A*S*H (1972-1983), born in New York City on January 28, 1936

January 29, 2018
Monday

Kansas Day (Kansas)

Objectives & reminders

____

____

____

Appointments

Early morning

8 a.m.

9 a.m.

10 a.m.

11 a.m.

Noon

1 p.m.

2 p.m.

3 p.m.

4 p.m.

5 p.m.

6 p.m.

Later evening

Happy birthday: Thomas Paine

Born in Thetford, Norfolk (England) on January 29, 1737, Paine worked in a variety of jobs early in his career, but for the most part lived in poverty for 37 years before meeting Benjamin Franklin in London in September 1774. Franklin encouraged Paine to travel to America, which he did a few weeks later. There, Paine fine-tuned his writing skills by writing a few articles for the *Pennsylvania Magazine.*

Then, in January 1776 -- only 14 months after arriving in America -- he published his best-selling and highly influential pamphlet, *Common Sense,* which called for America's independence. Almost 500,000 copies were sold. Paine went on to write several more political pamphlets and books.

Paine on hard work, commitment, courage and overcoming adversity

"The harder the conflict, the more glorious the triumph. What we obtain too cheap, we esteem too lightly; 'tis dearness only that gives everything its value. I love the man that can smile in trouble, that can gather strength from distress, and grow brave by reflection. 'Tis the business of little minds to shrink; but he whose heart is firm, and whose conscience approves his conduct, will pursue his principles until death." -- Thomas Paine

---

Happy birthday: William McKinley

Born in Niles, Ohio on January 29, 1843, McKinley served as a congressman, governor, and finally as the 25th President of the United States from 1897 until September 1901 when he died from a gunshot wound inflicted by an assassin. During most of his political career McKinley advocated tariffs and other protectionist measures. As a member of the U.S. House of Representatives, for example, he sponsored the McKinley Tariff Act of 1890.

Leadership by example

"That's all a man can hope for during his lifetime -- to set an example -- and when he is dead, to be an inspiration for history."
-- President William McKinley

January 30, 2018
Tuesday
Martyrs' Day (India)

Objectives & reminders

____

____

____

Appointments

Early morning

8 a.m.

9 a.m.

10 a.m.

11 a.m.

Noon

1 p.m.

2 p.m.

3 p.m.

4 p.m.

5 p.m.

6 p.m.

Later evening

Happy birthday: Franklin Delano Roosevelt

Roosevelt was born on January 30, 1882, in Hyde Park, New York. He went on to serve as the Governor of New York and as the 32nd President of the United States. His 12 years and 40 days as President (beginning March 4, 1933) was the longest presidential stint in U.S. history. During his presidency, Roosevelt successfully faced two of the nation's greatest challenges in history -- the Great Depression and World War II.

> **FDR's popularity**
> In 1939 almost 50,000 school children in Manhattan, New York were surveyed. They were asked to identify the most hated and most loved people in the world. In the "most hated" category, Adolph Hitler and Benito Mussolini "won," while President Roosevelt topped the voting for "most loved."

The great march

In 1937 President Roosevelt was involved in the birth of an extremely successful fundraising effort that not only raised money and heightened public awareness for a worthy social cause, but also spawned a non-profit organization that still exists today.

Stricken with polio himself, Roosevelt asked citizens across America to each send him a dime to be used for polio research. Soon his mailbox was filled with 150,000 letters *daily* -- each with dimes enclosed. He referred to the outpouring of support as the "March of Dimes."

> **Presidential endorsements: Worth more than a dime**
> Today, marketers for non-profit organizations (NPOs) understand that the political clout and media attention-getting ability of U.S. Presidents make them preferred supporters. However, there are thousands of NPOs in the U.S. today, so the competition for presidential support is enormous.

On his birthday in 1946, Roosevelt was honored by Congress with the authorization of his likeness to be used on the dime coin. The Roosevelt dime is still minted today.

January 31, 2018
Wednesday

Thaipusam Festival
(India, Malaysia, Singapore, South Africa, Sri Lanka, and elsewhere)

Appointments

Early morning

8 a.m.

9 a.m.

10 a.m.

11 a.m.

Noon

1 p.m.

2 p.m.

3 p.m.

4 p.m.

5 p.m.

6 p.m.

Later evening

Whose children are these?

Devoted and older television viewers may remember January 31, 1949 -- the day the first daytime television soap opera was broadcast. *These Are My Children* was shown on the NBC network.

Today, soap operas enjoy extremely loyal audiences. For some fans, watching their favorite soap opera takes precedence over all other activities in their life. Missing a daily episode is not an option for these devotees, because episodes are inseparably linked together. The drama of one episode spills into future episodes. Today's episode cannot be understood fully without understanding the context of past and future episodes within which it is nested.

Marketers in multiple industries can learn from the high loyalty factor enjoyed by today's soap operas. One lesson is to avoid discrete transactions that have a clearly delineated beginning and end. Rather, like soap operas, dealing with customers should be staged as a continuous series of linked episodes within which individual purchases are made. Each contact with a customer leads to a follow-up contact. Inquiries blossom into dialogues. A "Hello" on one day leads to "How's the family?" and "What's new?" on subsequent days. One purchase is linked to a service commitment, to accessories, to upgrades, to a "new and improved" model, to loyalty club points, and, of course, to "Thank you. Come again."

As relationships with customers develop, specific beginnings and endings are lost. As such, there is no discrete decision-point at which customers make conscious choices to continue or discontinue purchasing from the marketer -- much like devoted soap opera viewers never consciously decide whether to watch today's episode or not. Soap opera viewers simply watch; that's what they do.

Corporate soap opera challenge

"The solution of the problem affecting the regulation and control of the relations between the human factors essential in our industrial and corporation life – the employers, the wage-earners and consumers – so as to insure absolutely fair dealings among the three, is one of the principal tasks set before the enlightened statesmanship of the present day and the future."
– George W. Perkins, vice-president of New York Life Insurance Co. and partner at J.P. Morgan & Co., born in Chicago on January 31, 1862

February 1, 2018
Thursday
National Freedom Day

Mon	Tue	Wed	Thr	Fri	Sat	Sun
			1	2	3	4
5	6	7	8	9	10	11
12	13	14	15	16	17	18
19	20	21	22	23	24	25
26	27	28				

Objectives & reminders

Appointments

Early morning

8 a.m.

9 a.m.

10 a.m.

11 a.m.

Noon

1 p.m.

2 p.m.

3 p.m.

4 p.m.

5 p.m.

6 p.m.

Later evening

Welcome to February

February is the shortest month of the year, but it has several noteworthy holidays, occasions and events to celebrate or observe. In 2018, a few of these include:

- African-American History Month (all month)
- Groundhog Day (February 2)
- Super Bowl Sunday (February 4)
- Fat Tuesday, to begin Mardi Gras (February 13)
- Valentine's Day (February 14)
- Ash Wednesday, beginning of Lent (February 14)
- Chinese New Year (February 16)
- Presidents' Day [U.S.], (February 19)

Calendar-led marketing

When planning your promotion calendar, consider linking promotional efforts with these and other holidays, events and occasions. Also consider noteworthy local or regional dates, those of particular relevance to your industry or brand, and those most likely to resonate with buyers. Many other possibilities are noted throughout each edition of *Marketing FAME* and on websites such as http://www.holidayscalendar.com/ and http://www.holidayinsights.com/

Every day is special, with no exceptions

There's always something or someone to celebrate, observe, honor or remember.

First automobile insurance policy: Something to celebrate?

Hartford, Connecticut's Travelers Insurance Company became the first American firm to issue automobile insurance -- on February 1, 1898. The first policyholder was Buffalo, New York resident Dr. Truman J. Martin whose premium was $11.25. Clearly, his 1898 policy of $5,000 liability coverage would need to be updated in today's world.

In his book, *Celebrate Today*, John Kremer points out the potential for promotional tie-ins to capitalize on this historic date in the history of automobile insurance. For example, he suggests that automobile dealers could promote a sales event in early February, during which dealers could pay for new buyers' first month's insurance. Or, insurance agents might promote the occasion to remind policyholders to review the adequacy of their coverage.

February 2, 2018
Friday

Candlemas Day * Groundhog Day

Objectives & reminders

Appointments

Early morning

8 a.m.

9 a.m.

10 a.m.

11 a.m.

Noon

1 p.m.

2 p.m.

3 p.m.

4 p.m.

5 p.m.

6 p.m.

Later evening

Candlemas Day

Religious observers recognize February 2 as the anniversary of the day on which the baby Jesus was presented in the temple. The name "Candlemas" derives from the accompanying celebration involving the blessing of candles for sacred use.

Groundhog Day

Some beliefs and practices are driven more by tradition and custom than can be defensibly justified on their own merits. For example, one traditional forecasting belief maintains that if a groundhog can see his shadow on February 2, another six weeks of winter is inevitable.

Like most approaches to forecasting, however, the groundhog test is most accurate in the short-term. That is, if the groundhog can see his shadow today, the sun is probably shining *today*.

May I be excused?

On February 2, 1852, the first public lavatory (with a "water closet") was opened for "Gentlemen" on Fleet Street in London. Women had to hold their enthusiasm for nine more days until the first public "Ladies" lavatory opened in Strand (U.K.).

Publicly accessible restrooms are commonplace today -- thanks, in part, to marketing wisdom. About 100 years after the first public lavatory opened in London, marketing researchers in the U.S. working for The Coca-Cola Company learned that motorists tended to spend more money when they got out of their vehicles at gasoline "filling" stations. The company used the research to convince gasoline retailers to stock Coke products. "Refreshing" and "ice cold" Coca Colas, coupled with "clean" and "modern" restrooms became effective promotional lures to coax motorists out of their cars.

Automotive milestone

On February 2, 1925, Walter P. Chrysler introduced his first Chrysler automobile, priced at $1,595. To better understand design issues and alternatives, Mr. Chrysler disassembled and then reassembled competing vehicles over and over again before finalizing the design of the first Chrysler automobile. Today, competitors routinely scrutinize their competitors' products by taking them apart.

February 3, 2018
Saturday
Carrot Cake Day

Objectives & reminders

___

___

___

Appointments

Early morning

8 a.m.

9 a.m.

10 a.m.

11 a.m.

Noon

1 p.m.

2 p.m.

3 p.m.

4 p.m.

5 p.m.

6 p.m.

Later evening

Feedback can be painful

Twenty-two percent of surveyed office workers reported that they have cried after going through a structured performance review, while 20 percent said they have quit their jobs after such a review. The study surveyed 1,328 U.S. office workers who had participated in a structured performance evaluation review process and was summarized in the February 3, 2017 edition of *USA Today*, p. 1B.

Tips for supervisors to make performance evaluations more palatable

1. Don't focus solely on the negatives. Include positive accomplishments in the review too.
2. Focus on observable behaviors. Leave personalities out of the evaluation process.
3. Give workers the opportunity to point out their own perceived deficiencies. If they do, the self-criticism will sting less than if coming from the manager, plus employees tend to be more committed to closing the gaps in performance that they've identified themselves.
4. Identify paths for progress, i.e., show workers specific action steps to take to improve performance.
5. Avoid surprises. Don't wait for the formal *annual* review to let workers know that their performance is subpar. Instead provide feedback, training and coaching throughout the year.
6. Stay calm.

Service augmentation

In an effort to differentiate themselves from competitors and add value for customers, service providers often add extras to the service package. If customers are receptive to the augmented services, competitors tend to copy the innovations and begin including them as part of their service packages too.

In no industry is this phenomenon more apparent than in lodging. For example, in February 1932, the Hotel New Yorker in New York City became the first hotel to install television sets in guests' "deluxe suites." Guests could tune-in to five hours of programming daily. Today, of course, television sets in hotel rooms (in industrialized countries) are no longer considered extras; they're expected. Hotels have to look elsewhere for extras. Slippers?

February 4, 2018
Sunday
World Cancer Day
National Day (Sri Lanka)

Objectives & reminders

___

___

___

Appointments

Early morning

8 a.m.

9 a.m.

10 a.m.

11 a.m.

Noon

1 p.m.

2 p.m.

3 p.m.

4 p.m.

5 p.m.

6 p.m.

Later evening

Super Bowl 52

This year, the annual climatic concluding game of the National Football League season will be held today – February 4 – at U.S. Bank Stadium in Minneapolis, Minnesota.

Although the stadium will be sold out, there will be enough room in homes, sports bars and other gathering places around the country to accommodate an expected 110-120 million football fans who will watch at least a portion of the big game on television.

Besides football, food will be a common denominator of today's get-togethers – making the day second only to Thanksgiving in terms of food and beverage consumption in the U.S.

Are you a cute animal or a child?
According to an aytm.com study of 3,500 viewers of the 2014 Super Bowl, commercials involving cute animals and/or children were the most memorable.

Not surprisingly, the enormous number of viewers (quite likely the most viewed television event of 2018) means advertising spots during the telecast will be premium-priced – possibly exceeding the 2017 rates of $5.5 million for some of the most desirable 30-second time slots, such as the first commercial break after the kickoff.

Much to advertisers' delight, the Super Bowl telecast may be the only televised event during the year with an audience that actually looks forward to seeing the commercials.

Online retailers prepared for "revenge shopping" during Super Bowl
As is the case with many sporting events, online retailers are likely to be busy today serving shoppers who resent the attention their spouses, family and friends devote to the Super Bowl. To compensate for the perceived injustice, some snubbed consumers who have no interest in football may be expected to seek revenge today by looking for something to buy online. Accordingly, online marketers will be prepared for the day's upturn in customer traffic.

February 5, 2018
Monday
Constitution Day (Mexico)

Objectives & reminders

____

____

____

Appointments

Early morning

8 a.m.

9 a.m.

10 a.m.

11 a.m.

Noon

1 p.m.

2 p.m.

3 p.m.

4 p.m.

5 p.m.

6 p.m.

Later evening

Happy birthday: Mr. Potato Head

The most famous spud in the world was born on February 5, 1952. Shortly thereafter he helped to revolutionize the toy business by being the first toy advertised on network television. The advertising exposure not only boosted sales, but may have had something to do with him meeting and marrying Mrs. Potato Head in 1953.

Three children's markets

Today, advertising to children is common, as marketers recognize the enormous potential of reaching these *three* markets.

1. Children as *direct purchasers*, who collectively spend billions of dollars of their own money. According to a 2017 National Retail Federation study, 59% of young consumers (ages 13-21) report receiving an allowance, 24% work part-time and 22% make money online.

2. Children as *influencers*, who frequently sway family purchase decisions for food products, household items, and even automobiles. Similarly, children are not shy in offering product and brand suggestions to Santa Claus and other gift-givers.

3. Children as *future adults.* Research confirms that when consumers are exposed to brands as children, they are more likely to develop or maintain a loyalty to those brands as adults than if they were not exposed to the same brands until adulthood.

Since those early days, Mr. Potato Head has extended his exposure in several ways: (1) by helping to cross-promote other products offered by his parent company [e.g., Children's Educational Software], (2) by endorsing other organizations' products in advertising [e.g., Burger King french fries], (3) by supporting non-profit causes [e.g., in 1987 he gave up his pipe and became the official "spokespud" for the Great American Smokeout sponsored by the American Cancer Society], and (4) by appearing on television and in movies [e.g., *Toy Story*, *Toy Story 2*].

February 6, 2018
Tuesday
Waitangi Day (New Zealand)

Objectives & reminders

Appointments

Early morning

---

8 a.m.

---

9 a.m.

---

10 a.m.

---

11 a.m.

Noon

---

1 p.m.

---

2 p.m.

---

3 p.m.

---

4 p.m.

---

5 p.m.

---

6 p.m.

Later evening

Happy birthday: Thurl Arthur Ravenscroft

Born in Norfolk, Nebraska on February 6, 1914, Ravenscroft was a singer throughout much of his career, but his most remembered contribution to marketing began in 1952 when he landed the job as the voice of Tony the Tiger, spokescharacter for Kellogg's Frosted Flakes breakfast cereal.

For more than 50 years, Ravenscroft's deep booming voice helped Tony repeatedly reinforce Kellogg's assertion about Frosted Flakes, i.e., "Theeeey'rrrrre Grrrrreeeeeat!" At the turn of the century, *Advertising Age* magazine dubbed Tony the Tiger as one of the top 10 advertising icons of the 20th century.

After Ravenscroft died of cancer in May of 2005, Kellogg saluted him with an ad in *Advertising Age;* the headline read, "Behind every great character is an even greater man."

Why advertisers like spokescharacters

1. They help consumers identify with the brands the spokescharacters represent. Tony the Tiger reinforced the brand in consumers' minds by inseparably intertwining the product with its packaging and its advertising.
2. Spokescharacters provide continuity over time. Unlike human spokes-people, for more than 50 years Tony the Tiger never aged or gained weight. He was never involved in a scandal, and he never endorsed competing brands.
3. They help create a "personality" for the brand by symbolizing the brand's attributes or desired position in the marketplace. If it weren't for Tony the Tiger, Frosted Flakes might be... too flakey?
4. Young children are more likely to recognize spokescharacters used in ads, on packages or in displays, than they are to recognize human spokespeople.

February 7, 2018
Wednesday
National Signing Day (football)

Objectives & reminders

Appointments

Early morning

---
8 a.m.

---
9 a.m.

---
10 a.m.

---
11 a.m.

Noon

---
1 p.m.

---
2 p.m.

---
3 p.m.

---
4 p.m.

---
5 p.m.

---
6 p.m.

Later evening

All exchanges are not necessarily equal: Agree or disagree?

"Men may not get all they pay for in this world, but they must certainly pay for all they get." -- Frederick Douglass, American writer and abolitionist, born in Tucahoe, Maryland on February 7, 1817

Decision-making recommendation

"Take nothing on its looks; take everything on evidence. There's no better rule." -- Charles John Huffam Dickens, English novelist, born in Landport, England on February 7, 1812

What should managers manage?

"The trouble with organizing a thing is that pretty soon folks get to paying more attention to the organization than to what they're organized for." -- Laura Ingalls Wilder, American children's writer (*Little House on the Prairie* series), born near Pepin, Wisconsin on February 7, 1867

Managing crises and adversity

"You must not abandon the ship in a storm because you cannot control the winds... What you cannot turn to good, you must at least make as little bad as you can." -- Sir Thomas More, English lawyer, politician and writer, born in London on February 7, 1478

Substitute "business" for "country": Then agree or disagree?

"The trouble with this country is that there are too many people going about saying, 'The trouble with this country is...'" -- Sinclair Lewis, American writer, born in Sauk Centre, Minnesota on February 7, 1885

Green quality

"I will never put my name on a product that does not have in it the best that is in me." – John Deere, founder of Deere & Company (construction equipment, green tractors and lawn mowers), born in Rutland, Vermont on February 7, 1804

February 8, 2018
Thursday
Fat Thursday

Objectives & reminders

Appointments

Early morning

---
8 a.m.

---
9 a.m.

---
10 a.m.

---
11 a.m.

Noon

---
1 p.m.

---
2 p.m.

---
3 p.m.

---
4 p.m.

---
5 p.m.

---
6 p.m.

Later evening

Fat Thursday

As the last Thursday before Lent, German and Polish Catholics celebrate Fat Thursday as a festive day of feasting, during which they eat a large amount of cakes, candy and other food forbidden by their religion during the Lent season that follows. They often enjoy the day with family and friends. Accordingly, the day of celebration is somewhat similar to the more familiar French day known as Fat Tuesday that kicks off the Mardi Gras festival.

Although the specific date of Fat Thursday varies on the Gregorian calendar, it always precedes Ash Wednesday by six days and Easter Sunday by 52 days.

Books with wheels?

On February 8, 1957, the library "bookmobile" concept began rolling along -- first in front of City Hall (San Francisco according to some sources, New York according to others). Recognizing the difficulty some consumers had getting to libraries, the bookmobile concept was simple: Take the library to the consumers.

It wasn't long before bookmobiles were crisscrossing the streets of hundreds of U.S. cities. The over-sized vans would arrive at pre-publicized locations and times (e.g., in the local shopping center parking lot at 2:00 p.m. on Wednesdays) and would stay there for a couple of hours -- depending on demand -- before moving on to the next location in another neighborhood. Bookmobile patrons could browse a few hundred selections routinely carried on the bookmobile, check out specific library books previously requested, or return books already read. At the height of their popularity, bookmobiles made library services more accessible to more patrons, and at a cost that was considerably less than that required to build, staff, and maintain branch library buildings.

Fewer bookmobiles make their rounds today than in the 1960s, but marketers can and still do capitalize on the concept of taking the service to customer-convenient locations. This is especially true for marketers of services that require the physical presence of the customer or his possessions. For example, some automobile oil change firms take their "oilmobiles" to customers' homes or places of employment; they service customers' vehicles while customers do things that are more productive or more pleasurable than sitting in a service center's waiting room.

February 9, 2018
Friday

Winter Olympics begin (Pyeongchang County, South Korea)

Objectives & reminders

Appointments

Early morning

8 a.m.

9 a.m.

10 a.m.

11 a.m.

Noon

1 p.m.

2 p.m.

3 p.m.

4 p.m.

5 p.m.

6 p.m.

Later evening

Happy birthday: Bill Veeck

Born in Chicago on February 9, 1914, Veeck was a colorful contributor to the history of baseball – particularly to the marketing of baseball.

Working for the Chicago Cubs in 1937, Veeck decided to make the ball park (Wrigley Field) more aesthetically pleasing for fans, so he had ivy planted on the outfield walls – a key point of differentiation for several decades.

As owner of the Cleveland Indians, St. Louis Browns and Chicago White Sox, Veeck pioneered several other innovations that have been adopted almost universally by baseball marketers – fireworks, Bat Day and exploding scoreboards that lead the celebration when a home-team player hits a home run.

Further, it was Veeck's idea to put players' names on the backs of uniforms so fans could identify them more easily. Relationship marketers now know that learning names is an essential building block in forming lasting business relationships.

To boost attendance and generate publicity and excitement, Veeck wasn't afraid to exercise creativity and do what some baseball marketing purists (i.e., those who consider baseball to be solely a sport rather than entertainment) might consider outlandish and inappropriate. For example, in 1951 Veeck hired Eddie Gaedel – a three-foot, seven-inch midget whose tiny strike zone intimidated the opposing pitcher to the point that Gaedel actually got on base (apparently a "walk"). "The fans went wild," Gaedel later noted, "and continue to talk about the event." However, few people seem to remember which team won the game.

Guiding philosophy for sports marketers: Agree or disagree?

"There is in all of us a competitive spirit, but winning has become life and death. We lose sight that it's only a *game*. It's a delightful game that is occasionally played by skillful men. Phil Wrigley once said that all you need is a winning club. It's a damning comment. We all like winners, but winning without joy isn't worth the candle." – Bill Veeck

For more baseball stories and sports marketing insights, see Veeck's 1981 book, *Veeck As In Wreck*.

February 10, 2018
Saturday
Carnival Saturday (Brazil)

Objectives & reminders

____
____
____

Appointments

Early morning

8 a.m.

9 a.m.

10 a.m.

11 a.m.

Noon

1 p.m.

2 p.m.

3 p.m.

4 p.m.

5 p.m.

6 p.m.

Later evening

Fire safety: Do you know this about *then*?

The first U.S. patent for a fire extinguishing system for buildings was awarded on February 10, 1863. The recipient was Alanson Crane from Fortress Monroe, Virginia. In the event of fire, the system of pipes that extended across the ceiling could be operated by someone outside to flood the building with water to extinguish the fire.

Do you know this about *today*?
February 10 is a good day to familiarize yourself and your coworkers with fire safety. Begin with these questions:

1. Is there a fire extinguishing system in the building where you work? If not, are hand-held fire extinguishers available? Where are they located? Are they operable?
2. Further, does your organization have a fire safety plan? Is everyone in your organization familiar with it? Does everyone know what to do to prevent fires, and what to do in a fire emergency?

Short-term managers: Fighting fires and alligators

During times of crises -- such as fires -- long-term plans and strategic thinking are abandoned until the fires are extinguished. Accordingly, managers who are overly preoccupied with the day-to-day details of the business often use a fire metaphor to justify (rationalize?) their short-term orientation.

Although the strength of many businesses lies in their superior execution of day-to-day details, if managers spend too much time "putting out fires," so to speak, an organization's long-term may be sacrificed unnecessarily. So, effective managers think in terms of balancing the short-term with the long-term.

On February 10, 1982, U.S. President Ronald Reagan used another crisis management metaphor to illustrate the short-term/long-term balancing challenge that managers face: "I know it's hard when you're up to your armpits in alligators to remember you came here to drain the swamp."

February 11, 2018
Sunday
National Inventors' Day

Objectives & reminders

____

____

____

Appointments

Early morning

8 a.m.

9 a.m.

10 a.m.

11 a.m.

Noon

1 p.m.

2 p.m.

3 p.m.

4 p.m.

5 p.m.

6 p.m.

Later evening

Happy birthday: Edward Johnston

Born in San José, Uruguay on February 11, 1872, Johnston was an influential British calligrapher and letter designer. He spent most of his career teaching lettering design classes at the Royal College of Art where he authored two noteworthy books, *Writing and Illuminating and Lettering* (1906), and *Manuscript and Inscription Letters* (1909).

Today, lettering is much less of an artistic skill as word processing technology allows businesspeople to choose from dozens of fonts with the effortless click of a mouse. Still, it is useful to be sensitive to the impressions that alternative lettering designs are likely to make in readers' minds.

Font selection matters

If you're not convinced of the role that letter design has in advertising, signage, packaging and correspondence, consider the different impressions evoked by alternative letter designs for each of the businesses listed below.

Principle: Effective letter designs should reinforce – not contradict – the mental images that firms wish to evoke.

Forever Bridal Boutique
versus
FOREVER BRIDAL BOUTIQUE

Big Game Bar & Grill
versus
Big Game Bar & Grill

Party-Time Arcade
versus
Party-Time Arcade

Progressive Medical Associates
versus
Progressive Medical Associates

Speedy Delivery Service
versus
Speedy Delivery Service

Old-Fashion Barbeque
versus
Old-Fashion Barbeque

February 12, 2018
Monday
Shrove Monday

Objectives & reminders

____

____

____

Appointments

Early morning

8 a.m.

9 a.m.

10 a.m.

11 a.m.

Noon

1 p.m.

2 p.m.

3 p.m.

4 p.m.

5 p.m.

6 p.m.

Later evening

Happy Birthday: Peter Cooper

Born in New York City on February 12, 1791, Cooper dabbled with several mechanical inventions in the emerging industrial age, but unfortunately none of them became particularly profitable ventures.

However, Cooper was successful in several businesses that he started or purchased. One of these was a glue factory, in which he serendipitously created a flavored gelatin product -- the ancestor of what we now know as "Jell-O."

Today, we recognize that one of the keys to the longevity of many discretionary products is their suitability for new uses or new applications. That is, the identification and adoption of new uses helps to boost a product's sales and extend its life. New uses often attract new buyers to the product category. New uses can increase existing customers' usage rates and especially in the case of food products, keep customers from becoming bored with the product. Jell-O, for example, is not *just* Jell-O, per se; rather it is a key ingredient in more than 700 food recipes that help the product category and brand to thrive.

New applications are essential when old ones fade away
If you're not convinced, try counting the number of people you know who still use baking soda for baking.

____

Publicity to prove capability

What do you get when you marry 10,000 pounds of pound cake batter with 4,810 pounds of vanilla/almond frosting? A record-breaking wedding cake weighing more than five times as much as a Volkswagen Beetle and all the publicity its maker can eat.

The cake was unveiled at the New England Bridal Showcase on February 12, 2004, by Mohegan Sun (casino and hotel) to demonstrate its wedding services capabilities. The five-tiered, 22-feet tall cake took the company's 58-person team of chefs almost two weeks to create.

Presumably if the hotel's wedding chefs can prepare a cake of this size, they can handle the catering for almost any wedding that might be booked at the hotel.

February 13, 2018
Tuesday
Mardi Gras * Fat Tuesday
World Radio Day

Objectives & reminders

____

____

____

Appointments

Early morning

8 a.m.

9 a.m.

10 a.m.

11 a.m.

Noon

1 p.m.

2 p.m.

3 p.m.

4 p.m.

5 p.m.

6 p.m.

Later evening

Happy birthday: Paul Felix Lazarsfeld

Lazarsfeld was born in Vienna, Austria on February 13, 1901, and became a U.S. citizen in 1943. As a sociologist, Lazarsfeld's research at the Bureau of Applied Social Research at Columbia University in New York explored the marketing implications of sociological phenomena.

Among his many contributions to the field of marketing, Lazarsfeld demonstrated the important role that consumers' families, friends, co-workers and other people play in influencing consumers' purchase decisions. That is, *opinion leaders* may be found within most groups -- people who tend to be gregarious and are likely to have above-average knowledge of the brand or product category, and whose perspectives and recommendations are respected and sought by other consumers.

Lazarsfeld suggested that marketers aggressively target opinion leaders, especially for new products: "Once the advertiser knows who the marketing [opinion] leaders are, he can direct his advertising to this select group that will eventually, through its influence, establish the buying pattern of his total market."

School lesson

Born in London, England on February 13, 1910, William Shockley's inquisitive mind led him to co-develop and commercialize transistors in the 1950s and 1960s that would create California's Silicon Valley and change the world.

Shockley's reputation as a tenacious, objective-driven inventor and businessman were influenced by a negative experience he encountered in school. According to Shockley:

> "I had one experience which gave me some slant on the way large organizations run. I was not allowed to take spherical trigonometry because I'd sprained my ankle. Because I'd sprained my ankle I had an 'Incomplete' in gym, phys ed. And the rule was that if you had an Incomplete in anything, you were not allowed to take an overload. I argued with some clerical person in the administration office, and was stopped there. It's an experience which I've remembered since, and advised people not to be stopped at the first point."

February 14, 2018
Wednesday
Ash Wednesday
Valentine's Day

Objectives & reminders

____

____

____

Appointments

Early morning

8 a.m.

9 a.m.

10 a.m.

11 a.m.

Noon

1 p.m.

2 p.m.

3 p.m.

4 p.m.

5 p.m.

6 p.m.

Later evening

Valentine's Day research: What does $85.21 mean?

Many descriptive summary statistics are reported for holidays and occasions throughout the year -- including some for Valentine's Day, which is celebrated annually in the U.S. on February 14. The statistics typically provide a glimpse of how many consumers observe the occasion, how much they spend, what items they purchase, and so on.

However, the summary statistics are often singled-out and reported by the media with little or no context regarding the methodologies used – methodologies that could sway a study's findings considerably. So, before fully digesting or acting on these statistics, it can be helpful to locate the original research in order to scrutinize the methodologies and learn precisely what the statistics represent and how they were calculated.

To illustrate, on the day before Valentine's Day in 2017, *USA Today* reported a couple of Valentine's Day summary statistics they called "USA Snapshots." One asserted that the "average spending on significant other for Valentine's Day 2017" was $85.21. A footnote indicated that the finding stemmed from a "survey of 7,591 consumers."

So, what does "$85.21" represent? Consider how the answers to the following questions could affect the magnitude and meaning of the statistic:

1. Was "spending" operationalized as *actual* money spent, what respondents *remembered* spending, what they *planned* to spend, or something else?
2. Was the "average" calculated as the mean, median, mode or some other measure of average?
3. Did "spending" include only gifts, or were cards, dining and travel (airfare, mileage expense) also included? Was spending the day or two before Valentine's "*Day*" included or excluded?
4. Exactly what is a "significant other"? Was the statistic inflated by respondents with multiple significant others, or otherwise biased by those with different definitions of "significant other"?
5. Were "consumers" adults, or were teens and children surveyed too?
6. Was the survey conducted online – under-representing seniors, less-educated and rural consumers who are less likely to use the Internet?
7. Did consumers voluntarily take the survey, possibly excluding potential responses from those who don't observe Valentine's Day?

February 15, 2018
Thursday
Susan B. Anthony Day

Objectives & reminders

____

____

____

Appointments

Early morning

8 a.m.

9 a.m.

10 a.m.

11 a.m.

Noon

1 p.m.

2 p.m.

3 p.m.

4 p.m.

5 p.m.

6 p.m.

Later evening

Happy birthday: Cyrus Hall McCormick

McCormick was born in Virginia's Shenandoah Valley on February 15, 1809. Like most people of the era, McCormick was born into a family of farmers. His father helped instill in him an interest in easing the burden of farming work. When only 15 years old, he built a light-weight cradle used to harvest grain. At 22 he invented an efficient reaper, soon followed by a new threshing machine.

Although mechanically-inclined, McCormick's success probably had more to do with his aptitude as a marketer than as an inventor. For example, to convey the superiority of his reaper's design he challenged his key competitor -- Obed Hussey -- to a head-to-head contest in 1843. McCormick's reaper won in convincing fashion, cutting 17 acres in the same amount of time it took Hussey to cut only two acres.

McCormick was so interested in farmers' perspectives that he moved to the mid-western U.S. to be geographically closer to them. He listened to farmers and distributors, and adopted many of their suggestions for improvements. One reaper improvement we might consider an obvious need today, was not so apparent to his competitors -- a seat. The seat eliminated the need for farmers to walk alongside the reaper -- thus reducing farmer fatigue and increasing the reaper's appeal.

Recognizing that service quality is part of the bundle of benefits that buyers buy, McCormick also made building and maintaining a competent and service-oriented network of dealers a top priority -- a practice that marketers routinely recognize as key today, but one that was much more novel in McCormick's era.

Greatness can begin today!

"Greatness consists not in the holding of some future office, but really consists in doing great deeds with little means and the accomplishment of vast purposes from the private ranks of life. To be great at all one must be great here, now... [R]emember this, that if you wish to be great at all, you must begin where you are and what you are... now." – Russell Conwell, American lawyer, writer, Baptist minister, and founder and first president of Temple University. Conwell was born in South Worthington, Massachusetts on February 15, 1843.

February 16, 2018
Friday
Chinese New Year

Objectives & reminders

Appointments

Early morning

8 a.m.

9 a.m.

10 a.m.

11 a.m.

Noon

1 p.m.

2 p.m.

3 p.m.

4 p.m.

5 p.m.

6 p.m.

Later evening

Chinese New Year

The Chinese New Year (CNY) is considered the most important of the traditional Chinese holidays – celebrated in China, of course, as well as in countries with a significant Chinese population or cultural influence, including the U.S., Canada, Australia and the Philippines, among others.

Unlike the Gregorian calendar, the Chinese calendar is based on cycles of the moon, so the beginning of each CNY doesn't precisely correspond to the dates found on the Gregorian calendar. Typically, however, the first day of the CNY falls somewhere between late-January and mid-February.

Legend provides celebration clues

According to Chinese legend, Nian, a man-eating monster descended from the mountains annually on New Year's Eve to feast on humans. Over time, the Chinese learned that Nian feared the color red as well as loud noises, so in order to "Guo Nian" (survive the Nian), people learned to use red colors liberally and shoot fireworks. Once the annual Nian threat was repelled, additional fireworks, feasts, red clothing, and other traditions were used to celebrate the anticipation of another safe year.

The length of CNY celebrations varies around the world, but may begin on New Year's Eve with a family reunion and feast, and continue for up to 15 days, with each day celebrated or observed in a slightly different way. Generally, only the first day or the first few days of the CNY are recognized as public holidays, if at all. When CNY begins on the weekend, the public holidays may be pushed into the following work-week.

Marketing opportunities for this CNY tradition?

Chinese families give their homes a thorough cleaning prior to the beginning of the New Year – to rid homes of bad luck so that good luck may enter. Similarly, some apply a fresh coat of red paint to doors and window frames to keep bad luck at bay. Red clothing also is considered lucky and anyone wearing bright red during CNY celebrations is destined to have a bright future.

February 17, 2018
Saturday
Random Acts of Kindness Day

Objectives & reminders

___

___

___

Appointments

Early morning

8 a.m.

9 a.m.

10 a.m.

11 a.m.

Noon

1 p.m.

2 p.m.

3 p.m.

4 p.m.

5 p.m.

6 p.m.

Later evening

Happy birthday: Michael Jordan

Born in Brooklyn, New York on February 17, 1963, Jordan became what some people consider to be the best basketball player in the history of the game. One key to his basketball success was his positive attitude, which also can be applied to business pursuits. According to Jordan: "Obstacles don't have to stop you. If you run into a wall, don't turn around and give up. Figure out how to climb it, go through it, or work around it."

Athletes as advertising short-cuts: Agree or disagree?

"You can't explain much in 60 seconds [of advertising], but when you show Michael Jordan, you don't have to. It's that simple." – Phil Knight, co-founder and former CEO & chairman of Nike (Nike was one of Jordan's key endorsements)

Focus group innovation

The "transparent mirror" was invented more than 100 years ago, with the first patent issued on February 17, 1903, to Emil Bloch. The mirrors are reflective on one side, but allow viewers to see *through* the mirrors when viewed from a well lit room on the opposite side.

Today, transparent mirrors are often found in rooms constructed for focus group research. While the focus groups are conducted on one side of a mirror, researchers or clients unobtrusively observe the participants and listen to their comments while seated in another room on the other side of the mirror.

Marketing research was/is junk: Agree or disagree?

"[J]udging from papers which continue to be published in our most prestigious journals and from research reports which often form the basis for important marketing management and public policy decisions, it is all too apparent that *too large a proportion of the consumer (including marketing) research literature is not worth the paper it is printed on or the time it takes to read.*" -- Jacob Jacoby, consumer researcher, from an article published in the April 1978 issue of *Journal of Marketing*, "Consumer Research: A State of the Art Review," pp. 87-96. Jacoby was born in Brooklyn, New York on February 17, 1940.

February 18, 2018
Sunday
Independence Day (Gambia)

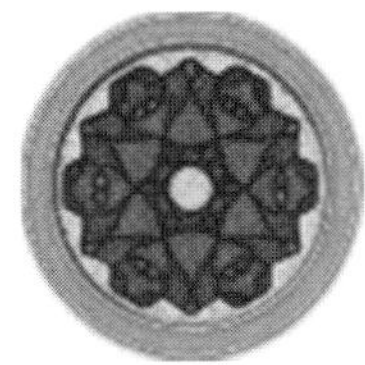

Objectives & reminders

____

____

____

Appointments

Early morning

8 a.m.

9 a.m.

10 a.m.

11 a.m.

Noon

1 p.m.

2 p.m.

3 p.m.

4 p.m.

5 p.m.

6 p.m.

Later evening

What has been the strongest non-advertised brand in the world?

It may be the one named after Enzo Ferrari, who was born on February 18, 1898. Ferrari's love of automobiles and racing led him to form his own car company and his own brand in 1947 -- Ferrari. Although Ferrari stayed away from advertising, his cars generated publicity and interest by winning races. According to *Automotive News Europe*, by the time Mr. Ferrari died in 1988, Ferrari racing cars had tallied nine Formula One world championships and 14 victories at the 24-hour race of LeMans.

Recently, managers of the Ferrari brand began to advertise on a limited basis. Not surprisingly, the first television commercial stressed speed, styling, speed, maneuverability, and more speed. See the ad yourself: www.youtube.com/watch?v=CPft8xiusTU

Happy birthday: Louis Comfort Tiffany

Born in New York City on February 18, 1848, Tiffany was the son of jeweler Charles L. Tiffany (founder of Tiffany & Co.). The younger Tiffany went on to establish his own career as a painter, designer, and interior decorator. Perhaps Louis Tiffany is best known for his work with iridescent and stained glass.

Aesthetic design: Three principles

1. A product's exterior design speaks before its functions do.
2. The more publicly visible a product's use, the greater the importance of an aesthetically pleasing design.
3. Glass is class.

Good day to make a sale

"We are all salesmen every day of our lives. We are selling our ideas, our plans, our enthusiasms to those with whom we come in contact." – Charles Michael Schwab, president of Carnegie Steel Co. (1896-1901), U.S. Steel Corp. (1901-1903), and Bethlehem Steel Corp. (1903-1913) – then chairman of Bethlehem Steel (1913-1939). Schwab was born in Williamsburg, Pennsylvania on February 18, 1862.

February 19, 2018
Monday
Presidents' Day

Objectives & reminders

____

____

____

Appointments

Early morning

8 a.m.

9 a.m.

10 a.m.

11 a.m.

Noon

1 p.m.

2 p.m.

3 p.m.

4 p.m.

5 p.m.

6 p.m.

Later evening

Presidents' Day

The third Monday of each February is set aside as Presidents' Day, on which all U.S. Presidents are honored. Because Presidents George Washington (1st President) and Abraham Lincoln (16th President) were born during the month of February (i.e., the 22nd and 12th of the month, respectively), the holiday recognizes these great Presidents, in particular.

> **What to say: Insight for building relationships with customers and co-workers**
> "Everybody likes a compliment."
> – President Abraham Lincoln

Accordingly, Presidents' Day celebrations and promotions often incorporate images of Washington and Lincoln, as well as more general patriotic themes using images of the U.S. flag or red, white and blue color combinations (i.e., colors of the U.S. flag). Also, fireworks and the playing of the national anthem are heard on Presidents' Day.

> **What *not* to say: Taking the "high" road**
> "Speak not injurious words, neither in jest nor earnest; scoff at none although they give occasion."
> – President George Washington

Finally, note that because Presidents' Day is a U.S. federal holiday, most federal workers and the thousands of businesses that adopt the federal government's holiday schedule as their own will have the day off from work today. Astute marketers know that when consumers don't have to report to their jobs, they have more time to shop, travel and pursue recreation and leisure activities.

> **Current and recent Presidents are too controversial to be honored today: Agree or disagree?**
> Although Presidents' Day presumably honors *all* U.S. Presidents, marketers tend to exclude current and recent Presidents from advertising and promotion campaigns, because they are viewed as too controversial and thus references to them might alienate a significant portion of targeted buyers.

February 20, 2018
Tuesday
Social Equality Justice Day

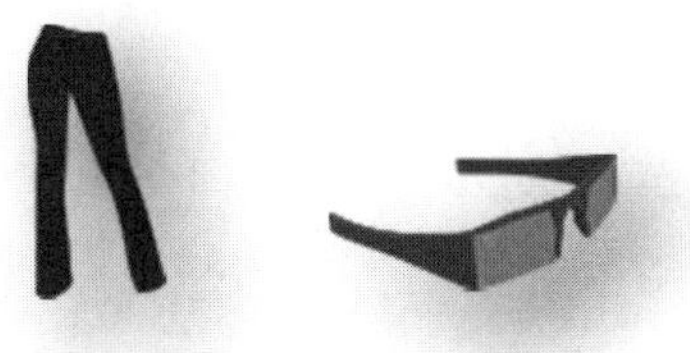

Objectives & reminders

___

___

___

Appointments

Early morning

8 a.m.

9 a.m.

10 a.m.

11 a.m.

Noon

1 p.m.

2 p.m.

3 p.m.

4 p.m.

5 p.m.

6 p.m.

Later evening

Happy birthday: Gloria Vanderbilt

Artist, actress, socialite, designer, and spokesperson Gloria Vanderbilt was born in New York City on February 20, 1924. After studying art at the Art Students' League in New York City, Vanderbilt built a reputation in oil paintings, watercolors and pastels.

Beginning in the late 1960s, Vanderbilt pursued a more commercial career by licensing her artwork to manufacturers of textiles (Bloomcraft) and paper products (Hallmark), and designing glassware, china, flatware, and linens. In the 1970s she licensed the use of her name to makers of products such as eyeglasses, perfume and clothing. In the late 1970s Gloria Vanderbilt designer jeans were introduced and popularized in a series of television ads featuring Vanderbilt herself.

Attitude is key
"I like the idea of showing that you can go through a lot and still be on your feet, still be working, and still be positive about life." -- Gloria Vanderbilt

Advertising pioneer born

Grayson, Kentucky is the birthplace of Helen Lansdowne Resor -- a business professional described by advertising legend David Ogilvy as "the greatest copywriter of her generation." Resor was born on February 20, 1886.

Resor's advertising career is noteworthy in many respects. More specifically, here are three ways Resor shaped the practice of advertising. First, she dared to use *sex appeal* in ads as early as 1910. For Woodbury facial soap, for example, she attracted readers' attention with what was a controversial and risqué headline at the time: "A skin you love to touch." Some magazines refused to print the ad.

Second, at a time when many advertisers used outrageous claims to hype products, Resor was a strong believer in the correlation between advertising *believability* and effectiveness. She insisted that advertising "copy must be believable."

Third, Resor was among the first to use *endorsements* of celebrities and well-known personalities to legitimize brands -- beginning in the 1920s (e.g., for Pond's cold cream).

February 21, 2018
Wednesday
International Mother Language Day

Objectives & reminders

____

____

____

Appointments

Early morning

8 a.m.

9 a.m.

10 a.m.

11 a.m.

Noon

1 p.m.

2 p.m.

3 p.m.

4 p.m.

5 p.m.

6 p.m.

Later evening

Some promotions are for the dogs, but apparently some are not

There tends to be an extra element of drama and accompanying publicity value when sales promotions and publicity stunts are staged "live."

But there's a downside of live events too if things don't go as planned. For example, on February 21, 1974, a dog food manufacturer invited journalists to a luncheon at which a pedigree dog sat at the table next to the company's president. When served the presumably tasty dog food, the dog refused to eat it. In an apparent effort to salvage the event, the president ate the dog food himself. Unfortunately, the dog's behavior had already discredited the dog food, while the president's bizarre behavior discredited himself.

Managing the evidence

Because services are intangible and typically not produced until after they're ordered, it can be difficult for consumers to evaluate services prior to purchase. So, consumers look for bits of evidence in the service environment that might be used as surrogate indicators of service quality. For example, is the service provider dressed professionally? Does the service equipment appear to be clean, operable and modern-looking? Because consumers notice these things, so should service businesses.

Inferential detail
"Never go to a doctor whose office plants have died." -- Erma Bombeck, American humorist, born in Bellbrook, Ohio on February 21, 1927

Innovations follow innovations

Innovations often create opportunities and demand for related innovations that follow. Examples: Mouse-pads followed the mouse, which followed personal computers. Automobile insurance followed automobiles. Microwavable cookware followed microwave ovens. And, in New Haven, Connecticut on February 21, 1878, the first telephone book was distributed -- only a few years after the telephone was introduced. The directory listed about 50 names.

What new product/service opportunities might stem from modern-day innovations such as electric cars, self-driving cars, and drone delivery services?

February 22, 2018
Thursday

Anniversary of People Power Revolution (Philippines)

Objectives & reminders

Appointments

Early morning

8 a.m.

9 a.m.

10 a.m.

11 a.m.

Noon

1 p.m.

2 p.m.

3 p.m.

4 p.m.

5 p.m.

6 p.m.

Later evening

Famous response to customer inquiry

Francis P. Church was born in Rochester, New York on February 22, 1839. Part of his career was spent as an editorial writer for the *New York Sun* where he reminded marketers of the importance of responding to customer comments in a thoughtful and respectful way.

Customer feedback is essential

Today, market-oriented businesses welcome customers' comments which include complaints, suggestions, compliments and inquiries. Such comments help businesses better understand what their customers value, how customers use the products, what they want, what they are thinking, and so on. Customer comments also provide businesses with opportunities to build relationships with customers.

Church recognized that well-crafted responses to readers' comments could help the newspaper strengthen its relationships with readers. Little did he know in 1897 that one such response would continue to make a memorable impression for generations to come. That is, rather than dismissing young Virginia O'Hanlon's inquiry about the existence of Santa Claus as childish or beyond the editorial scope of the newspaper, Church seized the relationship-building opportunity to reply, as shown in the accompanying box.

Yes there is!

"Yes Virginia, there is a Santa Claus. He exists as certainly as love and generosity and devotion exist, and you know that they abound and give to your life its highest beauty and joy. Alas! How dreary would be the world if there were no Santa Claus! It would be as dreary as if there were no Virginias. There would be no childlike faith then, no poetry, no romance to make tolerable this existence. We should have no enjoyment except in sense and sight. The eternal light with which childhood fills the world would be extinguished."
– Francis P. Church

February 23, 2018
Friday
National Banana Bread Day

Objectives & reminders

____

____

____

Appointments

Early morning

8 a.m.

9 a.m.

10 a.m.

11 a.m.

Noon

1 p.m.

2 p.m.

3 p.m.

4 p.m.

5 p.m.

6 p.m.

Later evening

Brands satisfy need for dignity: Agree or disagree?

When low-income consumers are shown how much money they can save by buying house brands at the grocery store instead of well-known national brands, some reject the seemingly rational argument. Why? Because they realize they may never live in an affluent neighborhood or drive a new car, or take an overseas vacation -- like more affluent consumers do -- but they know they can afford a premium grade jar of mustard, a set of tournament marbles or a bottle of the leading brand of soft drink -- like more affluent consumers do.

To market to the poor, first empathize

"To be a poor man is hard, but to be a poor race in a land of dollars is the very bottom of hardships." – William E.B. Du Bois, sociologist and founder of the National Association for the Advancement of Colored People (NAACP), born in Great Barrington, Massachusetts on February 23, 1868

Inventing a new category

One way to beat the competition is to differentiate your product so much that, in effect, a new product category is created. That's what Leo Hirshfield did on February 23, 1896, when he first produced a candy treat named after his five-year-old daughter, "Tootsie." Unlike competing treats, the Tootsie Roll wasn't exactly a chocolate drop, nor was it exactly a fudge piece. Consumers didn't exactly eat or suck Tootsie Rolls; they chewed them. Clearly, Tootsie Rolls were differentiated.

When Hirshfield began producing Tootsie Rolls, he made about 200 per day. Today, thanks to a strong brand reputation and plenty of automated equipment, the company cranks out 64 million Tootsie Rolls daily.

Staying customer-focused

"It's customers that made Dell great in the first place, and if we're smart enough and quick enough to listen to customer needs, we'll succeed." – Michael Dell, founder of Dell Computers, born in Houston, Texas on February 23, 1965

February 24, 2018
Saturday
Flag Day (Mexico)

Objectives & reminders

____

____

____

Appointments

Early morning

8 a.m.

9 a.m.

10 a.m.

11 a.m.

Noon

1 p.m.

2 p.m.

3 p.m.

4 p.m.

5 p.m.

6 p.m.

Later evening

Happy birthday: Elizabeth G. MacDonald

Ms. MacDonald was born on February 24, 1894. She was a homemaker in Saginaw, Michigan in the late 1920s who was dissatisfied with the household cleaners that were sold at the time. So, MacDonald researched various cleansing ingredients and formulated her own cleaner in about 1930. Dubbed Spic and Span, the brand name meant "perfectly clean."

Prior to the brand being sold in 2001, Spic and Span was produced by Procter & Gamble who advertised it heavily during television soap operas such as *Search for Tomorrow*. Several other soap products also sponsored the soap operas, which is why they are called "soap" operas or "soaps," for short. Today, Spic and Span is owned by Prestige Brands and is still available on retailers' soap aisles.

Leadership role

"My job is to listen to ideas, maybe cook up a few of my own, and make decisions based on what's good for the shareholders and for the company." – Phil Knight, co-founder and former CEO & chairman of Nike, born in Portland, Oregon on February 24, 1938

New calendar issued

Pope Gregory XIII announced a new calendar on February 24, 1582. Distinguished mathematicians and astronomers of the day agreed that the Julian calendar was ten days off, thus the need for the new calendar that went into effect later in the year.

In most Catholic countries the new *Gregorian* calendar replaced the previously used *Julian* calendar, although Great Britain and the American colonies did not adopt the Gregorian calendar until 1752. Today the Gregorian calendar is the most widely used calendar in the world.

Design as a product's soul

"In most people's vocabularies, design means veneer... But to me, nothing could be further from the meaning of design. Design is the fundamental soul of a man-made creation." – Steve Jobs, co-founder and former CEO of Apple Inc., born in San Francisco, California on February 24, 1955

February 25, 2018
Sunday
National Day (Kuwait)

Objectives & reminders

___

___

___

Appointments

Early morning

8 a.m.

9 a.m.

10 a.m.

11 a.m.

Noon

1 p.m.

2 p.m.

3 p.m.

4 p.m.

5 p.m.

6 p.m.

Later evening

Happy birthday: Adelle Davis

Born in Lizton, Indiana on February 25, 1905, Davis was a pioneering nutritionist who encouraged people to pursue healthy lifestyles, especially with regard to their diet. Two of her books included *Let's Cook It Right* (1947) and *Let's Eat Right to Keep Fit* (1954); both found receptive audiences.

She once observed that, "[t]housands upon thousands of persons have studied disease [but] [a]lmost no one has studied health," but is perhaps best known for her observation that, "[y]ou are what you eat" (she popularized the expression, although it originally appeared in a 1923 advertisement for beef).

Today, consumers, businesses and public policy-makers are increasingly health conscious. Consumers read government-mandated nutrition labels on food packages while food producers strive to produce healthier foods. Employers realize that healthy, fit employees tend to be more productive.

Continued relevance of nutrition and wellness

"We do need to be concerned about eating a sensible diet, because this is a fundamental area in which we can take charge of our own health... [T]wo thirds of all deaths in America are directly or indirectly related to diet..." – C. Everett Koop, former Surgeon General of the United States

"Each dollar invested in preventive health services saves $3.48 in health care costs and $5.82 in losses due to absenteeism... 80% of illness and disease is preventable." – www.wellnesswiz.com

"Nearly 60% of all companies and 95% of large companies have programs designed to encourage individuals to take some responsibility for their health." – www.fitnessworksatwork.com

Acting on the numbers

What are the possible marketing implications (including new product/service opportunities) of these statistics?

February 26, 2018
Monday
Liberation Day (Kuwait)

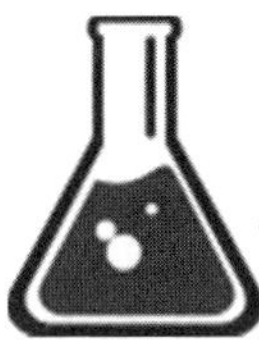

Objectives & reminders

____

____

____

Appointments

Early morning

8 a.m.

9 a.m.

10 a.m.

11 a.m.

Noon

1 p.m.

2 p.m.

3 p.m.

4 p.m.

5 p.m.

6 p.m.

Later evening

Dress casually today?

In honor of Levi Strauss's birthday, it's okay to dress casually today. Born in Buttenheim, Germany on February 26, 1829, Strauss created "Levi's" jeans in 1850 and founded the company that makes them, Levi Strauss & Company. One hundred and nineteen years later the popularity of Levi's prompted Donald Fisher to launch a new chain of retail clothing stores called "The Gap." In the early years, Gap stores sold only Levi's jeans.

> **The French connection**
> The fabric Strauss used to make pants was known as *serge de Nimes*, meaning that it came from Nimes, France. Later, the name of the fabric was shortened to "denim."

Happy birthday: Herbert Henry Dow

Born in Belleville, Ontario, Canada on February 26, 1866, Dow graduated from what is now Case Western Reserve University in Cleveland, Ohio with a degree in chemical engineering.

While still in his early 20s, Dow developed a process for manufacturing bromine from brine. To capitalize on this and other innovations, Dow formed various companies which eventually led to the formation of the Dow Chemical Company in 1897. By the time Dow died in 1930, Dow Chemical plants were producing more than 200 products. Dow himself received 100 patents during his lifetime.

> **Policy of excellence**
> "If you can't do it better, why do it?"
> – Herbert Henry Dow

Today, Dow Chemical, headquartered in Midland, Michigan is one of the largest chemical producers in the world, employing 54,000 people worldwide and tallying more than $48 billion in annual sales across 160 countries.

No such thing as "playing it safe": Agree or disagree?

"The ultimate risk is not taking a risk." -- James Goldsmith, financier and member of the European Parliament (1994-1997), born in Paris, France on February 26, 1933

February 27, 2018
Tuesday
World NGO Day

Objectives & reminders

______

______

______

Appointments

Early morning

8 a.m.

9 a.m.

10 a.m.

11 a.m.

Noon

1 p.m.

2 p.m.

3 p.m.

4 p.m.

5 p.m.

6 p.m.

Later evening

Dummer jokes are no laughing matter

Governor Dummer Academy, the oldest boarding school in America, opened for business in Newbury, Massachusetts on February 27, 1763. The school was named after its benefactor, William Dummer, who was the governor of Massachusetts in the 1720s.

Duh!

"Research has shown that the current name has been an impediment." -- Judith Klein, communications director, Governor Dummer Academy (upon revising the name)

Although the "Dummer" name has served as fodder for countless jokes over the years, the school continues to operate today. However, "Dummer" was expelled from the academy's name in 2006. Now the school is officially known as The Governor's Academy.

Not-so-dumb names

Not surprisingly, there should be a congruency between the desired image of a company, brand or institution and its name. Often the name is the first and sometimes only exposure consumers have to the organization or brand. So, if the inventor's, founder's or benefactor's name doesn't make a favorable impression (or if it's difficult to pronounce, spell or remember), it's probably a good idea to use another basis for selecting a brand or organization's name.

Here are three examples of company names that have carried the same names as their founders -- names that represent a good fit with the images the companies want to reinforce:

1. Strong Funds -- a mutual fund firm named after Richard Strong (now part of Wells Fargo).

2. Crisp Learning -- a series of short, concisely-written training and "how to" business books, named after the company's founding publisher, Mike Crisp (Crisp Learning is now an imprint of Axzo Press).

3. Price Club – chain of discount warehouse stores named after founder Sol Price.

February 28, 2018
Wednesday
Purim (begins in evening)

Objectives & reminders

Appointments

Early morning

8 a.m.

9 a.m.

10 a.m.

11 a.m.

Noon

1 p.m.

2 p.m.

3 p.m.

4 p.m.

5 p.m.

6 p.m.

Later evening

February as a political casualty

Under Julius Caesar's reign, February normally had 29 days (30 every fourth year), but when Augustus became the emperor of the Roman Empire, he chopped a day from February and added it to August -- the month named after him.

> 'Thirty days hath September,
> April, June, and November.
> All the rest have thirty-one,
> Excepting February alone
> Which hath but twenty-eight, in fine,
> Till leap year gives it twenty-nine."
> -- Anonymous

The February effect: More or less discretionary money available

Because February is the shortest month of the year, *salaried workers paid monthly or semi-monthly* may have a little *more* discretionary money to spend at the end of the month. That is, while their paycheck is the same size as their paychecks received in other months, some expenses are reduced. For example, instead of buying gasoline for 30 or 31 days of automobile transportation, only enough fuel for 28 days is required in February. Likewise, total food expenses may be lower during February.

In contrast, *workers paid on an hourly basis* may find that they have *less* discretionary money to spend in February. With only 28 days in the month, they are likely to work fewer hours at their jobs during February (and thus earn less money), yet payments for mortgage or rent, vehicle payments, and some other "monthly" bills may be the same size as those faced in other months.

Understanding the target market

The variability in February's effect on consumer spending serves as a reminder of the importance of being familiar with the target market. Knowing that customers are more likely to be salaried or paid hourly has implications for promotion appeals and other business practices. For example, salaried customers might be encouraged to "splurge" on items they ordinarily would not buy, whereas hourly workers might be more responsive to February appeals that stress "value" or "savings."

March 1, 2018
Thursday
World Civil Defense Day

Objectives & reminders

____

____

____

Appointments

Early morning

8 a.m.

9 a.m.

10 a.m.

11 a.m.

Noon

1 p.m.

2 p.m.

3 p.m.

4 p.m.

5 p.m.

6 p.m.

Later evening

First-of-month opportunities

Many consumer marketers begin to salivate as the first of the month approaches, because that's when many consumers receive income. When prospective buyers receive money, they're inclined to spend some of it right away. Indeed, a Gallup survey found that, on average, workers reported spending about $50 more in the weeks they get paid than in the weeks they're not paid.

> **Not sure when consumers receive income in your market area?**
> - Ask employees of major local businesses: "When do you get paid?"
> - Ask local bank tellers and retailers: "What are your busiest days of the week/month?"

Military pay received today

Active duty military personnel is one market segment to be paid today. As discussed in more detail on September 14, 1.4 million members of that market segment are paid an average of $1,900 about the 1st and 15th of each month. Another six million retired military and veterans' families are paid today too -- typically on the 1st of the month, or earlier if the 1st falls on a Saturday, Sunday or federal holiday.

SNAP benefits also arrive today

Another market segment that is particularly noteworthy for food retailers is made up of 46 million American recipients of SNAP benefits. SNAP is an acronym for Supplemental Nutrition Assistance Program – a government assistance program for low-income consumers that evolved from what was once known as "food stamps." The size of SNAP benefits varies by family size and income, but in 2015 averaged $1.40 per family member, per meal, up to a maximum of $632 per month for a family of four.

The timing of monthly SNAP distributions varies from state to state, but states tend to distribute most benefits earlier rather than later in the month. At the extreme, Idaho issues benefits to all of its SNAP recipients on the first day of the month, creating an enormous spike in the number of shoppers at Idaho Wal-Mart stores right after midnight and throughout the day on the first of the month. For state-by-state specifics, see: http://www.fns.usda.gov/snap/snap-monthly-benefit-issuance-schedule

March 2, 2018
Friday
Employee Appreciation Day

Objectives & reminders

___

___

___

Appointments

Early morning

8 a.m.

9 a.m.

10 a.m.

11 a.m.

Noon

1 p.m.

2 p.m.

3 p.m.

4 p.m.

5 p.m.

6 p.m.

Later evening

Unethical to spread rumors and superstitions to increase consumption: Agree or disagree?

Although the environmental movement encourages consumers to share (e.g., car-pooling) as a means of conserving resources, sometimes sharing may clash with businesspeople's interest in selling more of their goods. Apparently, that was the case with Ivar Kreuger, the Swedish financier born in Kalmar, Sweden on March 2, 1880.

In 1913, before the days of cigarette lighters, Kreuger began taking control of the match-making industry throughout the world. To discourage match sharing (thereby boosting demand), he ignited a match superstition that circulated widely and became known as "three on a match."

According to the superstition, it was unlucky to use the same match to light three individuals' cigarettes. Presumably, during World War I – according to the superstition – a soldier lighting his own cigarette would attract the enemy's attention. As the second soldier's cigarette was being lit, the enemy would take aim and finally fire at the unlucky soldiers while the third soldier's cigarette was being lit. Not surprisingly, the superstition caught the attention of soldiers who quickly avoided match-sharing, but soon the avoidance behavior spread through civilian ranks as well. Sharing the same match was "unlucky."

___

Cynical view of consultants

"A consultant is a person who knows nothing about your business to whom you pay more to tell you how to run it than you could earn if you ran it right instead of the way he tells you." – William Marsteller, co-founder and former CEO of Burson-Marsteller

"B-Mar" is one of the oldest public relations firms in the United States, headquartered in New York City. The firm began operations on March 2, 1953, and today operates in 98 countries and employs more than 2,000 people, not "consultants."

___

Poly first

It was March 1933 when the first polythene was made. R. O. Gibson gets the credit. The discovery was first put to practical use as insulating material in telecommunications cable. It wasn't until 1948 that ordinary household items made with polythene began to appear; wash basins led the way.

March 3, 2018
Saturday
World Wildlife Day

Objectives & reminders

____

____

____

Appointments

Early morning

8 a.m.

9 a.m.

10 a.m.

11 a.m.

Noon

1 p.m.

2 p.m.

3 p.m.

4 p.m.

5 p.m.

6 p.m.

Later evening

Big ideas about brands and branding

It's a branded world according to Michael Levine, founder of Levine Communications Office, Inc. (LCO), an entertainment public relations firm headquartered in Los Angeles.

On March 3, 2003, Levine's book was published: *A Branded World: Adventures in Public Relations and the Creation of Superbrands*. In it, Levine offered several insights about brands, their importance in today's competitive marketplace, and the processes that create them. In particular, here are three of his branding insights:

1. "Branding is a complex process, but its goal is simple: It is the creation and development of a specific identity for a company, product, commodity, group, or person" (p. 3).
2. "Before there can be a brand, there has to be a product. The bridge between product and recognizable brand is marketing" (p. 9).
3. "Too many marketing executives rely on their own concept of the brand's identity, and never bother to discover what attributes the public has assigned to a product" (p. 20).

Time for an idea tournament

"Nothing is more dangerous than an idea when it is the only one you have." -- Emile Chartier, French writer and philosopher, born in Mortagne-au-Perche, Orne, France, on March 3, 1868

Education shouldn't stop with formal graduation ceremony

"The most successful men in the end are those whose success is the result of steady accretion. It is the man who carefully advances step by step, with his mind becoming wider and wider -- and progressively better able to grasp any theme or situation." -- Alexander Graham Bell, inventor and co-founder of Bell Telephone Co. in 1877, born in Edinburgh, Scotland on March 3, 1847

Leadership insight

"Give the people not hell, but hope and courage."
-- Sir John Murray, marine scientist who coined the term "oceanography," born in Cobourg, Canada on March 3, 1841

March 4, 2018
Sunday
March Fourth and Do Something Day

ABCDEF
GHIJKLM
NOPQRS
TUVWXYZ

Objectives & reminders

___

___

___

Appointments

Early morning

8 a.m.

9 a.m.

10 a.m.

11 a.m.

Noon

1 p.m.

2 p.m.

3 p.m.

4 p.m.

5 p.m.

6 p.m.

Later evening

Happy 100th birthday: TIAA-CREF

Thanks to steel magnate Andrew Carnegie's foresight, leadership and generous endowment, the Teachers Insurance & Annuity Association of America (TIAA) was formed on March 4, 1918. The insurance company for teachers was part of Carnegie's broad vision "to do all things necessary to encourage, uphold, and dignify the profession of teaching." In 1952, TIAA expanded its offerings to facilitate variable annuity equity investments – under the banner of College Retirement Equities Fund (CREF).

TIAA-CREF has grown considerably and by 2016 employed almost 13,000 people and managed $889 billion of assets, making it one of the largest financial services firms in the United States.

Understandably, firms should consider avoiding a lengthy company name. Obviously it's a cumbersome mouthful to refer to "Teachers Insurance and Annuity Association of America – College Retirement Equities Fund" during a normal conversation or 30-second advertisement. So, not surprisingly, companies with long names frequently use easier-to-deal-with initials – such as TIAA-CREF.

However, "initial" companies tend to be at a disadvantage to "name" companies in terms of public awareness. To demonstrate the point, marketing analysts Al Ries and Jack Trout tested matched groups of "initial" versus "name" companies using subscribers to *Business Week* magazine.

Their research found that, on average, respondents were aware of the "initial" companies 49 percent of the time. In contrast, 68 percent of the respondents were aware of the "name" companies. So, if the goal of a company's public relations, investor relations and marketing professionals is to make the company name a memorable household word or phrase, the odds are better if the company relies on its name rather than its initials (to learn more, see Ries & Trout's book, *Positioning: The Battle for Your Mind*, 2001 edition, pp. 108-110).

___

Outside of America too

"Lots of folks think they are too good to sell. They have forgotten that every dollar that is made in America is made because somebody somewhere sold something." – Richard M. Devos, co-founder of Amway Corporation, born in Grand Rapids, Michigan on March 4, 1926

March 5, 2018
Monday
National Tree Planting Day (Iran)

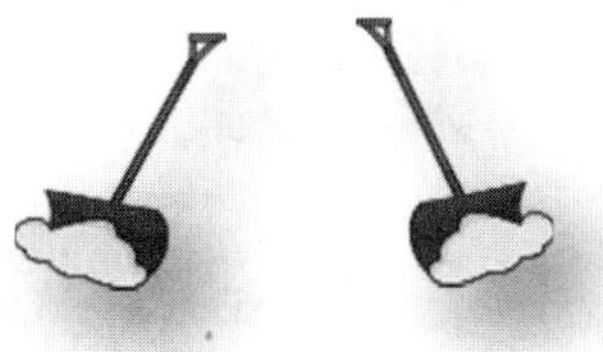

Objectives & reminders

___

___

___

Appointments

Early morning

8 a.m.

9 a.m.

10 a.m.

11 a.m.

Noon

1 p.m.

2 p.m.

3 p.m.

4 p.m.

5 p.m.

6 p.m.

Later evening

Happy birthday: Daniel "Danny" Kahneman

Born in Tel Aviv, Israel on March 5, 1934, Kahneman is a Professor Emeritus at Princeton University where he has researched business-relevant topics pertaining to behavioral finance and the psychology of decision-making.

Kahneman's research suggests that overconfidence in one's decision-making ability or the over-reliance on decision-making heuristics (rules-of-thumb) can lead to relatively poor decisions. In 2002, he won the Nobel Prize in Economics for his research.

In another marketing-relevant stream of research, Kahneman and his colleagues asked 107 consumers for their reaction to the following situation:

> "A hardware store has been selling snow shovels for $15. The morning after a large snowstorm, the store raises the price to $20. Please rate this action as: completely fair, acceptable, unfair, very unfair."

The results? Apparently 82 percent of those surveyed viewed the hypothetical hardware store's action as price gouging, rating the price increase after a snow storm as "unfair" or "very unfair." Several follow-up studies by Kahneman and other research teams also found large percentages of respondents perceived such a price increase to be unfair. The samples included groups of profit-minded business executives as well as typical consumers.

For more details regarding Kahneman's study, see "Fairness as a Constraint on Profit Seeking: Entitlements in the Market," *American Economic Review*, 76 (September 1986), pp. 728-741. For a broader discussion of Kahneman's study and other issues pertaining to buyers' perceptions of prices, see the thoughtful and thorough book by Sarah Maxwell, *The Price is Wrong...* (particularly pp. 43-44).

___

Vary the media: Agree or disagree?

"Not all minds react to the same stimuli... and there is no single means of communication which will transmit an idea to all persons with equal effectiveness."
– Clarence B. Randall, former president and chairman of Inland Steel (later part of Ispat International), born in Newark Valley, New York on March 5, 1891

March 6, 2018
Tuesday
Town Meeting Day (Vermont)

Objectives & reminders

______

______

______

Appointments

Early morning

8 a.m.

9 a.m.

10 a.m.

11 a.m.

Noon

1 p.m.

2 p.m.

3 p.m.

4 p.m.

5 p.m.

6 p.m.

Later evening

Perishability challenge addressed

New Yorker Clarence Birdseye addressed the "perishability" dilemma when he pioneered a method of quick-freezing vegetables without substantially changing their texture or taste. On March 6, 1930, his "Birds Eye Frosted Foods" were first available for sale in 18 test-market grocery stores in Springfield, Massachusetts. Within three months, the trial was considered a success. Additional foods were quick-frozen and made available. Today, Birdseye and competing frozen food brands are widely available in grocers' frozen food sections.

By freezing vegetables, Birdseye effectively extended their shelf life, which reduced the amount of rotten vegetables that had to be trashed -- thus saving money for both consumers and suppliers. Further, by extending veggies' shelf life, Birdseye eliminated much of the seasonal fluctuations in the supply of vegetables. This led to more stable prices and an increased ability of suppliers to meet demand throughout the year. As reinforced by many of the principles in the accompanying box, conquering the perishability dilemma is generally good for business.

Selected perishability principles

1. The less perishable an item, the greater the chances that its potential value will be realized. That is, non-perishables are not as likely to rot, spoil, or otherwise perish.

2. The more perishable a product, the more important it is for marketers to forecast demand and supply accurately, to avoid excess inventory that's wasted when it perishes.

3. As the shelf-life of products is extended, consumers are more likely to buy in larger quantities and "stock-up." By doing so, consumers relieve producers and intermediaries of inventory costs. Moreover, when consumers have ample supplies on hand, they tend to consume at a higher rate.

4. When a product is not particularly perishable, a greater degree of flexibility exists in the channels of distribution. Longer and more efficient channels are possible.

March 7, 2018
Wednesday
Alexander Graham Bell Day

Objectives & reminders

Appointments

Early morning

---

8 a.m.

---

9 a.m.

---

10 a.m.

---

11 a.m.

Noon

---

1 p.m.

---

2 p.m.

---

3 p.m.

---

4 p.m.

---

5 p.m.

---

6 p.m.

Later evening

The internal marketing difference

Managers may not always have a wide range of alternatives when making difficult decisions during difficult times. But they do have choices in the way they communicate their decisions -- in an insensitive and abrasive manner, or in a more palatable way.

Management writer Carl Heyel made this point in his 1942 book, *How to Create Job Enthusiasm*, when he showed how two different U.S. companies delivered bad news about employee pay cuts one week in early 1932, during the Great Depression. The two memos that the companies used to notify their respective employees are shown in the top and bottom boxes below. Which memo do you prefer, and why?

Hint

Memo to employees of Company A

"Effective Monday, March 7, 1932, there will be a ten per cent reduction in all salaries. The company will expect the same standards of service on the part of all employees. Those not willing to work without complaining about this adjustment will be subject to dismissal."

Key leadership concept: Internal marketing

Employees are an "internal" market. They choose to buy or reject their job roles and responsibilities. They choose to embrace or shun the firm's values and mission. Their choices can hinge upon the way management markets to them, including the impressions made by the internal marketing communications they receive.

Hint

Memo to employees of Company B

"Because of the continued depression suffered by the industries served by our [company], reflected in a sharp drop in our revenues, the Executive Committee has felt it necessary to institute a ten per cent reduction in all salaries, effective March 1, 1932. We want to assure our employees that this step was taken only after a careful survey of all other avenues of cost reduction. Many of the upper executives are taking much more drastic reductions. Needless to say, these reductions will be restored at the very earliest opportunity."

March 8, 2018
Thursday
International Women's Day

Objectives & reminders

____

____

____

Appointments

Early morning

8 a.m.

9 a.m.

10 a.m.

11 a.m.

Noon

1 p.m.

2 p.m.

3 p.m.

4 p.m.

5 p.m.

6 p.m.

Later evening

Happy birthday: Warren Bennis

Born in New York City on March 8, 1925, Bennis was a leading authority on leadership. He wrote dozens of books and articles on the topic and founded the Leadership Institute at the University of Southern California.

Leadership defined

"[Leadership is] the capacity to create a compelling vision, and to translate it into action and sustain it."
-- Warren Bennis

Distinction between management and leadership

"The manager asks how and when; the leader asks what and why."
-- Warren Bennis

Earlier in his career Bennis was the president of the University of Cincinnati. There he learned that his ability to lead UC would be limited if he could not gain control of his calendar and proactively manage his time.

Are calendars tools or tyrants?

"My moment of truth came toward the end of my first ten months [as president of the University of Cincinnati]. It was one of those nights in the office. The clock was moving toward four in the morning, and I was still not through with the incredible mass of paper stacked before me. I was bone weary and soul weary, and I found myself muttering, 'Either I can't manage this place, or it's unmanageable.'"

"I reached for my calendar and ran my eyes down each hour, half-hour, quarter-hour to see where my time had gone that day, the day before, the month before... My discovery was this: I had become the victim of a vast, amorphous, unwitting, unconscious conspiracy to prevent me from doing anything whatever to change the university's status quo."
-- Warren Bennis

March 9, 2018
Friday

Winter Paralympics begin
(Pyeongchang, South Korea)

Objectives & reminders

____

____

____

Appointments

Early morning

8 a.m.

9 a.m.

10 a.m.

11 a.m.

Noon

1 p.m.

2 p.m.

3 p.m.

4 p.m.

5 p.m.

6 p.m.

Later evening

Happy birthday:
Peter Andrew Georgescu

Born in Bucharest, Romania on March 9, 1939, Georgescu landed a job with the international advertising agency Young & Rubicam, Inc. in his early 20s (1963). He became the company's director of marketing in 1977 and president in 1994. Today, he serves as the company's chairman emeritus.

Not surprisingly, Georgescu's experience, insights and leadership have contributed greatly to the practice of marketing, in general, and advertising, in particular. For example, note in the accompanying box the important distinction he makes between brands and brand names.

> **A *brand* is more than a brand *name***
>
> "A clear distinction must be made between brand names, which are as old as the hills, and the new concept of brands evolving today. The brand, as I see it, is expressive of a relationship between the product or service and the customer -- a sense of kinship, affinity, or identification."
>
> "A brand is a set of differentiating promises that link products to customers. The brand contract offers two promises: (1) consistency of quality, and (2) an ingredient, or quality, that symbolizes something special, a clearly superior benefit. The specialness may arise from functional superiority or from some emotional gratification that the product or service engenders."
> -- Peter Andrew Georgescu

Design-driven vehicle brands

"In the car industry, superior design is critical. Product design defines the first impression the customer has about our products. With one look the customer makes their decision about their appeal. Of course, an attractive design is not enough to make a product a success, but it is necessary." -- Carlos Ghosn, chairman and CEO of Renault and Nissan Motors, born in Porto Velho, Brazil on March 9, 1954

March 10, 2018
Saturday
Harriet Tubman Day

Objectives & reminders

___

___

___

Appointments

Early morning

8 a.m.

9 a.m.

10 a.m.

11 a.m.

Noon

1 p.m.

2 p.m.

3 p.m.

4 p.m.

5 p.m.

6 p.m.

Later evening

"Mr. Watson, come here; I want to see you."

It was March 10, 1876, when Alexander Graham Bell spoke these famous words when he called for his assistant, Thomas Watson, during a telephone experiment. It was the first successful telephone transmission, coming only a few days after Bell received a patent for his new device.

Later that day, an exuberant Bell wrote to his father to share the news of the "great success" (he had to write, given that his father had no telephone). In that letter, Bell predicted that "the day is coming when [telephone] wires will be laid on to houses just like water and gas -- and friends converse with each other without leaving home."

The toughest sales job in history?
Would you have liked to work for Bell as a sales representative? How would you have sold the *first* telephone? (Hint: Who would the first buyer call?) This dilemma opened marketers' eyes to the importance of buyer networks for some products and how the size of networks can affect the speed with which new products are adopted.

In much the same way that children's toy "walkie talkies" are sold in pairs today, the first two telephones were sold as a pair -- to a physician who installed one telephone at home and one at his office so he could communicate with his wife throughout the day.

Quality insight

"Whatever is worth doing at all is worth doing well." -- Earl of Chesterfield, English statesman. The Earl penned these words in a letter to his son on March 10, 1746.

Entrepreneurial beginnings

On March 10, 1910, William Boeing purchased a shipyard on the Duwamish River in Seattle, Washington -- not to build ships, but airplanes. Today, the company that William Boeing founded is a leader in the manufacture of commercial aircraft.

March 11, 2018
Sunday
Johnny Appleseed Day

Objectives & reminders

Adjust clocks for DST.

Appointments

Early morning

8 a.m.

9 a.m.

10 a.m.

11 a.m.

Noon

1 p.m.

2 p.m.

3 p.m.

4 p.m.

5 p.m.

6 p.m.

Later evening

Daylight Saving Time (DST) begins

U.S. time-pieces are moved forward one hour (at 2:00 a.m.) on the second Sunday in March. That's today! That is, 2:00 a.m. suddenly becomes 3:00 a.m.

Although the practice was suggested as early as 1784 (by Benjamin Franklin) and advocated by others in subsequent years, DST did not become a reality until World War I when the U.S., Great Britain, and Australia adopted it to conserve fuel associated with artificial light. The practice was called upon again during the Second World War.

For several years, DST in the U.S. began on the *last* Sunday in April, but this starting period was moved up to the first Sunday in April by a 1986 act of Congress. Beginning in 2007, the starting date was moved up again – to the second Sunday in March – in response to rising fuel prices. In the U.S. DST now ends on the first Sunday in November.

DST not universally observed

Although DST runs from March until November throughout most of the United States, DST is not observed everywhere. Hawaii and most of Arizona, for example, do not observe DST, and neither do many U.S. territories such as Guam, Puerto Rico, and the Virgin Islands.

Several other countries are on DST during part of the year, but their timing differs slightly. Generally, in Western Europe DST begins on the last Sunday in March. When traveling abroad or when arranging communications in real time, familiarity with the correct time helps to avoid confusion and missing appointments.

Today, DST's popularity stems not from its contribution to the war effort, but because it allows people to enjoy outdoor activities for an extra hour each evening. This works to the advantage of marketers of outdoor-related goods and services such as outdoor recreation equipment, lawn and garden supplies, patio furniture, outdoor sporting events, and so on. Further, the extra hour of daylight prompts some consumers to extend the timing and duration of their shopping trips, leading many retailers to promote or extend their night-time operating hours.

March 12, 2018
Monday
Commonwealth Day

Objectives & reminders

____

____

____

Appointments

Early morning
8 a.m.
9 a.m.
10 a.m.
11 a.m.
Noon
1 p.m.
2 p.m.
3 p.m.
4 p.m.
5 p.m.
6 p.m.
Later evening

Commonwealth Day

Aay! Today, the second Monday in March, is a Canadian day of celebration to recognize Canada's membership in the British Commonwealth. Other Commonwealth countries also celebrate this day.

Spring Break: Marketing opportunity?

March is typically the month during which U.S. college students receive a one week break from classes to enjoy Spring Break. Accordingly, 70 percent of surveyed college students say that they intend to travel during Spring Break. Some banks report that ATM machines dispense 20 percent more cash during Spring Break than during average weeks.

Marketing-relevant history of March 12

1877 John Wanamaker opened the first major department store in the U.S., in Philadelphia, Pennsylvania. He used his planning calendar extensively to stage numerous events throughout the year to ensure that customers would have reasons to return to the store frequently; e.g., he was the first to stage annual "white sales."

1894 Coca Cola was sold in bottles for the first time. Bottling broadened Coca Cola's distribution potential, facilitated at-home consumption, and ensured greater product consistency.

1912 Girl Scouts of America was formed in Savannah, Georgia (then known as "Girl Guides"). They began selling cookies in the 1920s.

1956 *Time* magazine reported numerous uses and high expectations for the "newest wonder in U.S. industry" -- the transistor. According to Texas Instruments, "[Transistors] truly are the basis for the electronics of the future."

1980 Fixed mortgage rates rose to 16.25 percent (they would rise to 17 percent later in the month). In the short-term, many (most?) companies could have earned more for their shareholders by selling their tangible assets and buying CDs (Certificates of Deposit).

March 13, 2018
Tuesday

National Elephant Day (Thailand)

Objectives & reminders

___

___

___

Appointments

Early morning

8 a.m.

9 a.m.

10 a.m.

11 a.m.

Noon

1 p.m.

2 p.m.

3 p.m.

4 p.m.

5 p.m.

6 p.m.

Later evening

What's behind a brand promise?

"Integrity is not an option. A company's brand is its promise... The companies that accept that integrity is not an option in their dealings with all of their stakeholders will be the ones that thrive in the future." – John Luff, founder and CEO of Sustainable Marketing. Luff offered this perspective at The Financial Services Forum Annual Members' Conference in London on March 13, 2007.

___

How lengthy should advertising copy be?

Born in Hoboken, New Jersey on March 13, 1898, Victor O. Schwab began his advertising career at the age of 19. He went on to become what some people considered "the greatest mail-order copywriter of all time." Schwab was particularly noted for using coded coupons in ads to test the effectiveness of alternative headlines, layouts, appeals, action closings, copy length and other variables.

After amassing 44 years of copywriting experience, Schwab's book, *How to Write a Good Advertisement*, was published in 1962. In it he weighed-in on an important and frequently debated question: How lengthy should advertising copy be? According to Schwab:

> "Advertisers who are able to check their advertising and sales results carefully have discovered an astonishing relationship between effectiveness and number of words used. They have found that – unless copy is exceptionally fine or exceptionally bad – these ratios of resultfullness to copy length are fairly constant."
>
> "The LONGER your copy can hold interest of the greatest number of readers, the likelier you are to induce MORE of them to act..."
>
> "To sum up: The longer your copy can hold people, the more of them you will sell; and the more interesting your copy is, the longer you will hold them. If you can keep your reader interested, you'll have a better chance of propelling him to action. If you cannot do that, then too small an amount of copy won't push him far enough along that road anyway."

March 14, 2018
Wednesday
Pi Day (π or 3.14…)

Objectives & reminders

______

______

______

Appointments

Early morning

8 a.m.

9 a.m.

10 a.m.

11 a.m.

Noon

1 p.m.

2 p.m.

3 p.m.

4 p.m.

5 p.m.

6 p.m.

Later evening

Values-led marketing

"If your company has values, an essence, you need to capitalize on that strategic advantage and make sure your marketing expresses your values and your essence. A company with values is a company with soul. When you've got a soul, you can market from your values."

"If a traditional marketing campaign is really well done it makes people say, 'Great ads. I like those ads.' Values-led marketing evokes a different reaction. People say, 'Great company. I love that company.' Which response is likely to foster a more long-lasting relationship?" – Ben Cohen and Jerry Greenfield, co-founders of Ben & Jerry's Homemade, Inc. (ice cream). Interestingly, Cohen and Greenfield were born only four days apart, and in the same hospital in Brooklyn, New York – Greenfield on March 14, 1951, followed by Cohen on March 18, 1951.

Happy birthday: Rose Pierini

Born on March 14, 1911, Rose Pierini unwittingly became part of the consumerism movement in the early 1960s when she was involved in an automobile accident in Santa Barbara, California. The accident severed her left arm. Claiming the General Motors' Corvair she was driving to be defective and the cause of the accident, she sued General Motors and the local dealership. Three days into the trial, GM settled with Ms. Pierini for $70,000.

In his best-selling book that propelled the consumerism movement, *Unsafe at Any Speed* (1965), Ralph Nader detailed the story of Rose Pierini and bashed the automotive industry for not making safety a higher priority in automobile design.

Nader's book, the publicity surrounding the book, and Pierini's lawsuit (as well as several other lawsuits) were followed by a sharp decline in Corvair registrations – 42 percent in one year alone – proving the harmful effects that negative publicity can have on a company.

Although the fairness of Nader's allegations against the automotive industry have been debated and characterized by some as "fearmongering," a number of product safety measures for automobiles and other products did follow Nader's book and Rose Pierini's news-making experience.

March 15, 2018
Thursday
World Consumer Rights Day

Objectives & reminders

____

____

____

Appointments

Early morning

8 a.m.

9 a.m.

10 a.m.

11 a.m.

Noon

1 p.m.

2 p.m.

3 p.m.

4 p.m.

5 p.m.

6 p.m.

Later evening

The ideas of March

Always speak up: Agree or Disagree?
"A man with a worthless idea is better than a man with no ideas at all." -- H. Gordon Selfridge, founder of the British chain of Selfridge & Company department stores. Selfridge's first store opened on March 15, 1909.

Always have them in stock
"To stay ahead, you must have your next idea waiting in the wings." -- Rosabeth Moss Kanter, Professor, management consultant, researcher, and former Editor of the *Harvard Business Review*, born in Cleveland, Ohio on March 15, 1943

"March madness" underway this week

The latter half of March is filled with enough basketball excitement generated from the annual NCAA tournament to attract both television audiences and advertisers. During the single-elimination tournament in 2018, national advertisers will collectively spend an estimated $1.3 billion to reach tournament audiences. The air time for a single 30-second television ad during the championship game will cost about $1.7 million.

In addition to advertising expenditures, companies also spend heavily on basketball-related promotions during March madness. Intrust Bank, for example, uses a basketball theme to decorate their branch offices -- complete with school mascots from regional universities represented in the tournament.

March madness at work: Agree or disagree?
Fifty percent of senior-level managers surveyed in 2015 (reported on monster.com) said that March madness activities in the workplace had a positive effect on *employee morale*, while 43% said the tournament had no impact on employee morale. Regarding *employee productivity*, 36% of the respondents reported their belief in a positive effect of March madness activities in the workplace, while 49% claimed no impact on productivity.

March 16, 2018
Friday
Freedom of Information Day

Objectives & reminders

___

___

___

Appointments

Early morning

8 a.m.

9 a.m.

10 a.m.

11 a.m.

Noon

1 p.m.

2 p.m.

3 p.m.

4 p.m.

5 p.m.

6 p.m.

Later evening

Happy birthday: Sanford "Sandy" Weill

Born in Brooklyn, New York on March 16, 1933, Weill has held numerous banking/finance positions since landing his first Wall Street job in 1955 at Bear Stearns. Perhaps Weill is best known as the CEO of Travelers Group and later, when Travelers merged with Citicorp in 1998, the CEO and co-chairman of Citigroup.

The Mother of selling fears

Successful businesspeople often owe much to their parents. In the case of a newly minted college graduate named Sandy Weill who was working as a licensed broker at Bear Stearns in the mid-1950s, the help and encouragement -- push -- from his mother was instrumental. It seems that Weill suffered from a tendency that many new marketers have -- fear of contacting prospective customers.

Rather than picking up the telephone or personally visiting prospective clients, in those early days Weill chose to hide in his office and simply study companies' financial statements and related documents that streamed across his desk. His only client was his mother. Learning of this apparent fear, Weill's mother persuaded a friend to let Weill open an account for him. She also began telephoning her son's office daily -- sometimes several times a day -- to remind him to "get off your duff and make some calls."

Turning the corporate organizational chart upside down

"Really good ideas and innovative ideas come from the bottoms of organizations – not really the tops of organizations – where people are dealing directly with the customers and really understand what the market wants, rather than dictating what the market wants, where people can see the silly things that the chairman may be doing, or whatever, that's wasting a lot of money and there might be a better way to do it. We encourage people to think that way."
– Sandy Weill

March 17, 2018
Saturday

St. Patrick's Day
Submarine Day
Campfire Girls Day
Doctor-Patient Trust Day
National Irish Coffee Day
National Corned Beef & Cabbage Day
Children's Day (Bangladesh)

Observed on 3rd Saturday in March:
Maple Syrup Saturday
National Corndog Day
Worldwide Quilting Day
International Sports Car Racing Day

Appointments

Early morning

8 a.m.

9 a.m.

10 a.m.

11 a.m.

Noon

1 p.m.

2 p.m.

3 p.m.

4 p.m.

5 p.m.

6 p.m.

Later evening

St. Patrick's Day

Although St. Patrick's Day is observed today in many parts of the world (e.g., Canada, Australia, Japan, Singapore, and Russia), in the United States, in particular, it has evolved into a secular and non-cultural celebration -- enjoyed regardless of whether one is Irish or not.

Often St. Patrick's Day is celebrated with Irish green. Consumers observe the day by wearing green clothing and accessories, drinking green-colored beverages, wearing green make-up, adorning their homes and offices with green decorations, and so on.

Significantly green market segment
About 43 million Americans can trace their ancestry to Ireland. That's about 13 percent of the U.S. population.

Always something to celebrate

The United States is somewhat unique relative to other countries around the world in that there are only a few officially-designated federal holidays and their observance outside of the federal government is largely voluntary. State and local governments, as well as schools, banks and many businesses, often adopt the federal government's list of holidays as their own, but rarely are they required to do so.

Still, there are countless unofficial holidays and occasions throughout the year – dubbed so by Congressional or Presidential proclamations, ordained by the church, or simply invented by individuals or trade organizations. Without exception, several of these occur every day of the year.

Of course, unofficial holidays and occasions that are widely known and have established traditions represent obvious marketing opportunities (e.g., St. Patrick's Day, Valentine's Day, Mother's Day, Father's Day). Consumers plan to celebrate or observe these holidays and occasions, while the media and the collective efforts of businesses, trade associations and others help to promote them.

But windows of marketing opportunity may be open for lesser-known holidays and occasions too – especially those that are industry- or product-specific, or of local interest. And for holidays and occasions that are meaningful to target markets, it can be a bonus to promote those that competitors ignore.

March 18, 2018
Sunday

Flag Day (Aruba)

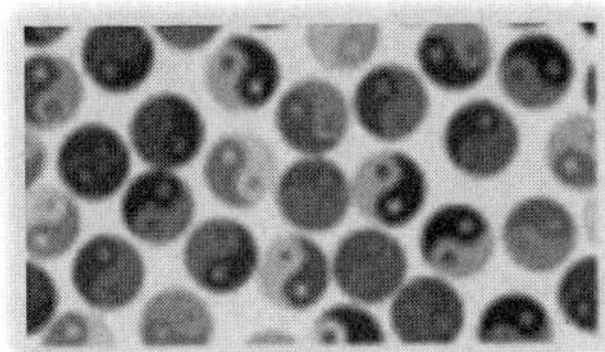

Objectives & reminders

____

____

____

Appointments

Early morning

8 a.m.

9 a.m.

10 a.m.

11 a.m.

Noon

1 p.m.

2 p.m.

3 p.m.

4 p.m.

5 p.m.

6 p.m.

Later evening

Happy birthday: Karol Adamiecki

Born in Poland on March 18, 1866, Adamiecki was an influential economist and business researcher in Central and Eastern Europe. In particular, he conceptualized the *managerial law of harmony* that suggests an organization's productivity is enhanced when harmony exists. According to Adamiecki, harmony consists of three pieces:

1. Harmony of choice, i.e., tools and equipment used in production should be compatible with each other.

2. Harmony of doing, i.e, the timing of processes should be coordinated and schedules thoughtfully developed.

3. Harmony of spirit, i.e., building competent teams of workers, and fostering a sense of teamwork with superordinate goals.

Like many business thinkers of his era, Adamiecki's focus dealt largely with questions of productivity and efficiency: How can companies produce more with fewer resources? What's the most efficient way to accomplish a particular job task? *Are we doing things right?*

More recent business thinkers (most notably Peter F. Drucker) have prompted managers to consider broader strategic questions of effectiveness as well: What business are we in? What are our priorities? *Are we doing the right things?*

Quest for convenience gone too far?

Part of the decades-long trend toward making products more convenient involves making them easier to acquire or less time-consuming to use. Sometimes it means making products so economical that little or no maintenance is involved; perhaps the ultimate is the disposable product.

In addition to customer convenience, disposables can be advantageous to producers if buyers continue to repurchase disposables to replace used and discarded ones. That was the hope of Scott Paper Company on March 18, 1966, when they began selling disposable paper dresses for $1.00 each. Despite the appealing price and the convenience of not having to laundry the dresses, the innovation was not well received by consumers. The paper dresses were soon dropped from the product mix.

March 19, 2018
Monday

St. Patrick's Day observed (Ireland)

St. Joseph's Day (Bolivia, Croatia, Honduras, Italy, Portugal, Spain and elsewhere)

Objectives & reminders

______

______

______

Appointments

Early morning

8 a.m.

9 a.m.

10 a.m.

11 a.m.

Noon

1 p.m.

2 p.m.

3 p.m.

4 p.m.

5 p.m.

6 p.m.

Later evening

Words and creative ambiguity

The creative element of advertising and promotion can be enhanced by playing with words. For example, the multiple meanings of some words can introduce an element of creative ambiguity into a message. Similarly, different words that are pronounced identically can prompt audiences to think about messages in new ways.

So, in much the same way that professional writers and comedians catch readers' attention and provoke thought by cleverly playing with words, marketers too can play with words to prompt audiences to notice and remember marketing messages. To illustrate, note below how historical figures born on March 19 played with words to give their messages a creative twist. Then in the accompanying box, note how advertising slogans sometimes use a similar approach.

☺ "Some folk are *wise*, and some are other*wise*." -- Tobias Smollett, Scottish writer, born on March 19, 1721

☺ "I am sitting in the smallest room of my house. I have your review *before* me. In a moment, it will be *behind* me." -- Max Reger, German composer in response to a critic. Reger was born on March 19, 1873.

☺ "Honey, that Totie Fields is one well-fed... woman. When that gal sits *around* the house, she sits *around* the house." -- Moms Mabley, American comedian, born on March 19, 1894

Playful business slogans

1. "If your nails aren't *becoming* to you, you should *be coming* to us." -- manicure shop
2. "Tell us the *plane* truth." -- headline on an airline's comment card to prompt passengers' feedback
3. "We take the *dent* out of acci*dent*." -- automobile body shop
4. "The *mark* of a good body shop is no *mark* at all." – another automobile body shop
5. "If you *fail* to *plan*, then *plan* to *fail*." -- small business consulting firm specializing in planning facilitation

March 20, 2018
Tuesday

Spring arrives in Northern Hemisphere at 12:15 p.m. EDT
International Day of Happiness

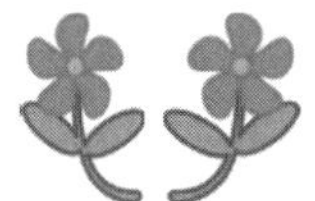  

Objectives & reminders

Appointments

Early morning

8 a.m.

9 a.m.

10 a.m.

11 a.m.

Noon 12:15 EDT: Spring arrives!

1 p.m.

2 p.m.

3 p.m.

4 p.m.

5 p.m.

6 p.m.

Later evening

Arrival of spring accompanied by marketing opportunities

Spring arrives a few minutes after noon today, in the Northern Hemisphere. Accompanying the transition from winter to spring are transitions in numerous buyer behaviors. Perhaps most apparent are changes in wardrobes and an increase in the pursuit of outdoor activities.

For marketers, the seasonal and behavioral transitions create opportunities that are likely to require marketing activities customized for the season. Initiatives may involve shelving or introducing new spring-related merchandise (e.g., shorts and sleeveless tops, outdoor cooking grills, patio furniture, lawn mowers), discounting the prices of winter-related items, suggesting seasonal uses for not-particularly-seasonal items (e.g., recipes for outdoor grilling with the company's brand of cooking sauce), or emphasizing more seasonal product appeals (e.g., shifting from an emphasis on the social appeal of a cold beverage in the winter to a thirst-quenching appeal in warmer weather), among other marketing actions.

However, marketers working for companies with a presence in multiple geographic areas should keep in mind that today's *official* arrival of spring does not necessarily coincide with the *practical* arrival of spring. For example, homeowners in College Station, Texas may have begun mowing their lawns in late February, whereas those in Fargo, North Dakota may not pull their mowers out of their garages before late April.

Career tip:
To become a "seasoned" management trainee, pay attention to seasons

Entering a management training program after graduation may involve various activities in the organization for one or more full cycles of the calendar year.

In part, this is to introduce future managers to the seasonal dynamics in the business – cyclical changes in buyers and buyers' needs, the product mix, promotional programs, pricing and a host of other seasonal variables throughout the year. The business may be quite different in each season (or month) of the year, so being familiar with the seasonal variation and anticipating it leads to more proactive and more effective marketing leadership.

March 21, 2018
Wednesday

First *full* day of spring in the Northern Hemisphere
World Poetry Day

Objectives & reminders

____

____

____

Appointments

Early morning

8 a.m.

9 a.m.

10 a.m.

11 a.m.

Noon

1 p.m.

2 p.m.

3 p.m.

4 p.m.

5 p.m.

6 p.m.

Later evening

Zodiac sign: Aries

March 21 marks the beginning of the month of Aries. According to believers of astrology, people born between March 21 and April 20 tend to be competitive, impulsive, youthful, proud, enthusiastic and open to change.

Surveys conducted by Pew Research, the National Science Foundation (NSF) and other organizations suggest that between 25 and 40 percent of American consumers believe that astrological claims have merit – with higher percentages reported for younger, less-educated and female respondents. In the NSF study, 15 percent of those surveyed claimed to read their horoscopes daily or "quite often" while another 30 percent said they read them at least occasionally.

Regardless of whether there is any legitimate association between personalities, fate and zodiac signs, or any validity to horoscopes, there may be marketing consequences nonetheless, as long as some individuals believe in astrology. For example, believers may reject a sales proposal if their horoscope warns them that today is not a good day to make a commitment or trust others. So, it might be worthwhile to consider timing marketing messages (and otherwise adjusting marketing programs) to coincide with horoscope-friendly days of the year.

Taco Bell's zodiac adaptation

In an apparent effort to capitalize on the public's interest in -- or amusement of -- astrology, Taco Bell restaurants printed a "personality guide" on placemats, but instead of a horoscope or description of the 12 signs of the zodiac, personalities were described for 12 menu items. "The noble burrito," for example, was described as "usually responsible for taking care of others," while "the sensible soft taco... loves to just go with the flow."

Wheeler-Lea Act

On March 21, 1938, the Wheeler-Lea Act became law in the United States. The purpose of the Act was to strengthen the Federal Trade Commission's power to protect the public from "unfair or deceptive acts or practices in commerce" -- particularly with regard to advertising. With the passing of the Wheeler-Lea Act, it was no longer necessary to show that deceptive practices harmed competitors.

March 22, 2018
Thursday

World Water Day
Emancipation Day (Puerto Rico)

Objectives & reminders

____

____

____

Appointments

Early morning

8 a.m.

9 a.m.

10 a.m.

11 a.m.

Noon

1 p.m.

2 p.m.

3 p.m.

4 p.m.

5 p.m.

6 p.m.

Later evening

Should advertisers keep newspapers in their media mix?

"Ted Turner [founder of CNN] said at a newspaper publishers' convention in Chicago in 1981 that newspapers would be dead by 1990. Didn't happen. The demise was predicted when radio came into being and again when television appeared. Now it's predicted with the Internet. I think it will dramatically affect newspapers but it will not mean their demise... I don't think there's anything in the [21st century] that's likely to kill off newspapers as we now know them, in terms of being printed on newsprint with colored ink and delivered to homes." – Allen "Al" H. Neuharth, who founded *USA Today* newspaper in 1982, born in Eureka, South Dakota on March 22, 1924

Television advertising threatened too: Early warning signs

The Association of National Advertisers (ANA) and Forrester Research, Inc. released the findings of a survey of 133 large national (U.S.) advertisers on March 22, 2006. Overall, the study found that major advertisers were concerned about the effectiveness of television advertising (especially the traditional 30-second spot) and, accordingly, were re-evaluating their advertising media mixes. More specifically, the survey found:

1. 80 percent of the respondents said they would spend more of their ad budgets on Web advertising. Sixty-eight percent reported that they would look to more search engine marketing.

2. 78 percent agreed that traditional television advertising had become less effective in the past two years.

3. Almost 70 percent expressed the belief that digital video recorders (DVRs) and video-on-demand will threaten the effectiveness of traditional 30-second television commercials.

4. Although television may continue to be an important medium for advertisers, many respondents reported their intention to consider alternatives to traditional 30-second commercials. Examples: TV program sponsorships (55%), interactive advertising during TV programs (48%), and product placement (44%).

March 23, 2018
Friday

Pakistan Day (Pakistan)

Marketing FAME is differentiated

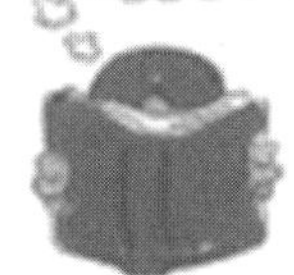

Objectives & reminders

____

____

____

Appointments

Early morning

8 a.m.

9 a.m.

10 a.m.

11 a.m.

Noon

1 p.m.

2 p.m.

3 p.m.

4 p.m.

5 p.m.

6 p.m.

Later evening

Marketing-relevant books published on March 23

Learn to think like the customer

"Customers buy for their reasons, not yours." – Orvel Ray Wilson, marketing and management consultant, speaker and writer. For more of Wilson's insights, see his best-selling book co-authored with William K. Gallagher and Jay Conrad Levinson, *Guerrilla Selling: Unconventional Weapons and Tactics for Increasing Your Sales*, published on March 23, 1992.

____

Differentiation is key

The paperback edition of Watts Wacker and Ryan Mathews' popular and thought-provoking book, *The Deviant's Advantage: How to Use Fringe Ideas to Create Mass Markets*, was published on March 23, 2004.

In their book, Wacker and Mathews pointed out that doing things that are different from the norm ("deviant") can lead to positive or negative consequences. For businesspeople in general, and marketers and entrepreneurs in particular, the practice of deviance "irrigates the imagination; offers an inexhaustible font of new ideas, products, and services; and in the end, is the source of all innovation, new market creation, and... ultimately represents the basis of all incremental profit. Deviance equals innovation and innovation equals opportunity."

____

Market share is not always profitable

"Market share is the most widely reported marketing metric in the world. But it's used in the wrong ways: as hindsight instead of foresight... Market share should be... [p]lanned to rise and fall to the level that maximizes earnings... [To do that] *spend money on market share until the profit from acquiring the last share point just equals its costs.* The main reason managers find the result of applying this rule so difficult to accept is too often it points to a significant decline in sales revenue." – Victor J. Cook, Jr., business researcher and writer whose work blends the fields of marketing and finance. For more of Cook's insights, read his well-regarded book published on March 23, 2006: *Competing for Customers and Capital.*

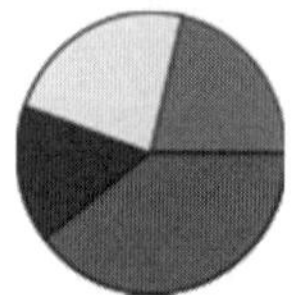

March 24, 2018
Saturday
World Tuberculosis Day

Objectives & reminders

____

____

____

Appointments

Early morning

8 a.m.

9 a.m.

10 a.m.

11 a.m.

Noon

1 p.m.

2 p.m.

3 p.m.

4 p.m.

5 p.m.

6 p.m.

Later evening

Animated day: Chapter One, 1901

Ubbe "Ub" Eert Iwerks (originally Iwwerks) was born in Kansas City, Missouri, on March 24, 1901. Although Iwerks excelled at art in high school, family problems forced him to leave school prematurely to help support his mother.

Fortunately, Iwerks landed a job doing lettering and airbrushing work at a commercial art studio where he soon met Walt Disney. The two worked on several projects together, became friends and after both had lost their jobs, teamed to form Iwerks-Disney Commercial Artists in 1920. Although the new venture failed, Iwerks and Disney continued to work together.

By the late 1920s, Iwerks had developed a creative flare for animated characters, when he accepted a job offer to work for Walt Disney. The two developed a new cartoon character in 1928 -- Mickey Mouse. Soon after that Iwerk left Disney, launched his own animation studio (Ub Iwerks Studio), then later returned to work for Disney again.

Animated day: Chapter Two, 1911

Exactly ten years after Ub Iwerks was born -- on March 24, 1911 -- another animation legend was born in New York City: Joseph Barbera. Creativity was central to Barbera's career as a cartoonist, television/movie producer and half of the famous "Hanna & Barbera" team. His creations included *The Flintstones, Tom & Jerry, Yogi Bear,* and *Scooby Doo*, among many others. His success formula was straightforward and focused: "I have a simple goal; make people laugh."

> **Reality of excellence**
> "I learned long ago to accept the fact that not everything I create will see the light of day." – Joseph Barbera

---

No laughing matter

On March 24, 1989, more than 11 million gallons of oil began spilling from the Exxon Valdez after the tanker ran aground on Bligh Reef in Alaska's Prince William Sound. The accident created one of the largest environmental disasters, most expensive clean-up projects, and largest public relations nightmares of all time.

March 25, 2018
Sunday
Palm Sunday

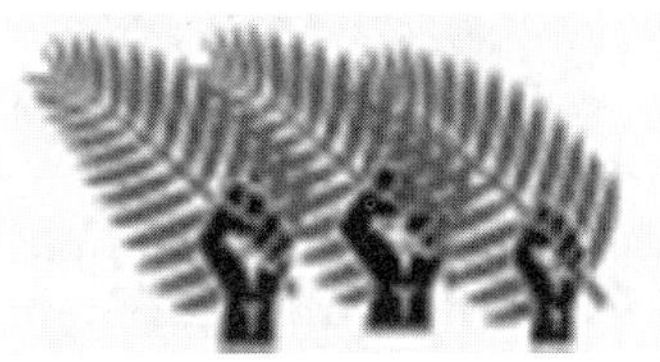

Objectives & reminders

Appointments

Early morning

8 a.m.

9 a.m.

10 a.m. https://www.youtube.com/watch?v=DQAKY1ntM9o

11 a.m.

Noon

1 p.m.

2 p.m.

3 p.m.

4 p.m.

5 p.m.

6 p.m.

Later evening

Palm Sunday

Palm Sunday is a Christian observance that falls one week before Easter Sunday. The holiday commemorates Jesus' triumphal entry into Jerusalem and is celebrated with feasts and worship services.

Palm Sunday sentiment
"Palm Sunday is like a glimpse of Easter. It's a little bit joyful after being somber during Lent." – Laura Gale

---

Every Sunday is special

Palm Sunday, along with Easter Sunday that follows next week, may be the two most important Sundays of the year for Christians. But that's not to say that other Sundays aren't special too – they are – for both religious and non-religious reasons.

In much the same way that every day of the year is unique and therefore special, every day of the week is special too. Buyers' moods, sentiments and how they spend their time and money tend to differ across the days of the week. Similarly, marketing professionals and the organizations they represent tend to vary their behavior across the weekly cycle.

Although exceptions abound, several day-of-week patterns of marketplace behavior are both pronounced and marketing-relevant. Accordingly, a few distinctions that characterize Sundays are listed in the box below. Noteworthy distinctions for other days of the week are featured every eight days for the next few weeks, i.e., Mondays discussed on April 2, Tuesdays on April 10, Wednesdays on April 18, and so on.

Sundayness

Consider the marketing implications of each of these characteristics of Sundays in the U.S.:

1. Sunday is most likely to be considered one's "favorite day of the week."
2. Sunday is the most popular day of the week to worship and the least likely day to work.
3. Consumers are more likely to dine out for breakfast on Sunday than on any other day of the week.
4. Sunday has more newspaper readers than any other day of the week.
5. Fewer emails are sent on Sundays than on other days of the week.

March 26, 2018
Monday
Purple Day (U.S. and Canada)

Objectives & reminders

____

____

____

Appointments

Early morning

8 a.m.

9 a.m.

10 a.m.

11 a.m.

Noon

1 p.m.

2 p.m.

3 p.m.

4 p.m.

5 p.m.

6 p.m.

Later evening

Happy birthday: Ernst Engel

Engel was a statistician born in what is now Dresden, Germany on March 26, 1821. Among other contributions, Engel is best known for his marketing-relevant Engel's Law, articulated in 1857.

Engel's Law suggests that consumers with lower incomes tend to spend a higher proportion of their income on food than do consumers at higher levels of income. As income rises, people do tend to spend greater *amounts* of money on food because they trade-up to higher quality or processed foods, but the *percentage* of their income spent on food decreases. Today, in the United States the typical household spends about 10 percent of its income on food, whereas in very poor countries consumers spend more than 50 percent of their income on food.

Engel's Law, in his own words

"The poorer is a family, the greater is the proportion of the total outgo which must be used for food... The proportion of the outgo used for food, other things being equal, is the best measure of the material standard of living of a population." -- Ernst Engel

Interestingly, Engel found that the relationship between income and the proportion of income spent on many other product categories differs. For example, the proportion of income spent on housing (including utilities) tends to remain fairly constant as income rises, while the proportion spent on services, major durables, luxury goods, and savings or investments tends to increase.

By understanding these income-expenditure relationships identified by Engel, marketers are able to estimate more accurately the potential demand for their products and brands in a particular market segment or geographic area. For example, the demand for luxury automobiles might be several times as high in an affluent community as in a poorer community, although the number of consumers living in each community might be comparable.

Engel's Law also applies to time expenditures: Agree or disagree?

"By working faithfully eight hours a day, you may eventually get to be boss and work twelve hours a day." -- Robert Frost, American poet, born in San Francisco, California on March 26, 1874

March 27, 2018
Tuesday
World Theatre Day

Objectives & reminders

Appointments

Early morning

8 a.m.

9 a.m.

10 a.m.

11 a.m.

Noon

1 p.m.

2 p.m.

3 p.m.

4 p.m.

5 p.m.

6 p.m.

Later evening

Time-management insight

Jack Welch, former chairman and CEO of General Electric, had a reputation for getting a great deal of work done. He worked hard and had a successful career, but he didn't believe in 16-hour work days, at least not on a regular basis. On March 27, 1989, he offered this time-management insight:

> "If someone tells me, 'I'm working 90 hours a week,' I say, 'You're doing something terribly wrong... Put down a list of the 20 things you're doing that make you work 90 hours, and 10 of them have to be nonsense -- or else somebody else has got to do them for you.'"

Sure about this?

"Some people, however long their experience or strong their intellect, are temperamentally incapable of reaching firm decisions." -- James Callaghan, former British prime minister (1976-1979), born in Portsmouth, England on March 27, 1912

Is "first to market" always an advantage?

"It is better to be good than to be original." -- Ludwig Mies van der Rohe, German-American architect, born in Aachen, Germany on March 27, 1886

Business is more than business

"Business is society. We touch an enormous number of people, and we have to touch everybody with care and concern, with gentleness and awareness." -- Lane Nemeth, founder of Discovery Toys (makers of Marbleworks), born on March 27, 1947

Unethical positioning: Agree or disagree?

Anita Roddick, founder and former CEO of the chain of environmentally-friendly cosmetic stores called "The Body Shop," opened her first store on March 27, 1976, in Brighton, England. Considerable publicity and criticism surrounded the store's opening -- not so much because the store had opened, per se, but because of what critics claimed was an incompatible fit between the store's name and the location of the store. Coincidentally or not, the first Body Shop was located next to a mortuary.

March 28, 2018
Wednesday

Teachers' Day
(Slovakia and Czech Republic)

Objectives & reminders

______

______

______

Appointments

Early morning

8 a.m.

9 a.m.

10 a.m.

11 a.m.

Noon

1 p.m.

2 p.m.

3 p.m.

4 p.m.

5 p.m.

6 p.m.

Later evening

Innovative beginnings on March 28

1897 Victor Mills was born in Milford, Nebraska. He was the American chemical engineer who, while working for Procter & Gamble, invented what became the Pampers brand of disposable diapers. The invention resulted from Mills' efforts to utilize the absorbent paper byproducts produced by a pulp mill P&G had acquired.

> **Byproduct principle**
> One process's waste is another process's raw materials.

1899 August "Gussie" Busch, Jr. was born in St. Louis, Missouri. Gussie was the grandson of Adolphus Busch who co-founded the Anheuser-Busch Brewing Co. Following in his grandfather's footsteps, the younger Busch joined the company in 1924 and served as chairman from 1946 to 1975.

Under Gussie's leadership, the firm bought the St. Louis Cardinals baseball team and the home stadium where the team played (guess which brand of beer is served at Busch Stadium?). During Gussie's leadership, the company began showcasing the firm's team of Clydesdale horses and became the first brewery to sponsor a radio network.

> **Advertising staying power**
> "King of Beers" – Anheuser-Busch's long-running slogan coined by Gussie Busch

1935 Arnold Reuben, restaurateur and inventor of several sandwiches (including the Reuben, of course), officially and ceremoniously held a "grand opening" event for his restaurant and delicatessen – Reubens – in New York City. Mayor Fiorello LaGuardia attended the event which was covered by *The New York Times*.

> **Advantage of grand opening events**
> Retail businesses are like babies; their ability to attract attention is greatest when they are first born.

March 29, 2018
Thursday
Martyrs' Day (Madagascar)

Objectives & reminders

______

______

______

Appointments

Early morning

8 a.m.

9 a.m.

10 a.m.

11 a.m.

Noon

1 p.m.

2 p.m.

3 p.m.

4 p.m.

5 p.m.

6 p.m.

Later evening

Happy 100th birthday: Samuel Moore "Sam" Walton

Walton was born in Kingfisher, Oklahoma on March 29, 1918. In Rogers, Arkansas in 1962 he opened what would become the first discount store in his Wal-Mart empire. Also in 1962, the first Kmart and the first Target stores opened.

Learning from competitors

"We're really not concerned with what [the competition is] doing wrong; we're concerned with what they're doing right. Everyone is doing something right."
– Sam Walton

Today, the company is enormous: Almost 12,000 Wal-Mart stores scattered across 28 countries, employing 2.3 million "associates" and generating annual revenues of more than one-half trillion dollars.

Sams do what Sams do!

One of the most admirable traits of Sam Walton was his enthusiastic tenacity. Although events did not always unfold as planned, no setback ever seemed to bother him. He just kept bouncing back, undaunted. For example, David Glass, who served as Wal-Mart's CEO after Walton's death in 1992, recalls a grand opening for one store in the early 1960s -- a grand opening that might have derailed growth plans and otherwise unnerved anyone except Sam Walton:

> "I drove down... to see a Wal-Mart opening. It was the worst retail store I had ever seen. Sam had brought a couple of trucks of watermelons in and stacked them on the sidewalk. He had a donkey ride out in the parking lot. It was about 115 degrees, and the watermelons began to pop, and the donkeys began to do what donkeys do, and it all mixed together and ran all over the parking lot. And when you went inside the store, the mess just continued, having been tracked in all over the floor."

March 30, 2018
Friday
Good Friday
Passover (begins)
World Marbles Day

 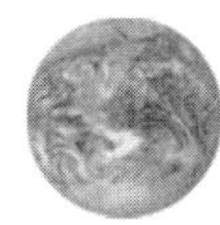 

Objectives & reminders

___

___

___

Appointments

Early morning

8 a.m.

9 a.m.

10 a.m.

11 a.m.

Noon

1 p.m.

2 p.m.

3 p.m.

4 p.m.

5 p.m.

6 p.m.

Later evening

5th Friday Windfall

March is one of only four months in 2018 with five Fridays. The others are June, August and November. For calendar-led marketers who serve household consumers, this fact is more than trivia; it is an opportunity. The following paragraphs explain why…

Friday is payday for more employed consumers in the U.S. than any other day of the week. Many workers receive a paycheck every Friday, while many others are paid on alternating Fridays. Regardless of the pay dates, however, it's typical for employers to withhold money from employees' *gross pay* for federal and state income taxes, healthcare insurance and other obligations. Because workers don't directly receive these deductions, they tend to think of their wages in terms of *net pay* or *take-home pay* received after the deductions are withheld.

The net pay for salaried workers and for hourly workers with consistent schedules tends to be about the same from one pay period to the next, so workers know about how much money they'll receive on payday. This consistency is maintained as long as payroll deductions are the same each pay period.

But payroll deductions can vary on the 5th Friday of the month for organizations with healthcare insurance plans and other deductions paid on a monthly basis. This occurs because months with 30 or 31 days are not evenly divisible by weekly or bi-weekly periods. So, as an example, suppose a worker's monthly healthcare insurance premium through her employer's plan is $400. If she is paid weekly on Fridays, her employer might deduct $100 from each paycheck for the first four Friday paydays. If she's paid every other Friday, $200 might be deducted from each of her first two Friday paydays of the month. Because her monthly insurance premium is already paid when an occasional 5th Friday payday occurs, the payroll deduction for insurance is skipped for 5th Friday paychecks – creating what the employee is likely to perceive as a $100 or $200 windfall or bonus for the pay period.

Although the 5th Friday phenomenon doesn't affect all workers, if those who are affected view the extra cash as a windfall, they may be quite willing to spend all or a portion of it on discretionary purchases. So, as 5th Fridays approach, astute calendar-led marketers are ready with marketing communications, sale events and other tactics to "help" employed workers spend their 5th Friday windfalls. Timing matters!

March 31, 2018
Saturday
César Chávez Day

Objectives & reminders

Appointments

Early morning

8 a.m.

9 a.m.

10 a.m.

11 a.m.

Noon

1 p.m.

2 p.m.

3 p.m.

4 p.m.

5 p.m.

6 p.m.

Later evening

César Chávez Day: Good day to salute farm workers

"It's ironic that those who till the soil, cultivate and harvest the fruits, vegetables, and other foods that fill your tables with abundance have nothing left for themselves." – César Estrada Chávez, American union organizer and social activist who founded the National Farm Workers Association (NFWA) and the United Farm Workers (UFW).

Chávez was born near Yuma, Arizona on March 31, 1927, and was posthumously awarded the Presidential Medal of Freedom in 1994. Today, Chávez's birthday is celebrated in at least 10 U.S. states, including six states where it is a state holiday: Arizona, California, Michigan, New Mexico, Utah and Wisconsin.

End of one era, but not its influence

John Wooden ended his illustrious career as basketball coach for the UCLA Bruins on March 31, 1975, when he coached his last game. The team won the game giving Coach Wooden his tenth national championship in a span of 12 years. Accordingly, Wooden is considered the most successful college basketball coach of all time.

While sport history is bound to remember Wooden for the number of victories and championships his teams tallied, his players and others who had the honor of knowing him are more likely to remember him as someone who shaped players' character; imparting basketball skills, per se, were secondary considerations.

Basketball-business wisdom from a legend
"Never criticize, nag, or razz a teammate. Be a team player always." – John Wooden

More emails & meetings needed: Agree or disagree?

"It's hard for me to imagine that you can over-communicate. I think many companies have some really wonderful policies, procedures, and intentions, but 90 percent of the people in the company don't know about them. Management thinks 'this is what's important,' but if they looked they'd discover nobody understands it." – Arthur "Art" D. Levinson, CEO of Calico and chairman of Apple Inc., born in Seattle, Washington on March 31, 1950

April 1, 2018
Sunday

Easter
April Fools' Day

Objectives & reminders

____

____

____

Appointments

Early morning

8 a.m.

9 a.m.

10 a.m.

11 a.m.

Noon

1 p.m.

2 p.m.

3 p.m.

4 p.m.

5 p.m.

6 p.m.

Later evening

Welcome to a new month!

April

In April Rome was founded; Shakespeare died;
The shot whose sound rang out from Concord town
And brought an avalanche of echoes down
Shaking all thrones of tyranny and pride,
Was fired in April' Sumter far and wide
Lifted a voice the years will never drown;
'Twas April when they laid the martyr's crown
On Lincoln's brow, with tears that scarce have dried.
O flowers that bloom in April; little wings
And voices that like happy sunbeams dart
Around us; budding trees and bubbling springs --
Ye all are beautiful; such is your part
In God's great world. And yet 'tis human things
Most stir the soul and move the thoughtful heart.
-- Samuel Valentine Cole, poet, educator, and 1st president of Wheaton College (Massachusetts)

Easter Sunday

Christians celebrate Easter to commemorate the resurrection of Jesus Christ. Church services are heavily attended on Easter, including sunrise services that coincide with the time of day Jesus was resurrected.

Over the years, more secular meanings have been associated with Easter. The tradition of the Easter Bunny visiting children to leave candy, eggs, and small gifts is widely observed in the U.S. The decoration and exchange of Easter eggs is popular too, as are Easter egg hunts for children. Because Easter is celebrated near the beginning of spring, Easter often is seen as the unofficial beginning of the new season -- prompting church-goers and others to don their new spring apparel.

Double-dip Easter promotion

Easter-related promotions such as egg hunts and egg decorating activities for children are good ways to build both goodwill and customer traffic.

Before the age of digital photography, at least one promotion scored extra points in terms of generating customer traffic for retail stores and malls, i.e., having children's pictures taken with the Easter Bunny. Parents brought their children *once* to have the pictures taken, and a *second* time to pick up the developed pictures.

April 2, 2018
Monday
International Children's Book Day

Objectives & reminders

____

____

____

Appointments

Early morning

8 a.m.

9 a.m.

10 a.m.

11 a.m.

Noon

1 p.m.

2 p.m.

3 p.m.

4 p.m.

5 p.m.

6 p.m.

Later evening

Welcome to Monday

Buyers and businesspeople are creatures of habit who establish routines that tend to repeat somewhat predictably across the four major calendar cycles: time of day, day of week, day/period of month, and day/period of year. Further, although there are plenty of exceptions, the timing of our individual habits, routines and accompanying sentiments frequently resembles that of other people. As a result, a unique identity and partially-shared meaning has evolved for each time period on the calendar – including each day of the week.

Today, we focus on Mondays. Knowing what behaviors and feelings coincide with Monday enables calendar-led marketers to fine-tune the timing and content of their marketing plans. Accordingly, consider the possible marketing implications of the following Monday characteristics.

1. Monday is the day of the week most likely to represent workers returning to their jobs after having one or more days off. However, along with Friday, Monday is one of the two most popular days for workers to claim as a "sick" day.

2. Especially for workers who don't enjoy their jobs, Monday is the day of the week most likely to be associated with negative mood states, i.e., the "Monday blues" are common.

Monday metaphor

Mondays are the "potholes in the road of life." – Tom Wilson, American comedian

3. Unless they have scheduled special Monday events, retailers tend to report fewer shoppers on Mondays than on other days. Their customers may have already shopped on the weekend.

4. Online shoppers are more likely to buy insurance on Monday than on any other day of the week – perhaps because they used part of the weekend to study alternatives and discuss their future with family members.

♫ ♪ Listen, learn and enjoy ♪ ♫

Learn more about the meanings associated with each day of the week by listening to hundreds of songs with lyrics about the uniqueness of a day of the week. Start with these two Monday favorites: https://g.co/kgs/EnvLDB and https://g.co/kgs/3UZN2h

April 3, 2018
Tuesday
World Party Day

Objectives & reminders

____

____

____

Appointments

Early morning

8 a.m.

9 a.m.

10 a.m.

11 a.m.

Noon

1 p.m.

2 p.m.

3 p.m.

4 p.m.

5 p.m.

6 p.m.

Later evening

Business-relevant celebrity birthdays on April 3

Wayne Newton

Born in Norfolk, Virginia on April 3, 1942, Newton is an American singer and entertainer. Known as "Mr. Las Vegas," Newton has performed more than 30,000 shows in Las Vegas since the late 1960s.

In his book, *Often Wrong, Never in Doubt*, former advertising executive and talk-show host, Donny Deutsch, used Newton to illustrate an important point about target marketing. That is, it is okay that some buyers dislike the brand (like some Las Vegas tourists shun the idea of seeing a Wayne Newton show), as long as a significant number love the brand – in much the same way that some Las Vegas tourists visit the city primarily to attend back-to-back Newton shows.

Deutsch asserts that too many marketers try to appeal to too broad of a market and end up appealing to no one: "It's better to have thirty-five percent of the people really charged up about you and the rest hate you than to have 100 percent not care" (p. 167).

Eddie Murphy

Born in Brooklyn, New York on April 3, 1961, Murphy was a successful American comedian in the early 1980s, including his role as a cast member on *Saturday Night Live* (1980-1984). He soon applied his comedic genius to the silver screen starring in a series of box office hits including *48 Hours, Trading Places, Beverly Hills Cop*, and several Disney films, among others.

In the 2003 movie, *Daddy Day Care*, Murphy's character, Charlie Hinton, became disenchanted with the life of a corporate marketing executive and left his job to start a children's day-care center with a colleague. He found the small business, hands-on world he entered to be quite different from the bureaucratic, disconnected and politically-charged corporate world he left behind.

While the sharp contrasts between the two work environments supplied the comical fodder to amuse audiences, they also high-lighted the reality that different businesses and jobs call for different skill sets. Although Charlie eventually flourished in his new business world, the transition was a bumpy ride.

April 4, 2018
Wednesday

Walk to Work Day *(also observed on April 6)*

Objectives & reminders

____

____

____

Appointments

Early morning

8 a.m.

9 a.m.

10 a.m.

11 a.m.

Noon

1 p.m.

2 p.m.

3 p.m.

4 p.m.

5 p.m.

6 p.m.

Later evening

A victory for women and a loss for mankind

Argonia, Kansas was the site for celebration on April 4, 1887. There, the first female in the United States was elected as mayor: 27-year-old Susanna Medora Salter.

In sharp contrast, there was no cause for celebration in Memphis, Tennessee on April 4, 1968, when civil rights leader and recipient of the 1964 Nobel Peace Prize, Dr. Martin Luther King, Jr., was assassinated shortly after 6:00 p.m.

> **Redemptive pricing**
> "If physical death is the price that I must pay to free my white brothers and sisters from a permanent death of the spirit, then nothing can be more redemptive."
> -- Martin Luther King, Jr.

Bad Guy, good O'guy

The infamous magazine publisher Guy Wayte was born on April 4, 1907. Like many publishers, he viewed his publications as vehicles to deliver audiences to advertisers and he knew that larger audiences commanded higher advertising rates.

But, unlike other publishers, he was an "unscrupulous humbug," as one judge called him, because he had a habit of falsifying his publications' circulation figures. As an example, over one six-month period he claimed sales of 295,570 copies instead of the true figure of 100,069. In February 1980 Wayte was found guilty of conspiracy to defraud advertisers.

In contrast, Kevin O'Connor, who was born in Livonia, Michigan on April 4, 1961, wanted to ensure that advertisers were not defrauded or misled. Along with Dwight Merriman, he founded DoubleClick in 1996 (now a subsidiary of Google [Alphabet, Inc.]). The firm serves as a middleman between websites and advertisers.

To the delight of advertisers, one of DoubleClick's strengths is its ability to track users so advertisers know precisely how many people are exposed to their ads, where those people first logged on, and what other sites they have visited. Using DoubleClick or other comparable services, online advertisers can gain a stronger sense of the effectiveness of their advertising. In other words, they no longer have to misplace their trust in people like Guy Wayte.

April 5, 2018
Thursday
Sikmogil (South Korea)

Objectives & reminders

____

____

____

Appointments

Early morning

8 a.m.

9 a.m.

10 a.m.

11 a.m.

Noon

1 p.m.

2 p.m.

3 p.m.

4 p.m.

5 p.m.

6 p.m.

Later evening

Happy birthday: Colin L. Powell

Born in New York City on April 5, 1937, Powell grew up to enjoy a distinguished military career for 35 years – rising to the rank of 4-star General. Then he served as the U.S. Secretary of State under President George W. Bush from 2001 to 2005. Among many other qualities, Powell is widely recognized for his leadership skills.

Powell on leadership: Three insights

1. "Plans don't accomplish work. Goal charts on walls don't accomplish work. Even talking papers don't accomplish work. It is people who get things done."
2. "Figure out what is crucial, then stay focused on that. Never allow side issues... to knock you off track."
3. "Be flexible, be willing to change your opinions in light of new facts, and don't get hung up on any particular course of action if it's not essential to your mission… [B]e willing to question and change your mission when new 'enemies' arise."

A calendar mistake: Agree or disagree?

Businesses learn from one another -- sometimes what to do, and sometimes what *not* to do. On April 5, 2005, a calendar-printer's booth at a trade show in Houston, Texas attempted to showcase their capabilities by giving visitors a free sample – a copy of the *previous* year's calendar they had printed. Although the out-of-date calendar was appreciated, its impact was far less than a more useable calendar for the *current* year would have been.

Cost savings could prove to be expensive

Don't count on leftover merchandise that the company can't sell to be well-received as effective promotional items. To make a positive impression, give customers something they will use and value.

April 6, 2018
Friday

Walk to Work Day *(also observed on April 4)*
Chakri Day (Thailand)

Objectives & reminders

____

____

____

Appointments

Early morning

8 a.m.

9 a.m.

10 a.m.

11 a.m.

Noon

1 p.m.

2 p.m.

3 p.m.

4 p.m.

5 p.m.

6 p.m.

Later evening

Potential for nostalgia appeal

"After the age of 80, everything reminds you of something else." – Lowell Jackson Thomas, explorer and journalist, born in Woodington, Ohio on April 6, 1892

Aiming low to aim high: Agree or disagree?

"It's necessary to be slightly underemployed if you are to do something significant." -- James D. Watson, geneticist, born in Chicago, Illinois on April 6, 1928

Ideas surround listeners

"In the industrial age, the CEO sat on the top of the hierarchy and didn't really have to listen to anybody... In the information age, you have to listen to the ideas of people regardless of where they are in the organization." -- John Sculley, former chairman and CEO of Apple Computers, born in New York City on April 6, 1939

Ambitious plans are the most challenging

"It is a hard rule of life, and I believe a healthy one, that no great plan is ever carried out without meeting and overcoming endless obstacles that come up to try the skill of man's hand, the quality of his courage, and the endurance of his faith." -- Donald Wills Douglas, aircraft designer and founder of Douglas Aircraft Company in the early 1920s. The company merged with McDonnell Aircraft Company in 1967, then with Boeing in 1997. Douglas was born in Brooklyn, New York on April 6, 1892.

Employee profile should mirror customer profile: Agree or disagree?

"You cannot understand your consumer, you cannot make the right products and attract the best people if you are fishing in a pond that represents a minority of the actual environment that you operate in.... The point is, to be a successful business, you really have to represent the culture that you serve." – Steven Reinemund, former chairman and CEO of PepsiCo (2001-2006) and Dean of the business school at Wake Forrest University (2008-2014), born in New York City on April 6, 1948

April 7, 2018
Saturday
World Health Day

Objectives & reminders

___

___

___

Appointments

Early morning

8 a.m.

9 a.m.

10 a.m.

11 a.m.

Noon

1 p.m.

2 p.m.

3 p.m.

4 p.m.

5 p.m.

6 p.m.

Later evening

The Texas Company

Founded in Beaumont, Texas by Joseph S. Cullinan, Walter Benona Sharp and Arnold Schlaet on April 7, 1902, The Texas Company became known as Texaco.

The oil company proved to have a strong respect for the role of marketing in the organization. For example, in 1932, Texaco introduced and branded Fire Chief gasoline, a blend with an octane rating sufficient for fire engines – an association the public viewed favorably. Texaco promoted the Fire Chief brand through their nationwide radio program hosted by entertainer Ed Winn who personified the brand as "The Texaco Fire Chief."

Another Texaco marketing coup stemmed from the company's realization that motorists were not solely interested in buying gasoline, per se, but in the larger refueling experience. Accordingly, Texaco introduced its "Registered Rest Room" program in 1939. The company insisted that station operators maintain high standards of cleanliness to earn Texaco's endorsement. With the assurance of clean rest rooms, motorists developed a preference for the 45,000 Texaco dealers throughout the United States. Not surprisingly, other oil companies copied the concept and began promoting their clean rest rooms too.

Also during the 1930s, Texaco hired suggestive selling expert Elmer Wheeler to help stimulate retail sales of New Texaco Oil. Wheeler tested numerous phrases such as "How about some oil?" and "Shall I check your oil?" but found that motorists were conditioned to say "No" in response to such suggestive selling efforts. So, his research determined that the most effective pitch was to ask motorists, "Is your oil at proper driving level?" According to Wheeler, this seven-word question succeeded 58 percent of the time, "because it capitalized on the word 'NO'! It invited a 'NO' – for in this case 'NO' meant 'YES'!"

___

Hiring Texaco's Fire Chief might have made brand fire proof?

"The fire is of no consequence. You can't burn down what we have registered in the mind of the American woman." -- Will Keith Kellogg, inventor of Kellogg's Corn Flakes and founder of the company that makes them, born in Battle Creek, Michigan on April 7, 1860. Kellogg made this comment in 1907 after a fire burned down one of his factories.

April 8, 2018
Sunday
Buddha's Birthday Holiday

Objectives & reminders

Appointments

Early morning
8 a.m.
9 a.m.
10 a.m.
11 a.m.
Noon
1 p.m.
2 p.m.
3 p.m.
4 p.m.
5 p.m.
6 p.m.
Later evening

Happy birthday: Gautama Buddha

Buddha, "the enlightened one," is the founder of Buddhism. He is believed to have been born in southern Nepal on April 8, 563 B.C., although there is some debate as to his precise date of birth.

Born Siddhartha Gautama, Buddha reached "supreme enlightenment" at the age of 35 and began to spread his doctrine which includes "four noble truths": (1) to exist is to suffer, (2) suffering stems from human cravings, (3) a state of nirvana is reached when the suffering ceases, and (4) an "eightfold path" leads to nirvana -- right views, right resolve, right speech, right action, right livelihood, right effort, right mindfulness, and right concentration.

Today, more than 500 million people (largely Asian) in about 100 countries are followers of Buddhism. For devoted Buddhists around the world, April 8 is their most important holiday.

Selected Buddha perspectives

Consider the extent to which Buddhist teachings are consistent with your own belief system. Here are some sample quotations from Gautama Buddha himself:

Experience

"Let yourself be open and life will be easier. A spoon of salt in a glass of water makes the water undrinkable. A spoon of salt in a lake is almost unnoticed."

Change

"Everything changes. Nothing remains without change."

Tolerance

"To understand everything is to forgive everything."

Destiny

"All that we are is the result of what we have thought... What we think we become."

April 9, 2018
Monday
Severe Weather Awareness Week begins

Objectives & reminders

___

___

___

Appointments

Early morning

8 a.m.

9 a.m.

10 a.m.

11 a.m.

Noon

1 p.m.

2 p.m.

3 p.m.

4 p.m.

5 p.m.

6 p.m.

Later evening

Happy birthday: Joseph F. Cullman, III

Born in New York City on April 9, 1912, Cullman was the president, chairman and CEO of the tobacco giant Philip Morris from 1957 until 1978. Under Cullman's leadership, Philip Morris established the "Marlboro Man" advertising icon which helped Marlboro become the best-selling cigarette brand in the world.

In the early 1960s only about one percent of Philip Morris' tobacco sales were generated outside of the United States. However, Cullman had the foresight to see that international was where the company's long-term opportunities were – especially given the domestic health community's concerns about the dangers of smoking.

So, Cullman assigned his top executive – George Weissman – the job of cultivating international markets. At the time, Weissman wasn't sure if his new role was a promotion or demotion: "Here I was running 99 percent of the company and the next day I'd be running one percent or less." Within 20 years, however, Cullman's decision proved to be the right one as Weissman's efforts propelled the company's international operations into the spotlight with sales exceeding those in the U.S. Philip Morris exported more cigarettes than any other firm in the world.

In his best-selling book, *Good to Great: Why Some Companies Make the Leap... and Others Don't*, Jim Collins calls Cullman's decision to put Weissman in charge of developing the international markets "a stroke of genius." Too often, Collins observes, business leaders ask their top talent to solve the company's biggest problems, rather than exploit the biggest opportunities. But business leaders that navigate their firms through the good-to-great transition are more likely to follow the lead of Cullman and think in terms of exploiting opportunities.

Think:
Exploit opportunities

"Put your best people on your biggest opportunities, not your biggest problems.... [M]anaging your problems can only make you good, whereas building your opportunities is the only way to become great." – Jim Collins, *Good to Great,* pp. 58-59

April 10, 2018
Tuesday
Siblings' Day

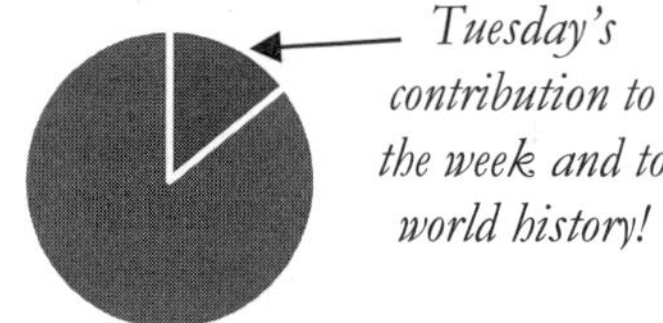
Tuesday's contribution to the week and to world history!

Objectives & reminders

____

____

____

Appointments

Early morning

8 a.m.

9 a.m.

10 a.m.

11 a.m.

Noon

1 p.m.

2 p.m.

3 p.m.

4 p.m.

5 p.m.

6 p.m.

Later evening

It's Tuesday!

Following the Sunday and Monday themes discussed on March 25 and April 2, respectively, today's focus is on the calendrical uniqueness of Tuesday – another important day of the week on which one-seventh of the world's history occurred. Knowledge of the uniqueness of each day of the week – including Tuesday – can enhance marketers' abilities to develop the content and time the execution of more effective marketing programs. Consider the possible marketing implications of these Tuesday tendencies:

1. Tuesday is the day of the week that workers are least likely to call their supervisors to claim a "sick" day.

2. B2B salespeople assert that Tuesday is the best day of the week to make cold calls – perhaps because buyers are less likely to be sick on Tuesdays.

3. Tuesday is the most popular day to send emails (Wednesdays and Thursdays are popular too), but as the number of Tuesday emails increases, the attention-getting potency of Tuesday emails may weaken.

4. Automobile dealerships tend to say that customer traffic is weakest on Tuesdays, which may mean that sales reps are able to spend more time with auto shoppers and may be more willing to negotiate on Tuesdays.

The weekly cycle in a calendar-led world

"Imagine for a moment that the week suddenly disappeared. What a havoc would be created in our time organization, in our behavior, in the co-ordination and synchronization of collective activities and social life, and especially in our time apprehension. Many of us would certainly mix our appointments, shift and change our activities, and fail many times to fulfill our engagements."

"If there were neither the names of the days nor weeks, we would be liable to be lost in an endless series of days – as gray as fog – and confuse one day with another. We think in week units… We live and feel and plan and wish in 'week' terms. It is one of the most important points of our 'orientation' in time and social reality." – Pitirim A. Sorokin, Russian-American sociologist

April 11, 2018
Wednesday

International Louie Louie Day

https://www.youtube.com/watch?v=4V1p1dM3snQ

Objectives & reminders

____

____

____

Appointments

Early morning

8 a.m.

9 a.m.

10 a.m.

11 a.m.

Noon

1 p.m.

2 p.m.

3 p.m.

4 p.m.

5 p.m.

6 p.m.

Later evening

Elimination of "price" from the marketing mix

On April 11, 1941, the U.S. marketplace was already suffering from the taxing effects of the war in Europe. To keep matters from getting worse, the Office of Price Administration and Civilian Supply (OPA) was established on this date. In effect, the regulations that followed took pricing out of the hands of businesses; the OPA had the authority to establish price ceilings or otherwise fix prices.

By controlling prices for many goods, the government hoped to prevent inflation, keep consumers from hoarding goods that were already in low supply, discourage businesses from reaping unrealistically high profits, and ensure that goods would be distributed fairly to consumers.

Not surprisingly, the price controls were unpopular with many businesspeople, but other than a black market that emerged for a few items (e.g., cigarettes, gasoline, meat), American consumers and businesses generally complied with OPA regulations. By 1946, the war had ended and business pressure prompted the easing of price controls and the dismantling of the OPA. A period of high inflation followed.

Not the end of price controls

The end of the OPA was not the end of price controls. Price controls continued for several years in some highly-regulated industries. Later, in a renewed effort to curb inflation, President Richard M. Nixon's administration imposed a general wage and price freeze.

Imitators can't succeed: Agree or disagree?

"The key to success for Sony, and to everything in business, science, and technology for that matter, is never to follow the others." – Masaru Ibuka, co-founder and former chairman of the electronics giant Sony, born in Nikko City, Japan on April 11, 1908

Is the past history?

"Whatever made you successful in the past, won't in the future." – Lewis E. Platt, former CEO of Hewlett-Packard, born in Johnson City, New York on April 11, 1941

April 12, 2018
Thursday

International Day of Human Space Flight

Can you catch the
the MISTAKE?
1 2 3 4 5 6 7 8 9

Objectives & reminders

Appointments

Early morning

8 a.m.

9 a.m.

10 a.m.

11 a.m.

Noon

1 p.m.

2 p.m.

3 p.m.

4 p.m.

5 p.m.

6 p.m.

ADMIT ONE MISTAKE

Later evening

Catching mistakes

We all make mistakes and each of us copes with mistakes in our own way. Some of us laugh at our follies and then bounce back. Other people deny their mistakes or downplay the consequences of mistakes, while others are busy blaming someone else. Still others redouble their efforts to prevent future mistakes.

Another approach is to accept the reality that mistakes are inevitable in most organizations -- at least occasional ones -- but that some reasonable precautions can help guard against their negative impact. Satisfaction guarantees, inspections, and safety gear are examples of such precautions. Apparently, the baseball community learned this too on April 12, 1877. That's when the first catcher's mask was worn in a baseball game.

Mistakes are only human

"The man who never makes any blunders is a very nice piece of machinery -- that's all." – Josh Billings, American humorist, born in Lanesborough, Massachusetts on April 12, 1818, or possibly on April 21, 1818 (sources disagree; apparently someone made a mistake recording Billings' date of birth)

Benefitting from mistakes

Mistakes are inevitable in business, and the consequences can be negative. But sometimes opportunities exist to capitalize on mistakes and turn them into something positive. That's what happened after a French newspaper mistakenly printed Alfred Nobel's obituary on April 12, 1888.

Apparently the newspaper had confused Alfred with his brother Ludwig, who had died. The obituary described Alfred as "a merchant of death" because his invention of dynamite had led to the death of so many people.

Troubled by such a legacy, Nobel decided to improve his image by doing something the public would regard more positively. So, he used his wealth to establish the Nobel Prizes, which continue to be awarded annually to individuals who make important contributions to society in the fields of chemistry, literature, medicine/physiology, physics and peace.

April 13, 2018
Friday
Katyn Memorial Day (Poland)

Objectives & reminders

Appointments

Early morning

8 a.m.

9 a.m.

10 a.m.

11 a.m.

Noon

1 p.m.

2 p.m.

3 p.m.

4 p.m.

5 p.m.

6 p.m.

Later evening

Diversified career

Born in Shadwell, Virginia on April 13, 1743, Thomas Jefferson was not only the primary author of the Declaration of Independence and the third President of the United States (1801-1809), but he was a businessman, architect, philosopher, ambassador, musician, inventor and astronomer, as well.

Jefferson's business insights

Consensus-building
"Great innovations should not be forced on slender majorities."

Decision-making
"The hole and the patch should be commensurate."

Future-orientation
"I like the dreams of the future better than the history of the past."

Conciseness
(formerly "being concise")
"The most valuable of all talents is that of never using two words when one will do."

Globalization
"Merchants have no country. The mere spot they stand on does not constitute so strong an attachment as that from which they draw their gains."

Is the sales force "connected"? Don't be so sure

"We're all linked to technology more than ever before. Many of us spend more time talking on our cell phones, checking email, or showing off the bells and whistles of our latest gadget, than we do actually connecting with people, especially new people. Selling is personal – very, very personal. We need to be present, involved, and connected. We need to connect – one human being to the other. It's then that we can make the person-to-person sale. Technology is a support for our sales process, not a substitute."
– Joanne S. Black, sales consultant and author of *No More Cold Calling: The Breakthrough System That Will Leave Your Competition in the Dust*, published on April 13, 2007

April 14, 2018
Saturday

Spring Takayama Festival begins
(Takayama, Gifu, Japan)

Objectives & reminders

______

______

______

Appointments

Early morning

8 a.m.

9 a.m.

10 a.m.

11 a.m.

Noon

1 p.m.

2 p.m.

3 p.m.

4 p.m.

5 p.m.

6 p.m.

Later evening

Consumers respond to rise in gasoline prices

In the spring of 2008, increases in gasoline prices continued to outpace the rate of inflation in the United States and $4.00-per-gallon gasoline became a reality. Accordingly, marketers in a variety of businesses contemplated the impact of gasoline prices on their customers and on their businesses.

To help businesses better understand the potential effects of rising gasoline prices, *Facts, Figures, & the Future* (a newsletter published by The Lempert Report/Consumer Insight, Inc.) reported a few relevant statistics and trends in their April 14, 2008 edition – derived from ACNielsen data for the U.S. Consider the marketing implications of the following findings:

1. For the year 2007, the average pump prices of regular gasoline ranged from $2.11 to $3.21 per gallon. Average weekly household gasoline purchases increased 46 percent throughout the year – from $32.02 to $46.72.

2. As the price of gasoline increased, so did the average number of gasoline-purchasing trips per gasoline-buying household – from 1.24 trips per week to 1.35 per week. During weeks when gasoline prices were high, consumers tended to make more trips to buy gasoline, but tended to buy fewer gallons each trip.

3. The percentage of household expenditures for gasoline (among gasoline-purchasing households) jumped from 12 percent to almost 19 percent of the typical household's budget.

4. Surveyed consumers most often reported combining errands and trips, dining out less, and spending more time at home, as ways they cope with rising gasoline prices.

5. Generally, lower-income consumers said they spend considerably less money in other product categories to offset the rising gasoline prices. Middle-income consumers claimed to reduce spending to a small degree, while higher-income consumers admitted that higher gasoline prices have little effect on their overall spending behavior.

April 15, 2018
Sunday

National Volunteer Week begins

Wafaa El-Nil [Flooding of the Nile] holiday period begins (Egypt)

Objectives & reminders

Appointments

Early morning

---

8 a.m.

---

9 a.m.

---

10 a.m.

---

11 a.m.

Noon

---

1 p.m.

---

2 p.m.

---

3 p.m.

---

4 p.m.

---

5 p.m.

---

6 p.m.

Later evening

Tax Day

April 15 is the standard deadline in the U.S. for tax-payers to file their individual tax returns for the previous calendar year. However, in recent years, the Internal Revenue Service (IRS) has extended the deadline when April 15 falls on the weekend.

> **"Celebrating" Tax Season**
> "These days, ya gotta hand it to the Internal Revenue Service (IRS); otherwise they'll come and get it."
> – Anonymous

About 70 percent of tax-payers receive a tax refund, now averaging about $2,800 -- a substantial windfall for consumers. Accordingly, marketers of appliances, automobiles, furniture, electronics and countless other product categories are happy to suggest ways for tax-payers to spend those "extra" dollars.

> **A calendar marketing principle**
> Because consumers are more inclined to spend when they have money available to spend, marketing efforts tend to be more effective when they're timed to coincide with the arrival of consumers' income.

Enron end-run broke too many rules

"[S]uccessful 'rule breakers' must have a clearly defined vision and a highly visible corporate image in order to attract the internal and external support needed to make revolutionary change possible -- and to keep it thriving." -- Kenneth L. Lay, former chairman and CEO of Enron Corporation, born in Tyrone, Missouri on April 15, 1942. Lay made this comment prior to his public admission that Enron was "missing" $1.2 billion, and prior to his 2006 conviction for breaking too many rules.

> **Lay should've listened to Leonardo**
> "He who wishes to be rich in a day will be hanged in a year."-- Leonardo da Vinci, Italian painter, sculptor, architect/draftsman, and mechanical engineer, born in Florence, Italy on April 15, 1452

April 16, 2018
Monday
Emancipation Day

Objectives & reminders

____

____

____

Appointments

Early morning

8 a.m.

9 a.m.

10 a.m.

11 a.m.

Noon

1 p.m.

2 p.m.

3 p.m.

4 p.m.

5 p.m.

6 p.m.

Later evening

Happy birthday: Charles "Charlie" Spencer Chaplin

Born in London on April 16, 1889, Charlie Chaplin enjoyed a career as an actor and director in the early days of cinema. He is most remembered for his entertaining comedies, such as *The Immigrant* (1917), *Easy Street* (1917), and *Shoulder Arms* (1918), although he was involved in more serious films as well.

Although Chaplin died in 1977, his career was extended after his death when his image became a spokesperson for IBM personal computers and other products. Some of those commercials may be viewed on YouTube, such as this one:
https://www.youtube.com/watch?v=_4oRVGbf9s0

Back from the dead

"Deceased people work as spokespeople... but only if the fit is unique, realistic, and done in good taste... In general though, this is a tricky category and 95 percent of the time not the right approach to take."
-- Steve Cone, *Steal These Ideas!* (p. 39)

Advertising guru Steve Cone examined the brilliance of using Chaplin in the IBM campaign. In his book, *Steal These Ideas!*, he points out that because Chaplin typically played the part of a common and frugal person, associating personal computers with Chaplin reinforced the notion that one need not be a genius to operate a PC or needlessly extravagant to buy one.

Look-alike promotions

A low cost promotion for small businesses is to stage a "look-alike" contest in which entrants receive prizes when they're judged to look most like a familiar celebrity, politician or news-maker. Such promotions could be calendar-timed to coincide with the celebrity's birthday or another key date associated with the individual.

During the middle part of the 20th century, Charlie Chaplin look-alike contests were popular. In one of these, Charlie Chaplin himself entered the competition, but somehow lost.

April 17, 2018
Tuesday
Flag Day (American Samoa)

Objectives & reminders

Appointments

Early morning

8 a.m.

9 a.m.

10 a.m.

11 a.m.

Noon

1 p.m.

2 p.m.

3 p.m.

4 p.m.

5 p.m.

6 p.m.

Later evening

Sweet day in 1895

Business history was made on April 17, 1895, when the first Hershey chocolate bar was sold. The company went on to become so successful that for several decades (until 1970) marketers at the company resisted the use of any general advertising.

However, the Hershey folks did reach agreements with their business customers to promote their use of Hershey chocolates on their customers' packages (e.g., cake mixes), i.e., "Made with real Hershey's chocolate."

Today, Hershey does include advertising as part of its promotion mix.

Hope for "C" students

Federal Express Corporation began operations on April 17, 1973, although planning for opening day began years in advance.

As a student enrolled in an economics course at Yale University in 1965, Frederick W. Smith who would later become the founder and CEO of Federal Express, wrote a term paper in which he outlined what he viewed as the coming need for overnight, door-to-door delivery services and how such services could benefit from a "hub and spoke" delivery system.

He reasoned that in an increasingly high-tech world there would be an increased demand for the delivery of documents and packages of computer-related components. Further, because of the need for speed in a high-tech world, customers would be willing to pay a premium price for a speedy and reliable delivery service.

Of course, what Smith described in his paper was his future company, Federal Express.

Apparently, Smith's professor was not impressed. When asked about the grade received on the term paper, Smith later admitted, "Well I don't really remember. I guess it was my usual gentlemanly 'C.'"

Prerequisite for marketing success
"Make sure you have a competitively superior and sustainable business service or product." -- Frederick W. Smith

April 18, 2018
Wednesday
Independence Day (Zimbabwe)

Objectives & reminders

____

____

____

Appointments

Early morning

8 a.m.

9 a.m.

10 a.m.

11 a.m.

Noon

1 p.m.

2 p.m.

3 p.m.

4 p.m.

5 p.m.

6 p.m.

Later evening

Recognition of Wednesdays

In much the same way that marketers benefit from understanding how the marketplace differs seasonally across buyers and organizations, marketers also can benefit by being sensitive to the uniqueness of each day of the week. That is, a different mix of marketing opportunities arises for each day of the week, in much the same way that the mix of marketing opportunities varies from season to season throughout the year. Accordingly, consider the possible marketing implications of these Wednesday characteristics.

1. More email promotions are opened by prospective buyers in the U.S. on Wednesdays than on other days of the week.

2. About 70 percent of U.S. Social Security recipients receive benefit payments on either the second, third or fourth Wednesday of each month (depending on date of birth).

3. Worldwide, Wednesday is the most popular day of the week to surf the Web.

It may be Wednesday, but does it "feel" like Saturday?

All of us are "calendar-led" in that calendar periods influence our behaviors, preferences, moods, and lifestyles. All four major calendar cycles affect us – time of day, day of week, day/period of month, and day/period of year. Because our orientation to time periods varies across the four cycles, each period seems to develop its own distinct meaning that somehow makes us feel different when we experience it.

Although the calendar-led effect can be subtle and hardly noticeable, it can become quite apparent when our orientation to time is confused or tricked – such as when our behavior or our environment doesn't seem to fit with what we consider normal for the time period. For example, do you sometimes ask yourself what day of the week it is and upon realizing the answer (let's say "Wednesday") you challenge the calendar, the environment and/or your own feelings by saying to yourself something like: "That's strange, it *feels* like Saturday" (or some other day of the week)?

April 19, 2018
Thursday
Dutch-American Friendship Day

Objectives & reminders

____

____

____

Appointments

Early morning

8 a.m.

9 a.m.

10 a.m.

11 a.m.

Noon

1 p.m.

2 p.m.

3 p.m.

4 p.m.

5 p.m.

6 p.m.

Later evening

Unofficial national anthem

It is not known with certainty when the song "Yankee Doodle" was first written or sung, but historians at the U.S. Library of Congress suggest the date may have been April 19, 1775.

On that day, British troops used it during the American Revolution to intimidate the colonials as they marched from Boston to reinforce soldiers fighting at Lexington and Concord (note that "Yankee" is a derogatory term to refer to the New England colonists and a "Doodle" is a silly person).

Yankee Doodle (1st verse)

Yankee Doodle went to town,
A riding on a pony;
Stuck a feather in his hat
and called it macaroni.

Yankee Doodle, keep it up,
Yankee Doodle Dandy,
Mind the Music and the step,
And with the girls be handy.

Hear more: ♪♫♪♫♪♫♪♫♪ https://www.youtube.com/watch?v=P_BMzqwSdW8 ♪♫♪♫♪♫

By 1777, as the American Revolutionary War raged, the familiar tune had become the colonies' unofficial national anthem -- as they adopted the song as their own. During the Revolutionary War, and since then, numerous verses have been written, modified, and forgotten.

Today, the song is widely recognized, stirs feelings of both patriotism and fun, and is appropriate during festive occasions. Some organizations have capitalized on the public's awareness of Yankee Doodle by adopting the song or title as part of their branding strategies. For example, see this 1976 television commercial for Yankee Doodle Dandy restaurants: https://www.youtube.com/watch?v=wW5OGRe-MdY

Yankee Doodle during the Civil War

"I only know two tunes. One is 'Yankee Doodle,' and the other isn't." – General Ulysses S. Grant, U.S. Civil War military leader who later became the 18th President of the United States (1869-1877)

April 20, 2018
Friday
Chinese Language Day

Objectives & reminders

____

____

____

Appointments

Early morning

8 a.m.

9 a.m.

10 a.m.

11 a.m.

Noon

1 p.m.

2 p.m.

3 p.m.

4 p.m.

5 p.m.

6 p.m.

Later evening

Keeping abreast of the war effort

On April 20, 1891, Mary Phelps Jacob was born. She grew up in a relatively affluent family and became accustomed to a life of privilege as a New York socialite.

Her initial claim to fame began in 1914 when she received the first U.S. patent for a brassier. Her design was more comfortable than the 350-year-old corsets it replaced. It was lightweight and soft, but was considered more "flattening" than "flattering."

Brassier battles

Some historians point out that the French fashion designer Paul Poiret invented the brassier in Europe in 1907 -- seven years before Jacob's patent. Fortunately for Poiret, he was much more successful in marketing his designs.

Coincidentally, in addition to their twin interests in brassieres, Poiret and Jacob share the same birthday -- April 20 -- with Poiret being born 12 years earlier, in 1879.

Jacob's invention attracted considerable attention, so she launched a business to capitalize on it. Unfortunately, however, she did not enjoy life as a businesswoman, so she soon sold the patent to the Warner Brothers Corset Company for $1,500.

Soon after that, in 1917, the bra business received a lift from the U.S. War Industries Board who asked women to stop buying corsets. Apparently corsets used too much material -- valuable material needed for the war effort instead (i.e., World War I).

Managing your own customer satisfaction

"How to improve goods and services? Learn to complain, politely and firmly, when you receive what you believe to be inferior goods or services. Don't register your complaint with the salesperson or the waiter, but with the boss or the owner. He'll listen."
– Stanley Marcus, former president and CEO of Neiman-Marcus department stores, born in Dallas, Texas on April 20, 1905

April 21, 2018
Saturday
Astronomy Day
(also observed on October 13)

Objectives & reminders

____

____

____

Appointments

Early morning

8 a.m.

9 a.m.

10 a.m.

11 a.m.

Noon

1 p.m.

2 p.m.

3 p.m.

4 p.m.

5 p.m.

6 p.m.

Later evening

Listen to customers and co-workers, but also listen to yourself

"If you do not express your own original ideas, if you do not listen to your own being, you will have betrayed yourself. Also, you will have betrayed your community in failing to make your contribution." -- Rollo May, American existential psychologist, born in Ada, Ohio on April 21, 1909

Just because several forecasters agree doesn't mean they're right

"The herd instinct among forecasters makes sheep look like independent thinkers." – Edgar R. Fiedler, American business economist who enjoyed a distinguished career in industry and federal government, born in Chapel Hill, North Carolina on April 21, 1929

Children's Online Privacy Protection Act (COPPA)

Legislation took a step toward catching up with parents' concern for websites' exploitation of children in 1998 when COPPA was signed into law. The Act, enforced by the U.S. Federal Trade Commission (FTC), went into effect on April 21, 2000, and generally applies to websites that collect personal information from children under the age of 13.

Among the detailed provisions of the Act, applicable websites must provide a clearly visible, clearly written and clearly understood notice stating all parties (and contact information) who are collecting the personal information, the kinds of personal information collected, how the information will be collected (e.g., by asking or through cookies?), how the information will be used, and whether the information will be disclosed or shared with others.

The Act also includes some provisions to allow parental involvement, review and consent of the personal information.

For more detailed information about COPPA, see the online publication available from the FTC and the Direct Marketing Association, *How to Comply With The Children's Online Privacy Protection Rule*: http://thedma.org/wp-content/uploads/COPPA-rule-sept2013.pdf

April 22, 2018
Sunday
Earth Day

Objectives & reminders

____

____

____

Appointments

Early morning

8 a.m.

9 a.m.

10 a.m.

11 a.m.

Noon

1 p.m.

2 p.m.

3 p.m.

4 p.m.

5 p.m.

6 p.m.

Later evening

Earth Day

First celebrated in the United States on April 22, 1970, Earth Day is observed in dozens of countries today. It is an ideal day for companies to publicize their "green" initiatives.

> **Capitalizing on Earth Day concerns**
>
> To capitalize on the public's interest in Earth Day, marketers include green terms on their websites – terms that online consumers search.
>
> One study investigated online search behavior as Earth Day approached and found recycling to be the most frequently searched green term, followed by global warming, endangered species, solar power, hybrid autos, pollution, composting, radon, wetlands, coral reefs, air pollution, pesticides and acid rain.
>
> Simply using the terms is the first step. Next, it's crucial to talk about what the organization is doing to address these concerns, or offer tips to empower consumers to take action.

Marlboro pricing mishap

April 22, 1993, was the day the Marlboro Man (character for Marlboro brand cigarettes) fell off his horse, so to speak. It seems that the company behind the brand, Philip Morris, thought they could compete more effectively with the lower-priced no-name cigarettes by slashing the price of Marlboro by 60 cents per pack. But, when they cut Marlboro's price, sales failed to climb as expected. Instead, the stock market reacted negatively and Philip Morris stock price fell 23 percent in a single day.

Apparently, both Marlboro smokers and investors interpreted the price reduction as an insult to the value of the brand that had been built over several decades. "The whole point of branding," noted James Twitchell, upon examining the debacle in his book, *20 Ads That Shook the World*, "is to make sure the consumer *pays* for the advertising by thinking that the interchangeable product is unique" (p. 135).

To reinforce his point, Twitchell noted a study that the branding cowboys at Philip Morris apparently ignored. That is, before Marlboro's infamous price cut, *Forbes* magazine conducted an experiment in which they offered Marlboro smokers their preferred brand for half price, but in a generic brown box. Only 21 percent accepted the offer.

April 23, 2018
Monday
World Book Day

Objectives & reminders

___

___

___

Appointments

Early morning

8 a.m.

9 a.m.

10 a.m.

11 a.m.

Noon

1 p.m.

2 p.m.

3 p.m.

4 p.m.

5 p.m.

6 p.m.

Later evening

Service performance is role-playing: Agree or disagree?

Poet and playwright William Shakespeare was born in Stratford, England on April 23, 1564. In one of his classic works, *As You Like It,* Shakespeare observed:

> "All the world's a stage,
> And all the men and women merely players:
> They have their exits and their entrances;
> And one man in his time plays many parts."

As in other spheres of life, Shakespeare's take on role-playing is certainly applicable in business. Employees, for example, often interact quite differently with supervisors than with co-workers or customers.

In customer service settings, Shakespeare's perspective is particularly important, because the way service providers "act" greatly affects customers' satisfaction and perceptions of service quality. Consistent with Shakespeare's observation, effective customer service providers exhibit *behavioral flexibility,* i.e., the ability to adjust one's comments and demeanor quickly and appropriately, given the circumstances and people with whom one is interacting.

A behaviorally flexible server at a restaurant, for example, might "put on her happy face" while laughing and singing a birthday tribute at one table, and then act more serious and attentive one minute later while listening to another party's complaints about the improperly prepared food.

As a general rule, the more varied the circumstances and the customers (or other people) with whom one interacts, the greater the need to be behaviorally flexible.

___

Women prepared for leadership roles

"The core values needed for managing a business are leadership, strategies, flexibility and understanding the issues. Women are equipped for these jobs -- we have been managing households for years." -- Ann M. Fudge, former director of the Federal Reserve Bank of New York. Fudge was also the president of Maxwell House Coffee (division of Philip Morris's Kraft Foods, and chairwoman and CEO of Young & Rubicam Brands. She was born in Washington, D.C. on April 23, 1951.

April 24, 2018
Tuesday
Fashion Revolution Day

Objectives & reminders

___

___

___

Appointments

Early morning

8 a.m.

9 a.m.

10 a.m.

11 a.m.

Noon

1 p.m.

2 p.m.

3 p.m.

4 p.m.

5 p.m.

6 p.m.

Later evening

Happy birthday: John Graunt

Born in London on April 24, 1620, Graunt was an English statistician who essentially founded the science of *demography* -- the statistical study of populations, including their size, composition, distribution and other characteristics.

Today, marketers routinely rely on demographic factors such as age, household size, occupation, gender, education, race/ethnicity, and other variables in two general and interrelated ways:

1. To understand better what drives consumer purchase behavior and consumption patterns. Demographic variables often correlate with sales data. Not surprisingly, for example, families with small children spend more money on diapers than do middle-age couples without children.

2. To segment the market and then target market segments that represent the best fit with the firm's competencies and goals. Knowing who is most likely to buy diapers in the near future, a diaper manufacturer might pay close attention to the diaper attributes that are most important to married couples in their twenties, then advertise in media vehicles of interest to these consumers.

Because there are considerable differences across consumers within demographic groups, rarely do demographics fully explain or predict consumer behavior. Accordingly, demographics rarely should be used as the sole basis of market segmentation. However, given that demographic data are often easy and inexpensive to obtain and to analyze, they can serve as appropriate and useful starting points for many marketing analyses. For most geographic markets, demographic data are widely available in public libraries and on the Internet.

Demography of brands?

University of Michigan professor Rajeev Batra was born 336 years after John Graunt – also on April 24. Research by Batra and his colleagues implies that brands also enjoy some demographic-like characteristics. For example, in developing countries, foreign brands' countries of origin often correlate with consumers' brand perceptions. Brands born in the right neighborhoods, so to speak, may be perceived quite positively in terms of their quality and the status they bestow on consumers who buy them.

April 25, 2018
Wednesday
Administrative Professionals Day

Objectives & reminders

Appointments

Early morning

8 a.m.

9 a.m.

10 a.m.

11 a.m.

Noon

1 p.m.

2 p.m.

3 p.m.

4 p.m.

5 p.m.

6 p.m.

Later evening

Administrative Professionals Day

Today is a great day to say "thank you" to the 4.4 million office workers in the United States with titles such as Secretary, Administrative Assistant, and Administrative Professional.

Thinking *inside* the box

April 25, 1956, was an important date in the history of physical distribution. That's when the *Ideal X*, anchored at the port of Newark, New Jersey pulled away from the dock with the first load of shipping containers.

The *Ideal X* "containership" was part of an innovative distribution concept that enabled manufacturers to load large shipping containers at the factory, have them hauled by truck or rail (or both) to the port where they are hoisted onto the ship, stacked with other containers, and then shipped to another port where they are unloaded onto waiting trucks or rail cars and hauled to warehouses or business customers -- all without handling the manufactured goods inside the containers.

Credit for the containerization method goes to Malcolm McLean, the owner of McLean Trucking of Maxton, North Carolina. He realized that keeping merchandise inside the containers throughout the transportation process would eliminate merchandise handling, which, in turn, would speed the process, reduce paperwork, protect the goods from damage, and increase security -- all of which would cut costs. McLean's concept proved to be so successful that the containerization method of shipping is common today.

Containerized distribution now includes retailing

After coalition forces liberated Iraq earlier this century, signs of an emerging free enterprise system surfaced. Specifically, hundreds of small, independent retail shops sprang up offering an array of merchandise.

How could an economically-depressed group of merchants afford to open shops in locations other than open-air markets? They converted discarded shipping containers into retail stores.

April 26, 2018
Thursday

Take Your Daughters and Sons to Work Day

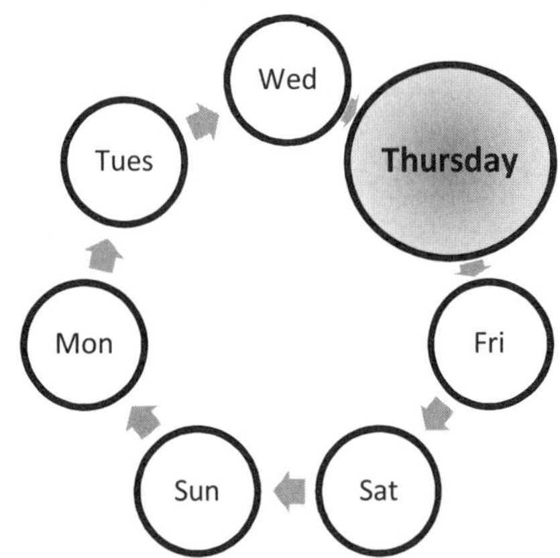

Appointments

Early morning

8 a.m.

9 a.m.

10 a.m.

11 a.m.

Noon

1 p.m.

2 p.m.

3 p.m.

4 p.m.

5 p.m.

6 p.m.

Later evening

Day-of-week tribute to Thursday

If you are not reading this edition of *Marketing FAME* from beginning to end (i.e., from pages denoted "January 1" through "December 31"), note that every 8th page beginning on "March 25" and continuing through "May 12" focuses on a different day of the week – including a few potentially marketing-relevant characteristics that make the featured day of the week noteworthy.

Accordingly, today's featured day of the week is Thursday and here are a few ways that Thursday is distinguished from other days of the week. Consider the potential marketing implications of each one.

1. Online bidding activity (such as on eBay) tends to be higher on Thursdays (for auctions that end on a weekday).

2. In the Hindu religion, Thursday is known as "guruvar" or the Guru's day.

3. Most Australian workers are paid on Thursdays – either weekly or on alternating Thursdays. In the U.S., Thursdays are the second most frequent paydays (Fridays are first).

4. Thursday is the heaviest day of the week for spam (unsolicited emails) in the U.S., according to one study.

5. In New Zealand, Thursday is the most popular day of the week to shop for groceries (Saturday is the top grocery-shopping day in the U.S.).

6. Given that many U.S. colleges and universities have eliminated or greatly reduced the number of Friday classes in recent years, increasingly Thursday nights are becoming party nights on many campuses.

Not yet convinced of the influence asserted by the calendar's weekly cycle?
How many activities do you normally engage in on one or more of the same days of the week each week, vs. those you participate in every five, six, eight, nine or other number of days not synchronized with the weekly calendar cycle?

April 27, 2018
Friday
Arbor Day

Objectives & reminders

Appointments

Early morning

8 a.m.

9 a.m.

10 a.m.

11 a.m.

Noon

1 p.m.

2 p.m.

3 p.m.

4 p.m.

5 p.m.

6 p.m.

Later evening

Arbor Day

First celebrated in Nebraska in 1872, Arbor Day is the United States' oldest environmental holiday. The holiday serves to salute the aesthetic, economic and environmental benefits of trees. Arbor Day is typically recognized on the last Friday in April, but in some states is observed on other dates too – determined by the best time of the year to plant trees in the region.

What if we planted 75 trees?
According to The National Arbor Day Foundation, $139,500 in air pollution control and $69,750 in erosion control can be saved annually for every 75 trees planted.

Fortunately for marketers, The Arbor Day Foundation's website provides a wealth of information about Arbor Day, including ideas and resources to help celebrate the occasion: https://www.arborday.org/celebrate/ways-to-celebrate.cfm

---

Happy birthday: Wallace H. Carothers

Born in Burlington, Iowa on April 27, 1896, Dr. Carothers received more than 50 patents during his life. In particular, his work on polymerization led to the development of a versatile man-made fiber at E. I. Du Pont de Nemours, Inc. The fiber -- nylon -- was first used in the late 1930s as toothbrush bristles, then in the manufacture of women's hosiery in late 1939 (read more about nylon hosiery on May 15). During World War II, nylon was used in the production of parachutes and tires. Since then, nylon's product life cycle has been continually extended as hundreds of new product applications have been discovered and new varieties developed.

Why some innovations become product categories instead of brands
Although not all stockings were made of nylon, "nylons" became synonymous with "stockings" due to their widespread popularity and because DuPont failed to register "nylon" as a trademark. However, DuPont did register subsequent varieties of nylon, such as Antron, Zytel, and Qiana.

April 28, 2018
Saturday
World Day for Safety and Health at Work

Objectives & reminders

Appointments

Early morning

8 a.m.

9 a.m.

10 a.m.

11 a.m.

Noon

1 p.m.

2 p.m.

3 p.m.

4 p.m.

5 p.m.

6 p.m.

Later evening

Happy birthday: Jay Leno

Comedian and host of *The Tonight Show* from 1992-2009, Leno was born in New Rochelle, New York on April 28, 1950. Although Leno has had a successful and profitable career, earning an estimated $16 million annually for hosting *The Tonight Show* and another $15 million for personal appearances, prosperity did not come immediately. He worked hard, was persistent, and took reasonable risks.

Several of the techniques Leno used early in his career are instructive. For example, salespeople should note how Leno focused on providing customer value. He also made a habit of backing up his sales assertions.

Early in his comedic career, he would stroll into a club, slap a $50-bill on the counter and explain to the proprietor that he'd like to go on stage. The $50 was for the proprietor to keep if Leno bombed, but rather than failing, Leno walked away with a commitment for a return *paid* engagement most of the time.

> **The power of nice**
> "[T]oday being nice is so surprising it becomes a news story.... We live in a society where common courtesy is so *uncommon* that it is treated as though you just saved someone's life by giving them the Heimlich maneuver.... So many of today's problems can be solved with simple acts of kindness." – Jay Leno

Another instructive lesson taken from Leno's early career was his reluctance to take "no" for an answer. For example, to supplement his income as a comedian, Leno applied for a job prepping cars at an auto dealership. After the manager refused to hire him, Leno simply showed up for work anyway. When the manager found out, he attempted to boot young Leno off the premises, but co-workers intervened and vouched that Leno was a valuable asset to the team. The manager was impressed enough to let Leno keep the job.

> **Success must be earned daily**
> "You're only as good as your last joke, right? I mean, if you think you're anything more than that, you're in a lot of trouble. You're delusional." -- Jay Leno

April 29, 2018
Sunday
International Dance Day

Objectives & reminders

____

____

____

Appointments

Early morning

8 a.m.

9 a.m.

10 a.m.

11 a.m.

Noon

1 p.m.

2 p.m.

3 p.m.

4 p.m.

5 p.m.

6 p.m.

Later evening

Advertising, realism and counterarguments

Some advertisements use unrealistic situations to dramatize the message. For example, when a vacuum cleaner is dropped from an airplane at 20,000 feet and then vacuums a living room, the message is clear: The vacuum cleaner is durable; it can take whatever abuse your family can subject it to. Such ads are effective because they entertain while making the point in a memorable way.

However, the downside of unrealistic ads is that the audience may view them as irrelevant, simply because they are so unrealistic. When viewing ads perceived as unrealistic, viewers may be so distracted by the counterarguments that come to mind, they completely miss the point the ad is trying to dramatize. They may ponder, "Who would take a vacuum cleaner with them on an airplane, and if they did, why would they toss it out of the plane? I'd never do that." Alternatively, they might ask themselves, "Do I *really* want to buy a vacuum cleaner from a company that tosses them out of airplanes?" Or, they might raise the most devastating counterargument of all, "It's all fake; vacuum cleaners couldn't really survive a fall from an airplane. You can't trust a company that advertises lies."

Advertising counterargument: A detergent example

"Now they show you how detergents take out bloodstains, a pretty violent image there. I think if you've got a t-shirt with a bloodstain all over it, maybe laundry isn't your biggest problem. Maybe you should get rid of the body before you do the wash." -- Jerry Seinfeld, American comedian, born in Brooklyn, New York on April 29, 1954

To reach your goals

"You must keep your mind on the objective, not on the obstacle." – William Randolph Hearst, American media magnate, born in San Francisco, California on April 29, 1863. Hearst once owned more than 40 major newspapers and magazines, plus a few radio stations and other media-related businesses.

April 30, 2018
Monday
National Honesty Day

Objectives & reminders

___

___

___

Appointments

Early morning

8 a.m.

9 a.m.

10 a.m.

11 a.m.

Noon

1 p.m.

2 p.m.

3 p.m.

4 p.m.

5 p.m.

6 p.m.

Later evening

National Honesty Day

Today, April 30, we recognize that "honesty is the best policy" -- hopefully, a belief that applies throughout the entire year. But apparently, not everyone agrees.

In a 2015 study, only 26 percent of those surveyed rated themselves as "very honest," but 85 percent claimed that they were more likely to support brands that they considered to be honest.

Possible to be too honest: Agree or disagree?
A 2015 study found that 62 percent of surveyed consumers agreed that it is sometimes possible to be too honest.

Another survey estimated that 75 percent of high school students are dishonest at school (if they were truthful in responding to the survey). Half of the surveyed students claimed that copying other students' answers during exams was *not* cheating. More than half admitted that they had plagiarized from the Internet.

A 2014 survey found that 19 percent of respondents admitted that they had lied on a resume and slightly more than 20 percent said they had lied on their Facebook profiles.

Further, data provided by the Federal Bureau of Investigation (FBI) suggest that American retailers lose about $9 billion annually to shoplifting.

Honesty as character
"Honesty is the cornerstone of character. The honest man or woman seeks not merely to avoid criminal or illegal acts, but to be scrupulously fair, upright, fearless in both action and expression. Honesty pays dividends both in dollars and in peace of mind." -- B.C. Forbes, co-founder of *Forbes* magazine in 1917

Honest exchanges
"He who freely praises what he means to purchase, and he who enumerates the faults of what he means to sell, may set up a partnership with honesty." -- Johann Lavater, Swiss philosopher, poet & theologian (18th century)

May 1, 2018
Tuesday
International Workers' Day
May Day

Objectives & reminders

____

____

What's already on your mind today?
♫♪ https://YOUTU.BE/rBJLoYd8xak ♫♪

Appointments

Early morning

8 a.m.

9 a.m.

10 a.m.

11 a.m.

Noon

1 p.m.

2 p.m.

3 p.m.

4 p.m.

5 p.m.

6 p.m.

Later evening

May loves spring...

"Then came fair May, the fairest maid on ground,
Deck'd all with dainties of the season's pride,
And throwing flowers out of her lap around."
--Edmund Spenser, 16th century English poet

...But who loves May? ☺
"My wife's jealousy is getting ridiculous. The other day she looked at my calendar and wanted to know who May was." -- Rodney Dangerfield, American comedian

---

Happy birthday: John Caples

Born in New York City on May 1, 1900, Caples was an advertising copywriter for Ruthrauff & Ryan (R&R) and then for Barton Durstine & Osborn (later BBDO). He blended creativity with somewhat of a scientific approach to writing copy for mail-order and direct response advertising.

Caples pioneered the cyclical advertising process of RUN-MONITOR-REVISE-REPEAT to improve the effectiveness of advertising. That is, he recognized that because customer response to mail-order offers were easily measured, responses should be monitored and then linked to the ads that generated the responses, which could then be reevaluated, revised and re-run. Today, Caples' legacy continues in the direct response advertising arena where practitioners routinely embrace the test-test-test philosophy.

Headlines rule!

Caples was a staunch supporter of strong headlines in print ads. If readers don't respond positively to the headline, they're not likely to read the more detailed copy that follows. Accordingly, Caples' experience taught him that the best headlines tend to exhibit one or more of the following five characteristics:

1. They appeal to readers' self-interest.
2. They are news-related or newsworthy.
3. They arouse readers' curiosity.
4. They maintain a positive point of view.
5. They suggest an easy way to do something.

May 2, 2018
Wednesday
National Education Day (Indonesia)

Objectives & reminders

____

____

____

Appointments

Early morning

8 a.m.

9 a.m.

10 a.m.

11 a.m.

Noon

1 p.m.

2 p.m.

3 p.m.

4 p.m.

5 p.m.

6 p.m.

Later evening

Spring cleaning month

May is a prime month for consumers' spring cleaning efforts, which often leads to household repairs and maintenance projects. In one 2016 survey of households in the U.K., 73 percent of respondents claimed to spring clean every year, with May being the most popular spring cleaning month.

For businesses, spring cleaning creates an obvious market for a wide range of cleaning supplies and equipment, shelving and storage containers, paint, do-it-yourself repair tools and materials, cleaning services, trash removal services, and so on. Less apparent demand for bulky goods -- such as furniture -- may surface when consumers free space in their homes by discarding items that are no longer needed.

Gender divide?

Reasons most frequently cited by males and females for not engaging in spring cleaning activities (2016 study):

- Males: "Can't be bothered" to spring clean. (33%)
- Females: "My house doesn't need it." (39%)

Spring cleaning can spell fundraising opportunities for nonprofit organizations. That is, nonprofits can encourage consumers to donate discarded items to the organizations for resale or distribution to less fortunate consumers. Businesses can partner with these nonprofits by helping to promote the spring donation drive, accepting trade-ins to be given to the nonprofits, or using the firms' locations as convenient collection points for donated items.

Happy birthday: Elijah McCoy

Born in Colchester, Ontario, Canada on May 2, 1844, McCoy invented a device that could be used to lubricate machinery while continuing to operate, thus saving operators the time and inconvenience of stopping the machinery, oiling the moving parts, and restarting it. Soon, McCoy's lubricating device was considered essential for heavy machinery and no substitute would suffice. That's why equipment inspectors began asking, "Is it the real McCoy?" Today, the phrase "real McCoy" is broadly used to refer to an original item of high quality.

May 3, 2018
Thursday
National Day of Prayer

Objectives & reminders

____

____

____

Appointments

Early morning

8 a.m.

9 a.m.

10 a.m.

11 a.m.

Noon

1 p.m.

2 p.m.

3 p.m.

4 p.m.

5 p.m.

6 p.m.

Later evening

May proms

May is prom month for this year's 3.5 million U.S. high school graduates. But unlike those of past generations, this year's proms are not as likely to be inexpensive dances held in the school gym.

Today, proms tend to be elegant affairs with more than four billion dollars spent annually by prom-goes and their families – an average of $978 per American prom-destined couple, according to a 2014 Visa survey. Interestingly, Canadian prom couples spend significantly less ($723), while the British spend quite a bit more ($1,500). Clearly, proms constitute a significant market for dresses, shoes, cosmetics, salon services, photographs, limos, flowers, catering services, and (unfortunately?) alcohol.

Happy birthday: Niccolò Machiavelli

Machiavelli was an Italian statesman, diplomat and political theorist born in Florence on May 3, 1469. His major contributions to business are found in his writings, particularly *The Prince* and *Discourses on the First Decade of Livy*. Although somewhat controversial, Machiavelli's books provide numerous insights about the dynamics and use of power in organizations.

Machiavelli also offered insights regarding business leadership, strategy, and planning. For example, according to Machiavelli, most leaders have competencies or capacities that enable them to develop and implement plans to capitalize upon opportunities.

But Machiavelli recognized that success can be planned only to a degree, because unanticipated circumstances or chance events can disrupt the most thoughtful and carefully conceived plans. Often, however, the unfolding of unanticipated events presents additional -- but not-so-apparent -- opportunities to truly effective leaders who are capable enough and quick enough to recognize and seize them.

Do you have a Machiavellian personality?
Researchers Richard Christie and Florence Geis developed a scale to measure the manipulative personality style for which Machiavelli is noted. Take the five-minute test at: http://personality-testing.info/tests/MACH-IV.php

May 4, 2018
Friday

Star Wars Day

(May the fourth be with you today!)

W
E
E
K
E
N
D

ON THE WAY!

Objective or reminder

___

Appointments

Early morning

8 a.m.

9 a.m.

10 a.m.

11 a.m.

Noon

1 p.m.

2 p.m.

3 p.m.

4 p.m.

5 p.m.

6 p.m.

Later evening

Festive Friday focus

Cultural, legal and organizational calendars have played important roles in shaping the meanings assigned to each day of the week and to a range of day-of-week behaviors, preferences and sentiments throughout the marketplace. Considering today's Friday focus, consider the uniqueness of this day of the week and the possible marketing implications.

1. Fridays are the most popular day of the week for U.S. decision-makers to leave work early – making Friday afternoons the worst time of the week to make B2B cold calls.

2. More U.S. workers (hint: who are also consumers) are paid on Fridays than on any other day of the week – either every Friday or on alternating Fridays.

3. For most U.S. workers, Friday is the last day of the workweek – followed by the weekend.

Will it always be Friday at Friday's?

TGI Friday's, a U.S.-based chain of more than 1,000 casual dining restaurants, frequently touts its advertising slogan: "It's always Friday at Friday's." The slogan, coupled with supporting "party" visual images, implies that Friday enjoys a special slot on the calendar to be envied by other days of the week – probably because Friday represents the end of the workweek for most U.S. workers. However, as the company expands beyond the U.S. and into countries where Friday is not the end of the workweek but a day of worship (e.g., some Middle Eastern and Asian countries), how well will the name of the company and its slogan resonate with consumers?

4. Overwhelmingly, Friday has more high school football games scheduled (U.S.) than any other day of the week.

5. Known as "Casual Friday" or "Dress-Down Friday," dress codes for workers are often relaxed on Fridays – in the U.S. and elsewhere.

6. More airline passengers in the U.S. *depart* on Friday than on any other day of the week.

Learn more

Also read the story for March 30 to learn the Friday marketing relevance of months with five Fridays.

May 5, 2018
Saturday
Cinco de Mayo

Objectives & reminders

______

______

Appointments

Early morning

8 a.m.

9 a.m.

10 a.m.

11 a.m.

Noon

1 p.m.

2 p.m.

3 p.m.

4 p.m.

5 p.m.

6 p.m.

Later evening

Cinco De Mayo

Mexico gained its independence by defeating French invaders at the Battle of Puebla de Los Angeles (a small town in east-central Mexico) on May 5, 1862. In Mexico, Cinco De Mayo is a national holiday celebrated with a variety of cultural festivities such as fairs, parades, food, dancing, and so on.

The day is also widely recognized and celebrated in the U.S. to promote the heritage and culture of the Hispanic community. About 12 percent of the U.S. population is Hispanic -- making it the largest ethnic group in the country, and one of the fastest growing. A disproportionately large number of Hispanics live in the southwestern U.S., California, and southern Florida.

Fun food fact
There are 367 tortilla manufacturing businesses in the U.S. Almost one-third are found in Texas.

No horsing around for promotion planning

First held in May of 1875, the most famous horse race in the United States now takes place on the first Saturday in May -- The Kentucky Derby, held at Churchill Downs in Louisville, Kentucky.

The event illustrates an extreme example of the planning principle known by promotion-minded planners everywhere. That is, event planning tends to be far more time consuming than the event itself. In the case of the Kentucky Derby, plans are developed, implemented and revised almost year-round. Horse-racing fans and the media must be informed, contestants determined, tickets and advertising sold, facilities prepared, and countless details addressed.

Further, because the race itself lasts for only about two minutes (2:03.59 in 2017), additional pre-race and post-race events must be developed, orchestrated and promoted to stretch the occasion beyond two minutes. By stretching the single event into multiple events spread over several days, publicity is stirred, anticipation is built, and additional sponsorship opportunities are created. Much like Christmas was once a day, but is now a "season," today marketers for the Kentucky Derby speak in terms of Kentucky Derby "week."

May 6, 2018
Sunday

National Nurses' Day

(also note International Nurses' Day on May 12)

Objectives & reminders

____

____

____

Appointments

Early morning

8 a.m.

9 a.m.

10 a.m.

11 a.m.

Noon

1 p.m.

2 p.m.

3 p.m.

4 p.m.

5 p.m.

6 p.m.

Later evening

What isn't thought possible, isn't done

When a challenge is believed to be unrealistic and unattainable, people tend to turn from it and never adopt it as a goal. Their failure to try, in turn, reinforces the belief that it can't be done. Such was the thinking during the first half of the 20th century in the world of track and field regarding the four-minute mile. Coaches and journalists asserted, "It can't be done. The human body is physically incapable of running that far that fast."

But then came 25-year-old Roger Bannister who proved the pundits wrong on May 6, 1954, when he ran a mile in 3 minutes and 59.4 seconds. Because Bannister broke the four-minute barrier other athletes learned that such a feat is within the realm of possibility. As a result, it is not uncommon today for top runners to finish a mile in less than four minutes.

It's your choice
"Just as no one can be forced into belief, so no one can be forced into unbelief."
-- Sigmund Freud, founder of psychoanalysis and coincidentally born in what is now Pribor, Czech Republic on May 6, 1856

It's your turn
What can you accomplish in less than four minutes? That is, what achievements are thought to be impossible in your college or where you work? Just because they have never been done, are they necessarily impossible?

Happy birthday: Sir Patrick Michael Meaney

Born in London on May 6, 1925, Meaney's business experience was extensive. He was a key figure in the British film industry as chairman of the Rank Organization, and also was involved as a high level executive for Rank Xerox Ltd. He ran his family's flour business as well.

From 1981 until 1991, Meaney served as the president of the Chartered Institute of Marketing (CIM), an international (although largely British) trade and professional organization for marketers. While Meaney was president, CIM's membership grew to 50,000. Today, there are more than 60,000 members in 144 countries. Learn more: http://www.cim.co.uk

May 7, 2018
Monday
Defender of the Fatherland Day (Kazakhstan)

Objectives & reminders

___

___

___

Appointments

Early morning

8 a.m.

9 a.m.

10 a.m.

11 a.m.

Noon

1 p.m.

2 p.m.

3 p.m.

4 p.m.

5 p.m.

6 p.m.

Later evening

Integrated marketing: Now and then

Today, the term "integrated marketing" refers to the synergistic blending of various marketing decisions and tools, especially those that are communications-related (e.g., advertising, sales promotion, publicity, sponsorship and personal selling).

But this wasn't always the case. In the 1960s integrated marketing was more likely to refer to the use of a racially diverse mix of actors or models in advertising.

New York Telephone, for example, was one of the first U.S. firms to feature an African-American in an advertisement targeting a general audience. They did so in a tasteful manner, in the *New York Herald Tribune* on May 7, 1963. In the ad, a professionally dressed model was shown as he was about to enter a telephone booth. The eye-catching headline explained, "A man of action knows -- you get action when you telephone."

> **Courage needed: Agree or disagree?**
> "Before most marketing practices became mainstream, someone had to have the insight to 'give em a try' and sometimes also had to have the courage to do so."
> – Carey Kickten, marketing analyst

Although using an African-American in such an ad today might not be particularly surprising (except that today he would probably use a smart phone instead of a telephone booth), the practice was far less common in the 1960s. In 1967, the Kerner Commission suggested that racial tension in the U.S. stemmed, in part, from the absence of African-Americans on television, including television advertising. In response, television programmers and advertisers began to increase their audiences' exposure to African-Americans.

By the 1990s about 11 percent of the models in general circulation ads were African-Americans, which approximated the 12.6 percent of African-Americans found in the general population.

In recent years, some of the most sought after spokespeople and commercial endorsers in the U.S. have been African-Americans. Examples include: Halle Berry, Michael Jordan, Vanessa Williams, and Tiger Woods. For additional information regarding the representation of African-Americans in advertising, see *Advertising Age's Encyclopedia of Advertising* (2003), pp. 1058-1059.

May 8, 2018
Tuesday

National Teacher Day
Victory in Europe (V-E) Day

Objectives & reminders

____

____

____

Appointments

Early morning

8 a.m.

9 a.m.

10 a.m.

11 a.m.

Noon

1 p.m.

2 p.m.

3 p.m.

4 p.m.

5 p.m.

6 p.m.

Later evening

Without the first sale, no marketing milestone is possible

The location was Jacob's Pharmacy in Atlanta, Georgia. The date was May 8, 1886. The event? The first sale of a new beverage called "Coca-Cola," invented by pharmacist John Pemberton. For the next 19 years, Coca-Cola was not positioned as the fun and sociable drink that it is today, but as a "brain and nerve tonic."

Happy birthday: Harry S Truman

Harry Truman was born in Lamar, Missouri on May 8, 1884. He was elected as President Franklin D. Roosevelt's vice-president in 1944, but served only 82 days as the Vice-President, rising to the presidency when Roosevelt died in April 1945. Truman served as the country's 33rd President until 1953.

Did you know?
Of the nine Presidents in U.S. history who did *not* attend college, Harry Truman was the most recent. All of the Presidents since Truman earned college degrees. Further, Presidents George W. Bush and Donald Trump earned MBA degrees (Masters in Business Administration).

President Truman faced a number of difficult decisions, including the decisions to drop atomic bombs on Hiroshima and Nagasaki, Japan to bring World War II to an end. But, like any great leader, he accepted the responsibility of his decisions and held himself accountable, as evidenced by a sign on his desk which read, "The buck stops here."

Don't wait for the "next" job
"I studied the lives of great men and famous women, and I found that the men and women who got to the top were those who did the jobs they had in hand, with everything they had of energy and enthusiasm and hard work." -- Harry Truman

Ever wondered where familiar expressions originated?
"If you can't stand the heat, get out of the kitchen." – Harry Truman

May 9, 2018
Wednesday
Third Shift Workers Day

Objectives & reminders

Appointments

Early morning

8 a.m.

9 a.m.

10 a.m.

11 a.m.

Noon

1 p.m.

2 p.m.

3 p.m.

4 p.m.

5 p.m.

6 p.m.

Later evening

Happy birthday: Henry John Kaiser

Born in Sprout Brook, New York on May 9, 1882, Henry Kaiser was a successful entrepreneur in a variety of businesses. He started a construction company in 1914, building highways, schools, and civic centers. He even played a role in the construction of the Hoover and Grand Coulee Dams.

Later, Kaiser pioneered several mass-production processes in building ships and delivered 1,450-plus ships to the U.S. Navy during World War II. After the war, Kaiser Motors produced Jeeps and cars in Michigan, then in Ohio and South America.

At one point Kaiser teamed with Howard Hughes to enter the aircraft business, and also ventured into aluminum (Kaiser Aluminum), residential real estate (Kaiser Community Homes Corporation), and the hotel/resort business (Kaiser Hawaiian Village Hotel).

Reflecting his interest in retaining valuable employees, in 1938 Kaiser offered employees what may have been the first large-scale prepaid health care plan in the country -- a plan that grew into one of the largest health maintenance organizations (HMOs), Kaiser Permanente.

Was Kaiser's business growth too risky?

Growing a business or a family of businesses can be very risky. Often businesses fail when they move too far away from what they know best. That's why experts often recommend that businesses "stick to their knitting" unless the future of their knitting business is in jeopardy.

Still, when considering growth alternatives, businesses can reduce risk by pursuing alternatives that capitalize upon existing business strengths and competencies. Answering "yes" to one or more of the following questions may create a risk-reduction advantage:

Will the new business or opportunity…
...serve the same or similar customers?
...utilize existing channels of distribution?
...have an image that fits with the existing business?
...utilize the same or similar technologies?
...help smooth peaks and valleys in demand?
...effectively utilize existing facilities, equipment and personnel?

May 10, 2018
Thursday
Mother's Day in several countries

Objectives & reminders

______

______

______

Appointments

Early morning

8 a.m.

9 a.m.

10 a.m.

11 a.m.

Noon

1 p.m.

2 p.m.

3 p.m.

4 p.m.

5 p.m.

6 p.m.

Later evening

Good day to honor mothers around the world

In the United States and several other countries, Mother's Day is celebrated on the second Sunday in May. However, May 10 is Mother's Day in many other places: Bahrain, Hong Kong, India, Malaysia, Mexico, Oman, Pakistan, Qatar, Saudi Arabia, Singapore, and United Arab Emirates. Most of South America also celebrates Mother's Day on May 10, with Argentina being an exception (Argentina celebrates the occasion on the second Sunday in October).

______

Internal marketing: Extreme name calling

St. Joseph Medical Center in Wichita, Kansas recognized each of its 1,900 employees on May 10, 1987. During National Hospital Week, the hospital had the names of all 1,900 employees published in the local newspaper -- *The Wichita Eagle-Beacon.* Above the rather overwhelmingly long list read the headline, "We'd like to call our employees names." Below the list the caption explained: "For a job well-done, they deserve to be named." The copy went on to attribute high patient satisfaction to the "unrelenting dedication," "hard work," and "commitment" of these "professionals."

The ad accomplished two sets of objectives; it recognized and reinforced the efforts of employees while reminding the community of the hospital's competencies.

> **What people never tire of hearing**
> "[A] person's name is to that person the sweetest and most important sound in any language." – Dale Carnegie, *How to Win Friends and Influence People*

______

Should all products be mass-marketed? ☺

"What about those red balls they have on car aerials so you can spot your car in a [parking lot]. I think all cars should have them!" – Homer Simpson, fictional character and questionable role model on the television comedy, *The Simpsons*, presumably born on May 10, 1955

May 11, 2018
Friday

National Technology Day (India)
Statehood Day (Minnesota)

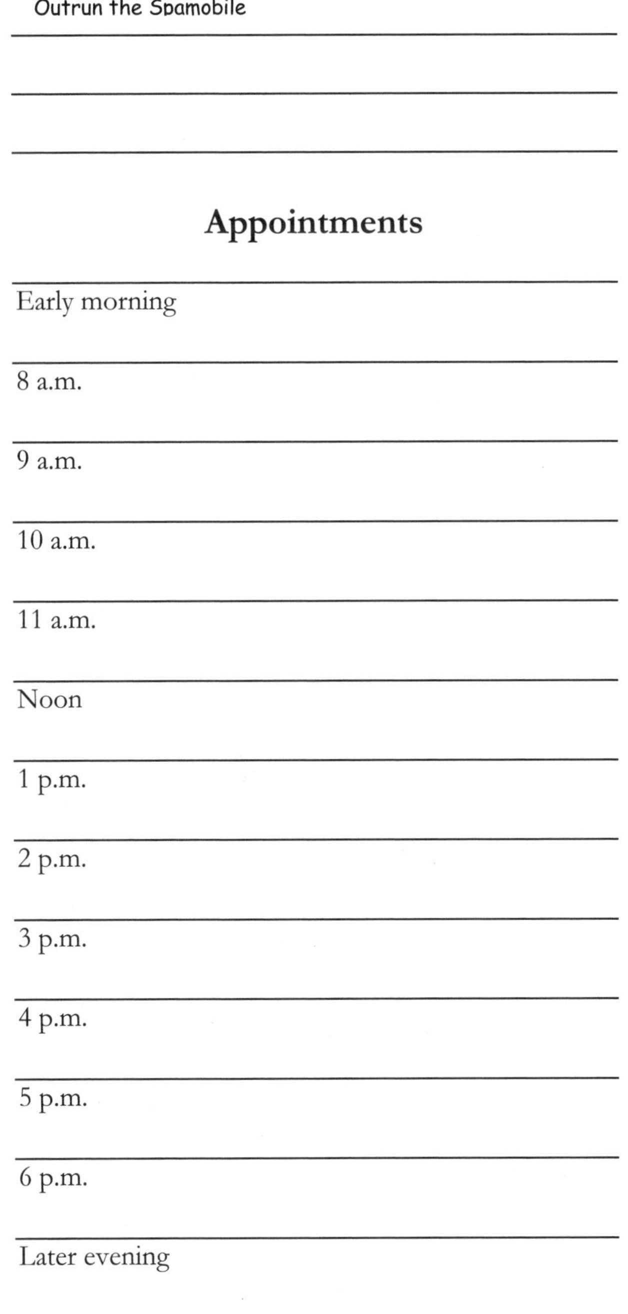

Objectives & reminders

Outrun the Spamobile

Appointments

Early morning

8 a.m.

9 a.m.

10 a.m.

11 a.m.

Noon

1 p.m.

2 p.m.

3 p.m.

4 p.m.

5 p.m.

6 p.m.

Later evening

Happy birthday: Spam

Long before spam referred to unwanted and unsolicited emails, Spam the meat product was conceived in the 1930s when meat processor Jay C. Hormel pondered what he could do with pork shoulder meat. Although pork shoulder was certainly edible and of reasonable quality, there was almost no market for it at the time. So, Hormel's team hit upon the idea of combining water, meat and a few spices and processing the mix in a can.

Two years after the first can was processed, the company registered the name as "Spam" on May 11, 1937. Like many new product concepts, consumers' initial response to Spam was less than positive. Although the company maintained that the meat could be refrigerated, many consumers at the time believed that whoever ate refrigerated meat would get sick the next day.

Soon, however, the affordable price coupled with the convenience of not having to cook Spam won the public's support. The same product appeals helped Spam to become a regular feature in soldiers' diets during World War II. The federal government purchased more than 150 million pounds of Spam for American military personnel during the war. War-weary consumers in England and Europe welcomed Spam as well.

Like many manufacturers, Hormel was interested in capitalizing on its brand's strength, so the company pursued a *brand extension* strategy in 1964 with the introduction of deviled Spam (later dubbed Spam Spread). Spam Smoked Flavored and Spam with Cheese Chunks debuted in 1971, followed by Spam Lite in 1986 and a "96 percent fat free" version of Spam in 1997.

Asking too much of Spam brand: Agree or disagree?

"Women want a brand to extend into their lives in as many ways as possible. They want a brand to speak to their heads and their hearts. To understand them. To recognize their needs, values, standards, and dreams.... Women don't buy brands, they join brands." -- Faith Popcorn and Lys Marigold. Popcorn is a trend-spotter/futurist, marketing consultant, and author or co-author of several best-selling books. She was born in New York City on May 11, 1947.

May 12, 2018
Saturday
Migratory Bird Day
International Nurses' Day
(also note National Nurses' Day on May 6)

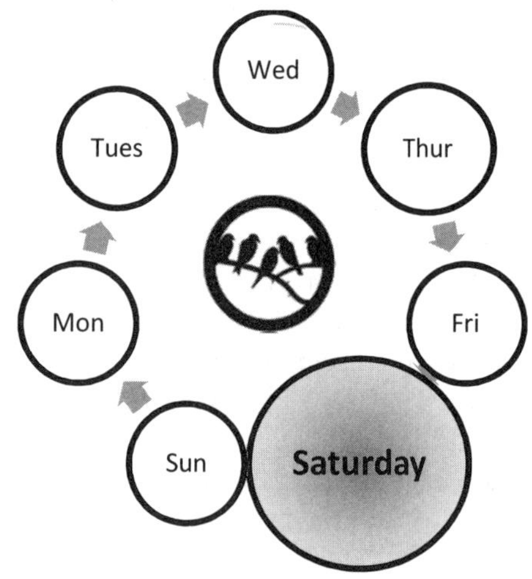

Appointments

Early morning

8 a.m.

9 a.m.

10 a.m.

11 a.m.

Noon

1 p.m.

2 p.m. -- Time to wake up and call your friends?
♫♪ https://YOUTU.BE/GVCzdpagXOQ ♫♪

3 p.m.

4 p.m.

5 p.m.

6 p.m.

Later evening

Saturday salute

To wrap-up the day-of-week focus that has featured a different day every eight days since Sunday, March 25, today's finale points out a few unique and potentially marketing-relevant aspects of Saturdays. Like every day of the week, Saturday is much like its own brand – clearly differentiated in meaning and marketplace behavior from other days of the week. Consider these points of Saturday distinction:

1. Across almost all product categories, Saturday is American's most popular day of the week to shop (e.g., 22 percent of groceries are purchased on Saturdays). Unfortunately, shoplifting also reaches its weekly peak on Saturday.

2. Restaurants appreciate Saturdays too, as U.S. consumers are more likely to dine out on Saturday than on any other day of the week.

3. In the Middle East, Saturday is typically the beginning of the six-day workweek.

4. For Jewish consumers, Saturday is the Sabbath day – a day of rest and worship.

5. Saturday is the most popular day of the week in the U.S. for weddings (Money-saving tip: If you're planning a wedding, you may qualify for discounts if you select another day of the week). For readers not contemplating marriage in the near future, note that Saturday is the most popular day for dancing.

6. Email scammers are busy on Saturdays and Sundays. They like to strike organizations on weekends and holidays when they hope to catch victims without access to assistance from their IT departments.

Why understanding how the marketplace differs across calendar periods is important

The ability to predict behavioral changes in the marketplace that accompany each calendar period almost always enhances the potential effectiveness and efficiency of marketing efforts. That is, marketers have a competitive advantage when they know in advance what buyers are likely to do during a specific time period.

May 13, 2018
Sunday
Mother's Day
Father's Day (Romania)

Objectives & reminders

___

___

___

Appointments

Early morning

8 a.m.

9 a.m.

10 a.m.

11 a.m.

Noon

1 p.m.

2 p.m.

3 p.m.

4 p.m.

5 p.m.

6 p.m.

Later evening

Mother's Day

Welcome to the second Sunday in May – Mother's Day in the United States, Australia, Belgium, Canada, Denmark, Finland, Italy, Japan, Turkey and about 85 other countries.

None of us fortunate enough to have a mother would be the same person without one. Accordingly, here's a sampling of what two noteworthy leaders said about their mothers.

> "[M]y mother has been my biggest fan over the years. She was proud of me when I graduated from college and got steady, indoor work without any heavy lifting. That was enough for her." -- Robert Eaton, former chairman and CEO of Chrysler Corporation

> "My mother taught me how to read good books quickly and correctly, and as this opened up a great world in literature, I have always been very thankful for this early training." -- Thomas Edison, prolific American inventor with 1,093 patents

Good news for imaginative marketers

"Any object may satisfy any need. To put it metaphorically, a need may have no inkling of what it needs." -- Henry A. Murray, American psychologist whose research on human needs is highly marketing-relevant. For additional reading, Murray's 1938 book, *Explorations in Personality*, is recommended. Murray was born in New York City on May 13, 1893.

Need defined

"A need is a hypothetical construct that stands for a force in the brain region that organizes and directs mind and body behavior so as to maintain the organism in its most desirable state." -- Henry A. Murray

Needs needed

"It is a rare marketing book that does not speak frequently of consumer needs... The reason is obvious: Most marketing activities are important only to the extent that they help the firm to satisfy consumer needs."
-- James U. McNeal, Professor Emeritus of Marketing, and Stephen W. McDaniel, Professor of Marketing, Texas A&M University

May 14, 2018
Monday

National Unification Day (Liberia)
Flag Day (Paraguay)

Objectives & reminders

Appointments

Early morning

8 a.m.

9 a.m.

10 a.m.

11 a.m.

Noon

1 p.m.

2 p.m.

3 p.m.

4 p.m.

5 p.m.

6 p.m.

Later evening

Business ethics insight

"Without consistency there is no moral strength." -- Robert Owen, British entrepreneur (cotton mills), born in Newtown, Wales on May 14, 1771

Marble marketing inspiration

"When I was younger, I had a collection of history books that I was addicted to, a whole series about famous people in history from Ancient Greece and Alexander the Great, up to the Civil War... I collected a whole library of them. I used to love to read those books. It started me on a lifelong love of history.... I was very interested in history -- why people do the things they do. As a kid I spent a lot of time trying to relate the past to the present." -- George W. Lucas, Jr., film-maker (*Star Wars, Indiana Jones* and many others), founder of Lucasfilm Ltd., born in Modesto, California on May 14, 1944

Happy birthday: Marion Harper, Jr.

Born in Oklahoma City, Oklahoma on May 14, 1916, Harper went to work for McCann-Erickson advertising agency shortly after graduating from college in 1938. By 1948, he had worked his way up the corporate ladder to president, and then to chairman 13 years after that.

Like many successful people in the field of advertising, Harper was an advocate of creativity and often prodded his team to "dare to be different." Yet, Harper did not define creativity in terms of "winging it." Rather, he believed that business decisions should be based on sound information and he supported the creation of a "Manager of Information" to "provide an intelligence service for the shaping of strategy and policy" so that managers would not be "drowned in a sea of data, spewed out by data-processing machines..."

To ensure that McCann-Erickson advertising would serve the agency's clients well, Harper focused on the search for the key appeal that would motivate buyers to purchase clients' products rather than those of competitors -- what he called "the purchase proposition." According to Harper, "We must find that out through application of sophisticated research, not just how many subscribe or don't subscribe to our copy themes, but why they do or why they don't. What is the one idea that moves them to buy our product instead of our competitor's? What is the best purchase proposition to use to bring this about?"

May 15, 2018
Tuesday
National Nylon Stocking Day

Objectives & reminders

____

____

____

Appointments

Early morning

8 a.m.

9 a.m.

10 a.m.

11 a.m.

Noon

1 p.m.

2 p.m.

3 p.m.

4 p.m.

5 p.m.

6 p.m.

Later evening

Getting two legs up on the competition

May 15, 1940, was a big promotional day for the Du Pont Corporation. That's the day the company declared as "Nylon Day" or "N-Day" -- the day when nylon hosiery were first offered for sale in stores throughout the United States, although "nylons" had been test marketed in Wilmington, Delaware since October 1939.

The synthetic stockings were promoted as "stronger than steel" and "run-proof," and thus promised to be superior to previously available silk stockings. At what was then considered a premium price of $1.15 per pair, all five million pairs of "nylons" available were sold on that day.

If Du Pont had agreed to Happy Meal stockings promotion, where would their sales be today?

On the same day that Du Pont celebrated Nylon Day -- May 15, 1940 -- two brothers named Dick and Mac McDonald opened their fast-food restaurant in San Bernardino, California with much less fanfare.

Although Du Pont sold more stockings on that day than the McDonald brothers sold hamburgers, McDonald's sales have caught up and surpassed nylon stockings sales since then.

Soon after Nylon Day, Du Pont diverted its nylon production from hosiery to parachutes and other military applications in support of the war effort (World War II). Not surprisingly, this led to shortages of nylon stockings which drove prices to $20 per pair on the black market.

Within days after World War II, Du Pont resumed production of nylon stockings but could not keep up with demand. Long lines of nylon-hungry customers were common, and several fights and riots were reported when stores' limited supplies were sold out. By March 1946 Du Pont was able to produce one million pairs of nylon stockings daily, which was finally enough to meet the demand.

May 16, 2018
Wednesday
Ramadan begins

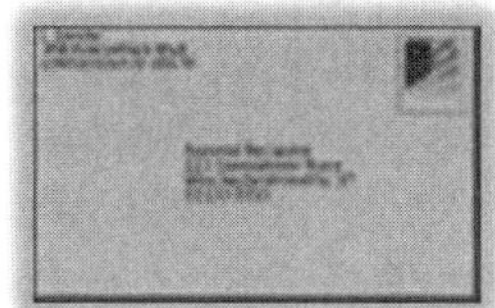

Objectives & reminders

____

____

____

Appointments

Early morning

8 a.m.

9 a.m.

10 a.m.

11 a.m.

Noon

1 p.m.

2 p.m.

3 p.m.

4 p.m.

5 p.m.

6 p.m.

Later evening

Enveloping ideas

Sir James Ogilvie achieved some distinction on May 16, 1696, when he became the first person known to use an envelope for mailing purposes, which he sent to British Secretary of State William Turnbull. The envelope measured 4¼" by 3."

Today, businesses, in general, and direct mail marketers, in particular, use billions of envelopes annually in which they enclose communications to their customers and prospective customers. The typical U.S. household receives an average of 16-17 pieces of mailed marketing communications weekly. About half of these are enclosed in envelopes.

Include marbles in the envelope?
"Be a smarty-pants -- tuck little ideas, frisky facts, notable quotables into your business bag of tricks." -- Harvey Mackay, Mackay Envelope Corp., in *Pushing the Envelope All the Way to the Top* (p. 266)

Not exactly something to celebrate
Exactly 275 years after Ogilvie mailed that first envelope, the price of doing so increased. That is, on May 16, 1971, the rate for first class mail in the U.S. increased from six to eight cents. By 2017, the price of a first class stamp had increased to 49 cents.

Understanding customers and co-workers from other cultures

"We should never denigrate any other culture but rather help people to understand the relationship between their own culture and the dominant culture. When you understand another culture or language, it does not mean that you have to lose your own culture." – Edward T. Hall, anthropologist and prolific author, born in Webster Groves, Missouri on May 16, 1914

Experience + luck = success

"Get as much experience as you can, so that you're ready when luck works. That's the luck." -- Henry Fonda, American actor, born in Grand Island, Nebraska on May 16, 1905

May 17, 2018
Thursday
Constitution Day (Norway)

Objectives & reminders

___

___

___

Appointments

Early morning
8 a.m.
9 a.m.
10 a.m.
11 a.m.
Noon
1 p.m.
2 p.m.
3 p.m.
4 p.m.
5 p.m.
6 p.m.
Later evening

Bundle of joy born

In marketing, one form of *bundling* involves combining related products together and charging a single price for the entire bundle. Generally, the price of the bundle is lower than the sum of the prices of the individual items in the bundle.

If the bundle includes add-on items that the buyer might not purchase separately (e.g., French fries in a fast-food meal bundle), bundling has the effect of prompting consumers to purchase more; "after all," the consumer may conclude, "the bundle's price is only a few cents more."

Further, bundles may speed the ordering process, simplify pricing and money-handling, provide a mechanism for the seller to encourage customers to try new items, facilitate planning, and possibly enable sellers to secure discounts or other consideration from suppliers.

Bundling tip

When offering a bundle, also allow buyers to purchase each item in the bundle separately. The prices of the individual items will serve as reference points to reinforce the value of the bundled price.

On May 17, 1861, Thomas Cook introduced an innovative travel concept -- the vacation package (bundle). For a specified lump-sum amount, Cook transported 1,700 vacationing workers and their families from London to Paris. He arranged for transportation, meals and lodging.

Cook's bundle proved to be convenient for travelers and their families. Moreover, the large size of the group enabled Cook to negotiate quantity discounts and pass some of the savings along to his customers. The concept caught on and within five years Cook was regularly advertising holiday vacation packages.

Marketer's belief in his product

"To travel is to feed the mind, humanize the soul, and rub off the rust of circumstance…" – Thomas Cook

Today, Cook's travel agency still exists and is known by the founder's name, Thomas Cook. Annually, the Thomas Cook Group serves more than 19 million customers and generates almost $10 billion in revenues.

May 18, 2018
Friday
Bike to Work Day

Objectives & reminders

___

___

___

Appointments

Early morning
8 a.m.
9 a.m.
10 a.m.
11 a.m.
Noon
1 p.m.
2 p.m.
3 p.m.
4 p.m.
5 p.m.
6 p.m.
Later evening

Happy birthday: Bertrand Russell

Born in Trelleck, Gwent, U.K., into an aristocratic family on May 18, 1872, Bertrand Arthur William Russell grew to become an influential and sometimes controversial philosopher, logician and writer. In 1950, he received the distinction of "Nobel Laureate in Literature" for championing "humanitarian ideals and freedom of thought."

One of the many business-relevant topics which Russell addressed had to do with the phenomenon of overconfidence. He seemed to believe that the world is filled with decision-makers who examine complex problems superficially; the superficial then tout their solutions backed more by confident-sounding rhetoric than merit.

Russell on overconfidence

"When a man tells you that he knows the exact truth about anything you are safe in inferring that he is an inexact man."

"The whole problem with the world is that fools and fanatics are always so certain of themselves, but wiser people so full of doubts."

___

Post-Russell overconfidence research

After Russell's death, a series of studies by J. Edward Russo and Paul J.H. Schoemaker indicated that Russell's concerns regarding overconfidence were justified. Their research found that when decision-makers lack information, they frequently develop estimates (or guesses) and then tend to be guilty of believing their estimates are more likely to be true or accurate than justified.

Why too much confidence is problematic

The greater confidence in one's decisions, the greater the reluctance to gather additional information and consider other possible alternatives. In other words, when one is overconfident, he or she is likely to make a decision or reach a conclusion too quickly.

Why too little confidence is problematic too

"Whether you believe you can or believe you cannot, you're probably right." – Henry Ford, founder of The Ford Motor Company

May 19, 2018
Saturday
Armed Forces Day

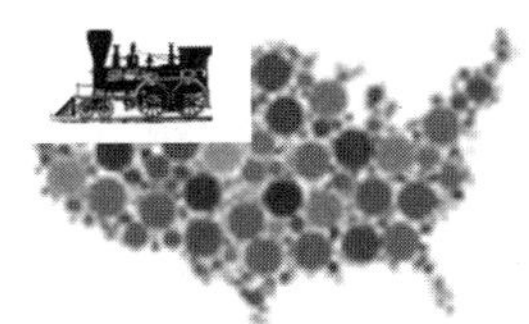

Objectives & reminders

___

___

___

Appointments

Early morning

8 a.m.

9 a.m.

10 a.m.

11 a.m.

Noon

1 p.m.

2 p.m.

3 p.m.

4 p.m.

5 p.m.

6 p.m.

Later evening

Happy birthday: Louis Warren Hill

Born in St. Paul, Minnesota on May 19, 1872, Louis Hill was the son of James Jerome Hill – the successful empire builder of the Great Northern Railway. Louis took control of the company in 1907 when his father retired.

Although both Hills were successful railroad executives, Louis proved to be more marketing-minded than his father. For example, he recognized the potential of tourism to drive the demand for passenger rail transportation, so he successfully lobbied Congress to establish Glacier National Park (Montana) in 1910. It was no coincidence that Hill's railroad skirted along the southern border of the park.

Enduring tourism slogan
"See America first." – slogan coined by Louis Hill to lure tourists to national parks. The slogan continues to be used today.

In the years that followed, Hill stimulated demand for passenger rail services by promoting the country's western national parks – especially Glacier National Park. He funded the production and distribution of park films to be shown to moviegoers in the East. He hired PR professionals to write stories about the parks and distribute them to newspapers around the country. He arranged two-week excursions of Glacier National Park specifically for newspaper editors, so they could experience the park firsthand. Hill even commissioned noteworthy painters to visit the West and capture the parks' scenic beauty on canvas.

Strong positive correlation between park attendance and sale of railroad tickets
"Every passenger that goes to the national parks, wherever they may be, represents practically a net earning."
– Louis Hill, 1911

___

Funny business

"Humor is by far the most significant activity of the human brain." -- Edward De Bono, physician and author who developed the concept of lateral thinking in his 1982 book, *Lateral Thinking for Management.* De Bono was born in Malta on May 19, 1933.

May 20, 2018
Sunday
Whit Sunday

Objectives & reminders

____

____

____

Appointments

Early morning

8 a.m.

9 a.m.

10 a.m.

11 a.m.

Noon

1 p.m.

2 p.m.

3 p.m.

4 p.m.

5 p.m.

6 p.m.

Later evening

What professional baseball player hit the most home runs during his career?

If you're thinking that Babe Ruth, Henry Aaron, or Barry Bonds holds the record, you're wrong.

Need a hint? He was born in Tokyo, Japan on May 20, 1940. The record-holder is Sadaharu Oh -- a retired first baseman who played professional baseball in Japan from 1959 to 1980. Oh, yes; he hit 868 home runs during his professional career -- more than Ruth (714), Aaron (755) and Bonds (762).

For U.S. and Canadian baseball fans who think this was an unfair or trick question, think again. Several countries around the world play baseball; it's not solely a North American sport. If your evoked set includes only North American players (e.g., Ruth, Aaron and Bonds), your *ethnocentricism* is showing.

> **Additional evidence**
> If you're still not convinced that North American baseball doesn't suffer from ethnocentric tendencies, consider how many countries participate in baseball's "*World* Series" each fall.

In business, ethnocentric tendencies surface when we assume a particular national or cultural perspective, rather than a global one. For example, one might define market share, market potential or the field of competitors in domestic, rather than international terms. Unlike answering questions about baseball records, defining markets too narrowly or the failure to consider international competitors can have serious consequences -- such as ignoring potentially valuable market opportunities, the failure to monitor competitors and counter their initiatives, and the underestimation of the firm's costs and power in the marketplace relative to those of current or prospective competitors.

Other examples include erroneous assumptions that business practices around the world correspond to what may be considered normal in the United States. Examples: Saturday and Sunday is not universally accepted as the weekend. Typical business hours are not necessarily 8:00 a.m. to 5:00 p.m. Despite one credit card company's advertising that suggests otherwise, not all businesses around the world accept credit cards. And only 16% of the world's population speaks English as their primary or secondary language.

May 21, 2018
Monday
Victoria Day
Whit Monday

Objectives & reminders

___

___

___

Appointments

Early morning

8 a.m.

9 a.m.

10 a.m.

11 a.m.

Noon

1 p.m.

2 p.m.

3 p.m.

4 p.m.

5 p.m.

6 p.m.

Later evening

Brand new day!

What is a successful brand?
"A successful brand is an identifiable product, service, person or place, augmented in such a way that the buyer or user perceives relevant, unique, sustainable added values which match their needs most closely."
-- Leslie de Chernatony and Malcolm McDonald

More than a brand: Agree or disagree?

"Since 1886... changes have been the order of the day, the month, the year. These changes, I may add, are partly or wholly the result of the very existence of the Coca-Cola Company and its product... They have created satisfactions, given pleasure, inspired imitators, intrigued crooks.... Coca-Cola is not an essential, as we would like it to be. It is an idea -- it is a symbol -- it is a mark of genius inspired." -- William C. D'Arcy, American advertising executive who handled the Coca-Cola account on May 21, 1942, when he made this comment

Gemini is a brand: Agree or disagree?

May 21 to June 21 is the month of Gemini (the twins), according to astrology followers. Presumably people born during this period tend to be interested in information, curious, persuasive, adaptable and absent-minded. According to one horoscope, Geminis should "[r]esist the urge to run away from a tough job."

Brand design principle

"Beauty of style and harmony and grace and good rhythm depend on simplicity." -- Plato, Greek philosopher, born in Athens, Greece on May 21, 0427

Perhaps wrong reason to buy a brand

Armand Hammer was a wealthy American industrialist and once the CEO of Occidental Petroleum (oil and natural gas firm). Over the years, he grew tired of people asking him if he was "related" to the brand of baking soda called Arm & Hammer, so he finally purchased it. Hammer was born in New York City on May 21, 1898.

May 22, 2018
Tuesday
National Maritime Day

Objectives & reminders

______

______

______

Appointments

Early morning

8 a.m.

9 a.m.

10 a.m.

11 a.m.

Noon

1 p.m.

2 p.m.

3 p.m.

4 p.m.

5 p.m.

6 p.m.

Later evening

Happy birthday: Vance Packard

Born in Granville Summit, Pennsylvania on May 22, 1914, Vance Packard was a journalist, author, and social critic. Many of his criticisms were leveled at consumers and marketers in his popular -- but controversial -- books such of *The Status Seekers* and *The Hidden Persuaders.*

The Hidden Persuaders, first published in 1957, sold more than one million copies. In it, Packard seems to argue that marketing is a world filled with master manipulators who have almost complete control over hordes of mindless consumers who purchase whatever merchandisers and advertisers command them to buy.

Packard's critics, in turn, find his analysis to be superficial, his assertions poorly developed, and many of his conclusions simply wrong. They ask, "if marketers are so powerful, why do so many products and companies fail when consumer demand fails to materialize?" Accordingly, advertising guru David Ogilvy pointed out that consumers are smart enough to make their own decisions when he observed, "the consumer isn't a moron, she's your wife."

Marketers as puppeteers: Agree or disagree?

"What the probers [i.e., marketing researchers] are looking for... are the *whys* of our behavior, so that they can more effectively manipulate our habits and choices in their favor. This has led them to probe why we are afraid of banks; why we love those big fat cars; why we really buy homes; why men smoke cigars; why the kind of car we drive reveals the brand of gasoline we will buy; why housewives typically fall into a hypnoidal trance when they get into a supermarket; why men are drawn into auto showrooms by convertibles but end up buying sedans; why junior loves cereal that pops, snaps, and crackles... [T]he probers... are systematically feeling out our hidden weaknesses and frailties in the hope that they can more efficiently influence our behavior... Seemingly, in the probing and manipulating nothing is immune or sacred." -- Vance Packard, in *The Hidden Persuaders* (pp. 2-3)

May 23, 2018
Wednesday
Students' Day (Mexico)

Objectives & reminders

Appointments

Early morning

8 a.m.

9 a.m.

10 a.m.

11 a.m.

Noon

1 p.m.

2 p.m.

3 p.m.

4 p.m.

5 p.m.

6 p.m.

Later evening

The Dwarf Grill opens, but not on Sunday

On Thursday, May 23, 1946, S. Truett Cathy and his brother, Ben, opened a 24-hour coffee shop in Hapeville, Georgia -- Dwarf Grill (later renamed the Dwarf House). Sales for that first day were $58.20.

The business experience Cathy gained during those early days in Georgia paved the way for his future national chain of Chick-fil-A restaurants. Today, there are more than 2,000 Chick-fil-A restaurants scattered across the U.S. and Canada generating annual sales in excess of $6 billion.

> **Too chicken to fail?**
> "The key to our success, I am convinced, was our commitment. When we're fully committed to something, we're not likely to give up or become discouraged, and we're not likely to fail."
> -- S. Truett Cathy

It's not clear what day of the week the first Chick-fil-A restaurant opened in 1967, but the ribbon probably was not cut on a Sunday. Throughout his business career, Cathy stood firm in his refusal to conduct business on Sundays. Being open on Sunday, according to Cathy, would violate his religious principles, but in his autobiography, *Eat Mor Chikin: Inspire More People*, he also notes other business benefits of the policy:

> "Why do we close on Sunday? Well... [a few days after opening the Dwarf Grill] I determined that if it took seven days a week to make a living, I should be in some other business. Too, it was my conscience that I had to live with; I just never could come to the idea of dealing with money on the Lord's Day.... I believe the Lord has blessed us because we recognize Him on this special day we call Sunday... I do not condemn a person for opening on Sunday: it is just a principle I stand very firmly on for my business..."

> "We find closing on Sunday attracts those people who give attention to spiritual growth and are family oriented. The fact that we have Sunday closing helps attract quality housewives and young people as employees."

May 24, 2018
Thursday
Brainstorm New Ideas Day

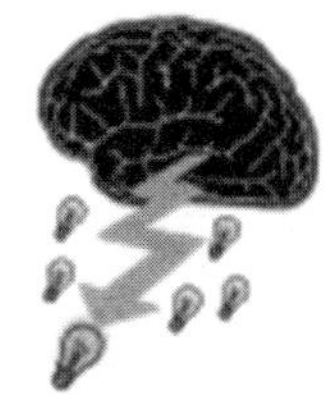

Objectives & reminders

______

______

______

Appointments

Early morning

8 a.m.

9 a.m.

10 a.m.

11 a.m.

Noon

1 p.m.

2 p.m.

3 p.m.

4 p.m.

5 p.m.

6 p.m.

Later evening

Happy birthday: Alex Faickney Osborn

Born in the Bronx, New York on May 24, 1888, Osborn was a journalist, publicist and sales rep early in his career, before he landed a job with the E.P. Remington advertising agency in Buffalo, New York. In 1919 he teamed with Bruce ***B***arton and Roy ***D***urstine to form their own agency, BDO. Nine years later BDO merged with the George ***B***atten Company to become the familiar BBDO agency.

Over the years, Osborn recognized the important role that creativity played in business in general, and in advertising in particular. Accordingly, he researched the topic and investigated methods to improve or stimulate people's creativity. His interest in creativity led him to write several books on the topic which included *Your Creative Power* (1948), and *Applied Imagination: The Principles and Procedures of Creative Thinking* (1953). In these books, Osborn described a technique that he had implemented at BBDO, called "brainstorming."

Brainstorming is essentially a group process in which members are encouraged to offer ideas in response to a clearly stated goal or problem, e.g., "How can we attract more new customers to our store?" or "What new products should we develop within the next two years?" As group members hear other members' ideas, additional ideas are stimulated -- creating a chain reaction of ideas that presumably leads to a larger volume of ideas than would result if group members listed ideas in isolation. So, the group is an important element of the brainstorming technique.

Brainstorming/creativity insight
"New facts often trigger new ideas."
– Alex F. Osborn

Another key element is suspended judgment. That is, the initial step of brainstorming is to list as many ideas as possible, including possibly outlandish ones. To avoid stifling ideas, group members are not allowed to make evaluative comments about the ideas until the list of ideas is complete.

Creativity as a delicate flower
"Creativity is so delicate a flower that praise tends to make it bloom, while discouragement often nips it in the bud." -- Alex F. Osborn

May 25, 2018
Friday
National Missing Children's Day

Objectives & reminders

______

______

______

Appointments

Early morning

8 a.m.

9 a.m.

10 a.m.

11 a.m.

Noon

1 p.m.

2 p.m.

3 p.m.

4 p.m.

5 p.m.

6 p.m.

Later evening

May 25 in the history of U.S. labor movement

1805
Members of the U.S.'s first and oldest trade union -- Federal Society of Journeymen Cordwainers -- were confronted by Philadelphia police while striking for better wages. Many strikers were arrested and charged with criminal conspiracy. Apparently a local judge had authorized the police's strike-breaking tactics at the request of the strikers' employers, marking the first (but not the last) time employers would turn to the courts to intervene.

1886
Philip Murray was born. He later founded the Congress of Industrial Organizations (CIO). According to Murray, "Unions are created to make living conditions just a little better than they were before they were created, and the union that does not manifest that kind of interest in human beings cannot endure."

1948
General Motors and the United Automobile Workers agreed to a sliding scale wage contract. The first of its kind, the agreement adjusted wages to the cost of living. The cost of living adjustment (COLA) was particularly important at that time because the rate of inflation was high (up 29% in two years). COLAs continue to be highly-relevant during inflationary periods.

1962
AFL-CIO unions began a campaign for 35-hour work weeks.

2005
A report by Genesys Telecom Labs noted the increasing number of customer-contact call centers that are outsourced, often across national borders. Not surprisingly, outsourcing was, and is, of great concern to labor unions.

May 26, 2018
Saturday
National Sorry Day (Australia)

Objectives & reminders

____

____

____

Appointments

Early morning

8 a.m.

9 a.m.

10 a.m.

11 a.m.

Noon

1 p.m.

2 p.m.

3 p.m.

4 p.m.

5 p.m.

6 p.m.

Later evening

Graduation Season

About this time of year – and especially on weekends – millions of high school and college seniors enjoy the graduation experience. This creates an obvious market for graduation-related products and services such as graduation gifts and celebrations.

Enrollment statistics

- An estimated 68% of this year's 3.5 million high school graduates in the U.S. will enroll in college for the Fall semester.
- American colleges and universities enrolled a total of 20.5 million students in 2016.
- 56% of college students in the U.S. earn a degree within six years of first enrolling.

But the *transition market* is even larger. That is, newly-minted graduates face inflexion points in their lifestyles and consumption habits as they transition from high school to college, or from being college students to pursuing careers and families. Moving to a new community, beginning a new job and marrying could be part of the transition mix – which in turn creates demand for numerous home-related items, clothing, automobiles, and other products and services to accompany the new lifestyle.

Graduation exercise

If you're not already convinced of the potential of the graduate transition market, brainstorm a list of purchases that you and your friends have postponed until after graduation. Stop when the length of the list reaches 1,000 items.

Marketers who win the race to reach new graduates during this critical transition period tend to reap the rewards that late-comers may miss.

Advice for graduates

"Be grateful... Keep a grateful journal. Every night list five things that happened this day, in days to come that you are grateful for. What it will begin to do is to change your perspective of your day and your life. I believe that if you can learn to focus on what you have, you will always see that the universe is abundant and you will have more. If you concentrate and focus in your life on what you don't have, you will never have enough. Be grateful. Keep a journal." -- Oprah Winfrey, talk-show hostess and businesswoman, during a commencement address at Wellesley College

May 27, 2018
Sunday
Trinity Sunday
Children's Day (Nigeria)

Objectives & reminders

____

____

Appointments

Early morning

8 a.m.

9 a.m.

10 a.m.

11 a.m.

Noon

1 p.m.

2 p.m.

3 p.m.

4 p.m.

5 p.m.

6 p.m.

Later evening

Happy birthday: Philip Kotler

Born in Chicago, Illinois on May 27, 1931, Kotler earned graduate degrees in economics at the University of Chicago and the Massachusetts Institute of Technology before embarking on a brief career teaching economics at Roosevelt University from 1957 to 1961.

In the early 1960s, Kotler developed an interest in marketing, so in 1962 he switched disciplines and began teaching marketing at Northwestern University's Kellogg School of Business, where he is now the SC Johnson Chair in Global Marketing.

> **Important role played by economists: Agree or disagree?**
> "Basically, economists exist to make astrologers look good." -- Philip Kotler

Over the years, Professor Kotler has played a key role in shaping the way businesspeople and scholars think about marketing. His texts and trade books have sold millions of copies around the world and have argued convincingly that marketing is much more than a bag of tricks companies employ to evoke desired buyer responses.

Rather, Kotler asserts that marketing is a philosophy of doing business that starts with an understanding of prospective customers' needs, wants and demands, which then works back to the company to determine how best to serve those prospective customers. Accordingly, marketing is not a peripheral activity, but is central to companies' justification for existence.

> **Best phrases to begin and end marketing essays ☺**
> Begin: "According to Kotler..."
> End: "Kotler concurs."

Speaking fluent marketing

In his book, *According to Kotler*, Dr. Kotler lists the following as the "main concepts used in marketing: segmentation, targeting, positioning, needs, wants, demand, offerings, brands, value and satisfaction, exchange, transactions, relationships and networks, marketing channels, supply chain, competition, the marketing environment, and marketing programs." Further, in his book, *Marketing Insights from A to Z*, Kotler provides a longer list and discussion of "80 concepts every manager needs to know."

May 28, 2018
Monday
Memorial Day

Objectives & reminders

___

___

___

Appointments

Early morning

8 a.m.

9 a.m.

10 a.m.

11 a.m.

Noon

1 p.m.

2 p.m.

3 p.m. *National Moment of Remembrance (3:00 p.m.)*

4 p.m.

5 p.m.

6 p.m.

Later evening

Memorial Day

First observed in May 1868, "Decoration Day" was set aside to decorate the graves of soldiers killed in the Civil War and to otherwise honor their memory.

Later, the annual commemoration became known as "Memorial Day" and fallen soldiers from all U.S. wars were honored in the observances. Some people honor the memory of all deceased veterans on Memorial Day, not just those who died in battle.

Since 1971, Memorial Day has been observed on the last Monday of May. Today, many other countries also designate a similar day to honor their military personnel killed in war (refer to the index).

Important to fine-tune your calendar marketing vocabulary: Agree or disagree?
Some holidays and occasions are to be celebrated, while others should be remembered, recognized, observed, honored or commemorated, but not "celebrated." Memorial Day is in the latter group.

"Soldier's Memorial Day"

When flow'ry Summer is at hand,
And Spring has gemm'd the earth with bloom,
We hither bring, with loving hand,
Bright flow'rs to deck our soldier's tomb.

Gentle birds above are sweetly singing
O'er the graves of heroes brave and true;
While the sweetest flow'rs we are bringing,
Wreath'd in garlands of red, white and blue.

With snowy hawthorn, clusters white,
Fair violets of heav'nly blue,
And early roses, fresh and bright,
We wreathe the red, and white, and blue.

-- Mary B.C. Slade (1870). Slade was a teacher, editor, poet and lifelong resident of Fall River, Massachusetts.

Americans and Memorial Day 2016
- 1.5 million watched the National Memorial Day Parade on television.
- 62% attended a cookout or barbeque.
- 39% traveled (89% of these traveled by car).

May 29, 2018
Tuesday
Veterans' Day (Sweden)

Objectives & reminders

Appointments

Early morning

8 a.m.

9 a.m.

10 a.m.

11 a.m.

Noon

1 p.m.

2 p.m.

3 p.m.

4 p.m.

5 p.m.

6 p.m.

Later evening

The competition within

"It is not the mountain we conquer but ourselves."
-- Sir Edmund Hillary, leader of the first team of mountain climbers to successfully reach the summit of Mt. Everest. He did so on May 29, 1953.

Consumer Credit Protection Act

The U.S. Consumer Credit Protection Act, also known as the Truth in Lending Act, went into effect on May 29, 1968, to eliminate some of the confusion regarding various credit terms, fees, and other costs associated with credit and therefore enable consumers to make more informed decisions about credit.

Among its several provisions, the Act requires lenders to disclose the costs of credit offers and do so in a common language. This provision helps reduce consumer confusion and enables consumers to compare competing credit options.

Eliminate confusion: Agree or disagree?

It is in the best interest of *both* consumers and businesses to eliminate confusion regarding credit arrangements, as well as any other potentially confusing stipulations of a business transaction (e.g., regarding post-sale service and product warranties).

The Act also bars unfair discrimination. For example, creditors are not allowed to withhold credit because of the consumer's gender or marital status. Further, if credit is denied, the consumer must be told why. The Act also mandates that credit records be made available to consumers and that processes be established to allow consumers to challenge billing errors or other disputes with creditors.

Credit insight

"A bank is a place that will lend you money if you can prove that you don't need it." – Bob Hope, American actor and comedian, born in Kent, England on May 29, 1903

May 30, 2018
Wednesday
Canary Islands Day (Spain)

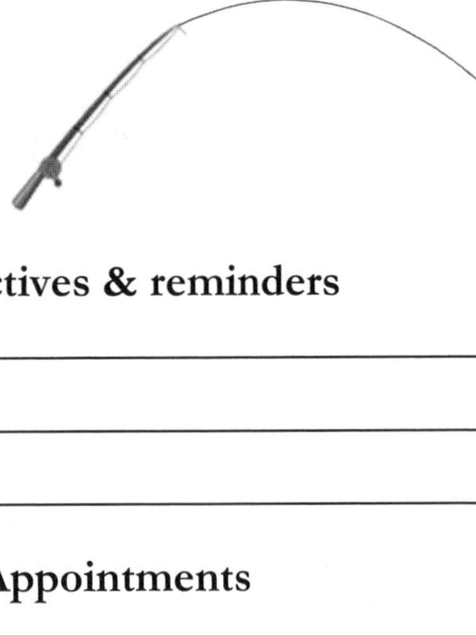

Objectives & reminders

Appointments

Early morning

8 a.m.

9 a.m.

10 a.m.

11 a.m.

Noon

1 p.m.

2 p.m.

3 p.m.

4 p.m.

5 p.m.

6 p.m.

Later evening

Misguided invention?

Louisville, Kentucky's George Cook received a patent for his "Automatic Fishing Device" on May 30, 1899. Tension on the line released a trip lever which caused a spring-loaded carriage to roll backwards while a spring-driven device would reel-in the fishing line. Although the concept was an interesting one, unfortunately for Mr. Cook the market was never "hooked" on the invention.

Contemplating why a new invention fails in the marketplace can be a useful exercise. In the case of the "automatic fishing device," history doesn't provide full disclosure of the reasons, but a classic reason for many new product failures (especially during Mr. Cook's era) is because they simply do not perform as well as the technology they attempt to replace, i.e., the fish may have been much smarter than the device.

Other possible reasons to explain the failure have to do with basic business issues. The inventor may have not had the capital, interest or business skills needed to bring the device to market. Clearly, inventing something that's potentially useful is one thing, but turning it into a commercial success is a different matter. It's not uncommon to have the skills needed for invention, but not have the skills needed to bring the invention to market, or vice versa.

Misunderstanding the marketplace explains other new product failures – in particular, misunderstanding why people might buy something and not knowing what their purchase requirements are. Although the idea of removing the fisherman from the fishing process might appeal to someone who's forced to fish to provide food for the family, recreational fisherman may shun the automatic fishing device if they enjoy doing the fishing themselves. In short, labor-saving devices may not be welcomed by prospective buyers who don't consider their involvement in the consumption process as "labor."

Marketing time machine: Your turn

Suppose you were a marketing consultant in the late 1800s and George Cook approached you before developing his automatic fishing device. What marketing-related suggestions would you offer? If you believe that a consumer survey is needed, who should be asked to participate and what key questions should they be asked?

May 31, 2018
Thursday

World No-Tobacco Day
Feast of Corpus Christi

Objectives & reminders

______

______

______

Appointments

Early morning

8 a.m.

9 a.m.

10 a.m.

11 a.m.

Noon

1 p.m.

2 p.m.

3 p.m.

4 p.m.

5 p.m.

6 p.m.

Later evening

Happy birthday: Johnny Paycheck

Born in Greenfield, Ohio on May 31, 1938 as Donald Eugene Lytle, Paycheck was an American country and western singer. In the 1960s, Lytle changed his name to Johnny Paycheck -- some say as a positioning strategy to compete against the already established and hugely popular country singer Johnny Cash.

Among Paycheck's 11 top-ten recordings, he is best known for his 1977 hit song written by David Allan Coe, "Take This Job and Shove It." The song reflects a worker's frustrations with his job – telling his boss, upon resignation, what he can do with the job. ♫♪ https://www.youtube.com/watch?v=EzGoDtmTllg

Tips: Before resigning in anger...

1. Count to 10, as in 10 *days*.
2. Remember that you may leave the job behind, but not the reputation as a hothead if you quit in anger.
3. Ask yourself, "Am I *sure* I'll be able to find another job in a timely manner?"

One study somewhat quantifies the take-this-job-and-shove-it phenomenon. Conducted by Vault, Inc., the survey of 706 American workers across several industries found that 61 percent had left jobs on "bad terms." Of these, 42 percent had involved screaming matches. Another 24 percent of disgruntled employees sent negative mass emails just prior to their departure, while 18 percent gave negative speeches at company meetings. Twelve percent stole or vandalized company property while four percent were involved in physical scuffles.

The study also explored the effect that a co-worker's exit has on those who remain. Fifty-two percent of the respondents claimed that they or other workers also had left the company soon after observing a co-worker's departure. This "me too" phenomenon can be particularly problematic when competent and respected employees leave the company in anger.

Reinforcing the value of strong employee relations

"When a natural leader gets the shaft and can't take it anymore, their decision to leave often impassions the desire of others to do the same." – Anonymous survey respondent in the Vault study

June 1, 2018
Friday
Children's Day (China)

Objectives & reminders

Appointments

Early morning

8 a.m.

9 a.m.

10 a.m.

11 a.m.

Noon

1 p.m.

2 p.m.

3 p.m.

4 p.m.

5 p.m.

6 p.m.

Later evening

Making the month more tangible for more effective seasonal communications

The alexandrite, moonstone, and pearl are June's gems. The rose is the month's flower.

Potential marketing appeals for June?

"It is the month of June,
The month of leaves and roses,
When pleasant sights salute the eyes,
And pleasant scents the noses."
-- Nathaniel Parker Willis, 19th century American poet, editor and literary critic

Marketing moves in June

June is the most popular month of the year to move. According to the U.S. Census Bureau, 13.1 percent of household moves each year occur in June. August is the second busiest moving month, accounting for 12.6 percent of all moves. A high proportion of these moves involve families with school-age children.

Obviously, moving-related businesses such as realtors and moving/storage companies have a lot to gain by identifying and contacting households on the move. Generally, advertising and promotion activities tend to be the most effective when they are timed to coincide with buyers' decision-making process.

But dozens of other home-related businesses also could benefit by being aware of and capitalizing on the annual moving patterns. One survey found that recent home buyers were several times more likely to express an interest in buying carpeting or flooring products, paint, furniture and fixtures, lawn and garden equipment, and many other house-related products and services than were consumers who had not moved recently.

Further, marketers of grocery stores, drug stores, banks, restaurants, auto repair services and a host of other businesses that sell products and services locally tend to have a competitive advantage if they are the first in their category to contact consumers who are new to the community. So, it's to these local firms' advantage to identify and contact new residents.

June 2, 2018
Saturday
Decoration Day (Canada)

Objectives & reminders

___

___

___

Appointments

Early morning

8 a.m.

9 a.m.

10 a.m.

11 a.m.

Noon

1 p.m.

2 p.m.

3 p.m.

4 p.m.

5 p.m.

6 p.m.

Later evening

Happy birthday: Jerry Mathers

Born in Sioux City, Iowa on June 2, 1948, actor Jerry Mathers is best known for his role as "the Beaver" in the 1950s/1960s television series, *Leave It to Beaver.* Reruns of the popular program are still shown today.

The show attempted to portray a middle-class suburban American household – the Cleavers – consisting of a husband and wife with two children (Beaver and his brother Wally) under the age of 18. At the time of the television series, almost half of all U.S. households consisted of a similar composition (i.e., husband, wife and one or more children under the age of 18) and it was common for marketers to target such households.

Today, the "traditional" family market is still significant and is still targeted, but it is not as typical as it once was -- now representing less than one-in-four U.S. households, compared to about one-in-two households during the *Leave It to Beaver* days. The marketing implications of this long-term trend are numerous. Here are three:

1. Today, slice-of-life scenes in advertisements are more likely to include non-traditional families, e.g., grandparents with grandchildren, parents with 20-something children, single-parents with children, couples without children, and so on.

2. The large-volume "family" sizes of food products, laundry detergent, and other household items are less popular because household sizes are smaller today. And, they are more likely to be called "economy" or "value" sizes rather than "family" sizes.

3. Similarly, many service businesses that previously offered "family" rates or discounts now offer "group" prices. Otherwise, trying to define what constitutes a "family" is too likely to offend non-traditional families.

First television generation

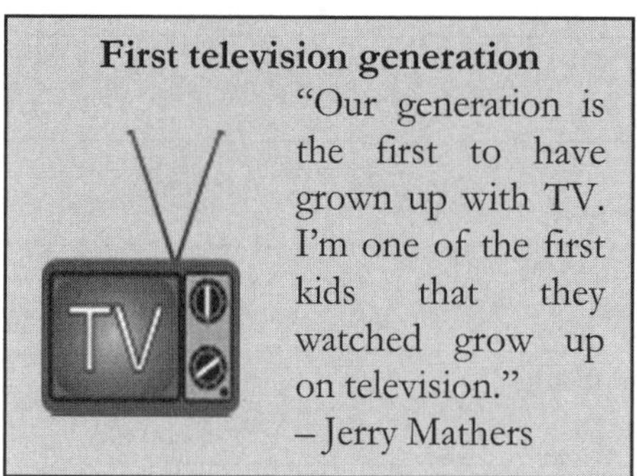

"Our generation is the first to have grown up with TV. I'm one of the first kids that they watched grow up on television."
– Jerry Mathers

June 3, 2018
Sunday
Martyrs' Day (Uganda)

Objectives & reminders

____

____

____

Appointments

Early morning

8 a.m.

9 a.m.

10 a.m.

11 a.m.

Noon

1 p.m.

2 p.m.

3 p.m.

4 p.m.

5 p.m.

6 p.m.

Later evening

Uniform decisions for women

The International Ladies' Garment Workers Union was founded on June 3, 1900. The organization's mission was to improve the deplorable working conditions too commonly found in the sweatshops where women worked. On June 3, 1974, the U.S. Supreme Court ruled that men and women should receive equal pay if they perform equal jobs.

Another uniform decision made

Baseball uniforms were worn for the first time on June 3, 1851. The honor and distinction belonged to the New York Knickerbockers. The new outfits included white shirts and long blue trousers, topped off with straw hats.

Today, uniforms are routinely worn by sports teams and are commonly found among employees in retail and service businesses. Uniforms serve a variety of purposes. For sports teams, they not only help spectators identify players and teams, but they help create a sense of belongingness, loyalty, pride and professionalism among team members -- a sense that is extended to fans through the merchandising of uniforms and other team-licensed apparel.

Uniforms also can help cultivate a similar sense of team spirit and professionalism among retail and service workers. Employee uniforms minimize the need for overly detailed, potentially ambiguous, and debatably subjective dress codes. If thoughtfully selected, uniforms can be chosen to reflect the desired image of the company. Further, employee uniforms enable customers to identify employees more easily -- a definite plus when customers need assistance.

Uniform placement discouraged

In June 1990, the Outdoor Advertising Association of America (OAAA) recommended that the placement of billboards near schools, churches and minority neighborhoods be voluntarily limited if the billboards advertised cigarettes or alcohol products. About 80 percent of billboard companies in the U.S. were OAAA members. By the end of the decade, several state laws and local ordinances banned or restricted outdoor advertising of cigarettes and alcohol near schools.

June 4, 2018
Monday
National Unity Day (Hungary)

Objectives & reminders

____

____

____

Appointments

Early morning

8 a.m.

9 a.m.

10 a.m.

11 a.m.

Noon

1 p.m.

2 p.m.

3 p.m.

4 p.m.

5 p.m.

6 p.m.

Later evening

Planning: Details, details, and more details

Thousands of details can be involved in the production, sale and delivery of a product or service -- so many, in fact, that it is difficult to anticipate each and every one. Even with careful planning, some details are likely to be overlooked.

That was the case at 2:00 a.m. on June 4, 1896, when Henry Ford's first automobile -- then known as a "quadricycle -- was completed in a Detroit, Michigan work-shed. Unfortunately, the road test had to be delayed by about an hour while workmen used an ax to knock bricks out of the shed's framework. Why did they do that? Because the new automobile was wider than the shed's door.

Teamwork lessons from kindergarten

"Live a balanced life -- learn some and think some and draw and paint and sing and dance and play and work every day some." -- Robert Fulghum, former IBM salesman and author of the best-selling book, *All I Really Need To Know I Learned in Kindergarten*, born in Waco, Texas on June 4, 1937

Nineteenth Amendment approved

The U.S. Congress approved the women's suffrage amendment on June 4, 1919, after congressmen showed their support for the amendment by about a three-to-one margin. The amendment would become part of the U.S. Constitution when ratified by two-thirds of the state legislatures during the 15 months that followed. The campaign for women's right to vote had begun at least 71 years earlier.

In most U.S. elections today, a slightly higher percentage of women vote than men. Of particular interest to today's marketers is the increased frequency of women who "vote" in the marketplace with their dollars. According to some estimates, women spend or influence the spending of 80 percent of all consumer expenditures in the U.S.

Where there is need, there is opportunity

"The war against hunger is truly mankind's war of liberation." -- U.S. President John F. Kennedy, speech at the World Food Congress on June 4, 1963

June 5, 2018
Tuesday
World Environment Day

Objectives & reminders

____

____

____

Appointments

Early morning

8 a.m.

9 a.m.

10 a.m.

11 a.m.

Noon

1 p.m.

2 p.m.

3 p.m.

4 p.m.

5 p.m.

6 p.m.

Later evening

Happy birthday: William E. Upjohn

Born in Richland Township, Michigan on June 5, 1853, Upjohn was trained to practice medicine but left his practice in 1885 after inventing the "fiable" pill, i.e., one that was easily digestible. Before the fiable pill, medicine was generally available in liquid form; available pills were frequently hard and insoluble. Upjohn's innovation led him into the pill business, forming what would become known as the Upjohn Company.

Like any new innovation, Upjohn's digestible pills didn't sell themselves. Upjohn employed sales reps to visit physicians and tell the company's story. One memorable way sales reps dramatized the fact that Upjohn pills could be easily absorbed was to challenge physicians to crush Upjohn's pills with their thumb, which they could. Then physicians were asked to do the same with competitors' pills, which they could not.

More P's for business success

Leslie Yerkes and Charles Decker added to the proliferation of business-relevant p-words when their book, *Beans: Four Principles for Running a Business in Good Times or Bad*, was published on June 5, 2003. Their four pet-P's include *passion, people, personal* and *product* which they assert are the key ingredients in their "recipe for life and work."

Yerkes and Decker recommend pouring "some of each [P] into your work and working relationships to experience satisfaction and success in all that you do." More specifically:

Passion: "Do what you love and you won't work another day in your life."

People: "Look for people who share your values.... Clearly communicate and develop shared expectations."

Personal: "Practice simple gestures of courtesy. Be authentic and well intentioned in all situations."

Product: "Be as passionate about your product as you are about the people. Find little ways to differentiate and delight.... Earn a reputation for having a product that your customers cannot stop talking about." (pp. 119-122)

June 6, 2018
Wednesday
D-Day Anniversary

Objectives & reminders

___

___

___

Appointments

Early morning

8 a.m.

9 a.m.

10 a.m.

11 a.m.

Noon

1 p.m.

2 p.m.

3 p.m.

4 p.m.

5 p.m.

6 p.m.

Later evening

D-Day: Operation Overlord

The largest invasion of any war in history occurred on June 6, 1944, when World War II Allied forces landed on France's Normandy beaches. The invasion involved 5,300 ships and 11,000 airplanes. Although thousands of lives were lost that day and during the days that followed, the operation was considered a success as it hastened the end of the war. Today, June 6, 1944, is remembered at this time each year for the sacrifices made and the acts of heroism exhibited at Normandy. It's a great day to salute veterans.

D-day: Did you know?

The Normandy invasion is often referred to as "D-day," but actually it was only one of perhaps 100 or more D-days during World War II.

D-day is a military term used to designate the initial day on which a major military operation begins. For planning purposes, "D-day" is referred to rather than the actual date because the actual date may not be known when the plans are made, the date may be confidential, or the date may be subject to revision.

It follows that "D-day minus 1," "D-day minus 2," "D-day minus 3," and so on, refer to the days *prior* to D-day, while "D-day plus 1," "D-day plus 2," etc. refer to the days *following* D-day.

Home is where the "re" is: Ag-re or disag-re?

"Home is a tremendously powerful archetype in the American culture... Americans may have a stronger sense of home than any other culture on the planet... When we [Americans] think of home, we think of words that begin with the prefix "re." Words like return, reunite, reconnect, reconfirm, and renew... Selling any household item with the notion that it can become part of a family ritual (anything from popcorn to coffee to laundry detergent) is a valuable way to ignite our affection for home." – Clotaire Rapaille, *The Culture Code: An Ingenious Way to Understand Why People Around the World Live and Buy as They Do* (pp. 95, 101), published on June 6, 2006

June 7, 2018
Thursday
Flag Day (Peru)

Objectives & reminders

Appointments

Early morning

8 a.m.

9 a.m.

10 a.m.

11 a.m.

Noon

1 p.m.

2 p.m.

3 p.m.

4 p.m.

5 p.m.

6 p.m.

Later evening

Price takes many forms

"Price" is an essential element of the marketing mix, usually thought of in terms of money. But organizations frequently "charge" indirect prices and non-monetary prices too.

Buyers may pay *indirect* or *systems prices* to install, operate, maintain, finance, and insure a durable good, such as an automobile. Or, they may incur non-monetary prices, such as *time* price (the time it takes to acquire a product, become familiar with it, use it, register it, maintain it, and so on), *psychic* price (the mental anxiety or hassle associated with acquiring, using, repairing or worrying about a product), or *lifestyle* price (altering one's lifestyle as required by the product, e.g., changing one's eating habits as part of a weight-control service).

Sometimes non-monetary prices become indirect monetary prices, such as when a business customer pays an employee's wages for the time the worker spends buying, transporting and installing a new piece of office equipment.

Today, marketers frequently gain an advantage in the marketplace by reducing some of the indirect or non-monetary prices associated with their product offerings, and/or by recognizing that many buyers are willing to make trade-offs between one type of price and others (e.g., by paying more money is exchange for faster service [i.e., lower time price] or assurance of higher quality [i.e., lower psychic price]).

Happy birthday: Vivien Kellems

Born in Des Moines, Iowa on June 7, 1896, Kellems grew to become a prosperous industrialist. She also was outspoken and didn't appreciate the imposition of having to deduct taxes from her employees' wages. At one point she refused to withhold payroll taxes unless she was appointed as an agent of the Internal Revenue Service (IRS) and reimbursed for the time and expense involved in collecting her employees' taxes. It is probably a safe assumption that many other employers have felt the same way.

Price analysis: Your turn
What tax-related prices were Vivien Kellems expected to pay? What might the IRS have done to offset these prices or otherwise make them more palatable for Kellems?

June 8, 2018
Friday

World Oceans Day

Objectives & reminders

______

______

______

Appointments

Early morning

8 a.m.

9 a.m.

10 a.m.

11 a.m.

Noon

1 p.m.

2 p.m.

3 p.m.

4 p.m.

5 p.m.

6 p.m.

Later evening

Happy birthday: Scott Adams

Born in Windham, New York on June 8, 1957, Adams' career took a few twists and turns before he became well-recognized for his cynical views of business, as expressed in his *Dilbert* cartoons.

Dilbert's popularity stems from readers' ability to recognize and relate to the absurdities and maladies depicted by Dilbert and his supporting cast of characters. In short, people seem to see their own co-workers, bosses, and companies (and sometimes themselves) whenever they read a *Dilbert* cartoon.

The cartoon's popularity is perpetuated by Adams' continual contact with readers. Unlike authors of most comic strips, Adams includes his email address on each cartoon so readers can provide feedback whenever they wish – which is a great idea according to Dr. Martin, Charles.Martin@wichita.edu

> **Business according to *Dilbert***
> "Informed decision-making comes from a long tradition of guessing and then blaming others for inadequate results." -- Scott Adams

De-marketing behaviors

Marketing is usually thought of in terms of commercially traded goods and services, but not-for-profit organizations (NPOs) also engage in marketing. Often the "products" NPOs market are intangible and abstract -- like causes or behaviors -- which can be difficult for "buyers" to understand and want to buy. Often NPOs' marketing objectives involve efforts to convince consumers to *stop* buying or doing something, which is called *de-marketing.*

The American Heart Association responded to the de-marketing challenge in 1963 when they launched a campaign on June 8 to encourage people to stop smoking. At the time, more than four of every 10 American adults smoked. Early efforts in the anti-smoking movement emphasized that non-smokers were likely to live longer than smokers. But, because the benefit of an extended life was not immediate enough for younger consumers, emphasis shifted to shorter-term benefits that younger people could relate to: "Who'd want to kiss someone whose mouth tastes like an ashtray?" Today, about 15 percent of U.S. adults and 9 percent of high school students smoke.

June 9, 2018
Saturday
National Heroes' Day (Uganda)

Objectives & reminders

____

____

____

Appointments

Early morning

8 a.m.

9 a.m.

10 a.m.

11 a.m.

Noon

1 p.m.

2 p.m.

3 p.m.

4 p.m.

5 p.m.

6 p.m.

Later evening

June 9 in food marketing history

1876 Hires Root Beer was first sold at the U.S. Centennial Exposition in Philadelphia by its creator, Charles Elmer Hires. Today, the brand is still available as one of the 50 brands produced by the Plano, Texas-based Dr. Pepper Snapple Group.

1902 Also in Philadelphia, the first Automat was opened by entrepreneurs Frank Hardart and Joe Horn. The concept was a vending machine restaurant. Patrons bought the food on one floor. Then the food was sent to a lower floor for cooking and then lifted back to the upper floor on small elevators.

1938 Leo's Hawaiian Punch was trademarked. Later the "Leo's" was dropped from the brand's name. The seven-fruits-flavored tropical blend was first sold in California, but was available nationwide by the mid-1950s.

2003 ACNielsen's online newsletter, *Facts, Figures & the Future*, reported the trend toward alternative channels of distribution for food products, including "super vending machines" to be installed in some Washington D.C. train stations. The vending machines were to carry milk and other chilled products. However, 74 percent of consumers surveyed by Nielsen said they would not buy groceries from such vending machines.

American Marketing Association

In June 1915, the National Association of Teachers of Advertising (NATA) was formed in Chicago during a convention held by the Association of Advertising Clubs of the World. In 1937, NATA merged with the American Marketing Society, which had formed six years earlier, to become the American Marketing Association (AMA).

Since those early days, the AMA's membership has grown considerably – approaching 40,000 by 2017. Today, the AMA hosts numerous conferences and workshops for both members and non-members. The organization also publishes several marketing-related publications and journals such as the *Journal of Marketing*. Additional information about the AMA, as well as resources for marketing practitioners and students, may be found on the AMA's website, www.MarketingPower.com.

June 10, 2018
Sunday

Father's Day (Austria and Belgium)
Day of Portugal (Portugal)

Objectives & reminders

Appointments

Early morning

8 a.m.

9 a.m.

10 a.m.

11 a.m.

Noon

1 p.m.

2 p.m.

3 p.m.

4 p.m.

5 p.m.

6 p.m.

Later evening

Current Tax Payment Bill

On June 10, 1943, U.S. President Franklin D. Roosevelt signed the new bill that allowed taxes to be deducted directly from workers' paychecks. Although the new system was criticized by Vivien Kellems (discussed on June 7) and others, the "pay as you go" system continues today and has paved the way for other payroll deductions that followed.

Today, marketers of non-profit organizations also benefit from payroll deductions. They understand that payroll deductions tend to be less painful to donors than cash payments. The principle is that if donors never see the money, they are less likely to miss it. Systematic payroll deductions have other advantages too:

1. Frequent deductions of small amounts often seem more affordable than infrequent lump-sum donations.

2. An agreed-upon amount to be deducted from each paycheck means workers only have to make one positive decision to donate. That is, donors don't have to decide each pay period if they wish to donate. Otherwise, independent donation decisions are likely to lead to some (many?) decisions *not* to donate.

3. As a matter of convenience, payroll deductions require no extra effort or time on the part of the donor, further enhancing the palatability of giving.

Perhaps the next best alternatives to automatic payroll deductions are automatic electronic deductions from donors' checking accounts. Like payroll deductions, this method of payment is convenient and relatively painless for donors. Automatic electronic deductions tend to increase the volume and consistency of donations.

Advertising and PR are *not* crutches

"Advertising and public relations alone will not create a successful business. Putting a spotlight on a pile of manure only makes it smell worse." – William Rosenberg, founder of Dunkin' Donuts (1950) and the International Franchise Association (1960). He was born in Boston, Massachusetts on June 10, 1916.

June 11, 2018
Monday
Kamehameha Day (Hawaii)

Objectives & reminders

____

____

____

Appointments

Early morning

8 a.m.

9 a.m.

10 a.m.

11 a.m.

Noon

1 p.m.

2 p.m.

3 p.m.

4 p.m.

5 p.m.

6 p.m.

Later evening

Merchandising lifts sales

Retail sales tend to increase when related items are displayed together. For example, when the three key ingredients for banana pudding – bananas, pudding mix, and vanilla wafers – are displayed together, consumers' desire for banana pudding is aroused. Displayed separately, shoppers might not think about how much they enjoy banana pudding.

> **Another important combo ☺**
> "Man cannot live by bread alone. He must have peanut butter."
> -- Dave Gardner, American comedian, born in Jackson, Tennessee on June 11, 1926

Trade promotions also lift sales

ACNielsen data released on June 11, 2007, point to the prevalence of trade promotions in grocery and drug stores. The data indicate that promotions account for 36 percent of sales dollars generated in grocery stores, and 32 percent in drug stores (the data exclude Wal-Mart's sales).

Interestingly, Nielsen's research found that sales in some product categories are more responsive to promotional efforts than others. For example, sales for meats and nonfood grocery categories tend to increase more substantially when promoted than do sales of health and beauty care items or beverages (including alcohol). Across all product categories studied, temporary price reductions boost sales by the least amount (45%), in contrast to displayed items which realize an average 89 percent increase in sales.

Truth and character more generally uplifting

"Leadership rests not only upon ability, not only upon capacity; having the capacity to lead is not enough. The leader must be willing to use it. His leadership is then based on truth and character. There must be truth in the purpose and will power in the character." – Vince Lombardi, legendary football coach of the Green Bay Packers (1959-1967), born in New York City on June 11, 1913

June 12, 2018
Tuesday
Independence Day (Philippines)

Objectives & reminders

Appointments

Early morning

---
8 a.m.

---
9 a.m.

---
10 a.m.

---
11 a.m.

Noon

---
1 p.m.

---
2 p.m.

---
3 p.m.

---
4 p.m.

---
5 p.m.

---
6 p.m.

Later evening

June 12 in baseball history: Good day to hit a home run with baseball-related promotions

1839 First baseball game was played in the United States. Abner Doubleday invented the sport.

1880 First perfect game was pitched, by John Richmond of Worcester, Massachusetts.

1939 Baseball Hall of Fame was opened in Cooperstown, New York.

1959 Little League Baseball Week was first declared in U.S. by presidential proclamation, now celebrated annually beginning on the second Monday in June.

1981 Baseball players began a 49-day strike, largely regarding the issue of free-agent compensation. ☹

Baseball's enduring intergenerational appeal

"Baseball in continuous, like nothing else among American things, an endless game of repeated summers, joining the long generations of all the fathers and all the sons." – Donald Hall, poet

Sales promotions most popular among Minor League fans

(with *percentage* of surveyed fans indicating positive attitude toward the promotion)

Fireworks (77)
Bat night (77)
Proof of purchase [discounts involving collection of cereal box tops] (74)
Cap day (71)
Coupon books [discounts as part of entertainment coupon book] (70)
Seat cushion (69)
Baseball night (69)
Pennant night (68)
Helmet night (67)

Source: Wakefield, K.L. and V. Bush (1998), "Promoting Leisure Services…" *Journal of Services Marketing*, 12(3), p. 214.

June 13, 2018
Wednesday
Inventors' Day (Hungary)

Objectives & reminders

___

___

___

Appointments

Early morning

8 a.m.

9 a.m.

10 a.m.

11 a.m.

Noon

1 p.m.

2 p.m.

3 p.m.

4 p.m.

5 p.m.

6 p.m.

Later evening

Happy birthday: Robert E. Wood

Born in Kansas City, Missouri on June 13, 1879, Wood enjoyed two careers -- first in the military where he rose to the rank of brigadier general and gained valuable experience in logistics and distribution as acting quartermaster general.

In 1919, General Wood launched his second career -- in retailing. He worked for the mail-order firm Montgomery Ward for about five years before joining Sears, Roebuck & Co. in 1924 where he soon spearheaded Sears' expansion program to build retail stores in suburban communities. The growth strategy was such a success that Wood was named President in 1928, then Chairman in 1939. In 1954, Wood retired as Sears' chairman, but remained on the board of directors until 1968.

Forecasting matters

Sears and Montgomery Ward were American retailing rivals prior to World War II. Both companies were successful at the time, but their paths departed immediately after WWII when the two firms anticipated and acted upon very different economic scenarios.

Montgomery Ward envisioned a post-war economic downturn and tough times for retailers. In response, the company opted for a no-growth strategy, limited investment in the company, and tried to build cash reserves. They "hunkered down" for several years while waiting for a depression that never materialized.

In contrast, Sears believed the post-war period would be a prosperous one. Decision-makers at Sears reasoned that the war had created pent-up demand for consumer goods that would need to be satisfied after the war. Further, they believed that recent technological advances and the expanded labor pool created by soldiers returning to civilian life would drive business innovation and productivity. So, during the eight years following the war (1945-1953), Sears invested $300 million to open new stores and upgrade existing ones – all in anticipation of the economic boon that *did* materialize.

Sears' forecast proved to be the correct one. Their sales almost tripled during the eight-year period following the war, and continued to expand throughout the 1950s and 1960s. Montgomery Ward never caught up.

June 14, 2018
Thursday
Flag Day

Objectives & reminders

Appointments

Early morning

8 a.m.

9 a.m.

10 a.m.

11 a.m.

Noon

1 p.m.

2 p.m.

3 p.m.

4 p.m.

5 p.m.

6 p.m.

Later evening

Flag Day
The Pledge of Allegiance

On Flag Day – today – and at other times of the year too, the American flag is celebrated with salutes and recitals of The Pledge of Allegiance.

These traditions give Americans the opportunity to pay their respect to the flag and express their patriotism. However, a Supreme Court ruling on June 14, 1943, found that the constitutional right of free speech denies anyone or any institution the authority to force anyone to salute the American flag or recite the Pledge against their will.

The Pledge of Allegiance
"I pledge allegiance to the flag of the United States of America, and to the Republic for which it stands -- one nation, under God, indivisible, with liberty and justice for all."

Flag Day is for Hope ☺

"I returned to Cleveland for a really big homecoming. I remember it well. How they welcomed me... flags waving, bands playing, big parades and everything. Yes sir! Lucky for me I arrived on Flag Day."
– Bob Hope, American comedian and actor

Flag waving guidelines

Cracker Barrel, the restaurant chain headquartered in Lebanon, Tennessee with 600+ locations, printed and distributed to customers 8.5" x 3.66" cards in time for Flag Day in 2017. The cards offered several guidelines for displaying and handling the American flag, e.g., "The flag should be kept from touching the ground, floor, water or anything beneath it."

Experience waving his own flag

"Experience taught me a few things. One is to listen to your gut, no matter how good something sounds on paper. The second is that you're generally better off sticking with what you know. And the third is that sometimes your best investments are the ones you don't make." -- Donald Trump, former real estate developer and entrepreneur, and since January 2017, the 45th President of the U.S. President Trump was born in New York City on Flag Day -- June 14, 1946.

June 15, 2018
Friday
Eid al-Fitr

Objectives & reminders

______

______

______

Appointments

Early morning

8 a.m.

9 a.m.

10 a.m.

11 a.m.

Noon

1 p.m.

2 p.m.

3 p.m.

4 p.m.

5 p.m.

6 p.m.

Later evening

Adaptability must surface when uncertainty does

"Although uncertainty does not... make intelligent choice impossible, it places a premium on robust adaptive procedures instead of strategies that work well only when finely tuned to precisely known environments." -- Herbert Simon, social scientist, computer scientist, economist, philosopher, author, etc., etc., born in Milwaukee, Wisconsin on June 15, 1916

Least likely to succeed?

Born on June 15, 1914, Robert C. "Bob" Wian, was voted by his high-school classmates as "*least* likely to succeed." In 1936, Wian bought a small 10-stool restaurant in Glendale, California which he renamed Bob's Pantry. He grew the business and opened additional restaurants under the "Bob's Big Boy" banner. In 1967, the "least likely to succeed" sold his empire of 600 restaurants to Marriott Corporation.

Voting for customers as *most* likely to succeed

"There is nothing fantastic in anything I ever did. It was all little things, but it was all for the customer, to let him know we cared." -- Robert C. Wian, 1979

Fair characterization of discrimination: Agree or disagree?

"Negroes are not discriminated against because of the color of their skin. They are discriminated against because they have not anything to offer that people want to buy. The minute that they can develop themselves so they excel in whatever they do -- then they are going to find that they don't have any real problems." -- S.B. Fuller, founder of Fuller Products Company (soap manufacturer) and one of the wealthiest African-Americans in the U.S. during the 1950s and early 1960s. Fuller was born in Monroe, Louisiana on June 15, 1905. Fuller offered this perspective in an interview in 1963.

June 16, 2018
Saturday
Engineers' Day (Argentina)

Objectives & reminders

____

____

____

Appointments

Early morning

8 a.m.

9 a.m.

10 a.m.

11 a.m.

Noon

1 p.m.

2 p.m.

3 p.m.

4 p.m.

5 p.m.

6 p.m.

Later evening

Ford Motor Company anniversary

After working for other people for several years and tinkering with his own designs of internal combustion engines, Henry Ford took the transitional plunge from mechanical engineer to entrepreneur and corporate businessman on June 16, 1903, when he formed The Ford Motor Company in Detroit, Michigan. That's the day the company was incorporated.

> **Teamwork requires the entire team**
> "You will find men who want to be carried on the shoulders of others, who think that the world owes them a living. They don't seem to see that we must all lift together and pull together."
> -- Henry Ford

Thirty four days after incorporation, the company sold its first vehicle. Seven years later (1910) Ford announced that it had produced its millionth automobile. By continuously improving production efficiencies, Ford was able to lower costs and pass along the savings to customers. The lower prices, in turn, expanded the size of the market. By June 16, 1924, Ford had manufactured ten million automobiles -- with the 10th million requiring only 132 working days to produce.

> **Quality, costs, wages**
> "There is one rule for industrialists and that is: Make the best quality of goods possible at the lowest cost possible, paying the highest wages possible."
> -- Henry Ford

Citigroup anniversary

When The Ford Motor Company was incorporated on June 16, 1903, City Bank of New York was celebrating its 91st anniversary. Formed on June 16, 1812, the bank was launched with two million dollars of capital. Like The Ford Motor Company, the bank still exists today -- but changed its name to Citibank in the mid-1970s, then merged with Travelers Group in 1998 to become Citigroup.

> **Age matters: Agree or disagree?**
> What are the marketing advantages, if any, of organizations like Ford and Citigroup that have been in business for a very long time? Any disadvantages?

June 17, 2018
Sunday
Father's Day

Objectives & reminders

____

____

____

Appointments

Early morning

8 a.m.

9 a.m.

10 a.m.

11 a.m.

Noon

1 p.m.

2 p.m.

3 p.m.

4 p.m.

5 p.m.

6 p.m.

Later evening

Father's Day

Celebrated annually in the U.S. and about 75 other countries on the third Sunday in June, Father's Day is a special time to honor fathers and to thank them for all that they do for their families.

Fathers get smarter

"When I was a boy of 14, my father was so ignorant I could hardly stand to have the old man around. But when I got to be 21, I was astonished at how much the old man had learned in seven years." -- Mark Twain, writer and humorist

Not surprisingly, fathers typically receive gifts on Father's Day, with cards, apparel and dinner being the most frequently bestowed gifts. Interestingly women tend to spend about 43 percent more money for Father's Day gifts than men spend. Further, consumers between the ages of 25 and 44 tend to spend more than younger or older groups of consumers.

Marbleous fatherly advice

Keep moving

"You mustn't let a few minor mistakes discourage you. Keep going, and I know you'll come out on top. If you do that, success will be yours forever." -- Herman Menasche's advice to his daughter, Lillian Vernon, who later built the Lillian Vernon catalog business

Arrange your priorities

"Chuck, your health comes first; without that you have nothing. The family comes second. Your business comes third. You better recognize and organize those first two so that you can take care of the third." -- advice given by Chuck Emerson's father. The younger Emerson became the chairman and CEO of Emerson Electric.

Visualize success

"Try to *see yourself* doing what you want to do, and you'll be able to do it." -- advice given to Wolf Schmitt as a young boy, by his father. As an adult, Wolf Schmitt landed the job he visualized -- CEO of Rubbermaid.

June 18, 2018
Monday
Dragon Boat Festival (China)

Objectives & reminders

____

____

____

Appointments

Early morning

8 a.m.

9 a.m.

10 a.m.

11 a.m.

Noon

1 p.m.

2 p.m.

3 p.m.

4 p.m.

5 p.m.

6 p.m.

Later evening

Leapfrog marketing

Students at Hanover High School in Hanover, New Hampshire set a world's record for leapfrogging on June 18, 1988. For almost 190 hours, they leapfrogged a distance equal to 888.1 miles.

In the game of leapfrog, participants are always slightly behind or ahead of other participants, but are never equal. That's why there is never a "tie" in leapfrog and never a clear point at which the game ends.

Although they don't always call it leapfrogging, marketers sometimes play leapfrog with their customers by ensuring that the relationship with customers, or the equity in the relationship, is never quite even -- thus prompting customers to continue to play the game. For example, manufacturers of hot dog buns tend to package fewer buns per package than do manufacturers of hot dogs. Consumers buying initial packages of buns and hot dogs find that extra hot dogs remain after the buns have been eaten, which prompts them to purchase more buns to use the extra hot dogs. This of course, leads to a surplus of buns, which prompts the purchase of more hot dogs, and so the game of leapfrog continues.

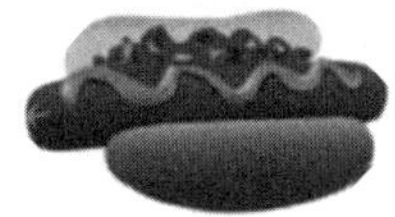

As another food-related example, a pizza delivery service may include a *bounce-back* coupon with a pizza order -- good for a discount on the *next* pizza order. Not to purchase a pizza in the future is to waste the coupon and therefore lose the game of leapfrog -- a psychologically uncomfortable state for many consumers. So, the coupon is redeemed with the purchase of another pizza, which generates another coupon to keep the game of leapfrog going.

Big idea:
Ensure no "ties" in leapfrog marketing

To extend customer relationships, ensure that there are no discrete points in the relationship at which customers conclude that they have paid all that they owe the company and have received all that they are entitled to. Leapfrog over customers by promising extra value or benefits that can be redeemed ***if*** customers leap in return.

June 19, 2018
Tuesday
Juneteenth

Objectives & reminders

Appointments

Early morning

8 a.m.

9 a.m.

10 a.m.

11 a.m.

Noon

1 p.m.

2 p.m.

3 p.m.

4 p.m.

5 p.m.

6 p.m.

Later evening

Happy birthday: James R. Adams

Born on a small farm in southwestern Indiana on June 19, 1898, Adams began his career as a college instructor (Indiana University) and a journalist before making the transition into advertising – first writing the advertising copy for Straube Piano Company, then working for an ad agency (Critchfield and Company) in Chicago beginning in 1925.

Nine years later (1934), Adams teamed with Theodore F. McManus and W.A.P. John to form a new agency, McManus, John & Adams, Inc. There he served in various leadership roles including president and chairman while building a reputation for effective automotive advertising. For 30 years he was closely involved with numerous Cadillac ad campaigns.

Fortunately for students of advertising, Adams passed along much of his experience by writing two best-selling books, *More Power to Advertising* (1937) and *Sparks Off My Anvil, from Thirty Years in Advertising* (1958). Adams was inducted into the Advertising Hall of Fame in 1960.

The true beauty of advertising
"Great designers seldom make great advertising men, because they get overcome by the beauty of the picture – and forget that merchandise must be sold." – James Randolph Adams

Content and advertising decisions should be kept separate: Agree or disagree?

Typically newspapers, magazines, television stations and other media vehicles keep their editorial or content departments separate from their advertising departments. Operating independently presumably avoids conflicts of interest. For example, a newspaper reporter should not be tempted to suppress a negative story that might jeopardize a company's reputation simply because the company is a high-volume advertiser in the newspaper.

In 1930, the "separation" policy of one newspaper led to unanticipated consequences. It seems that labor leader James Kimber died on June 19 of that year. His obituary was printed in the local newspaper. Also appearing on the same page was a testimonial ad featuring the same James Kimber providing the testimony. The ad touted a cure-all wonder medicine.

June 20, 2018
Wednesday
World Refugee Day

Objectives & reminders

Appointments

Early morning

8 a.m.

9 a.m.

10 a.m.

11 a.m.

Noon

1 p.m.

2 p.m.

3 p.m.

4 p.m.

5 p.m.

6 p.m.

Later evening

Happy birthday: George Pepperdine

Born near Mound Valley, Kansas on June 20, 1886, Pepperdine attended business college in Parsons, Kansas as a teenager. After his business school training Pepperdine worked for a brief time as a bookkeeper and then as a farmer.

In 1909, Pepperdine moved to Kansas City, Missouri where, with an initial investment of only five dollars, he founded the Western Auto Supply Company that same year (later the company became known as Western Auto Corporation). A few years later (1916 or 1920, sources disagree) Pepperdine moved his family and business to California where he founded George Pepperdine College in 1937 (now Pepperdine University). About two years after that, in 1939, he sold his interest in Western Auto.

Adjusting prices for inflation

Although there are exceptions, inflation causes the price of most items to creep upward over the years. Consider, for example, some of the prices students were charged at Pepperdine College in 1937:

- Room, board, tuition, and fees for the academic school year -- $420
- Tuition and fees for students who live at home and commute to campus -- $135
- Hamburger and soft drink in the college's cafeteria -- 20 cents
- Breakfast (eggs, pancakes and coffee) in the college's cafeteria -- 30 cents

---

A decade of free advertising

Billboards in Anniston, Alabama on both the west- and east-bound sides of U.S. Interstate 20 advertised Exit 185's "Super Buffet" restaurant on June 20, 2008. The billboards went on to note the restaurant's location: "Behind Shoney's."

Thanks to the free advertising, Shoney's, a competing restaurant with an established brand, saves about $1,200 per month on billboard advertising. A follow-up interview with the Shoney's manager evoked both laughter and a "no" response when asked if Shoney's paid the Super Buffet to mention Shoney's on the billboards.

June 21, 2018
Thursday
World Music Day

Objectives & reminders

______

______

______

Appointments

Early morning

8 a.m.

9 a.m.

10 a.m.

11 a.m.

Noon

1 p.m.

2 p.m.

3 p.m.

4 p.m.

5 p.m.

6 p.m.

Later evening

Summer solstice

Summer in the Northern Hemisphere begins with the arrival of the summer solstice at 6:07 a.m. EDT. That's when the sun is at its highest point in the sky – thus creating more daylight today than any other day of the year. Tomorrow is recognized as the first *full* day of summer.

For seasonal products and businesses, shifts in demand are likely to coincide with changes in the seasons. Obviously, demand for swimwear, lawn and garden equipment, air conditioners, family vacations (while children are out of school), and many outdoor sporting activities is higher in summer than in winter. For many products, however, seasonal variation in demand can be much less apparent, but real nonetheless. That's why it is useful to examine a company's or product category's historical sales records to identify seasonal peaks and valleys in demand.

The potency of seasonality

"Virtually every product in every industry in every country is seasonal… Seasonality dictates business strategy in highly seasonal businesses…" – Sonja Radas and Steven M. Shugan, in "Seasonal marketing and timing new product introductions," *Journal of Marketing Research*, 1998, Vol. 35, #3, p. 296

______

Summer appeals

As seasons change, the inclusion of seasonal images and verbiage in marketing communications can evoke positive meanings associated with the new season – associations that can transfer to the brand. Ads featuring backyard cookouts, baseball games or swimmers frolicking at the beach might evoke positive summer sentiments, as examples. Accordingly, marketers who learn how each season is special to their customers are poised to develop seasonal messages that resonate.

Summer afternoon

"Summer afternoon -- summer afternoon; to me those have always been the two most beautiful words in the English language." -- Henry James, American novelist, in *A Backward Glance*

June 22, 2018 Friday

First *full* day of summer in Northern Hemisphere

Teachers' Day (El Salvador)

Objectives & reminders

Appointments

Early morning

8 a.m.

9 a.m.

10 a.m.

11 a.m.

Noon

1 p.m.

2 p.m.

3 p.m.

4 p.m.

5 p.m.

6 p.m.

Later evening

From Servicemen's Readjustment Act to suburbia

U.S. President Franklin D. Roosevelt signed the Servicemen's Readjustment Act (also known as the "G.I. Bill") on June 22, 1944. The Act and subsequent updates enabled veterans returning from World War II to go to college or a vo-tech school, or get a low-interest government loan to buy a house, farm or to start a business.

Homecoming

More than 16.3 million Americans served in World War II, of which 405,000 died in the war. About 1.5 million remained in the military after the end of the war. The great majority of military personnel returned home, eager to resume their civilian lives.

The high number of soldiers returning home after the war, coupled with the availability of the low-interest loans drove-up demand for housing. Unfortunately, housing construction in the U.S. had slowed during the War, so available housing was in short supply. A Roper poll at the time showed that 19 percent of American families were looking for suitable housing and 19 percent were "doubled up," i.e., two or more families living together under the same roof.

So, the high housing demand spurred by the G.I. Bill and the influx of soldiers returning home after the war sparked what was probably the greatest housing boom in U.S. history. Builders like William Levitt used mass-production techniques, labor specialization, and bulk-purchasing to build inexpensive houses and partially close the supply-demand gap.

In particular, housing construction in the suburbs accelerated causing a tremendous population migration from urban centers to suburbia. From 1950 to 1960, for example, the U.S. population living in the suburbs increased dramatically – from 21 million to 37 million. Not surprisingly, the population migration led to a corresponding migration of retailers interested in serving the rapidly growing suburban markets.

Retailing migration principle

When consumers change their addresses, retailers follow.

June 23, 2018
Saturday

United Nations' Public Service Day

35 today!

Objectives & reminders

______

______

______

Appointments

Early morning

8 a.m.

9 a.m.

10 a.m.

11 a.m.

Noon

1 p.m.

2 p.m.

3 p.m.

4 p.m.

5 p.m.

6 p.m.

Later evening

The family test

"Never write an advertisement which you wouldn't want your own family to read. You wouldn't tell lies to your own wife. Don't tell them to mine." – David M. Ogilvy, founder of Hewitt, Ogilvy, Benson, & Mather International ad agency (later known as Ogilvy & Mather Worldwide), and probably the most frequently quoted advertising authority in history, born in West Horsley, England on June 23, 1911

Happy birthday: URL

The Internet's domain name system was born on June 23, 1983, thanks to the foresight and work of Paul Mockapetris, Jon Postel and Craig Partridge. Before that date, the few hundred Internet users around the world had to remember 12-digit numbers to direct their messages.

Today, the 3.7 billion Internet users throughout the world may lean on easier-to-remember domain names. This is an obvious convenience for users, and an obvious benefit for marketers who want audiences to connect with them without looking up their web addresses.

> **Memory principle**
> Letters and numbers organized in a meaningful way are easier to remember than those that appear to be arranged in a random fashion. Example: OK4U2B12 vs. O4B2U21K

Internet not solely a technological phenomenon

"The Internet is a place, an environment, made up of people and their myriad interactions. It is not merely a technology but a new way of cooperating, sharing and caring. Businesses that recognize the human aspect of the Internet will be more likely to find success in the artificial worlds of the Digital Age, for they will understand that the artificial is rooted in reality and reality is rooted in our hearts." – Vint Cerf, American computer scientist who played a key role in the creation of the Internet and the TCP/IP protocols, and thus is sometimes referred to as one of the "founding fathers of the Internet." He also co-founded the Internet Society (ISOC) in 1992. Cerf was born in New Haven, Connecticut on June 23, 1943.

June 24, 2018
Sunday
St. John's Day

Objectives & reminders

____

____

____

Appointments

Early morning

8 a.m.

9 a.m.

10 a.m.

11 a.m.

Noon

1 p.m.

2 p.m.

3 p.m.

4 p.m.

5 p.m.

6 p.m.

Later evening

Happy birthday: Ernst Heinrich Weber

Born in Wittenberg, Germany on June 24, 1795, Weber became a professor of anatomy at the University of Leipzig in 1818. There he developed a particular interest in the study of physiology. His research investigated the ability of people to distinguish between varying degrees of sensations or physical stimuli -- e.g., weight, pressure, temperature, light, sound, and so on.

In what has become known as *Weber's Law* or the law of *just noticeable differences*, Weber found that an individual's ability to detect a difference or change has more to do with the *percentage* of difference or change than with the *absolute* difference. For example, although a person handling objects may be able to tell that a ten-ounce object is heavier than an otherwise comparable nine-ounce object, the same individual may not be able to detect a difference between a 90-ounce object and one that weighs 91 ounces – even though the absolute differences are the same in both examples (i.e., one ounce). But, if the heavier objects vary by the same proportion as the lighter weights – 90 ounces versus 100 ounces – the difference between them is likely to be noticed.

Weber's Law succinctly stated

The change in stimulus required to produce a noticeable sensation is not fixed, rather it depends on the magnitude of the initial stimulus. The greater the ratio between the initial and subsequent levels of stimulus, the more likely the difference or change will be noticed.

Weber's Law has several applications in marketing – especially with regard to buyers' ability to discriminate between competing brands' attributes, such as price points or physical attributes (e.g., size, weight, color intensity). For example, whereas consumers may notice and object to a 25-cent increase in the price of a beverage, they may not notice or object to an increase of $250 in the price of an automobile – because the percentage increase in the automobile is much less than the percentage increase in the beverage.

So, marketers of higher-priced goods and services tend to enjoy a bit more pricing flexibility than those of lower-priced products.

June 25, 2018
Monday
Statehood Day (Virginia)

Objectives & reminders

___

___

___

Appointments

Early morning

8 a.m.

9 a.m.

10 a.m.

11 a.m.

Noon

1 p.m.

2 p.m.

3 p.m.

4 p.m.

5 p.m.

6 p.m.

Later evening

Half way to Christmas

Today is a key planning milestone for retailers and other businesses that rely heavily on the Christmas season. The day marks the approximate mid-point on the calendar between *last* Christmas and *next* Christmas. As the upcoming Christmas increasingly comes into focus, the need to finalize and begin implementing Christmas plans also comes into focus. Sufficient lead times for ordering and stocking merchandise, designing and placing advertising and promotional materials, hiring and training seasonal employees, and numerous other details must be incorporated into the planning process. Businesses that postpone holiday planning until the holiday season arrives are likely to find that they've waited too long.

Seasonal employment: Elves to the rescue

About 800,000 seasonal workers are hired annually in the U.S. to help businesses handle the increased demand during the Christmas season.

Relationships make the work-world go around

"Build personal relationships by making sincere connections with people and building trust with them. Strong relationships with colleagues and clients will fuel your passion and enthusiasm for your work." – Audrey Curtis Hane, communications professor at Newman University, born on June 25, 1969

Say it to communicate, not to impress

"Never use a long word where a short one will do, and never use jargon if you can think of an everyday English equivalent." – George Orwell, English novelist, born in what is now East Champaran, Bihar, India on June 25, 1903

Quest for convenience is marketing opportunity

"The most popular labor-saving device is still money." – Phyllis George-Brown, entrepreneur and former Miss America (1971), First Lady of Kentucky (1979-1983) and one of the first female sportscasters in the U.S. (1974-1985), born in Denton, Texas on June 25, 1949

June 26, 2018
Tuesday

Chocolate Pudding Day
Independence Day (Madagascar)

Objectives & reminders

______

______

______

Appointments

Early morning

8 a.m.

9 a.m.

10 a.m.

11 a.m.

Noon

1 p.m.

2 p.m.

3 p.m.

4 p.m.

5 p.m.

6 p.m.

Later evening

First of four billion!

At one minute after eight o'clock in the morning on June 26, 1974, the bar code on a pack of Wrigley's chewing gum was scanned at the Marsh Supermarket in Troy, Ohio.

Today, this sort of event is commonplace as an estimated four billion items are scanned *daily* in the U.S. and Canada. However, the pack of gum holds the distinction as being the first retail item scanned.

The point-of-sale scanning technology, coupled with the accompanying database/computers that support it, has revolutionized retailing. Scanning benefits both consumers and retailers. The technology saves time at the checkout stand (about 10%, on average) and provides customers with itemized receipts. Retailers also save time and money by not having to mark prices on individual items. Further, marketers can mine the database and quickly identify which items are selling well, which items need to be reordered, and which promotions are effective. Because this sort of information can be obtained quickly and easily, retailers can make adjustments in merchandising, promotions and prices in a timelier manner than they could prior to the introduction of scanning technology.

Being franc about technology

A computer glitch downed almost half of the automatic teller machines in France on June 26, 1993 -- leaving many consumers without francs to spend, and thus leaving many retail stores without customers. The crisis shows how technology-related problems can be problematic for both consumers and businesses. Such problems may not be entirely avoidable, but contingency plans may be developed before they occur. Does your company have back-up plans in place in case you get cut by cutting-edge technology?

Is "okay" okay?

"A temporary tolerance of mediocre performance leads to a permanent acceptance of poor performance." – John B. Fuqua, former head of Fuqua Industries ($2 billion conglomerate), born in Prince Edward County, Virginia 100 years ago today

June 27, 2018
Wednesday
Helen Keller Day

Objectives & reminders

Appointments

Early morning

8 a.m.

9 a.m.

10 a.m.

11 a.m.

Noon

1 p.m.

2 p.m.

3 p.m.

4 p.m.

5 p.m.

6 p.m.

Later evening

Happy birthday: H. Ross Perot

Born in Texarkana, Texas on June 27, 1930, Perot became widely known during his unsuccessful 1992 bid for the U.S. presidency. Prior to his brief stint in politics, however, Perot had established himself as a successful businessman.

After serving in the navy, Perot landed a sales job with IBM in 1957, then founded his own computer company in 1962, Electronic Data Systems (EDS). Twenty-two years later he sold EDS to General Motors for $2.4 billion. Since then, he has been involved in a number of business pursuits, including Perot Systems which he founded in 1988. As a businessman, Perot has a reputation for speaking his mind. He takes a direct, no-nonsense approach to business.

Business as a marathon

"Again and again, I have seen... people approach business as a hundred-yard dash. They initially had great energy, great ambition; but they poured so much energy into their efforts for a brief period of time that they were unable to produce a great sustained performance, month in and month out. Never forget that a business career is a marathon, not a sprint. You must perform consistently over a period of many years." – H. Ross Perot

---

Life and shopping as social/teamwork experiences?

"It must be obvious to those who take the time to look at human life that its greatest values lie not in getting things, but in doing them, in doing them together, in all working toward a common aim, in the experience of comradeship, of warmhearted 100 percent human life." – William Thomas Grant, founder of W.T. Grant retail stores, born in Stevensville, Pennsylvania on June 27, 1876

Grant's first store opened in 1906, "W.T. Grant Co. 25 Cent Store." By the time of his death in 1972, the chain included 1,200 stores. In 1975, after assuming too much debt (including the extension of too much credit to less-than-creditworthy customers) the firm folded, earning the dubious distinction at that time of being the largest bankruptcy in the history of retailing.

June 28, 2018
Thursday
Tau Day
$(2\pi, or\ 2\ x\ 3.14 \ldots = 6.28 \ldots)$

High demand

Peaks and valleys of seasonal demand

Low demand

Objectives & reminders

___

___

___

Appointments

Early morning

8 a.m.

9 a.m.

10 a.m.

11 a.m.

Noon

1 p.m.

2 p.m.

3 p.m.

4 p.m.

5 p.m.

6 p.m.

Later evening

Not enough snow in June

Eighteen-year-old Ralph Samuelson reasoned that if people could ski on snow, they should be able to ski on water as well. So, on June 28, 1922, he and his brother Ben attempted to ski on Lake Pepin in Lake City, Minnesota. Samuelson experimented for a few days with barrel staves and snow skis, then finally designed and shaped his own water skis from lumber and leather strips. Unfortunately, Samuelson never patented his water skis, so in 1925 someone else did -- Fred Waller.

Counter-seasonal innovation

Water skiing is a great example of how the adaptation of a product or activity can lead to business opportunities during what might otherwise be considered the "off" season. Consider how businesses have adapted other products or found alternative uses to accomplish the same counter-seasonal objective. Here are three examples:

1. Hot tea consumed during winter transformed into cold tea consumed in summer.

2. Riding lawn mowers fitted with front-end plows for snow removal during the winter.

3. Winter ski resorts transformed into campgrounds and hiking trails during the summer.

Hot idea for a cold product

A trademark patent was issued on June 28, 1887, to John Pemberton for his beverage concoction, known as Coca-Cola. Not surprisingly, it soon became apparent that consumers' preference for Coke was concentrated in the summer, not winter. Concerned about the seasonal peaks and valleys in their sales curve and interested in lifting the wintry lull sales, the company launched a campaign in the early 1920s to encourage more wintertime consumption. In one print ad, for example, snow skiers were shown gliding down a slope while holding bottles of Coca-Cola. The headline reminded readers that "Thirst knows no season." More recently, in 2006, the company tested a hot wintertime version of Coke to boost off-season sales, but the results were only lukewarm.

June 29, 2018
Friday
Veterans' Day (Netherlands)

Objectives & reminders

____

____

____

Appointments

Early morning

8 a.m.

9 a.m.

10 a.m.

11 a.m.

Noon

1 p.m.

2 p.m.

3 p.m.

4 p.m.

5 p.m.

6 p.m.

Later evening

5th Friday windfall: Something to celebrate

Today is only one of four Fridays in 2018 that is also the 5th Friday of the month. As discussed in more detail on the first 5th Friday of the year, March 30, 5th Fridays are accompanied by a small windfall for many workers paid on Fridays, i.e., their payroll deductions are generally lower when payday falls on the 5th Friday of the month. Accordingly, some retailers and other consumer marketers time marketing communications and promotions to coincide with 5th Friday weekends.

Federal-Aid Highway Act

After experiencing a number of delays and crowded roads while on a cross-country trip, U.S. President Dwight Eisenhower became an avid supporter of the Federal-Aid Highway Act which he signed on June 29, 1956. The Act paved the way for the construction of the 41,000-mile U.S. interstate system.

In hindsight, today we can see the multiple business implications of the interstate system. Because interstate travel tends to save time, consumers living near an interstate are more willing to travel farther distances to shop -- in effect expanding the geographic size of many markets. People are more willing to commute farther distances to work as well, thus spawning the growth of suburban communities and hastening the decay of many centrally-located neighborhoods. The interstates make trucking more efficient too, thereby facilitating timelier, more dependable, and less costly distribution of manufactured goods. Numerous small towns located along interstates have found the interstate traffic to provide an economic boost for the community, while many other towns bypassed by the interstate system have been negatively affected.

Consider the advantages and disadvantages of locating these businesses along an interstate: (1) Nationally-known restaurant, (2) Local restaurant, (3) Motel, (4) Manufacturing plant, (5) Convenience store with gasoline, and a (6) Movie theater.

Billboard advertising principle

Q: What are the two most powerful words included on billboard advertisements found along interstate highways?

A: "Next exit"

June 30, 2018
Saturday
International Asteroid Day

Objectives & reminders

___

___

___

Appointments

Early morning

8 a.m.

9 a.m.

10 a.m.

11 a.m.

Noon

1 p.m.

2 p.m.

3 p.m.

4 p.m.

5 p.m.

6 p.m.

Later evening

"May I have your attention please?"

The first open-air public address (PA) system was demonstrated on Staten Island, New York on June 30, 1916, by Bell Telephone. The system used large loud-speakers to reach audiences too large for human voices to reach without amplification.

Today, PA systems serve a variety of purposes. In large retail and service environments they are used to page individuals, summon assistance, and relay important safety information. Marketers use PA systems to broadcast pleasant music, announce sales events and focus customers' attention on merchandise.

The "Blue Light Special"

During its heyday, Kmart interjected some excitement into the shopping experience by promoting sale items throughout the day. Specially-priced sale items were touted on the store's PA system while push carts loaded with the items were rolled into an aisle. A pole topped with a flashing blue light rose from the carts high into the air so shoppers throughout the store could locate the sale merchandise easily.

More recently, Kmart tried to resurrect the "Blue Light Special," but a combination of shopper apathy and implementation inconsistencies killed the concept.

Profit is not a dirty word: Agree or disagree?

"To the economically illiterate, if some company makes a million dollars in profit, this means that their products cost a million dollars more than they would have without profits. It never occurs to such people that these products might cost several million dollars more... without the incentives to be efficient created by the prospect of profits." – Thomas Sowell, American economist and political analyst, born in Gastonia, North Carolina on June 30, 1930

When planning, anticipate setbacks and prepare contingency plans

"Everybody's got plans... until they get hit." – Mike Tyson, American professional boxer, born in Brooklyn, New York on June 30, 1966

July 1, 2018
Sunday
NAIDOC Week begins (Australia)

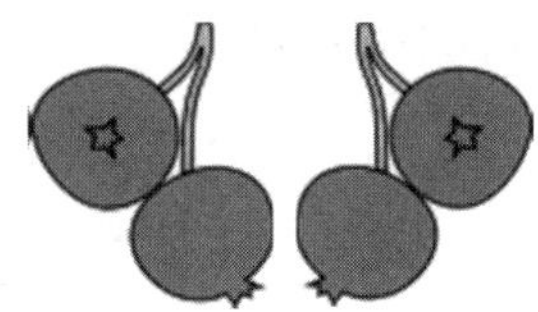

Objectives & reminders

____

____

____

Appointments

____

Early morning

____

8 a.m.

____

9 a.m.

____

10 a.m.

____

11 a.m.

____

Noon

____

1 p.m.

____

2 p.m.

____

3 p.m.

____

4 p.m.

____

5 p.m.

____

6 p.m.

____

Later evening

____

Calendar timing: Blueberries

Blueberries are at their peak during July! That's why July is Blueberry Month. What types of businesses could benefit by knowing this?

Calendar timing: Need a car?

July and August are good months to buy automobiles. That's when car dealers' sales are at lull points, so many dealers are ready to deal. January also tends to be a slow month for car dealers as consumers are still recovering from the Christmas season's financial hangover.

Bikini Atoll earns double distinction

On July 1, 1946, the U.S. detonated an atomic bomb at Bikini Atoll in the South Pacific. The bomb was recognized as the "ultimate" weapon and inspired French fashion designer Louis Réard who introduced the "ultimate" in two-piece bathing suits only four days later -- the "bikini." See the "1946" story on July 5 to learn more.

The power of involving customers in sales demonstrations

"Once you put the product in their hands, it will speak for itself." -- Estée Lauder, founder of the cosmetics company that bears her name, born on July 1, 1906, 1907, 1908, 1909 or 1910 (sources disagree)

Creative problem-solving: The fantasy approach

"Everybody has the ability to free associate, but society tends to frown on active fantasies. Beyond a certain age, we stop playing games, 'let's pretend,' 'what if,' and all that. It goes on in your head anyway, but at some point you start to feel guilty. You know, you listen to a symphony and imagine that you're the conductor, and there you are, conducting like crazy, but then you get to be a grown man, and you say, 'Gee, I'd hate for anybody to know that I'm pretending I'm conducting the symphony.' But that kind of fantasy life is the real key to problem-solving at every level." -- Sydney Pollack, American actor, director and producer, born in Lafayette, Indiana on July 1, 1934

July 2, 2018
Monday
Mother's Day (South Sudan)

Objectives & reminders

____

____

____

Appointments

Early morning

8 a.m.

9 a.m.

10 a.m.

11 a.m.

Noon

1 p.m.

2 p.m.

3 p.m.

4 p.m.

5 p.m.

6 p.m.

Later evening

Sherman Anti-Trust Act

On July 2, 1890, the U.S. Congress passed the Sherman Anti-Trust Act which discouraged unfair monopolistic business practices and outlawed trade practices that restricted competition and trade. Stemming from the philosophy that a healthy competitive environment is good for the consumer and in the long run, good for society, the intent of the Sherman Anti-Trust Act was to create a level playing field, so to speak, so that organizations could compete in a fair manner.

More specifically, the Act prohibited "every contract, combination in the form of trust or otherwise, or conspiracy, in restraint of trade or commerce among the several States." *Prior* to the Act, "competing" businesses had considerable latitude to form contracts with other businesses, e.g., to fix prices, assign customers or territorial boundaries (e.g., "I won't sell on the North side of town if you'll agree not to sell on the South side."), agree not to ship goods to certain areas, and so on. However, as the Sayre quote in the accompanying box suggests, not everyone is supportive of antitrust legislation.

Competing views on competition and monopolies: Agree or disagree?

"A monopoly is a terrible thing until you've got one." -- Rupert Murdoch, media magnate

"Without the spur of competition we'd loaf out our life." -- Arnold Glasow, American businessman, author and publisher

"The idea of imposing restrictions on a free economy to assure freedom of competition is like breaking a man's leg to make him run faster."
-- Morris R. Sayre, American industrialist

____

Discounters enter the competitive race

On July 2, 1962, Sam Walton opened what would become the first store in the Wal-Mart empire – in Rogers, Arkansas. Today, Wal-Mart is among the largest companies in the world, operating almost 12,000 stores in 28 countries. Also in 1962, the first Kmart and Target stores were opened.

July 3, 2018
Tuesday
Dog Days of summer begin

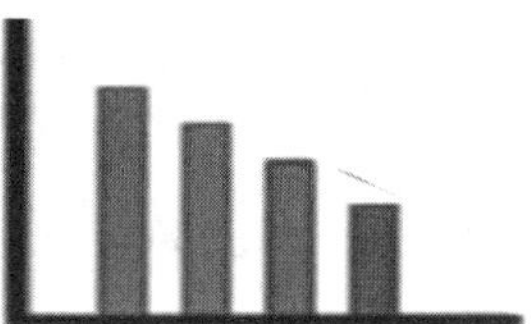

Objectives & reminders

___

___

___

Appointments

Early morning

8 a.m.

9 a.m.

10 a.m.

11 a.m.

Noon

1 p.m.

2 p.m.

3 p.m.

4 p.m.

5 p.m.

6 p.m.

Later evening

"Above-average" as both a marketing problem and opportunity

"The one thing that unites all human beings, regardless of age, gender, religion or ethnic background, is that we all believe we are above-average drivers." – David "Dave" Barry, American journalist and humorist, born in Armonk, New York on July 3, 1947

Although Barry offered this observation in jest, consider it seriously. Research (at least among college students) does somewhat confirm Barry's assertion that a disproportionate number of people do believe they are above-average drivers. But also consider other skills or traits that consumers may believe they have more of than most other people: A sense of humor? Memory? Intelligence? "Common sense"? Patriotism? Commitment to "family values"? Safety consciousness? Heath? Financial literacy? Shopping skills? And so on.

Consumers' overconfidence or inflated assessments of themselves could be problematic for marketers in several ways. For example, consider the challenge of marketing improve-your-driving-skills seminars if most people believe they already rate above average. Or, how accurate are survey responses likely to be if consumers are asked to retrieve information from memory (e.g., "When was the last time you purchased _____?") if most respondents rely only on their faulty memories that they consider to be better than average?

> **What is isn't necessarily what is**
> Buyers make purchase decisions based on what they believe, which may or may not reflect reality.

On the other hand, "above-average" beliefs may represent marketing opportunities. If everyone believes they have superior "common sense," for example, prospective buyers may be persuaded to adopt a marketer's commonsensical rationale for purchase; to do otherwise could be perceived as an admission that they really don't have common sense – an inconsistency to be avoided. Or, as another example, when marketers link their businesses, brands or promotions to personal values such as family values or patriotism, "above-average" consumers may believe the message is particularly relevant to them and thus may be more likely to respond favorably.

July 4, 2018
Wednesday
Independence Day

Objectives & reminders

____

____

____

Appointments

Early morning

8 a.m.

9 a.m.

10 a.m.

11 a.m.

Noon

1 p.m.

2 p.m.

3 p.m.

4 p.m.

5 p.m.

6 p.m.

Later evening

Independence Day

The Declaration of Independence was signed on July 4, 1776. As one of America's most important documents, the Declaration proclaimed the United States' freedom from Great Britain's rule. However, it took almost four decades for the occasion to be widely celebrated. Today, according to a recent survey of American consumers, 88 percent celebrate Independence Day.

Timely insight about teamwork

"We must all hang together, else we will all hang separately." -- Benjamin Franklin, on the signing of the Declaration of Independence

Time for a cross-cultural promotion?

Of course, the United States isn't the only country that celebrates its independence. In fact, several other countries also observe their independence during the first two weeks of July:

July 1: Burundi, Canada, Rwanda
July 5: Cape Verde Islands, Venezuela
July 9: Argentina
July 10: Bahamas
July 14: France

Celebration of independent variables?

"An experiment is taken to mean a scientific investigation in which an investigator manipulates and controls one or more independent variables and observes the dependent variable or variables for variation concomitant to the manipulation of the independent variables. An *experimental design*, then, is one in which the investigator has *direct* control over at least one independent variable and *manipulates* at least one independent variable." – Fred N. Kerlinger, *Foundations of Behavioral Research*, 1973, p. 315. Kerlinger was born in New York City on July 4, 1910.

What then is a *field* experiment?
"A field experiment is a research study in a realistic situation in which one or more independent variables are manipulated by the experimenter under as carefully controlled conditions as the situation will permit." (p. 401)

July 5, 2018
Thursday
Workaholics Day

Objectives & reminders

______

______

______

Appointments

Early morning

8 a.m.

9 a.m.

10 a.m.

11 a.m.

Noon

1 p.m.

2 p.m.

3 p.m.

4 p.m.

5 p.m.

6 p.m.

Later evening

July 5 in the marketing of sex

1878

Minna Lester was born near Louisville, Kentucky. In 1898, she opened a high-class brothel in Omaha, Nebraska with her sister, Ada. Within two years the sisters had doubled their $35,000 investment, which they used to launch another, larger, brothel in Chicago -- the Everleigh Club. Of the 600 brothels in Chicago during the early 1900s, the Everleigh Club was the most widely-recognized, most opulent, and the most expensive. Unfortunately for the Everleigh Club and its supporters, political pressure led to the brothel's closing in 1911.

Premium pricing at the Everleigh Club	
Admission	$10
Bottle of wine	$12
Dinner	$50
An evening with a "trained hostess"	$50

1920

James Tector "Jimmy" O'Brien was born in Clonroche, Co. Wexford (England). In the early 1950s he opened the Eve Club in London where scantily-clad showgirls paraded fig-leaf costumes. "Eve girls" were allowed to dance with customers or sit at their tables, but were not allowed to leave the premises with customers. A 1962 brochure for the club put it this way: "Her attractions are stunning, her talent is extraordinary and her telephone number, sir, is none of your business."

1946

French designer Louis Réard introduced the two-piece "bikini" swimsuit in Paris. Exotic dancer Micheline Bernardi modeled the fashion innovation. Although two-piece swimsuits had emerged in the 1930s, Réard's new design was much more revealing than earlier designs. He promoted his creation as "smaller than the world's smallest bathing suit." To dramatize his design and differentiate it from those of imitators, Réard advertised that a genuine bikini "could be pulled through a wedding ring." In the early 1960s the bikini became popular in the U.S. -- partially propelled into the mainstream by Brian Hyland's hit song, "Itsy Bitsy Teenie Weenie Yellow Polka-Dot Bikini."

July 6, 2018
Friday

Kupala Night (Belarus, Lithuania, Poland, Russia and Ukraine)

Objectives & reminders

____

____

____

Appointments

Early morning

8 a.m.

9 a.m.

10 a.m.

11 a.m.

Noon

1 p.m.

2 p.m.

3 p.m.

4 p.m.

5 p.m.

6 p.m.

Later evening

Breakthrough in classified advertisements

On July 6, 1882, the British newspaper, *Daily Telegraph*, became the first newspaper to use box numbers in classified ads. By asking readers to respond to a box number, the identity of the person or organization placing the ad could be kept confidential.

One benefit of using anonymous box numbers is to channel all inquiries through the box, thus discouraging personal visits, telephone calls, and other forms of contact that the advertiser might find distracting or otherwise unwelcome.

The anonymity of box numbers is beneficial in many other instances too. For example, companies trying to replace an incompetent worker could advertise for the position without divulging the fact to the incumbent (sometimes workers who know they are about to be fired do not act in the best interest of the company). More strategically, companies might use box numbers in classified ads to avoid prematurely divulging their growth or other plans to competitors.

He should have used a P.O. box number ☺

A jewelry store owner placed a classified ad in the local newspaper -- for a night watchman. Proving the effectiveness of advertising, the next night the store was robbed.

Good day to salute the U.S. Navy

John Paul Jones was born in Scotland on July 6, 1747. During the Revolutionary War, Jones distinguished himself as a naval commander and was later dubbed as "the founder of the American navy."

Faith over fear

"If fear is cultivated it will become stronger. If faith is cultivated it will achieve the mastery. We have a right to believe that faith is the stronger emotion because it is positive whereas fear is negative." -- John Paul Jones

July 7, 2018
Saturday
Satchel Day
World Chocolate Day

Objectives & reminders

___

___

___

Appointments

Early morning

8 a.m.

9 a.m.

10 a.m.

11 a.m.

Noon

1 p.m.

2 p.m.

3 p.m.

4 p.m.

5 p.m.

6 p.m.

Later evening

Each date carries multiple meanings: The case for localizing themed promotions

What is obvious from reading *Marketing FAME* is that every date has its own history. Every date commemorates something -- often several things. Worldwide or across market segments, the same date may be remembered for quite different things that evoke quite different moods, emotions and behaviors. Accordingly, when planning themed promotional events, it's useful to research what the targeted dates mean to their target markets. A joyous celebration in one market may be inappropriate elsewhere.

For example, marketers in Boston might be interested in seizing the opportunity to celebrate the anniversary of the opening of the first practical subway in the United States – an event that occurred in that city on July 7, 1897. Businesses located along the Boston subway routes might sponsor festivals and parades, promote sale events, and talk-up the city's rich history and economic development attributed to the subway – while reminding consumers of the convenience and low cost of riding the subway.

> **Take-away for calendar-led marketers**
> The knowledge of a date's history can be critical when planning marketing programs, because every date has multiple meanings. History matters.

Meanwhile, a more solemn subway observation for the date would be appropriate in London. On July 7, 2005, four bomb blasts terrorized that city's subway passengers – killing more than 50 and injuring another 700. Whereas subway-related festivals and parades in London would be tasteless on July 7, the distribution of armbands to remember the victims, fundraisers for the victims' families, and recognition ceremonies to thank the rescue workers who saved lives on that day in 2005 might be well received.

___

Satchel Day in Cleveland, Ohio

"Work like you don't need the money. Love like you've never been hurt. Dance like nobody's watching." – Leroy "Satchel" Paige, legendary American baseball pitcher, born in Mobile, Alabama on July 7, 1906, and signed by the Cleveland Indians on July 7, 1948

July 8, 2018
Sunday
Video Game Day

Objectives & reminders

Appointments

Early morning	
8 a.m.	
9 a.m.	
10 a.m.	
11 a.m.	
Noon	
1 p.m.	
2 p.m.	
3 p.m.	
4 p.m.	
5 p.m.	
6 p.m.	
Later evening	

Calendar play ✈

Boeing's new 787 Dreamliner was first rolled out for cheering dignitaries and employees to see on July 8, 2007, i.e., on 7-8-7.

Happy Birthday: John Davison Rockefeller

Rockefeller was born on July 8, 1839, in Richford, New York. He went on to make a fortune in the oil business, largely through a strategy of vertical integration against which competitors could not compete. Like other industrialists of his day, Rockefeller amassed great wealth during his career and then played the role of philanthropist later in his life and gave much of it away.

Rockefeller's business principles

Leaders bring out the best in others
"Good management consists of showing average people how to do the work of superior people." -- JDR

People skills are critical in business
"The ability to deal with people is as purchasable a commodity as sugar or coffee and I will pay more for that ability than for any other under the sun."-- JDR

Leveraged efforts produce results
"I would rather earn one percent off a 100 people's efforts than 100 percent [from] my own efforts." -- JDR

Focus, avoid distractions
"Singleness of purpose is one of the chief essentials for success in life, no matter what may be one's aim." -- JDR

Corporate responsibility has limits
"[T]he world owes no man a living but... it owes every man an opportunity to make a living." -- JDR

July 9, 2018
Monday
Constitution Day (Australia)

Objectives & reminders

____

____

____

Appointments

Early morning

8 a.m.

9 a.m.

10 a.m.

11 a.m.

Noon

1 p.m.

2 p.m.

3 p.m.

4 p.m.

5 p.m.

6 p.m.

Later evening

Commitment

"I had a veritable mania for finishing whatever I began..." -- Nikola Tesla, inventor. In 1883 he invented the first alternating current induction motor. Tesla was born in Smiljan, Croatia on July 9 or 10, 1856 (sources disagree).

Don't be duped

"Beware when any idea is promoted primarily because it is 'bold, exciting, innovative, and new.' There are many ideas that are 'bold, exciting, innovative and new,' but foolish." – Donald Rumsfeld, former Secretary of Defense and business executive, born in Chicago, Illinois on July 9, 1932

Marketers should avoid an over-reliance on price: Agree or disagree?

"There is too much emphasis on price at the expense of brand advertising and this can only lead to long-term category decline." -- Hans-Joachim Körber, chairman and CEO of Metro Group (Germany-based self-service wholesale trade company), born in Brunswick, Germany on July 9, 1946

Merchandise prizes to sales contest winners are preferable to cash prizes: Agree or disagree?

In 1938, Curtis L. Carlson earned a gold wristwatch and a $330 bonus for being the most successful soap salesperson in his Procter & Gamble territory. Later, Carlson reflected on the awards: "It was the watch that by far meant the most to me. It was the watch, also, that taught me something about the value of prizes as awards in incentive programs. Because long after the bonus money was spent and forgotten, that watch would signify my accomplishment."

Soon after winning the watch and bonus, Carlson went on to found his own group of companies, beginning with the Gold Bond Stamp Company. By the time of Carlson's death in 1999, Carlson Companies' annual revenues exceeded $22 billion. Mr. Carlson was born in Minneapolis, Minnesota on July 9, 1914.

July 10, 2018
Tuesday
Statehood Day (Wyoming)

Objectives & reminders

____

____

____

Appointments

Early morning

8 a.m.

9 a.m.

10 a.m.

11 a.m.

Noon

1 p.m.

2 p.m.

3 p.m.

4 p.m.

5 p.m.

6 p.m.

Later evening

Bull marketing

An advertising "first" occurred on July 10, 1842, when a full-page illustrated newspaper ad appeared in the *Courier* and *West End Advertiser*. The brand was British Cornflour and the illustration was a large bull's head. As a precursor of display advertising it would be about six more decades before this form of newspaper advertising would catch on.

Cow marketing

"The person with real influence on the success of a product today gets to sit at the table when the original seeds for a project are being sown. If you are a marketer who doesn't know how to invent, design, influence, adapt, and ultimately discard products, then you're no longer a marketer. You're deadwood."
-- Seth Godin, marketing analyst and author of *Purple Cow* (p. 98), born in Mount Vernon, New York on July 10, 1960

Vestus verum reddit?
(Latin for "clothes make the man?")

"Clothes and manners do not make the man; but when he is made, they greatly improve his appearance."
-- Arthur Ashe, pro tennis star of the 1960s and 1970s, born in Richmond, Virginia on July 10, 1943

Another fashion perspective 
"Clothes make the man. Naked people have little or no influence on society." -- Mark Twain, humorist

Product research jobs that stink?

On July 10, 1974, *Fortune* magazine reported some of the bizarre ways Procter & Gamble tested the interactions between people and products. For example, users of toothpastes and mouthwashes would breathe through a hole in a wall. On the other side of the wall researchers would smell and rate the odors. P&G also employed "professional armpit sniffers" to rate the effectiveness of deodorants.

Media marketing?

"The one function that TV news performs very well is that when there is no news we give it to you with the same emphasis as if it were." -- David Brinkley, former television journalist, born in Wilmington, North Carolina on July 10, 1920

July 11, 2018
Wednesday

Free Slurpee Day

(at participating 7-Eleven convenience stores in Canada and U.S.)

Objectives & reminders

Appointments

Early morning

8 a.m.

9 a.m.

10 a.m.

11 a.m.

Noon

1 p.m.

2 p.m.

3 p.m.

4 p.m.

5 p.m.

6 p.m.

Later evening

Customers are not stupid

"In writing advertising it must always be kept in mind that the customer often knows more about the goods than the advertising writers because they have had experience in buying them..." -- John Wanamaker, founder of Wanamaker's (one of the first department stores in the U.S.) and avid advertiser, born in Philadelphia, Pennsylvania on July 11, 1838

The winds of publicity

"There are always protests, whether you do something good or bad. Even if you do something beneficial, people say you do it because it's advertising."
-- Giorgio Armani, Italian fashion designer, born in Piacenza, Italy on July 11, 1934

Managing the product mix: You can't be all things to all people, but increasingly you can be more things to more people

"Every retailer has its own economic threshold, but they all cut off what they carry somewhere. Things that are likely to sell if the necessary number get carried; things that aren't, don't. In our hit-driven culture, people get ahead by focusing obsessively on the left side of the curve and trying to guess what will make it there." – Chris Anderson, on page 20 in his book, *The Long Tail: Why the Future of Business is Selling Less of More*, published on July 11, 2006

In *The Long Tail*, Anderson argues that the traditional hit-driven business mentality is changing because online retailing and improved distribution enable more businesses to profitably reach and serve market niches that have unique needs and product preferences.

Today, thanks to technology and being spurred by increasingly intense competition, niche markets are easier and more economical to reach and serve than ever before. Accordingly, the size of the critical mass of prospective buyers required to justify a marketing program is becoming smaller. So, rather than being overly obsessed with the mass market, more businesses are finding numerous opportunities in "the long tail" of prospective buyers that is beginning to wag the mass market.

July 12, 2018
Thursday
National Simplicity Day

Objectives & reminders

____

____

____

Appointments

Early morning

8 a.m.

9 a.m.

10 a.m.

11 a.m.

Noon

1 p.m.

2 p.m.

3 p.m.

4 p.m.

5 p.m.

6 p.m.

Later evening

New retail concept emerges

One of the first warehouse "club" stores was opened in San Diego, California by Sol Price on July 12, 1976 – Price Club. The members-only store featured a "no frills" shopping environment and discounted prices. In 1993, Price Club merged with rival Costco to become PriceCostco, and later Costco Companies.

Today, there are several warehouse club stores throughout the U.S. other than Costco – most notably Sam's Club, a division of Wal-Mart. By packaging in bulk quantities, the club stores discourage low-volume purchasers. In contrast to discount retailers, the club stores also focus on a more narrow range of merchandise – usually fast-moving items. Whereas a typical Wal-Mart store might carry 70,000 items, a nearby Sam's Club store might have only 3,500 to 4,000 items. By appealing to bulk purchasers (often small businesses), carrying a narrow range of fast-moving merchandise, and not offering too many extra services or expensive shopping facilities, the club stores are able to keep prices low.

Convenience appeal for the non-technical market

"You press the button; we do the rest." – early slogan for the Eastman Kodak Company. Roll-film photography was pioneered by the founder of Kodak, George Eastman, who was born in Waterville, New York on July 12, 1854. By making photography easy for amateur photographers, Eastman and Kodak greatly expanded the market for cameras and film.

> **Why Eastman chose "Kodak"**
> "[A] trademark should be short, vigorous; incapable of being misspelled... It must mean nothing. If the name has no dictionary definition, it must be associated only with your product." – George Eastman

---

Bias for action

"How often I found where I should be going only by setting out for somewhere else." – Richard Buckminster Fuller, American inventor (who specialized in architectural design) and philosopher, born in Milton, Massachusetts on July 12, 1895

July 13, 2018
Friday
Statehood Day (Montenegro)

Objectives & reminders

____

____

____

Appointments

Early morning

8 a.m.

9 a.m.

10 a.m.

11 a.m.

Noon

1 p.m.

2 p.m.

3 p.m.

4 p.m.

5 p.m.

6 p.m.

Later evening

Hooked on Krispy Kreme

Vernon Rudolph, Krispy Kreme founder, borrowed ingredients from a local grocer to cook his first batch of Krispy Kreme doughnuts in Winston-Salem, North Carolina on July 13, 1937. Retail customers paid a nickel (five cents) for a single doughnut, but received a deep discount for buying in quantity -- only 25 cents for a dozen.

Vernon Rudolph's quantity discount wisdom

Although quantity discounts are not uncommon, some consider Rudolph's quantity discount too extreme. Early retail customers buying a dozen doughnuts received more than a 58 percent discount, compared to the price of 12 individually-purchased doughnuts.

Perhaps a smaller discount would have prompted just as many customers to opt for a dozen, but consider the wisdom of Rudolph's deep discount pricing strategy. Because doughnuts are perishable, it is doubtful that quantity purchasers were able to stock up, and not many people have an appetite for a dozen doughnuts in a single day. Consequently, quantity purchasers found themselves sharing their boxes of doughnuts with their friends, families and co-workers which helped spread word-of-mouth communications at a much faster rate than would have occurred otherwise -- a vital ingredient in the company's success.

The sluggish rate that positive word-of-mouth spreads is one reason contributing to the failure of many new businesses with quality products -- even today. So, rather than taking a passive approach to word-of-mouth and assuming it will automatically materialize, marketers should think proactively in terms of what they can do to accelerate the spread of word-of-mouth.

Sixty-five years later, on July 13, 2002, Krispy Kreme celebrated its founding and successful history by setting a Guinness World Record for the largest doughnut cake. The doughnut weighed 2,413 pounds.

July 14, 2018
Saturday
Bastille Day (France)

Objectives & reminders

____

____

____

Appointments

Early morning

8 a.m.

9 a.m.

10 a.m.

11 a.m.

Noon

1 p.m.

2 p.m.

3 p.m.

4 p.m.

5 p.m.

6 p.m.

Later evening

Inflation worries

On July 14, 1974, the results of a Gallup poll of 1,509 American consumers were released. Forty-eight percent of those surveyed claimed that the high cost of living was the country's biggest problem. No other problem issue in the survey came close to the level of concern for inflation. A disproportionately high number of middle-income consumers expressed a concern about the inflation problem.

Many consumers in the inflation-plagued 1970s learned to shop for value – and today they continue to emphasize value as a primary purchase criterion. One popular value proposition that proliferated during the 1970s was that of self-service. By allowing customers to provide a portion of the labor (e.g., pumping their own gasoline), businesses were able to lower their costs, limit price increases and attract value-conscious customers.

Is inflation still relevant today?
Although the rate of inflation in the U.S. has been low in recent years, the inflation woes of the 1970s could return someday. Also, inflation continues to be problematic in many countries around the world. Finally, the rate of inflation tends to be greater in some industries and product categories than in others (e.g., health care).

Inflation appeals
What should marketers say to customers during periods of high inflation? Consider these three possibilities:

1. *The future is uncertain:* "If you go ahead and sign the paperwork today, we can lock-in your order at today's prices. I can't guarantee these prices tomorrow."

2. *Do-it-yourself:* "We offer discounts to customers who pick-up and deliver the merchandise themselves, assemble it, install it, and service it."

3. *You deserve it! (when directly asked about recent price hikes):* "Yes, we did have to raise our prices to make sure we would be able to continue to provide you with the high level of quality and service that you deserve."

July 15, 2018
Sunday

Democracy and National Unity Day (Turkey)

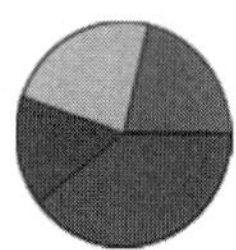

Objectives & reminders

______

______

______

Appointments

______

Early morning

______

8 a.m.

______

9 a.m.

______

10 a.m.

______

11 a.m.

______

Noon

______

1 p.m.

______

2 p.m.

______

3 p.m.

______

4 p.m.

______

5 p.m.

______

6 p.m.

______

Later evening

______

Happy birthday: Darrell Huff

Born in Gowrie, Iowa on July 15, 1913, Huff worked as a journalist and editor early in his career – for local newspapers in Iowa and for magazines such as *Look, Better Homes and Gardens* and *Liberty*. Soon after World War II, Huff focused on a career as a freelance writer, churning out hundreds of "how to" articles and at least 16 books. Six or more of his books dealt with quantitative literacy, including *How to Take a Chance* (1959), *Score: The Strategy of Taking Tests* (1961), *How to Figure the Odds on Everything* (1972), and the best-selling statistics book for which he is most remembered, *How to Lie with Statistics* (1954).

Statisticulation

"Misinforming people by the use of statistical material might be called statistical manipulation; in a word (though not a very good one), statisticulation." – Darrell Huff, *How to Lie with Statistics* (p. 100)

To date, *How to Lie with Statistics* has sold more copies than any other statistics book in history – more than 500,000 copies of the English edition alone. Interestingly, despite the accuracy, insightfulness and timeless relevance of the book, Huff had no formal training in statistics – which may be why the book is so easily read and understood by laymen who also lack statistical training. Although the book's title implies that readers could use the contents to deceive others, its greater value lies in its use as a series of alerts to prevent readers from being misled (intentionally or not) by biased, abusive, unaware or careless statisticians or users of statistics.

One phenomenon, many statistical faces

"There are often many ways of expressing any figure. You can, for instance, express exactly the same fact by calling it a one percent return on sales, a fifteen percent return on investment, a ten-million-dollar profit, an increase in profits of forty percent [compared with a recent five-year average], or a decrease of sixty percent from last year."
– Darrell Huff, *How to Lie with Statistics* (p. 82)

July 16, 2018
Monday

Holocaust Memorial Day (France)

Objectives & reminders

___

___

___

Appointments

Early morning

8 a.m.

9 a.m.

10 a.m.

11 a.m.

Noon

1 p.m.

2 p.m.

3 p.m.

4 p.m.

5 p.m.

6 p.m.

Later evening

Happy birthday: Dan Brinklin

Born in Philadelphia, Pennsylvania on July 16, 1951, Brinklin is credited with co-developing (along with Bob Frankston) the first major business application for the personal computer – the VisiCalc spreadsheet, introduced in 1979.

The market for electronic spreadsheets began to grow rapidly within months of Brinklin and Frankston's innovation, although a competing spreadsheet developed soon afterward by Mitch Kapor – Lotus 1-2-3 – emerged as the category leader for the next several years.

By 1989, Microsoft's spreadsheet software – Excel – had become one of that company's flagship products.

Marketing and spreadsheets

Accountants and decision-makers use spreadsheets to organize and analyze data in multiple dimensions. For example, calendar-led marketers develop spreadsheets to examine sales for customers over time, with each *row* in the spreadsheet representing a unique customer and each *column* representing a unique time period, such as a month.

By recording each customer's monthly sales in the intersecting *cells*, marketers can track sales trends per month, per customer, or both. Total month-to-month sales may be increasing, but declining sales for individual customers may be indicative of customer-specific problems to be investigated and addressed. Tracking only total sales without the help of a spreadsheet may mask potentially important data trends or patterns of interest to marketers.

___

Don't put the cart before the horse: Agree or disagree?

"Good service in the public interest must precede any calls for public support." – Ivy L. Lee, co-founder of one of the first public relations firms in the U.S. (in 1904) and considered by many to be the founder of modern public relations. Lee was born in Cedartown, Georgia on July 16, 1877.

July 17, 2018
Tuesday

Constitution Day (South Korea)

Objectives & reminders

Appointments

Early morning

8 a.m.

9 a.m.

10 a.m.

11 a.m.

Noon

1 p.m.

2 p.m.

3 p.m.

4 p.m.

5 p.m.

6 p.m.

Later evening

Happy birthday: Warren Weaver

Born in Reedsberg, Wisconsin on July 17, 1894, Weaver spent a great deal of his career studying communication processes. In his seminal book co-authored with C.E. Shannon, *The Mathematical Theory of Communication* (1949), Weaver outlined three key categories of communication concerns that should be of interest to businesspeople whose success depends on their ability to communicate with others:

1. Technical issues: To what extent do communications survive the transmission without being disrupted, delayed, or mutated?

2. Semantic issues: To what extent do recipients of communications understand the messages? Is their understanding the same as that intended by the sender?

3. Impact or effectiveness issues: To what extent do communications impact recipients? That is, will the messages change the audience's behavior or lead the audience to act in the same way the sender intended? For example, will recipients remember the message? Will they follow the instructions included in the message?

Marketing miscommunications

Classify the following communication mishaps according to the three categories identified by Weaver. Then consider how they might be prevented or otherwise addressed:

- An advertisement asks buyers to visit the company's website for more information, but some prospective buyers don't have Internet access.

- A sales rep tries to contact a prospect by telephone, but the prospect's assistant intercepts the call. The assistant promises to relay the message to the prospect, but important details are omitted when only a brief summary of the message is relayed to the prospect.

- A retail store advertises a "Fortnight Sale," but several customers ignore it because they don't know what a fortnight is or conclude that they have no need for any fortnights.

July 18, 2018
Wednesday
Nelson Mandela International Day

Objectives & reminders

____

____

____

Appointments

Early morning

8 a.m.

9 a.m.

10 a.m.

11 a.m.

Noon

1 p.m.

2 p.m.

3 p.m.

4 p.m.

5 p.m.

6 p.m.

Later evening

The 1948 vision of shopping centers

"It is our belief that there is much need for actual shopping centers – market places that are also centers of community and cultural activity. We are convinced that the real shopping center will be the most profitable type of chain store location yet developed for the simple reason it will include features to induce people to drive considerable distances to enjoy its advantages." – Victor Gruen, commercial architect who is sometimes described as the "father of the modern American shopping mall," born in Vienna, Austria on July 18, 1903 (moved to the U.S. in 1938)

In a review of Gruen's biography, *Mall Maker* (2003), Richard Longstreth described Gruen as one of the first American architects "to immerse himself in the intricacies of retailing and then seek dramatically new environments to improve the retail business."

We know when and where you were born: Hunter S. Thompson

Born in Louisville, Kentucky on July 18, 1937, Thompson was a gonzo journalist known for his anti-establishment views and unorthodox ways of doing things. For several years, he served as the editor of the publication *Rolling Stone.*

While *Rolling Stone* editor, Thompson used an unusual letter to encourage subscribers to renew their subscriptions. He combined threats with a self-serving sympathy appeal. He begged for renewals, pointing out that the publication was his only source of income; he implied that he would lose his job if recipients of the letter didn't renew. Further, Thompson demanded a response to his letter, "or else." A handwritten blurb on the outside of the envelope reinforced the threat: "I KNOW WHERE YOU LIVE."

In response, a high percentage of *Rolling Stone* subscribers did renew their subscriptions – prompting the publication to include similar appeals with future renewal notices.

Education matters

"A good head and good heart are always a formidable combination. But when you add to that a literate tongue or pen, then you have something very special." – Nelson Mandela, first President of South Africa (1994-1999), born 100 years ago today, in Mvezo, South Africa on July 18, 1918

July 19, 2018
Thursday
Martyrs' Day (Myanmar/Burma)

Objectives & reminders

______

______

Appointments

Early morning

8 a.m.

9 a.m.

10 a.m.

11 a.m.

Noon

1 p.m.

2 p.m.

3 p.m.

4 p.m.

5 p.m.

6 p.m.

Later evening

Help Wanted

John Houghton's publication, *Collection for the Improvement of Husbandry and Trade,* ran the first known matrimonial advertisement on July 19, 1695:

> "A Gentleman about 30 years of age, that says he has a very good estate, would willingly match himself to some young Gentlewoman that has a fortune of £3,000 or thereabouts..."

For several years that followed, society permitted only males to advertise for prospective spouses. When Helen Morison tried to use the same advertising approach to attract a husband in 1727, she was committed to "a lunatic asylum."

Pet projects for marketers to bark about: Agree or disagree?

Canadian Wesley McLellan designed a waterbed for pets in 1994. His pet project was patented on July 19 of that year. Recognizing that many people consider their pets as members of the family, McLellan, like other inventors of pet products, took what was originally a human concept and adapted it for pets.

Other examples include clothing for pets, multi-room dog houses, HMOs for pets, gourmet food for pets, day care centers for pets, and snack shops for pets.

What other products traditionally thought to be for humans also could be adapted for the pet market?

Starbucks' more about people than coffee: Agree or disagree?

"We believed very early on that people's interaction with the Starbucks experience was going to determine the success of the brand. The culture and values of how we related to our customers, which is reflected in how the company relates to our [work force], would determine our success. And we thought the best way to have those kinds of universal values was to build... company-owned stores and then to provide stock options to every employee, to give them a financial and psychological stake in the company. We thought the best way to get to those values would be to have all the employees working for us. [Consequently], Starbucks has the lowest employee turnover of any food and beverage company." – Howard Schultz, Executive Chairman for Starbucks Coffee Company, born in Brooklyn, New York on July 19, 1953

July 20, 2018
Friday
International Chess Day

Objectives & reminders

___

___

___

Appointments

Early morning

8 a.m.

9 a.m.

10 a.m.

11 a.m.

Noon

1 p.m.

2 p.m.

3 p.m.

4 p.m.

5 p.m.

6 p.m.

Later evening

Early infomercial?

Strictly speaking, infomercials didn't appear in the U.S. until the mid-1980s when the Federal Communications Commission (FCC) discarded previous rules that limited the time television stations devoted to commercials.

However, long before infomercials arrived in the form we know today, there was *The Arthur Murray Party* -- a variety show that premiered on July 20, 1950. The show merged dance lessons with guest performances and talk-show-type conversations with hostess Kathryn Murray. The show entertained audiences for ten years, but while doing so, it also promoted the chain of successful dance studios built by Arthur and Kathryn Murray.

Since then, the infomercial-like influence of television has been apparent. Spinach sales soared in the 1950s and 1960s largely because Popeye ate so much of it on television. Similarly, cruise ships' bookings jumped in the 1970s when *The Love Boat* romanticized cruise vacations. And for more than five decades, animated television programming for children has served as a merchandising springboard for dolls, action figures, food products, clothing and other items that resemble or are endorsed by the characters children idolize.

Synergistic effect: Agree or disagree? Television works. Advertising works. When television programming becomes advertising, both work overtime.

___

Flexible planning: Adapting to teammates' suggestions

"There are a lot of very successful explorers who choose their plan and their path and stick to it very closely indeed, following it very methodically through. This... wasn't my attitude. The main objective remained, but there were always a multitude of alternatives of how you achieve these objectives. So if someone came up with a good idea, I was perfectly prepared to accept it... [I]f the circumstances seemed suitable [I would] change a complete plan, to go in a different direction or use a different method." – Sir Edmund Hillary, New Zealand mountaineer who, along with Tenzing Norgay, first reached the summit of the world's highest peak -- Mount Everest -- on May 29, 1953. Hillary was born in Auckland, New Zealand on July 20, 1919.

July 21, 2018
Saturday
Racial Harmony Day (Singapore)

Objectives & reminders

____

____

____

Appointments

Early morning

8 a.m.

9 a.m.

10 a.m.

11 a.m.

Noon

1 p.m.

2 p.m.

3 p.m.

4 p.m.

5 p.m.

6 p.m.

Later evening

Homicide by robot: "Unanticipated consequence"

On July 21, 1984, Harry Allen, a diecast operator in Jackson, Michigan was accidentally crushed by a robot. Five days later, Allen died.

This tragic event points out the reality that so-called advanced technologies are sometimes (often?) accompanied by what sociologist Robert Merton called "unanticipated consequences." Numerous examples abound, although perhaps less tragic than the robot homicide example above:

1. The convenience of email means co-workers can communicate with each other with little or no face-to-face contact -- potentially jeopardizing the personal connections that satisfy workers' social needs and contribute to a sense of teamwork.

2. Many of today's golf club manufacturers have engineered clubs to help less skilled golfers hit golf balls much farther and straighter than yesterday's clubs -- potentially diminishing the challenge for skilled golfers and rendering some golf courses "too easy."

3. Computerized registration systems enable hotel clerks to capture and find relevant information when checking-in guests -- but guests may feel neglected when clerks seem to pay closer attention to computer monitors than to the guests themselves.

When developing new technologies or considering their adoption, it's useful to consider the effect of the technology on people and how people will react to the "advances." That is, how will the technologies affect patterns of human behavior and interpersonal communication? Can measures be taken to capitalize on the promised benefits of the technology without suffering from the potentially less desirable human consequences? And, as the example of the robot homicide reminds us, how safe is the technology?

Technology framework

"It is the framework which changes with each new technology and not just the picture within the frame." – Marshall McLuhan, researcher and writer, born in Edmonton, Alberta, Canada on July 21, 1911

July 22, 2018
Sunday
Parents' Day

Objectives & reminders

Appointments

Early morning

8 a.m.

9 a.m.

10 a.m.

11 a.m.

Noon

1 p.m.

2 p.m.

3 p.m.

4 p.m.

5 p.m.

6 p.m.

Later evening

Parents' Day salute to parents

"The guidance and unconditional love of parents help create a nurturing environment so children can grow and reach their full potential. Parents work to impart to their children the strength and determination to follow their dreams and the courage to do what is right. They shape the character of their children by sharing their wisdom and setting a positive example. As role models, parents also instill the values and principles that help prepare children to be responsible adults and good citizens." – U.S. President George W. Bush (2001-2009)

Happy birthday: Amy Vanderbilt

In the U.S., Amy Vanderbilt became known as an authority on matters of etiquette. However, since she was born in Staten Island, New York on July 22, 1908, many rules of etiquette have come and gone, such as women not riding bicycles except "side-saddle" and never riding alone.

Other manner matters have been relaxed somewhat, but not equally so by all generations – a point that customer-contact personnel should keep in mind when interacting with customers from different generations.

For example, a 1990 study of bowling center customers found that most seniors appreciated and expected to be thanked when making a purchase. Further, seniors tended to notice and were negatively impressed when they were not thanked. For younger consumers, however, the study found that hearing a "thank you" tended to be less of an expectation, although a significant portion of younger consumers still appreciated being thanked. For more information about the study, see "The Employee/Customer Interface: An Empirical Investigation of Employee Behaviors and Customer Perceptions," *Journal of Sport Management*, (1990), volume 4, #1, pp. 1-20.

Planning insight
"We must learn which ceremonies may be breached occasionally at our convenience and which ones may never be if we are to live pleasantly with our fellow man."
– Amy Vanderbilt

Interpersonal skills insight
"Good manners have much to do with the emotions. To make them ring true, one must feel them, not merely exhibit them."
– Amy Vanderbilt

July 23, 2018
Monday
Revolution Day (Egypt)

Objectives & reminders

____

____

____

Appointments

Early morning

8 a.m.

9 a.m.

10 a.m.

11 a.m.

Noon

1 p.m.

2 p.m.

3 p.m.

4 p.m.

5 p.m.

6 p.m.

Later evening

Lion's share of market?

People born during the month beginning on July 23 fall under the Leo – "The Lion" – zodiac sign. Presumably, Leos are proud yet stubborn, extroverted yet vain, courageous, optimistic, and open to change. Astrologers also claim that Leos often demonstrate leadership qualities.

> **Daily horoscopes can affect buyer behavior even if astrology doesn't: Agree or disagree?**
> Be cautious of strangers today. They may be persuasive but their best interests may be at odds with your best interests.

Happy birthday: Samuel A. Maverick

Born in Pendleton, South Carolina on July 23, 1803, Maverick was a land investor and lawyer who moved to Texas in the 1830s. There, from the late 1830s to the mid-1860s he served in various government roles – as a state legislator, congressman, mayor of San Antonio, and other offices. Maverick County, in southwest Texas, is named after him.

Maverick's contribution to marketing has to do with branding, sort of. It seems that while living in Texas in 1847, Maverick reluctantly accepted a herd of 400 cattle to settle a debt. However, Maverick wasn't personally interested in caring for the animals so he delegated the task to others. Unfortunately, the caretakers neglected their responsibilities and the cattle began to roam throughout the area. New calves were born but were not branded. Soon neighbors assumed that unbranded cattle more than a year old were *Maverick's* cattle. Over time the reference to generic, unbranded cattle became generic as well; i.e., they became known as *mavericks*.

> **Brand names**
> Despite Samuel Maverick's reluctance to brand his cattle, his ten children were not generic "children." Each child was given his or her own name.

Today, the term *maverick*s has an even more generic meaning; it refers to nonconformists who go their own way and refuse to act as part of the group or "herd" -- people whose ideas and practices defy "branding." Business leaders who successfully work with mavericks know not to "fence" them in with too many rigid rules and procedures.

July 24, 2018
Tuesday
Pioneer Day (Utah)

Objectives & reminders

Appointments

Early morning

8 a.m.

9 a.m.

10 a.m.

11 a.m.

Noon

1 p.m.

2 p.m.

3 p.m.

4 p.m.

5 p.m.

6 p.m.

Later evening

First public opinion poll

532 electors were polled regarding the U.S. Presidential election of 1824. On July 24 of that year, the results were published in the Harrisburg *Pennsylvanian* and the Raleigh *Star* indicating a clear lead for Andrew Jackson over his political rivals, including John Quincy Adams.

When the actual election was held, Jackson did receive more votes than his opponents, but not a majority, so the House of Representatives decided the outcome. In the House, Adams won -- not Jackson. Jackson bounced back, however, and defeated Adams in the 1828 election.

Today, opinion polls or surveys are used extensively by political organizations and businesses alike to gauge public sentiment.

Although useful, caution must be exercised when interpreting the results. The 1824 poll accurately predicted that Jackson would receive more votes than Adams, but it did not and could not predict the persuasive debate and political arm-twisting in the House of Representatives that would sway the election in Adams' favor.

In a similar fashion, surveyed consumers might express an overwhelming preference for one brand over competing brands, but that doesn't mean the winning brand is destined to be purchased most frequently. Companies producing competing brands may have more clout in securing distribution, they may price and promote more aggressively, or they may offer a money-back guarantee or more convenient packaging – among many factors that could sway the "election" in the marketplace.

Tip for reporting survey findings: Use words like "said," "claimed," and "expressed"

Gaps between what buyers *say* when surveyed and what *actually happens* in the marketplace means that marketing researchers must be careful when reporting the results of surveys.

For example, it may be that "63% of the respondents expressed a purchase preference for Acme Ace brand," but that doesn't necessarily mean that "63% of the respondents would purchase Acme Ace brand."

July 25, 2018 Wednesday

Republic Day (Tunisia)

Objectives & reminders

Appointments

Early morning

8 a.m.

9 a.m.

10 a.m.

11 a.m.

Noon

1 p.m.

2 p.m.

3 p.m.

4 p.m.

5 p.m.

6 p.m.

Later evening

Fall River was for children too

Labor conditions for mill workers in Fall River, Massachusetts were poor in the late 1800s and early 1900s – prompting about 25,000 workers to begin a strike on July 25, 1904, that lasted for several weeks. The protesters did not accomplish all of their goals, but they did manage to attract the attention of the nation – especially with regard to the long hours and tough conditions faced by the many children who worked at the mills. The public interest led to the formation of the National Child Labor Committee a few months later, which led to child labor reforms.

Child labor: Did you know?
In 1900, about the time of the Fall River strike, an estimated 250,000 children worked in U.S. factories, mills and mines – children who had not yet reached their 16th birthday.

Market research tool patented

On July 25, 1995, Harvard Business School marketing scholar Gerald Zaltman received one of the first U.S. patents ever granted for a market research tool – the Zaltman Metaphor Elicitation Technique (ZMET). The technique recognizes the shortcomings of traditional marketing research methods such as surveys; i.e., because most thoughts occur at the unconscious level, consumers are usually not able to articulate why they buy one brand instead of a competing brand or otherwise why they behave in the marketplace as they do.

So, the ZMET technique probes consumers' minds to understand the deep metaphors used to guide their orientation to life, in general, and to the marketplace, in particular. Marketers can enhance the effectiveness of marketing efforts -- including communications -- by understanding consumers' metaphors. Learn more by reading Zaltman's 2008 book, *Marketing Metaphoria.*

What drives consumers' purchase decisions?
"Consumer preferences and motivation are far less influenced by the functional attributes of products and services than the subconscious sensory and emotional elements derived by the total experience."
– Professor Gerald Zaltman

July 26, 2018
Thursday

Day of National Significance (Barbados)

Objectives & reminders

Appointments

Early morning

8 a.m.

9 a.m.

10 a.m.

11 a.m.

Noon

1 p.m.

2 p.m.

3 p.m.

4 p.m.

5 p.m.

6 p.m.

Later evening

Americans with Disabilities Act (ADA)

U.S. President George H.W. Bush signed the ADA on July 26, 1990. The Act went into effect exactly two years later, on July 26, 1992.

The ADA was developed to prohibit employers from discriminating against disabled employees and job applicants who are qualified to perform job duties if reasonable accommodations can be made for them. A wide range of physical and mental disabilities exist that should not be used as automatic applicant "knock-out" factors. So, employers should refrain from asking job applicants about past or current medical conditions. Similarly, applicants should not be asked to take a medical exam before job offers are made. And, of course, work environments should be free of extensive material barriers that might restrict the passage of physically disabled workers.

Several ADA provisions are marketing-relevant too – especially regarding the design of physical facilities. New or renovated businesses that customers normally would be expected to visit (e.g., retail stores, restaurants, hotels) should not prevent physically disabled patrons from entering and using the business space. For example, ramps or elevators should be available for customers in wheel chairs.

To learn more

For more information about the ADA and related matters – including marketing implications – see the informative article by Stacy Menzel Baker and Carol Kaufman-Scarborough, "Marketing and Public Accommodation: A Retrospective on the Americans with Disabilities Act," in volume 20 (Fall 2001) of the *Journal of Public Policy & Marketing*, pp. 297-304.

Gender stereotypes as disabilities?

"I hate the idea that women are more nurturing than men. That makes women nurse-mommy to the company. It's a trap.... It sounds like nurse-mommy is coming to run the company, and I don't want the bravery and the natural leadership of women to be obscured by that kind of analysis." – Charlotte Beers, former president of Ogilvy & Mather Worldwide (advertising agency) and former chair of J. Walter Thompson (ad agency), once dubbed as "the most powerful woman in advertising," born in Beaumont, Texas on July 26, 1935

July 27, 2018
Friday

National Korean War Veterans Armistice Day (U.S.)

Objectives & reminders

____

____

____

Appointments

Early morning

8 a.m.

9 a.m.

10 a.m.

11 a.m.

Noon

1 p.m.

2 p.m.

3 p.m.

4 p.m.

5 p.m.

6 p.m.

Later evening

Consumers and food marketers warned

On July 27, 1988, the top health official in the U.S. – Surgeon General C. Everett Koop – released the most comprehensive report regarding nutrition and health ever issued by the U.S. government. Among other conclusions, the report asserted that fat was a leading cause of disease; eating too much fat leads to a number of major health problems.

The report caught the media's and the public's attention, which prompted more Americans to at least notice their fat intake, if not reduce it. In response, food producers began searching for ways to reduce the fat content of their products. And, not surprisingly, producers of low-fat items began promoting their brands' health benefits.

Zany Americans, zany marketers?

"Americans are zany about food and diet. No other country gorges itself on junk food the way we do, and no other country has as many 'experts' on health diets. We have become more concerned about what we should not eat than what we should." – C. Everett Koop

Your opinion please: Do health appeals face "up-hill battle" for marketers?

1. Are consumers more likely to be interested in low-fat food items to improve or maintain their *health*, or to improve or maintain their *appearance*?

2. To what extent is *taste* a more salient attribute for consumers than low-fat, *health-related* appeals?

3. Suppose 100 consumers were to learn that their favorite brand of cookies now contains *half* as much fat as the same brand did last week (but the taste is the same). How many would interpret the information to mean that now they can eat *twice* as many cookies as they did previously without increasing their fat intake?

July 28, 2018
Saturday
World Hepatitis Day

Objectives & reminders

____

____

____

Appointments

Early morning

8 a.m.

9 a.m.

10 a.m.

11 a.m.

Noon

1 p.m.

2 p.m.

3 p.m.

4 p.m.

5 p.m.

6 p.m.

Later evening

Happy birthday: Karl Raimund Popper

Born in Vienna, Austria on July 28, 1902, Popper became a British citizen in 1945. He was a thought leader in the philosophy of science and offered a number of insights as to how researchers should approach their work. Two of his influential books along these lines were *The Logic of Scientific Discovery* (1959, 1968), and *Objective Knowledge: An Evolutionary Approach* (1972, 1974).

Insight for all problem-solvers

Many of Karl Popper's insights are relevant not only to scientists and researchers, but to anyone – including businesspeople – who must grapple with problems and search for solutions. In his quotation below, note the implication that researchers, like the rest of us, are human too, and as such, are prone to ego-related biases and lapses in their objectivity.

> "Whenever we propose a solution to a problem we ought to try as hard as we can to overthrow our solution rather than defend it. Few of us, unfortunately, practice this precept; but other people, fortunately, will supply the criticism for us if we fail to supply it ourselves." -- Karl R. Popper

In agreement with Popper

"In all life one should comfort the afflicted, but verily, also, one should afflict the comfortable, and especially when they are comfortably, contentedly, even happily wrong." – John Kenneth Galbraith, economist and writer, quoted on July 28, 1989

____

Climb trees, have fruit

"The fruits of life fall into the hands of those who climb the tree and pick them." -- Earl Tupper, founder of the company that makes containers for the left-over fruits gathered while climbing trees -- Tupperware. Tupper was born in Berlin, New Hampshire on July 28, 1907.

July 29, 2018
Sunday
International Tiger Day

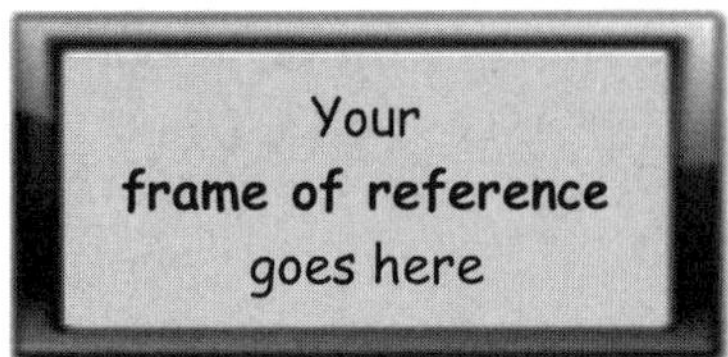

Objectives & reminders

Appointments

Early morning

8 a.m.

9 a.m.

10 a.m.

11 a.m.

Noon

1 p.m.

2 p.m.

3 p.m.

4 p.m.

5 p.m.

6 p.m.

Later evening

Happy birthday: Muzafer Sherif

Born in Odemis, Izmir, Turkey on July 29, 1906, Sherif was a social scientist whose work is very much business-relevant. For example, he coined the phrase "frame of reference" to convey the notion that people view and experience the world in different ways.

Customers, employees, and other people with whom businesspeople interact are likely to have different perspectives -- different frames of reference -- especially if their backgrounds, cultures, religions, and life experiences differ. It follows that to work with others, to persuade them to do something (e.g., make a purchase) or otherwise gain their cooperation, one must first understand their frame of reference.

In their 1947 book, *The Psychology of Ego-Involvements*, Sherif and his co-author, Hadley Cantril, linked the frame of reference idea to the concept of ego-involvement. They suggested that an individual's level of involvement greatly influences his frame of reference.

Involvement defined
Involvement has been defined in several ways, but it is essentially one's degree of psychological identification with an attitude object. Or, to put it in more common terms, involvement has to do with the extent to which someone is "into" a product, brand, company, advertisement, person, activity or something else.

In the 1970s and 1980s, several marketing scholars examined the construct of involvement which led to opportunities to use involvement as a basis of market segmentation.

One series of tenpin bowling marketing studies, for example, found that low-involvement bowlers perceived bowling to be a game or recreation not to be pursued seriously -- an activity that could be substituted for alternative forms of entertainment. In contrast, high-involvement bowlers tended to view bowling as a challenging sport to which they were committed. Whereas low-involvement bowlers tended to respond favorably to advertising appeals that stressed social interaction and ease of play, many high-involvement bowlers found such appeals to be trivial, demeaning or offensive.

July 30, 2018
Monday
International Day of Friendship

Objectives & reminders

______

______

______

Appointments

Early morning

8 a.m.

9 a.m.

10 a.m.

11 a.m.

Noon

1 p.m.

2 p.m.

3 p.m.

4 p.m.

5 p.m.

6 p.m.

Later evening

Conspicuous consumption

"The superior gratification derived from the use and contemplation of costly and supposedly beautiful products is, commonly, in great measure a gratification of our sense of costliness masquerading under the name of beauty." – Thorstein B. Veblen, American economist and social scientist who coined the phrase "conspicuous consumption," born in Manitowoc County, Wisconsin on July 30, 1857

______

The Marketingator

"The mind is the limit. As long as the mind can envision the fact that you can do something, you can do it, as long as you really believe 100 percent."
– Arnold Schwarzenegger, body-builder, movie star, businessman, and governor of California – all *after* studying marketing for two years at the University of Munich, in Germany. Schwarzenegger was born in Thal, Austria on July 30, 1947.

______

Comparative advertising is a good thing: Agree or disagree?

"Comparative advertising is not only a good idea; it is also one that marketers must increasingly embrace because it does three very important things at once. It positions you or your product as having valuable traits; it helps you control the dialogue in the market by defining the standards for judgment; and it narrows the position of your competition to an area where it is weaker than you are." – Sergio Zyman, former marketing director for The Coca-Cola Company, born in Mexico City, Mexico on July 30, 1945

Contrasting consideration regarding comparative advertising

Six months after you've talked about both your brand and your competitor's brand in the same ad, will consumers remember which brand was supposedly superior, and why? Or, will they simply remember that the ad featured *two* leading brands?

July 31, 2018
Tuesday
Warriors' Day (Malaysia)

Objectives & reminders

____

____

____

Appointments

Early morning

8 a.m.

9 a.m.

10 a.m.

11 a.m.

Noon

1 p.m.

2 p.m.

3 p.m.

4 p.m.

5 p.m.

6 p.m.

Later evening

Happy birthday: Sebastian S. Kresge

Born in Bald Mount, Pennsylvania on July 31, 1867, Kresge studied business in college. Then he gained about eight years of business experience working as a traveling tinware salesman.

Then, with a modest $8,000-investment, he opened his first two five-and-dime discount stores in 1899. By 1912, there were 85 stores in the S.S. Kresge Company chain collectively generating more than $10 million in annual sales revenue.

For the next few decades, Kresge's concept of the discount store evolved and was fine-tuned as additional stores were opened and the merchandise mix expanded to include higher-priced items.

> **Retail partnership**
> "Find out where you can render a service, and then render it. The rest is up to the Lord."
> – Sebastian S. Kresge

Finally, in 1962, the first Kmart store was opened – in Garden City, Michigan. Hundreds of Kmart stores followed in the 1960s and 1970s, although Mr. Kresge himself died in 1966. There were more than 2,000 Kmart stores by the early 1980s, followed by company expansion and subsequent sell-off of stores in other retail categories, such as Builders Square, Borders Books, Payless Drugs, and OfficeMax.

In January 2002, Kmart Corporation filed for bankruptcy and soon closed more than 300 stores. Then in May of the following year, the company emerged from bankruptcy as Kmart Holdings Corporation. In 2005, the company merged with Sears, Roebuck & Co. to become Sears Holdings Corporation.

Today, less than 700 Kmart and Kmart Super Center stores remain as part of Sears Holdings – about one-third as many stores that existed during Kmart's heyday. Collectively, Kmart stores generate $25 billion in annual revenues. Between 60,000 and 80,000 stock-keeping units (SKUs) are carried in each store.

> **Value-added commitment**
> "I really want to leave the world better than I found it."
> – Sebastian S. Kresge

August 1, 2018
Wednesday
National Girlfriend's Day

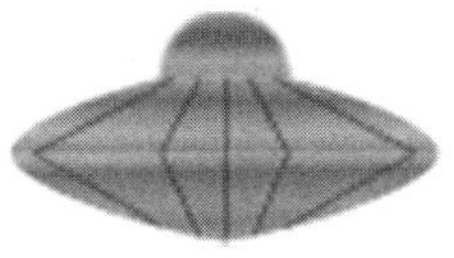

Objectives & reminders

____

____

____

Appointments

Early morning

8 a.m.

9 a.m.

10 a.m.

11 a.m.

Noon

1 p.m.

2 p.m.

3 p.m.

4 p.m.

5 p.m.

6 p.m.

Later evening

Welcome to August: Did you know?

The poppy and gladiolus are August's flowers while the peridot and the sardonyx are the month's gemstones.

Circular reasoning in August

More crop circles are found during August than during any other month. Perhaps the month is known as Artistica on planet Zebuli?

UFOs

Although it's not certain how many people believe that crop circles are made by aliens, a 2003 survey of consumers found that 34 percent claimed they believed in UFOs (55% said they did not and 11% were "not sure").

Culture as an export

MTV first hit the airwaves on August 1, 1981. Six years later, also on August 1 (1987), MTV *Europe* debuted. Originally, MTV, which stands for "*M*usic *T*ele*V*ision," was all about music. Since then the network has evolved to include other content of interest to teens and young adults. Today, MTV is an attractive vehicle for advertisers -- reaching 400 million households in 166 countries with 42 different channels.

The potency of MTV

"Teens who watch MTV music videos are much more likely than other teens to wear the teen 'uniform' of jeans, running shoes, and denim jacket... They are also much more likely to own electronics and consume 'teen' items such as candy, sodas, cookies and fast food. They are much more likely to use a wide range of personal-care products too." – Chip Walker, director of the New World Teen Study

MTV: *M*uch *T*oo *V*exing?

"MTV International has become the most compelling global catalog for the modern branded life." – Naomi Klein, marketing critic

August 2, 2018
Thursday
Republic Day (Macedonia)

Objectives & reminders

____

____

____

Appointments

Early morning

8 a.m.

9 a.m.

10 a.m.

11 a.m.

Noon

1 p.m.

2 p.m.

3 p.m.

4 p.m.

5 p.m.

6 p.m.

Later evening

Low-income market insight

"Anyone who has ever struggled with poverty knows how extremely expensive it is to be poor." -- James Baldwin, American author, born in Harlem, New York on August 2, 1924

Invitation to discuss

- Why is it expensive to be poor, or is it?
- If it is expensive to be poor, what are the potential marketing challenges and opportunities involved in serving the poor?

Buy one and get another for a penny

August 2 is a good day for a "one cent" sale in the U.S., because on that day in 1909, the Lincoln-head penny was first minted. Other penny promotions are also possibilities. Here are a couple of examples:

1. Lead a fundraiser for local charities by asking customers to drop their spare pennies into charity-specific containers to "vote" for their favorite cause. Donate the pennies to the charities.

2. Fill a large jar with pennies and stage a contest by asking patrons to guess the number of pennies in the jar, or guess the weight of the jar. The closest guess wins.

Today, the future of the penny is in question. Inflation has driven down the purchasing power of a penny and driven up the cost of making one. It costs far more than a penny to make one.

Marketing metrics the P&G way

"Market shares are the best litmus test I have found to see if we are indeed doing better than the competition in giving consumers products of superior quality and value. There are other measures. A very critical measure for us is the percentage of our product sales that have clear-cut superiority to the competition as the consumer sees it. We're looking for that number to be up in the nineties. We measure that through blind consumer testing. And we watch the results like a hawk. If that number falls, we are really unhappy campers." -- John Pepper, former chairman and CEO of Procter & Gamble, born in Pottsville, Pennsylvania on August 2, 1938

August 3, 2018
Friday
Flag Day (Venezuela)

Objectives & reminders

____

____

____

Appointments

Early morning

8 a.m.

9 a.m.

10 a.m.

11 a.m.

Noon

1 p.m.

2 p.m.

3 p.m.

4 p.m.

5 p.m.

6 p.m.

Later evening

State sales tax holidays

New Mexico kicks-off the back-to-school (B2S) season with sales tax holidays. This weekend, the sales tax is waived in New Mexico and about seven other states for qualifying B2S purchases. About a half dozen other states celebrate B2S state sales tax holidays later in August. A couple of others schedule the sales tax holidays in July or September.

To help families cope with the annual B2S financial burden that averages $688 for school children's families (according to a 2017 study by the National Retail Federation), several states now call time-out on sales taxes for qualifying B2S items purchased on designated days. Not surprisingly, retailers in these states often time their sale events and other B2S promotions to coincide with the sales tax holidays to create maximum value for their customers.

Joining New Mexico, other states that have designated one or more B2S sales tax holidays include: Alabama, Arkansas, Connecticut, Florida, Georgia, Iowa, Louisiana, Massachusetts, Maryland, Missouri, New York, Oklahoma, South Carolina, Tennessee, Texas and Virginia. Specific dates for each state and other details regarding sales tax holidays may be found at www.taxadmin.org

U.S. Back-to-school (B2S) statistics

The findings of the 2017 National Retail Federation studies indicate that:

- 77 percent of families with school-children are required to buy school supplies.
- 68 percent of these parents receive B2S supply lists at least one month before the school year begins.
- B2S shoppers say they plan to purchase from an average of three websites, but 84 percent insist on free shipping.

Back-to-school spending not limited to parents

According to the Census Bureau's Survey of Local Government Finances, U.S. public school districts spend lots of money too -- an average of $11,009 per student in 2014. States that spend the most money per student include New York ($20,610), New Jersey ($17,907), Connecticut ($17,745) and Vermont ($16,988). Idaho ($6,621) and Utah ($6,500) spend the least.

August 4, 2018
Saturday
Coast Guard Day

Objectives & reminders

Appointments

Early morning

8 a.m.

9 a.m.

10 a.m.

11 a.m.

Noon

1 p.m.

2 p.m.

3 p.m.

4 p.m.

5 p.m.

6 p.m.

Later evening

Merry Christmas in August!

Founder of the British department store chain that's named after him, Harry Gordon Selfridge may be best known in marketing circles for coining the debatable assertion that "the customer is always right." But he's also known for pioneering the practice of accelerating the start of the Christmas shopping season in an effort to stimulate more gift-buying.

In the early 1900s Selfridge observed that shoppers were reluctant to buy Christmas gifts until a few days before Christmas when they were in the Christmas spirit or mood for gift-shopping. So, to nudge shoppers into the Christmas spirit he began reminding them of how many "shopping days" remained until Christmas. The countdown raised shoppers' Christmas-consciousness and prompted them to avoid gift-giving procrastination. Later, Selfridge added mood-stimulating Christmas music and decorations to his store's atmosphere.

Early is too early: Agree or disagree?

- Although few retailers start promoting the Christmas season as early as Selfridges, how early is "too early"?
- Are Labor Day, Halloween, Thanksgiving and other holiday opportunities short-changed, so to speak, when the Christmas season begins before them?

Now in the 21st century, the most famous Selfridges store in London unveils its Christmas Shop annually on or about August 4 -- enabling the company to claim to be the earliest or among the earliest department stores in the world to launch what we now know as the Christmas "season."

Gift-giving facts

- About half of all U.S. Christmas shoppers will purchase at least one gift (for someone else) by the first week in November.
- The earlier in the season consumers begin shopping for Christmas gifts, the more likely they are to buy "gifts" for themselves.

August 5, 2018
Sunday
Independence Day (Burkina Faso)

Objectives & reminders

____

____

____

Appointments

Early morning

8 a.m.

9 a.m.

10 a.m.

11 a.m.

Noon

1 p.m.

2 p.m.

3 p.m.

4 p.m.

5 p.m.

6 p.m.

Later evening

Team insight

"The greater the loyalty of a group toward the group, the greater is the motivation among the members to achieve the goals of the group, and the greater the probability that the group will achieve its goals."
-- Rensis Likert, industrial psychologist and researcher who developed techniques to measure or "scale" attitudes -- techniques such as "the method of summated ratings" (also known as Likert scaling) which continues to be used by business researchers today. Likert was born in Cheyenne, Wyoming on August 5, 1903.

Example: Measuring team loyalty using Likert scaling approach

Rate the extent to which you agree or disagree with each of the following statements regarding your team, where:

1 = Strongly disagree
2 = Disagree
3 = Neither agree nor disagree
4 = Agree
5 = Strongly agree

A. Team members are supportive of each other._____

B. Team members feel honored to be part of the group. _____

C. Team members support the goals of the group. _____

D. Team members are interested in remaining on the team. _____

Analysis

After a team member responds to the four statements, her responses are added together to determine a "summated score" which, in this example, would range from a low of 4 (team members regarded as having very little loyalty) to a high of 20 (team members perceived as extremely loyal).

Why Likert scaling is popular among marketing researchers

- Easy to explain to respondents and easy for them to understand.
- Easy to analyze, present and interpret findings.

August 6, 2018
Monday
National Sisters' Day

Objectives & reminders

______

______

______

Appointments

Early morning

8 a.m.

9 a.m.

10 a.m.

11 a.m.

Noon

1 p.m.

2 p.m.

3 p.m.

4 p.m.

5 p.m.

6 p.m.

Later evening

Brand marketing fame

One of the most influential American artists and pop culture icons of the last fifty years was Andy Warhol, born in Pittsburgh, Pennsylvania on August 6, 1928.

In 1962, the art world applauded Warhol for one of his exhibits, which included paintings of Coca-Cola bottles and Campbell soup cans, as well as wooden carvings of Brillo soap-pad boxes. The next year, he began silk-screening prints of other consumer brands. Today, more than 4,000 of Warhol's creations can be seen at the Andy Warhol Museum in Pittsburgh.

Brands bond Americans: Agree or disagree?
"What's great about this country is that America started the tradition where the richest consumers buy essentially the same things as the poorest. You can be watching TV and see Coca-Cola, and you know that the President drinks Coke, Liz Taylor drinks Coke, and just think, you can drink Coke, too. A Coke is a Coke and no amount of money can get you a better Coke than the one the bum on the corner is drinking. All the Cokes are the same and all the Cokes are good. Liz Taylor knows it, the President knows it, the bum knows it, and you know it..." – Andy Warhol

---

Fair season underway

The state fairs for Indiana, Wisconsin and New Jersey are underway this week as are hundreds of county and local fairs, festivals and related events. An estimated 40,000 of these are staged annually in the U.S., with a disproportionate number scheduled for the latter half of the summer and early fall.

It's not uncommon for fairs to provide opportunities for small and not-so-small businesses to rent space and erect exhibits to drum-up business from fair-goers – prospective buyers that otherwise might be difficult or expensive to reach.

Fairs as venues to fine-tune salesmanship
"Selling at a fair is a great way to test your product. It can also help establish your salesmanship and lead you down the road to infomercials and TV sales." – Ron Popeil, founder of Ronco branded products (e.g., The Pocket Fisherman, The Showtime Rotisserie, and many others) that have generated more than $2 billion in revenues

August 7, 2018
Tuesday
Republic Day (Ivory Coast)

Objectives & reminders

____

____

____

Appointments

Early morning

8 a.m.

9 a.m.

10 a.m.

11 a.m.

Noon

1 p.m.

2 p.m.

3 p.m.

4 p.m.

5 p.m.

6 p.m.

Later evening

Happy birthday: Felipe Korzenny

Born in Mexico City on August 7, 1947, Dr. Korzenny earned advanced degrees in communication research at Michigan State University before becoming the Director of the Center for Hispanic Marketing Communication at Florida State University (FSU). His 2005 book, *Hispanic Marketing: A Cultural Perspective* (co-authored with Betty Ann Korzenny) was a finalist for the American Marketing Association's book-of-the-year award.

In one study published by FSU's Center for Hispanic Marketing Communications – *The Multicultural Marketing Equation: Media, Attitudes, Brands, and Spending* – Korzenny and his colleagues surveyed 3,000 consumers, including Hispanics (H), African-Americans (AA), Asians (A) and Non-Hispanic Whites (NHW). The study found several consumption-related similarities across the groups of consumers, but also found a few significant and marketing-relevant differences. Here are a few of the findings, along with the researchers' comments regarding implications:

1. In contrast to A and NHW consumers, AA and H consumers tend to spend much more time listening to CDs. "The role of music as a cultural expression… makes music on demand via CDs an important medium."

2. AA and H consumers were found to be much less cynical and more interested in commercial messages – generally "more positive towards advertising and marketing…" "[C]ommunicating with [these] consumers via commercial messages is more likely to be well received."

3. AA and H consumers tend to be particularly interested in what businesses do for their local communities. These consumers also say they are willing to pay more for products from companies that give back to the community. "Marketers who get involved in helping AA and H communities are likely to gain their favor."

Invitation to evaluate methodology

The survey was conducted online and in English. How might the findings have differed if the survey had been conducted face-to-face and in each respondent's language of choice?

August 8, 2018
Wednesday
World Cat Day

Objectives & reminders

___

___

___

Appointments

Early morning

8 a.m.

9 a.m.

10 a.m.

11 a.m.

Noon

1 p.m.

2 p.m.

3 p.m.

4 p.m.

5 p.m.

6 p.m.

Later evening

Pre-need versus at-need services

The marketing of funeral, legal, and other services on a "pre-need" basis has caught-on during the last three decades as businesses find that marketing on a pre-need basis offers several advantages for both businesses and consumers. In contrast to "at-need" services, pre-need affords the opportunity for consumers to plan ahead, shop around, ask questions and not rush their purchase decisions.

> **Pre-planning principle**
> The more advance notice a business has of future demand, the easier it is to plan for the efficient and effective satisfaction of that demand.

Marketers often find that pre-need services can be provided more flexibly and smoothly than at-need services; i.e., the advance notice of likely future demand allows them to plan more efficiently and more effectively. For example, scheduling meetings with pre-need clients can be arranged well in advance to accommodate both the buyers' and sellers' busy schedules. Further, selling services on a pre-need basis is one way to beat competitors to sales opportunities. And pre-need services accelerate cash flow by generating revenues earlier than the same services provided on an at-need basis.

One of the first pre-need legal services was launched on August 8, 1972, when Harland Stonecipher formed The Sportsman's Motor Club -- essentially a form of legal insurance for members.

The company and the concept grew into Pre-Paid Legal Services, now a subsidiary of LegalShield, headquartered in Ada, Oklahoma. The firm offers its members an array of legal services provided by a network of 6,900 independent law firms scattered across the U.S. and Canada.

___

Pre-infomercial infomercial

"And to think that this cake is not one of my own recipes, but a recipe I took right off the flour box."
-- Mother Moran, guest teacher on *Today's Children* (as she admired her finished cake), August 8, 1933. Along with host Irma Phillips, Moran frequently mixed cooking instructions, selling and entertainment on the Pillsbury-sponsored radio show.

August 9, 2018
Thursday
National Day of Singapore

Objectives & reminders

____

____

____

Appointments

Early morning

8 a.m.

9 a.m.

10 a.m.

11 a.m.

Noon

1 p.m.

2 p.m.

3 p.m.

4 p.m.

5 p.m.

6 p.m.

Later evening

Happy birthday: Smokey the Bear

Born on August 9, 1944, Smokey continues to be an effective spokesbear for fire safety. Over the years he has stressed repeatedly that, "only you can prevent forest fires."

In addition to fire prevention, marketers can learn at least a couple of lessons from Smokey. First, when the "product" is somewhat abstract and intangible, (such as a social cause or specific consumer behaviors), it helps to tangibilize the product or the message -- thus making it easier for consumers to recognize and remember. The birth of Smokey helped to accomplish that.

Second, there's a lot to be said for a consistent message, frequently communicated and reinforced over the years, e.g., "Only you can prevent forest fires." Advertisers and decision-makers are sometimes guilty of becoming bored with ad campaigns and their creative juices urge them to tamper with effective campaigns prematurely. Smokey's guardians, however, recognize the need to continually teach and remind new generations of consumers about fire safety. Smokey and his message may be in their 70s, but most of their audience is younger.

Innovations that may not sell themselves

While high-tech and lifestyle-changing innovations tend to grab the media's attention and create a "buzz" in the marketplace, they are not likely to come along every day, at least not for most companies. Rather, most patents are issued for fairly incremental advances that may not generate much excitement.

These ho-hum innovations may be appealing only to small niches of prospective customers, yet they may represent potentially profitable opportunities nonetheless. For example, on August 9, 1994, a patent was issued for an electric machine to clean eyeglasses. On the same day, another patent was granted to an inventor of a device used to squeeze tea bags, while another went to the designer of a door-knob cover.

Escaping media attention
Most innovations are low-tech. – Peter Drucker, world-renowned business consultant, educator and author

August 10, 2018
Friday
International Biodiesel Day

Objectives & reminders

____

____

____

Appointments

Early morning

8 a.m.

9 a.m.

10 a.m.

11 a.m.

Noon

1 p.m.

2 p.m.

3 p.m.

4 p.m.

5 p.m.

6 p.m.

Later evening

Lifetime achievement

On August 10, 1990, psychologist Burrus Frederick "B.F." Skinner made his last public appearance at an American Psychological Association (APA) conference where he was awarded the APA's first Citation for Lifetime Contributions to Psychology. Eight days later, Skinner died of leukemia.

Skinner was a leading figure in behavioral psychology. He relied heavily on techniques of operant conditioning or instrumental conditioning. His work developed the notion that an individual's behavior can be shaped through reinforcement.

Behavior's "bottom line"

"Behavior is shaped and maintained by its consequences." -- B.F. Skinner

Today, we know that people tend to gravitate toward behaviors that are consistently reinforced. For example, if a salesperson earns greater kudos for landing new accounts than for retaining existing ones, over time he or she is likely to place greater emphasis on finding new customers.

The potency of "thank you"

What explains the findings of these two studies?

Study 1

An insurance company sent "thank you" letters to a group of randomly selected customers a few weeks prior to mailing renewal notices to them. Policyholders receiving the thank you letters were more likely to renew their policies than customers not receiving the letters.

Study 2

A jewelry store's sales clerks telephoned a group of randomly selected customers the day after the customers made a purchase. The clerks thanked the customers for shopping at the store the day before. Interestingly, customers receiving the telephone calls were more likely to visit the store and make another purchase within the next 12 months than customers not receiving the follow-up "thank you" calls.

August 11, 2018
Saturday
Flag Day (Pakistan)

Objectives & reminders

____

____

Appointments

Early morning

8 a.m.

9 a.m.

10 a.m.

11 a.m.

Noon

1 p.m.

2 p.m.

3 p.m.

4 p.m.

5 p.m.

6 p.m.

Later evening

Leadership insight

"Autonomy is really a central part of my life. I believe that it drives the kind of behavior in individuals that we want.... [M]y belief is that if you pass autonomy as far down in any grouping of people as you can, you will get extraordinary results if you ask for a lot. The greatest burden you can put on someone is trust."
-- Craig O. McCaw, who as a college student began building McCaw Communications into what became an $11.5 billion business only 25 years later. McCaw was born in Centralia, Washington on August 11, 1949.

____

Brands are tangible products *and* experiences

"We view the experience of a Krispy Kreme store (where customers watch their donuts being baked behind glass) as the defining element of the brand."
– Scott Livengood, then CEO of Krispy Kreme, born in Salisbury, North Carolina on August 11, 1952

____

Organizations are about people: Agree or disagree?

"Companies die because their managers focus on the economic activity of producing goods and services, and they forget that their organizations' true nature is that of a community of humans." – Arie De Geus, former business executive with Royal Dutch/Shell (1951-1989) and author of *The Living Company...* (1997), born in Rotterdam, Netherlands on August 11, 1930

____

Plan for the unplanned

"Innovations never happen as planned." – Gifford Pinchot, Governor of Pennsylvania (1923-1927, 1931-1935), born in Simsbury, Connecticut on August 11, 1865

____

Consequence of advancing technology: Agree or disagree?

"Technology has become the great enabler, the steam roller that is flattening organizations." – Patrick J. McGovern, Jr., American entrepreneur who founded IDG (International Data Group), publishers of hundreds of newspapers, magazines, and books (especially those for "dummies"), born in Queens, New York on August 11, 1937

August 12, 2018
Sunday

International Youth Day
Father's Day (Brazil)
Mother's Day (Thailand)

Objectives & reminders

____

____

Appointments

____
Early morning
____
8 a.m.
____
9 a.m.
____
10 a.m.
____
11 a.m.
____
Noon
____
1 p.m.
____
2 p.m.
____
3 p.m.
____
4 p.m.
____
5 p.m.
____
6 p.m.
____
Later evening
____

Examples of both positive and negative points of differentiation today

Happy birthday: Frederick T. Stanley

Born on August 12, 1802, Frederick T. Stanley started his own company in 1843 manufacturing and selling bolts and other hardware items -- such as hinges. At the time, there was no shortage of hinge-makers, and competition was fierce. Hinges were thought to be commodities that did not particularly lend themselves to differentiation.

However, Stanley soon learned to differentiate his hinges in a meaningful way; he began including screws in the hinge packages. This convenience was a big hit among buyers who rewarded Stanley with their repeat patronage.

Today, Frederick T. Stanley's company still exists -- Stanley Works -- and the company continues to include screws with many of their hinges and other hardware items.

Commodities don't exist: Agree or disagree?

Long after Stanley figured out how to differentiate his "commodity," Harvard University business professor Theodore Levitt concluded: "There's no such thing as a commodity. All goods and services are differentiable."

Signs as *marketing* communications

On August 12, 1990, a sign was posted near the cash register at "Jerry's" restaurant in Carlsbad, New Mexico. Consider the impression the sign might have had on customers and how the posted check-cashing policies might be revised.

"Jerry's Check Cashing Policies

1. Checks must be numbered 500 or over.
2. Local checks only... No out of town checks.
3. Two forms of I.D. must be presented (with current address).
4. Current work and home telephone numbers.
5. No second party checks.
6. Absolutely no student checks.

A $17.50 charge plus tax will be added to all returned checks."

August 13, 2018
Monday
International Lefthanders' Day

Objectives & reminders

____

____

____

Appointments

Early morning

8 a.m.

9 a.m.

10 a.m.

11 a.m.

Noon

1 p.m.

2 p.m.

3 p.m.

4 p.m.

5 p.m.

6 p.m.

Later evening

Wall of fear

On August 13, 1961, Communist-controlled soldiers strung barbed wire around East Berlin, Germany to stop the daily exodus of 2,000 refugees who were leaving East Germany and another 50,000 who crossed the border regularly to work in West Berlin. Fear was reinforced by machine-gun armed guards positioned along the border. Although the U.S. and its allies called the action, "illegal, brutal and callous," the barbed wire stayed -- until replaced within a few short weeks by a concrete wall.

It wasn't until late in 1989 that the wall fell, and East and West Germany began the reunification process. Marketers played a role in the reunification process in that they introduced or reintroduced a number of products that the East Germans had gone without during the "wall" era of Communist control. For example, an entire generation of East Germans had never eaten bananas.

Invitation to discuss

How would campaigns to market bananas (or other consumer items) in markets with consumers who are largely unfamiliar with bananas differ from marketing bananas in markets with consumers who are already quite familiar with bananas?

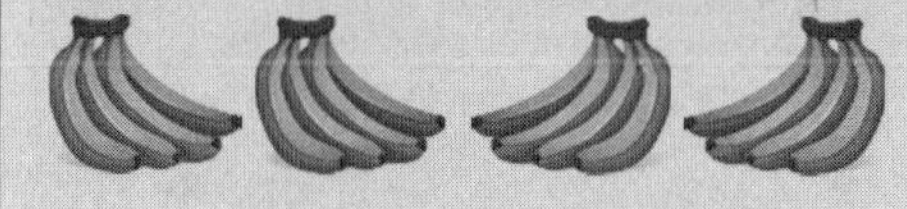

On a lighter note ☺

Born in Manchester, England on August 13, 1930, Bernard Manning grew up to make us laugh: "I once bought my kids a set of batteries for Christmas with a note on it saying 'toys not included.'"

Advertising is a potent cultural force: Agree or disagree?

"We are so busy measuring public opinion that we forget we can mold it." -- William Bernbach, one of the most influential advertising practitioners of all time and founder of Doyle Dane Bernbach (DDB) advertising agency. Bernbach was born in New York City on August 13, 1911.

August 14, 2018
Tuesday
Independence Day (Pakistan)

Objectives & reminders

____

____

____

Appointments

Early morning

8 a.m.

9 a.m.

10 a.m.

11 a.m.

Noon

1 p.m.

2 p.m.

3 p.m.

4 p.m.

5 p.m.

6 p.m.

Later evening

Product placement likely to increase: Agree or disagree?

"I think the advertising model is going to have to change for a lot of people. Because we now have the technology in our homes to zap through some of the commercials. And so, if you are a manufacturer and a marketer... you need to make sure [your products] get exposed in the right environment. And what better way to do that, than in the content or the body of the television show or the video game?" – Robert "Bob" A. Eckert, former chairman and CEO of Mattel, Inc. (toy- and game-maker), born in Elmhurst, Illinois on August 14, 1954

New old product ideas

A number of methods exist for finding or generating ideas for new products. Marketers interested in feeding the new product pipeline may look to customers for new ideas, ask sales and customer service reps (who talk to customers), monitor competitors to see what new products they're introducing, and so on.

One approach is to study Patent Office records to see what's been invented recently or not-so-recently. Such inventions may represent market opportunities themselves, or they may help to identify needs in the marketplace and thus spark ideas for alternative inventions that could be marketable.

On August 14, 1939, *Time* magazine reviewed recent patents and reported several interesting inventions. Here are five examples:

1. Motor-driven fan for removing foam from mugs of beer.

2. "Police claws" that could be mounted on the front of a police car to grab a speeder's rear bumper.

3. Portable toilet for city dogs -- attachable to their rear ends for convenience.

4. Hearing aid for the deaf, installed inside a set of false teeth.

5. Extendable rear automobile bumper that parallel parkers could extend to discourage others from parking too close.

August 15, 2018 Wednesday

Assumption of Mary

Objectives & reminders

Appointments

Early morning

8 a.m.

9 a.m.

10 a.m.

11 a.m.

Noon

1 p.m.

2 p.m.

3 p.m.

4 p.m.

5 p.m.

6 p.m.

Later evening

Animal fat-free day?

Procter & Gamble introduced Crisco brand shortening on August 15, 1911. Because Crisco was the first shortening made entirely from vegetable oils rather than animal fats, the brand was less expensive than alternatives and thus proved to be a big hit with consumers. Since Crisco's introduction, consumers have become increasingly concerned about the possible health hazards associated with animal fats, which may help explain Crisco's continuing popularity.

"Pull" strategy using free samples

To overcome grocers' initial reluctance to carry Crisco, Procter & Gamble's early marketing plan included the blanketing of the U.S. with free samples of their "modern product." Accompanying the samples were booklets and recipes -- also free -- to teach women how to cook with Crisco instead of butter. Not surprisingly, grocers began to carry the brand when consumers asked them to do so.

In a largely unrelated story, a pig farmer from Craftsbury, Vermont -- Earl Mayo -- wrote a letter of protest on August 15, 1995, in response to accusations that his pigs were developing heart disease after being fed a diet of Ben & Jerry's waste ice cream for more than seven years. According to Mr. Mayo, "[my] pigs live as long and are as healthy and productive as the pigs I kept before I started feeding them waste ice cream." Mr. Mayo's letter did not indicate whether his pigs prefer other meals prepared with Crisco or butter.

Negative word-of-mouth more potent than positive word-of-mouth

"The most common source of negative buzz comes from a negative experience... Customers will try to ease the tension they feel by 'getting even'... Negative information is given more weight in the purchase decision and spreads faster than positive information." -- Emanuel Rosen, former Vice President of Marketing for Niles Software (responsible for marketing Endnotes bibliographic software), and author of *The Anatomy of Buzz: How to Create Word-of-Mouth Marketing.* Rosen was born in Tel Aviv, Israel on August 15, 1962.

August 16, 2018
Thursday
National Airborne Day

Objectives & reminders

____

____

____

Appointments

Early morning

8 a.m.

9 a.m.

10 a.m.

11 a.m.

Noon

1 p.m.

2 p.m.

3 p.m.

4 p.m.

5 p.m.

6 p.m.

Later evening

Happy birthday: Apple Computer

Founded by two college dropouts in a California garage on August 16, 1976, Apple Computer quickly grew to become a key player in the computer world. Unlike most start-up businesses that are challenged by the problems of slow or no growth, Apple faced the opposite problem: how to manage its rapid rate of growth.

Recognizing the challenges of rapid growth and his own lack of business experience, co-founder Steve Jobs hired John Sculley to help run the company. Soon after that, Jobs left the company's management team for a few years.

Potential challenges of growing too rapidly

1. Rapid growth may pressure the company to promote people before they are adequately experienced or trained to handle the added responsibilities.
2. While some personnel find rapid growth exciting and challenging, others perceive it as stressful, burdensome or overwhelming.
3. Growth tends to consume cash. Substantial investments may be needed in plant and equipment, logistics support, inventory, hiring and training, and marketing efforts. Rapidly growing companies may run out of cash before revenues offset those investments.
4. Growth plans may preoccupy managers and marketers to the point that existing operations and existing customers are neglected. The glamour of growth may mean that mundane but important tasks are neglected.
5. An influx of new customers may introduce additional risk, and the greater the influx, the greater the risk. Relative to an established customer base, new customers can be more time-consuming and more expensive to serve. They tend to purchase less, and if they were attracted by price discounts they may be more likely to sever the relationship with the business when a competing business comes along with a lower price. In addition, it can be a challenge to learn and understand their buying habits and preferences.

August 17, 2018
Friday

Qixi Festival
(Chinese Valentine's Day)

Objectives & reminders

___

___

___

Appointments

Early morning

8 a.m.

9 a.m.

10 a.m.

11 a.m.

Noon

1 p.m.

2 p.m.

3 p.m.

4 p.m.

5 p.m.

6 p.m.

Later evening

Indonesia Independence Day

August 17 is a national holiday in Indonesia. In 1945, within days after the end of World War II and the Japanese withdrawal of troops, Indonesia declared itself a republic.

Located between the Pacific and Indian Oceans, today Indonesia is home to more than 261 million consumers, making it the fourth most populous country in the world (behind China, India and the United States). Seventy-six percent of Indonesian consumers are Muslim and 60 percent have not yet reached their 30th birthday. More than one-third of Indonesia's consumers who are at least 25 years old have no formal education.

Beanie Babies invade academia

On August 17, 2000, the front page of the *Wall Street Journal* reported an academic case study that helped to explain the enormous popularity of Beanie Baby stuffed toy animals. Published in the *Journal of Product and Brand Management*, the study pinpointed ten attributes of Beanie Babies and their manufacturer's business methods to explain why so many consumers seem to form "relationships" with Beanie Babies. Many of the principles could be incorporated in the design and marketing of other brands too.

Why consumers are attached to Beanie Babies: Two key principles

Principle of personification

"A brand may be personified by attributing human characteristics to it or designing it with subtle human-like features." Each Beanie Baby toy has its own name and each has a facial expression that conveys its unique personality.

Principle of engagement

"Brands may be made more engaging by designing them to increase customer interactivity with the products... Could the brand be augmented with a fastener, zipper, control knob, adjustable handle, or accessories?" In the case of Beanie Babies, the toys are intentionally under-stuffed so owners can manipulate the arms and legs and otherwise pose the toys.

August 18, 2018
Saturday
National Mail Order Catalog Day

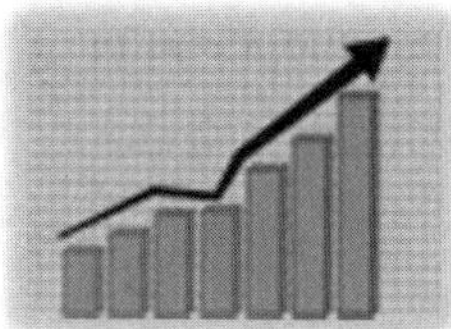

Objectives & reminders

____

____

____

Appointments

Early morning

8 a.m.

9 a.m.

10 a.m.

11 a.m.

Noon

1 p.m.

2 p.m.

3 p.m.

4 p.m.

5 p.m.

6 p.m.

Later evening

Increasing income

The U.S. Commerce Department released a report on August 18, 1951, showing that the per capita income in the United States for 1950 had reached a record high of $1,436 -- up nine percent from 1949.

The data also indicated substantial geographic differences in incomes, ranging from a low of $698 in Mississippi to a high of $1,986 in Washington, D.C.

> **Interpreting the statistics**
> The 1950 income statistic of $1,436 is the *mean* income, not the *median.* It is also a *per capita* statistic (i.e., it averages the incomes of every man, woman and child), rather than the income per worker, per adult between the ages of 18 and 65, or per household. Consider how businesses might use this statistic and how the knowledge or misunderstanding of the calculations involved could have an effect on its interpretation.

Welcoming complaints

"Those who enter to buy, support me. Those who come to flatter, please me. Those who complain, teach me how I may please others so that more will come. Only those hurt me who are displeased but do not complain." -- Marshall Field, co-founder of one of America's first department stores (in Chicago, 1868) which became known as Marshall Field's. Mr. Field was born in Conway, Massachusetts on August 18, 1834.

Show the value, then prove it

"Customers... [expect] suppliers to add value at much deeper levels than what was traditionally delivered to their organizations. Historically, we presented our products and customers connected the value to their business. Today, successful sales professionals are actively guiding those connections." – Jeff Thull, professional selling consultant and CEO of Prime Resource Group. To learn more about Thull's perspective of professional selling, see his book published on August 18, 2006 – *Exceptional Selling: How the Best Connect and Win in High Stakes Sales.*

August 19, 2018
Sunday
Hajj begins

Objectives & reminders

___

___

___

Appointments

Early morning

8 a.m.

9 a.m.

10 a.m.

11 a.m.

Noon

1 p.m.

2 p.m.

3 p.m.

4 p.m.

5 p.m.

6 p.m.

Later evening

Only in an industrial market?

Consumer marketers typically invest a great deal of time and money trying to find the "right" names for their new brands. Although brand names are important for industrial products too, industrial buyers -- arguably -- are less likely than household consumers to make purchase decisions based solely on an item's name appeal.

Perhaps that was part of the rationale for Lockheed dubbing one of its planes with the not-so-catchy name, L-1011. Apparently so much money was poured into the development of the L-1011 that Lockheed managers joked that they'd have to plead Chapter 10 or Chapter 11 bankruptcy if the plane failed -- thus the name "1011." Fortunately, Lockheed never had to find out, but the last L-1011 was produced on August 19, 1983.

Organizational buyers are objective: Agree or disagree?

According to some experts, organizational buyers are professionals. Because millions (sometimes billions) of dollars may be at stake, organizational buyers systematically develop purchase criteria and carefully compare purchase alternatives against those criteria. They're not likely to be swayed by emotional or irrelevant factors such as whether they like or dislike a particular sales rep, whether a brand's producer spends a lot of money on non-specific image advertising, whether a particular brand's color is their personal favorite, or as noted in the Lockheed example, whether the brand has a catchy or not-so-catchy name.

Other experts disagree, arguing that organizational buyers are people too -- just like household consumers -- and, as such, they are subject to many (most?) of the same personal biases, whims and subjective decision-making heuristics. In other words, experts in this camp argue that two organizational buyers employed by the same company evaluating the same purchase alternatives may reach quite different conclusions as to which alternative should be purchased.

What's your opinion? Consider the implications of your perspective for both *buying* organizations and *selling* organizations.

August 20, 2018
Monday
Eid al-Adha begins
(Festival of the Sacrifice)

Objectives & reminders

____

____

____

Appointments

Early morning

8 a.m.

9 a.m.

10 a.m.

11 a.m.

Noon

1 p.m.

2 p.m.

3 p.m.

4 p.m.

5 p.m.

6 p.m.

Later evening

8MK

On August 20, 1920, the first commercial radio station in the United States began broadcasting daily. The Detroit, Michigan station was 8MK, but the station's name was later changed to WWJ. In the early days of radio, it was not uncommon for a receiver to cost consumers a few hundred dollars -- the equivalent of about $5,800 today.

Deflating the inflation assumption

The Consumer Price Index (CPI) indicates that most retail prices have risen over the years. A basket of goods that cost American consumers $10 on August 20, 1920 cost $18.22 on August 20, 1969 and about $124 on August 20, 2018. But, because the CPI is an average of prices, the price of individual items in the basket may increase faster or slower than the average.

Some prices actually decrease – like those for radios. Pocket calculators, personal computers and printers are other examples. Such decreases can be attributed to several interrelated business factors, e.g., economies of scale, automation of production processes, increased learning of efficiencies, higher rates of consumption, accessibility to lower-cost labor and materials, and improved technologies.

So, while managers may be interested in controlling their costs to remain price competitive, the CPI may not be a particularly realistic benchmark. Better benchmarks are the costs of the company's chief competitors.

Business as tennis?

"All you can do is the best you can. Stay on the balls of your feet as you might in a tennis game. Be ready to change directions if you need to, but don't do it in haste (as one might have to in tennis), and above all, worry about your customers. Customers can go away in a drop of a hat." – Martha Ingram, chairman of Ingram Industries, Inc. (distribution conglomerate with annual sales exceeding $2 billion) and one of the wealthiest businesswomen in the United States, born in Charleston, South Carolina on August 20, 1935

August 21, 2018
Tuesday
Senior Citizens' Day

Objectives & reminders

______

______

______

Appointments

Early morning

8 a.m.

9 a.m.

10 a.m.

11 a.m.

Noon

1 p.m.

2 p.m.

3 p.m.

4 p.m.

5 p.m.

6 p.m.

Later evening

Happy birthday: Sergey Brin

Born in Moscow on August 21, 1973, Brin left the Soviet Union at the age of six and headed for the United States where he graduated from the University of Maryland with a degree in math and computer science -- at the age of 19. While still in his twenties, Brin successfully ventured into Internet entrepreneurship, i.e., he co-founded Google with Larry Page.

Word-of-mouse?
"Google actually relies on our users to help with our marketing. We have a very high percentage of our users who often tell others about our search engine."
-- Sergey Brin

Today, Google's effectiveness in streamlining the online search process explains why Google receives 3.5 billion search queries daily, and why Brin is very wealthy.

Up late at night with Sergey
The research behind the *Marketing FAME* series has included more than 17,000 online Google searches, so far.

Although successful, Brin has not lost the sense of humor and playfulness that he inherited from his parents -- which helps explain the name "Google." One year Sergey's father -- Michael Brin -- wrote a birthday poem to his son and posted it on the Internet. Here's an excerpt:

"You are tough, you mine data,
You surf first and think later,
And your crawler fast as light
Wanders madly in the night.
You work hard to squeeze a thesis
From the world wide web of feces.
You live abroad on the sunny coast
To you, my son I propose a toast."

Motivation for success
"Obviously everyone wants to be successful, but I want to be looked back on as being very innovative, very trusted and ethical and ultimately making a big difference in the world." -- Sergey Brin

August 22, 2018
Wednesday
Flag Day (Russia)

Objectives & reminders

____

____

____

Appointments

Early morning

8 a.m.

9 a.m.

10 a.m.

11 a.m.

Noon

1 p.m.

2 p.m.

3 p.m.

4 p.m.

5 p.m.

6 p.m.

Later evening

Beating around the Bush

Marketing isn't confined to goods and services. Ideas, causes and people can be marketed as well. U.S. presidential candidate Bill Clinton understood this on August 22, 1992, when he bashed what he considered to be President George H. Bush's (Sr.) failed economic policies. On that day, Clinton spoke of Bush's proposed tax cuts as "fools' gold," and reminded Bush that, "It's the economy, stupid."

These and other carefully worded accusations and labels helped crystallize voters' focus during the campaign while conveying a sense of empathy for the plight of those negatively affected by the recent economic slump. Less than three months later, Clinton won the election.

Lessons from "Professor" Clinton

Consider the marketing-relevant lessons that may be gleaned from President Clinton's campaign success:

1. Focus on salient issues that resonate with the audience. Although most voters may have a low level of economic literacy, they know what it means to be out of work or to fear losing their jobs.

2. Before Clinton's accusation that "It's the economy, stupid," was the "***KISS***" principle, "***K***eep ***I***t ***S***imple, ***S***tupid." When trying to persuade an audience, avoid confusing them with messages that are unnecessarily complicat-ed. Further, concisely packaged ideas are more easily understood, remembered and quoted by the media.

3. Because ideas often are abstract and intangible (and thus easy to misunderstand and forget), carefully chosen words to describe them can paint memorable pictures for the audience. "Fools' gold" evokes vivid images of both worthless stones and the gullible and duped miners who find them.

August 23, 2018
Thursday

International Day for the Remembrance of the Slave Trade and its Abolition

Objectives & reminders

Appointments

Early morning

8 a.m.

9 a.m.

10 a.m.

11 a.m.

Noon

1 p.m.

2 p.m.

3 p.m.

4 p.m.

5 p.m.

6 p.m.

Later evening

Avoid being canned

Some workers are hesitant to share very much knowledge with their employers for fear of losing their jobs. "If my job 'secrets' become common knowledge," they reason, "the company can train others to do my job and then they can replace me." Apparently, this fear of being "canned" was very much the mentality in canneries during the early 1900s. It's difficult to comprehend today, but in those days the top managers of canneries often did not understand how the canning process worked, because plant supervisors considered their knowledge of canning processes to be proprietary.

The canning secrecy was countered with more secrecy by George F. Winter on August 23, 1916. Winter was a Green Giant employee who was curious to learn about the canning process. So, he climbed into the rafters overlooking the company's vegetable canning operations and hid. Throughout the day, he observed the canning process and took notes. He went on to share his observations and notes with management and eventually became a member of the company's board of directors.

Should employees share information?

Agree?

Employees have a responsibility to share job-related information (including suggestions for improving or speeding the work process) with their employers and with their co-workers. Because employees are compensated by the company for their work, anything they learn or accomplish on the job "belongs" to the company. Moreover, the willingness to share information and suggest work-related process improvements is an important way for workers to demonstrate that they are competent and promotable.

Disagree?

It is *not* in employees' best interests to share job-related information with employers. Managers are paid more than rank-and-file workers, in part, because they are responsible for designing the work processes. It is unreasonable to expect employees to do "management work" by sharing suggestions for process improvements unless they are compensated for doing so. Furthermore, when job "secrets" are shared, workers become interchangeable and their job security is lost.

August 24, 2018
Friday
National Waffle Day

Objectives & reminders

____

____

____

Appointments

Early morning

8 a.m.

9 a.m.

10 a.m.

11 a.m.

Noon

1 p.m.

2 p.m.

3 p.m.

4 p.m.

5 p.m.

6 p.m.

Later evening

Mexican independence

After 11 years of fighting the Mexican War of Independence, the Treaty of Córdoba was signed on August 24, 1821, to end the hostilities and establish Mexico's independence from Spain.

Today, Mexico is one of the United States' major trading partners. More than 13 percent of all goods imported by the U.S. are *from* Mexico, while almost 16 percent of all U.S.-exported goods are destined *for* Mexico.

Mexico is home to more than 120 million consumers (slightly more than one-third the size of the U.S. population). Compared to those in the U.S., Mexican consumers tend to be much younger, with a median age of 27 (vs. 37 in the U.S.). Further, the median annual household income in Mexico tends to be much smaller – about $7,000 (vs. $57,000 in the U.S.).

Tips for budding entrepreneurs

On August 24, 1945, Vince McMahon was born in Pinehurst, North Carolina – possibly with an entrepreneurial flair for promotion already racing through his veins.

Like many big businesspeople, McMahon, the legendary entertainment promoter who built the World Wrestling Federation, started out as a small one. Then, through a series of calculated, deliberate and sometimes lucky decisions, he grew the business into the multi-billion dollar enterprise that it is today.

For readers wrestling with their own entrepreneurial aspirations, consider McMahon's take-down tips in the accompanying boxes.

Step into the entrepreneurship ring
"Sometimes you have to take a half step back to take two forward."

Think "team event"
"You need to surround yourself with quality human beings that are intelligent and have a vision."

Be willing to tag your teammates
"You do have to delegate as you grow."

Pin down quality
"Regardless of how well a [business] is run, it's only as good as the product it produces."

August 25, 2018
Saturday

Ghost Festival (Asia)

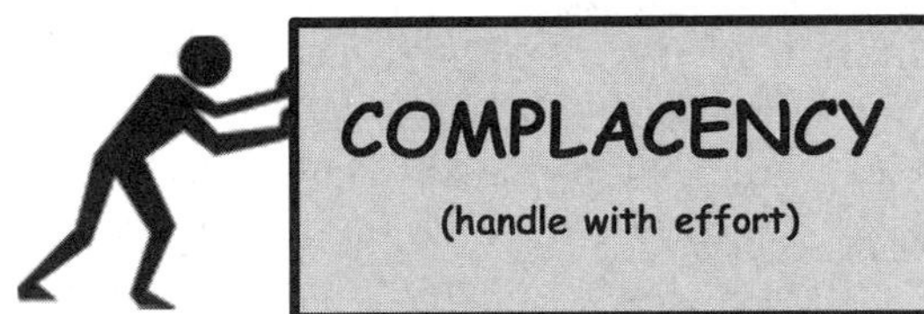

Objectives & reminders

Appointments

Early morning

8 a.m.

9 a.m.

10 a.m.

11 a.m.

Noon

1 p.m.

2 p.m.

3 p.m.

4 p.m.

5 p.m.

6 p.m.

Later evening

Motivation and Personality

On August 25, 1954, the classic book *Motivation and Personality* was published. In it, author Abraham H. Maslow explained his hierarchical theory of human motivation that he had previously reported in various journal articles. He suggested that people tend to satisfy basic physiological needs first, then gravitate to increasingly higher order needs for safety and security, social affiliation, self-esteem, and finally self-actualization. While many needs operate simultaneously, Maslow observed that unsatisfied needs at the next higher level are likely to be the most motivating.

Although the validity of Maslow's theory has been scrutinized and debated since 1954, businesspeople have used the theory to understand and motivate both employees and consumers. The mix of job attributes and working conditions that is important to an employee early in his or her career might be quite different several years later. Similarly, the mix of product attributes and appeals to which a consumer favorably responds may evolve over time.

Moving up the hierarchy

"All the evidence that we have indicates that it is reasonable to assume in practically every human being, and certainly in almost every newborn baby, that there is an active will toward health, an impulse towards growth, or towards the actualization."
-- Abraham Maslow

If marketers don't follow-up, neither will customers

"Once you have sold a customer, make sure he is satisfied with your goods. Stay with him until the goods are used up or worn out. Your product may be of such long life that you will never sell him again, but he will sell you and your product to his friends."
-- William Feather, American writer and publisher, born in Jamestown, New York on August 25, 1889

August 26, 2018
Sunday
Women's Equality Day

Chevrolet

Buick

Objectives & reminders

____

____

____

Appointments

Early morning

8 a.m.

9 a.m.

10 a.m.

11 a.m.

Noon

1 p.m.

2 p.m.

3 p.m.

4 p.m.

5 p.m.

6 p.m.

Later evening

Goodbye Alfred Sloan, Jr.

General Motors' Chairman Alfred Sloan officially retired on August 26, 1956, after leading the company for more than 32 years. One of Sloan's many contributions to business thought was the idea of segmenting the market -- partially in an effort to maximize market coverage, and partially to minimize competition among GM divisions. He summarized the GM segmentation plan as follows: "Chevy for the *hoi pallloi*, Pontiac for the poor but proud, Oldsmobile for the comfortable but discreet, Buick for the striving, and Cadillac for the rich."

Sloan's best-selling 1964 book, *My Years with General Motors*, contains numerous business insights that remain relevant today.

> **Invitation to discuss:**
> **"Class system" for automobile buyers**
> Although widely recognized by marketers today, Sloan's product-market segmentation scheme was somewhat of a secret for several years. Consider the extent to which buyers might have been offended or otherwise dissuaded from buying GM automobiles if the company's target markets were publicly defined as Sloan described them. More generally, is it a good idea for companies to publicly articulate precisely how they define their target markets?

Ugly Duckling waddles onto market

On August 26, 1957, The Ford Motor Company rolled out the first Edsel model with great anticipation. Dated marketing research conducted up to nine years earlier suggested American consumers wanted some of the Edsel's unique features – including tailfins and wraparound windshield. But consumer tastes had changed during the nine years.

Other marketing research suggested that naming the vehicle after founder Henry Ford's son – Edsel Bryant Ford – was a mistake, but the company proceeded with the name anyway. The name evoked negative images and connotations, such as "hard sell."

Partially because of these marketing research mishaps, significant sales never materialized. So, in less than two and a half years Ford discontinued the Edsel, swallowed losses of more than $350 million, and committed to more timely research in the future.

August 27, 2018
Monday
National Heroes' Day (Philippines)

Objectives & reminders

____

____

____

Appointments

Early morning

8 a.m.

9 a.m.

10 a.m.

11 a.m.

Noon

1 p.m.

2 p.m.

3 p.m.

4 p.m.

5 p.m.

6 p.m.

Later evening

Dayton Foundation's 100th anniversary

On August 27, 1918, George Draper Dayton (founder of Dayton department stores, which has evolved into Target) and his family formally established the Dayton Foundation, with an initial endowment of $1 million.

Later, in 1946, the "long-standing policy" of donating five percent of pretax profits to worthy causes was formalized. Bruce Dayton, grandson of George Draper Dayton, explained the rationale behind the company's decision by pointing out, "The health of [the community] in which you're operating is as important as the way you operate."

Strategic win-win, but must be real

"You do community involvement because community involvement is strategically important for the company... If you try to do it for any other reason, you're worse off, because people see it as just shameless public relations. No one is interested in shameless public relations. What they want to see is the real stuff, real engagement, real involvement." -- Peter Hutchinson, former Dayton Foundation director

Don't wait for corporate help

While corporations help to address community needs, individuals too can make a major impact in the community. As an example, consider the tireless efforts of the Roman Catholic missionary born in 1910 and known as Mother Teresa.

Mother Teresa dedicated herself to helping the poor and the sick around the world. She founded the Missionaries of Charity in Calcutta, India. In 1979, her efforts were formally recognized when she was granted the Nobel Peace Prize. Today, August 27 -- Mother Teresa's birthday -- is a great day to remind ourselves of the admirable example she set.

Strive for perfection

"You have not lived a perfect day, even though you have earned your money, unless you have done something for someone who will never be able to repay you." -- Ruth Smeltzer

August 28, 2018
Tuesday
Bow Tie Day

Objectives & reminders

______

______

______

Appointments

Early morning

8 a.m.

9 a.m.

10 a.m.

11 a.m.

Noon

1 p.m.

2 p.m.

3 p.m.

4 p.m.

5 p.m.

6 p.m.

Later evening

Happy birthday: Johann Wolfgang von Goethe

Goethe was born in Frankfurt, Germany on August 28, 1749. He is best known as a poet, novelist, dramatist and philosopher, but he also was somewhat of a scientist and pioneer of the modern-day scientific process. Many of the bits of wisdom he offered remain highly relevant in today's business world. Accordingly, some of his insights are included in the accompanying boxes.

Business bursts of insight

The need for a vision or plan
"One never goes so far as when one doesn't know where one is going."
-- JWG

Implementation of ideas
"Thinking is easy, acting is difficult, and to put one's thoughts into action is the most difficult thing in the world." -- JWG

Moving forward
"In the realm of ideas everything depends on enthusiasm... In the real world all rests on perseverance."
-- JWG

Professional development
"Accepting good advice increases one's own ability."
-- JWG

Working with others
"Human relations means treating people as if they were what they ought to be and you help them to become what they are capable of being."
--JWG

______

Insight for motivating others

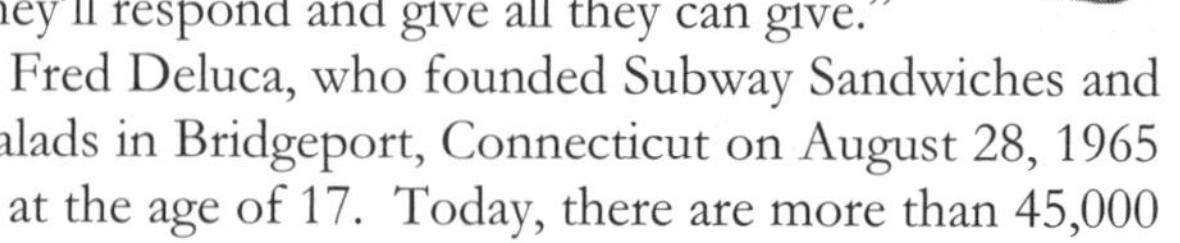

"People have inside of them a certain work ethic, and if you appeal to them nicely, they'll respond and give all they can give."
– Fred Deluca, who founded Subway Sandwiches and Salads in Bridgeport, Connecticut on August 28, 1965 – at the age of 17. Today, there are more than 45,000 Subway restaurants in 113 countries.

August 29, 2018
Wednesday
National Sports Day (India)

Objectives & reminders

Appointments

Early morning

8 a.m.

9 a.m.

10 a.m.

11 a.m.

Noon

1 p.m.

2 p.m.

3 p.m.

4 p.m.

5 p.m.

6 p.m.

Later evening

Happy birthday: Dorothy Hustead

Born in Colman, South Dakota on August 29, 1904, Dorothy Hustead and her husband, Ted, were instrumental in putting the small town of Wall, South Dakota on the map. The young couple moved to Wall where they opened Wall Drug in 1931.

After four and a half years, the drug store was drowning from the common business malady called "not enough customers." Dorothy Hustead's prescription was to offer free ice water to passing travelers. Ted agreed and helped promote the concept with eight signs placed along the nearby highway. The water lure made a splash with consumers (especially in the hot summer) and kept the business afloat. Not surprisingly, the Husteads became big believers in both free water and outdoor advertising.

Prescription for success
"I believe any person with patience, faith, humility, and courage can -- by hard work, enthusiasm, and by following a plan -- succeed."
-- Dorothy Hustead

Today, Wall remains a very small town with a population of about 766, but Wall Drug continues to thrive. The store gives away thousands of servings of free water daily. The business invests hundreds of thousands of dollars annually (estimates vary) for advertising on hundreds of billboards – some of which are placed more than 300 miles from the store.

The free water and billboards have proven to be an effective combination -- attracting up to 20,000 visitors on some hot summer days. Guests drink the free water and spend more than $11 million annually on refreshments, snacks, souvenirs, and other items.

Faith in marketing
"Free Ice Water. It brought us Husteads a long way and it taught me my greatest lesson, and that's that there's absolutely no place on God's earth that's Godforsaken. No matter where you live, you can succeed, because wherever you are, you can reach out to other people with something that they need!"
– Ted Hustead

August 30, 2018
Thursday
Constitution Day (Kazakhstan)

Objectives & reminders

____

____

____

Appointments

Early morning

8 a.m.

9 a.m.

10 a.m.

11 a.m.

Noon

1 p.m.

2 p.m.

3 p.m.

4 p.m.

5 p.m.

6 p.m.

Later evening

Q: What's more effective than a publicity stunt?
A: A *nationally televised* publicity stunt.

That's what Carvel's (the U.S.'s first retail ice cream chain) pulled off on August 30, 2002, when the company made the largest ice cream pyramid on the *CBS Early Show*. Establishing a new Guinness World Record, the 1,005-pound pyramid was built with 3,894 scoops (278 gallons) of Carvel's vanilla ice cream.

Capitalizing on the publicity opportunity, Carvel's president, Steve Romaniello commented: "Setting the new world record was an incredible opportunity for us to share the Carvel experience. Thanks to our dedicated employees and franchisees, our creamy, crunchy product has been an industry favorite for more than 68 years."

If you're a sales rep, do *not* try to break this record

Salespeople often use humor to relax prospects and establish rapport, but busy buyers are likely to interpret too many jokes as a waste of valuable time. It follows that salespeople should avoid trying to break Felipe Carbonnel's record-breaking joke marathon, which began on August 30, 1990. At the Lima Sheraton Hotel in Lima, Peru, Mr. Carbonnel began telling jokes on that day and didn't stop for 100 hours.

Humor tip: Make it relevant

In selling situations, humor is likely to work best when it pertains to the product or the message. For example, a candy salesman might use the following riddles when interacting with a grocery store's candy buyer:

Q: What do you call a bear without teeth?
A: A gummie bear. ☺

Q: Why is working in the Produce Department easier than working in the Candy Department?
A: Because it's much easier to peel bananas than M&Ms. ☺

August 31, 2018
Friday
Trail Mix Day

Objectives & reminders

___

___

___

Appointments

Early morning

8 a.m.

9 a.m.

10 a.m.

11 a.m.

Noon

1 p.m.

2 p.m.

3 p.m.

4 p.m.

5 p.m.

6 p.m.

Later evening

Footnote

Footnotes:
Quiet material can be quite material

In what one analyst described as "the ultimate in creative accounting," the annual report of the National Student Marketing Corporation (dated August 31, 1969) disclosed their deficit of more than $3.7 million -- a significant amount for an organization of its size. The deficit was not featured as a central topic in the report; rather it was quietly reported in a footnote.[1]

Obvious tip about the not-so-obvious
Read the footnotes!

August 31 in innovation history

1830 Edwin B. Budding, from Stroud, Gloucestershire, England patented his innovation -- the first lawn mower. Blades were mounted on a cylinder between two wheels. When the mower was pushed, the cylinders rotated which spun the blades to cut the grass. Today, mowers utilizing essentially the same technology are still available for purchase.

1920 John Lloyd Wright received a patent for his invention that continues to stimulate children's creativity -- Lincoln Logs. Positioned as educational toys, Lincoln Logs were an immediate success. The toy blocks were among the first toys advertised on television, i.e., on *Pioneer Playhouse* in 1953.

1955 The first solar-powered automobile in the world was demonstrated by William G. Cobb. Since then, dozens of solar-powered automobile competitions have been held, but the market is still waiting for a widely-available solar-powered vehicle.

[1] If you think you may be the first student from your college or university to read this footnote on or before August 31, 2018, let the author know. If you are the first, there's a free gift waiting for you, plus your name and the distinction of being first may be noted in future editions of *Marketing FAME*. Email Dr. Martin directly at Charles.Martin@wichita.edu or reach him through the "Contact" page on *Marketing FAME*'s official website, www.MarketingMarbles.com Be sure to include your name, of course, your mailing address, the name of your college or university, and the name of your instructor. Winners will be notified by return email and gifts will be shipped to the winners in October. Good luck and thanks for reading the fine print!

September 1, 2018
Saturday
Disaster Prevention Day (Japan)

Objectives & reminders

Appointments

Early morning

8 a.m.

9 a.m.

10 a.m.

11 a.m.

Noon

1 p.m.

2 p.m.

3 p.m.

4 p.m.

5 p.m.

6 p.m.

Later evening

Poetic content

"My favorite poem is the one that starts, 'Thirty days hath September' because it actually tells you something." -- Groucho Marx, comedian

September symbols to know

September's gem is the sapphire, and the month's flower is the morning glory.

Marketing-relevant U.S. legislation on September 1

1916 The Keating-Owen Act was signed by President Woodrow Wilson. Among other provisions, the Act prohibited companies from selling goods across state lines if the goods were made by children under the age of 14.

1940 The Federal Communications Commission (FCC) began allowing limited broadcasting of commercial messages on television, but warned that "emphasis on the commercial aspects of the operation at the expense of program research is to be avoided."

1954 The Social Security Act was amended to include an additional seven million people under the Social Security umbrella -- mostly self-employed farmers.

1997 The hourly minimum wage increased from $4.75 to $5.15.

Blackout period begins

Fund-raisers for non-profits affiliated with the United Way should note that certain periods of the year are designated as "Blackout Periods." During these periods, the United Way stages its fundraising drive and asks that member organizations call "time-out" on most individual fundraising activities that might conflict with the United Way's efforts.

The timing of the blackout periods varies throughout the country but often runs from September 1 through the middle of November. Businesses interested in teaming with non-profits should note the blackout periods and contact their local United Way office to learn more about which fundraising activities are prohibited or permitted during these times.

September 2, 2018
Sunday

Father's Day (Australia, Fiji, New Zealand and Papua New Guinea)

Objectives & reminders

___

___

___

Appointments

Early morning

8 a.m.

9 a.m.

10 a.m.

11 a.m.

Noon

1 p.m.

2 p.m.

3 p.m.

4 p.m.

5 p.m.

6 p.m.

Later evening

Only the paranoid survive

"I believe in the value of paranoia. Business success contains the seeds of its own destruction. The more successful you are, the more people want a chunk of your business and then another chunk and then another until there is nothing left. I believe that the prime responsibility of a manager is to guard constantly against other people's attacks and to inculcate this guardian attitude in the people under his or her management." – Andrew S. Grove, former chairman and CEO of Intel Corporation and author of the best-selling book, *Only the Paranoid Survive* (1996). Grove was born in Budapest, Hungary on September 2, 1936.

Time to be paranoid about Christmas plans

"Prepare marketing materials well in advance. With Black Friday, Cyber Monday, Thanksgiving, Christmas and [New Year's Day] all contained in a short period of time, it can be easy to be overwhelmed and to overlook important money-making opportunities. Have a holiday calendar with all promotions and plans scheduled so your team is ready; timing is key!" – Kyle Goguen, founder and president of Pawstruck.com (online retailer and manufacturer of dog treats)

Intuition not to be discounted: Agree or disagree?

"Organizational effectiveness does not lie in that narrow-minded concept called rationality. It lies in the blend of clear-headed logic and powerful intuition." – Henry Mintzberg, world renowned Canadian business/management scholar, born in Montreal, Canada on September 2, 1939

Self-empowerment is up for grabs: Agree or disagree?

"Authority is 20 percent given and 80 percent taken. Take it." – Peter Ueberroth, former chair of the United States Olympic Committee (USOC) and head of the committee in charge of organizing and hosting the 1984 Olympic Games in Los Angeles, and commissioner of Major League Baseball (1984-1989). Ueberroth was born in Evanston, Illinois on September 2, 1937.

September 3, 2018
Monday
Labor Day

Objectives & reminders

____

____

____

Appointments

Early morning

8 a.m.

9 a.m.

10 a.m.

11 a.m.

Noon

1 p.m.

2 p.m.

3 p.m.

4 p.m.

5 p.m.

6 p.m.

Later evening

Labor Day

Originally observed in the 1890s to honor workers' efforts and accomplishments, Labor Day is celebrated in the United States and Canada with parades, speeches, and other ceremonies on the first Monday of September.

Labor Day is one of the most widely observed holidays in the U.S. in terms of the number of employers who give workers the day off. Because the day off from work creates a three-day weekend for many consumers, about 11 percent seize the opportunity to travel. Many others view the weekend as one of a few remaining seasonal opportunities to engage in outdoor activities such as picnics and cookouts, swimming, camping, and boating.

Tip for workaholics only

American workaholics who believe Labor Day should be celebrated by working could "enjoy" the day by traveling overseas. In Europe, for example, the first Monday in September is a normal work day. Many European countries celebrate the equivalent of Labor Day on May 1.

Happy birthday: Glen William Bell, Jr.

Born in southern California on September 3, 1923, much of Bell's childhood was spent with his family trying to survive the Great Depression. After serving in World War II, Bell returned to California where he opened and then sold a series of fast-food restaurants, many of which were successful businesses.

Then in 1962, Bell opened a Mexican restaurant in Los Angeles -- "Taco Bell." Within the next two years Bell opened eight more Taco Bell locations and then began selling franchises in 1965. Bell grew the business for the next few years and then sold Taco Bell to PepsiCo in 1978. Today, Taco Bell is part of Yum! Brands and its 7,000 restaurants in the U.S. and Canada fill more than two billion orders annually.

Calendar-led marketing effort

Knowing that hectic American lifestyles prevent many consumers from eating at "traditional" times, Taco Bell introduced its "Fourth Meal" concept to promote guilt-free dining during evening hours.

September 4, 2018
Tuesday
National Macadamia Nut Day

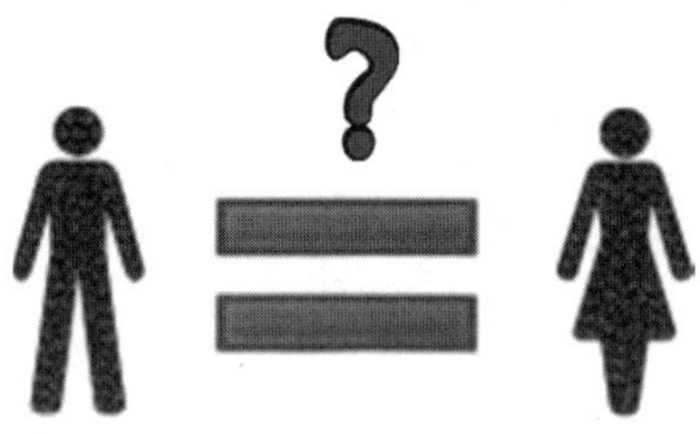

Objectives & reminders

____

____

Appointments

Early morning

8 a.m.

9 a.m.

10 a.m.

11 a.m.

Noon

1 p.m.

2 p.m.

3 p.m.

4 p.m.

5 p.m.

6 p.m.

Later evening

Learning from market research: Gender matters

"We learned that the most discriminating shoppers are female. We knew that if we could win over the loyalty of the female shopper, men would follow. Men are very simplistic. If you've got the... stuff in stock and it's at a good price, and they can get out in a hurry, they're happy. They say, 'I've got a golf game this afternoon, so let me go get this done.'"

"Women shop. And they shop intelligently. They know the prices of things. They know what's available. They look at magazines. They look at *Home and Garden Television.* How many men watch decorating shows when a football game is on? Women are different customers, and you have to market to them differently. We needed to create a more inviting environment -- a store that was lighter and brighter, with bigger aisles and clean floors."

– Robert L. Tillman, retired chairman, president and CEO of Lowe's Companies, Inc., born on September 4, 1943

First breakfast cereal trademark

Little did he know it at the time, but the Quaker on Quaker Oats cereal would be recognized around the world in the 21st century. That is, on September 4, 1877, the Quaker man's image was registered as part of the Quaker Mill Company's trademark – the first trademark in the breakfast cereal category. The company's co-founder, Henry Seymour, chose the Quaker image to symbolize quality and honesty – favorable attributes to be associated with the company and the brand. Since 1877, the now famous trademarked image has been revised only a few times.

Prior to Seymour's introduction of his Quaker brand, oats were considered a commodity product. Retailers purchased oats from multiple suppliers and sold them from large nondescript barrels. Quality varied.

Quaker Oats, however, were individually packaged in cardboard canisters and soon earned a reputation for high and consistent quality. The reputation was reinforced by the picture of the Quaker man on the package, as Quaker merchants were known for their high integrity and honesty in dealing with customers.

Today, oats continue to play an integral role in the company's product portfolio that generates annual sales in excess of $800 million.

September 5, 2018
Wednesday
International Day of Charity

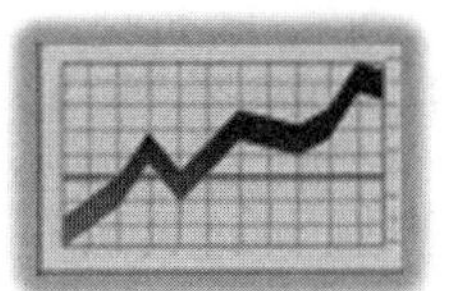

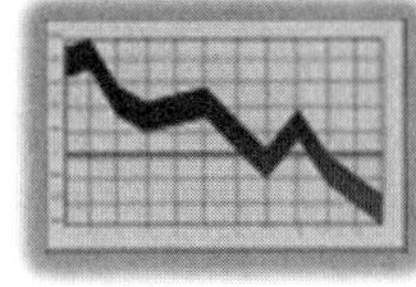

Objectives & reminders

____

____

____

Appointments

Early morning

8 a.m.

9 a.m.

10 a.m.

11 a.m.

Noon

1 p.m.

2 p.m.

3 p.m.

4 p.m.

5 p.m.

6 p.m.

Later evening

Impending crisis

"Sooner or later a crash is coming... Wise are those investors who now... reef their sails... Investment trusts will first begin to sell... and then there may be a stampede for selling which will exceed anything that the Stock Exchange has ever witnessed." – Roger W. Babson, financial analyst and founder of the Babson Institute. Babson offered this forecast on September 5, 1929. He was one of the few financial forecasters who correctly predicted the crash in the U.S. stock market that occurred less than two months later.

Microtrends shape America, shape marketing

On September 5, 2007, Mark Penn's book was published: *Microtrends: The Small Forces Behind Tomorrow's Big Changes*. In it, Penn asserts that the "melting pot" metaphor used to describe the U.S. population in the past has become less appropriate as the country becomes more of a collection of small communities, each with its own lifestyles, tastes, and preferences. Accordingly, says Penn, we should look to small "microtrends" that occur within each of these communities if we expect to understand and capitalize on the changing nature of society.

Penn identified about six dozen microtrends – many of which continue to have implications for marketers. For example, consider how the effectiveness of marketing communications might be enhanced by recognizing the following microtrends, or what new product opportunities might emerge to serve the market segments most closely associated with them.

1. Today's generation of fathers are older than those of the past, and they're spending more time with their children.

2. More children are home-schooled today than a generation or two ago.

3. In contrast to past generations of seniors, a greater percentage of people over the age of 65 are employed today – at least part-time.

4. Increasingly, Geeks are cool.

5. People are spending more time commuting to work than did past generations of workers. Many spend one hour or more commuting each way.

September 6, 2018
Thursday
Unification Day (Bulgaria)

Objectives & reminders

______

______

______

Appointments

______

Early morning

______

8 a.m.

______

9 a.m.

______

10 a.m.

______

11 a.m.

______

Noon

______

1 p.m.

______

2 p.m.

______

3 p.m.

______

4 p.m.

______

5 p.m.

______

6 p.m.

______

Later evening

______

Self-service revolution begins

Grocer Clarence Saunders changed food retailing forever on September 6, 1916, when he opened the first *self-service* Piggly Wiggly grocery store – in Memphis, Tennessee. Although commonplace today, the idea of allowing customers to roam the aisles by themselves while handling, inspecting, selecting and rejecting merchandise along the way was innovative in 1916. Some businesspeople viewed the practice as risky: "What if customers damage the merchandise while handling it?"

In hindsight, we now realize that the advantages of customer involvement in self-service stores outweigh the disadvantages. Labor costs are lower (customers provide much of the "labor") and the stepped-up role played by customers means they tend to purchase more items and are more likely to be satisfied with their purchase decisions. The concept was well-received by Piggly Wiggly's customers. By 1922, the grocery chain operated 1,200 stores in 29 states. A decade later they had grown to 2,660 stores.

______

Business reality

"Business is about more than facts. It's also about powerful emotions and how people react to them."
– Carly Fiorina, former CEO of Hewlett-Packard and 2016 Republican presidential candidate, born in Austin, Texas on September 6, 1954

______

Time to "fire up"

"I rate enthusiasm even above professional skill."
– Sir Edward Appleton, British physicist and Nobel Prize winner, born in Bradford, England on September 6, 1892

______

Ideas as products

"Whether we keep our free economy or trade it for something about which we know very little is the big political issue ahead. It is up to businessmen to sell our economic system to the public. They must do as good a job on that as they do on their own products. Unless the advantages of our system over others are brought home to everyone, there is no reason to believe that the trend toward more and more government will be checked." – Joseph P. Kennedy, industrialist and patriarch of the Kennedy family (father of President John F. Kennedy), born in Boston, Massachusetts on September 6, 1888

September 7, 2018 Friday

Independence Day (Brazil)

Objectives & reminders

______

______

______

Appointments

Early morning

8 a.m.

9 a.m.

10 a.m.

11 a.m.

Noon

1 p.m.

2 p.m.

3 p.m.

4 p.m.

5 p.m.

6 p.m.

Later evening

Chrysler's low is not investor-friendly

In the late 1970s, many large U.S. corporations experienced financial problems -- including the auto giant Chrysler Corporation. On September 7, 1979, Chrysler announced the likelihood that it would set a new record for pre-tax losses in a single year (the previous record was held by Bethlehem Steel, $911 million).

Chrysler management, led by Lee Iacocca, put together a "rescue plan" for the company which included an overhaul of the company involving a reduction in labor costs and a revamping of their product mix. The plan also involved asking the Federal government for a loan of approximately $1 billion, which Chrysler received and repaid.

Government as a safety net: Agree or disagree?

To what extent or under what circumstances should the government come to the aid of struggling businesses? Should the government adopt a "hands off" policy and let the marketplace forces of the free enterprise system determine which companies survive and which ones do not? Consider the effects on the struggling businesses' workforce, customers, suppliers and investors, as well as competitors, local communities where the struggling businesses are located, and other factors.

Chrysler's "Hi" is buyer-friendly

On the same day of the year, but 14 years later -- September 7, 1993 -- Chrysler Corporation broke automobile marketing tradition when the company introduced the Neon at the Frankfurt Auto Show.

Rather than positioning the Neon in terms of performance, styling or economy, per se, Chrysler chose to emphasize *friendliness* with their multi-million dollar "Hi" advertising campaign. The campaign suggested that the Neon was loaded with "friendly" attributes -- ease of handling, a welcoming design, and comfortable seats. The theme of the campaign was topped off by the apparently friendly and outgoing personality of the Neon who introduced itself by saying, "Hi. I'm Neon."

September 8, 2018
Saturday
International Literacy Day

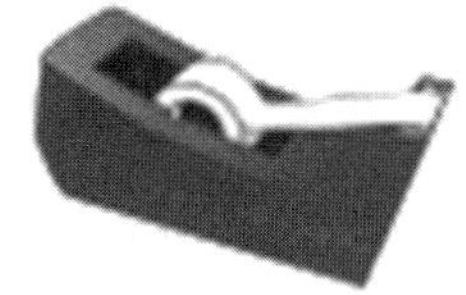

Objectives & reminders

____

____

____

Appointments

Early morning

8 a.m.

9 a.m.

10 a.m.

11 a.m.

Noon

1 p.m.

2 p.m.

3 p.m.

4 p.m.

5 p.m.

6 p.m.

Later evening

Sticking to it

Not all inventions are an immediate hit. Often inventors must try and try again before overcoming the technical problems of development. Then when commercialized, some innovations are not particularly well received by the market segments initially targeted. This was the experience of Richard G. Drew whose invention of cellophane tape enabled 3M to roll out the first roll of Scotch tape on September 8, 1930.

Scotch tape was first marketed to business markets, including grocers, bakers and meat packers, but the concept of cellophane tape didn't stick with them, so 3M began targeting household consumers in the U.S. Because the country was still very much in the grips of the Great Depression, consumers of the day were somewhat hesitant to try any new and unproven product.

But, the depression also brought out consumers' creative and thrifty instincts. So, consumers began using Scotch tape for a wide variety of purposes, including the mending and repair of personal belongings.

Today, Scotch tape is used in both homes and offices and its maker -- 3M -- commands a whopping 90 percent share of the cellophane tape market in the United States.

A national star is born

138 television stations in the United States carried the *Oprah Winfrey Show* on September 8, 1986 -- the day the show went national. The show's initial projected income was $125 million, of which Winfrey herself would receive $30 million. Soon Winfrey became a television star, and later became a successful businesswoman too – starting her own company to produce her show, Harpo Productions.

The Winfrey way

"To me, one of the most important things about being a good manager is to rule with a heart. You have to know the business, but you also have to know what's at the heart of the business, and that's the people. People matter."
-- Oprah Winfrey

September 9, 2018
Sunday

National Grandparents Day
Rosh Hashanah begins

Objectives & reminders

____

____

____

Appointments

Early morning

8 a.m.

9 a.m.

10 a.m.

11 a.m.

Noon

1 p.m.

2 p.m.

3 p.m.

4 p.m.

5 p.m.

6 p.m.

Later evening

Grandfatherly advice on National Grandparents Day

"What advice would I give my grandchildren? That's the easiest question in the world. Do something you enjoy -- music, business, public service, whatever. If they don't enjoy going to work, I don't care if their IQ is 30 points higher, the guy with the inferior IQ who loves what he is doing will beat them to death." – Alan C. "Ace" Greenberg, former chairman of the Executive Committee for Bear Stearns (securities firm)

For future reference
Since 1978, Grandparents Day falls on the first Sunday after the first Monday in September, i.e., Sunday after Labor Day.

Happy birthday: Colonel Harland Sanders

Sanders was born in Henryville, Kentucky on September 9, 1890, and enjoyed a fairly lackluster career in a variety of jobs and business ventures until the mid-1950s when his career took off -- at a time when others his age were making the transition into retirement. That's when Sanders hit upon the idea of licensing the use of his chicken preparation process in exchange for royalties on each chicken sold.

At the time, Sanders' marketing strategy was straightforward: he traveled throughout the southern United States and personally prepared sample batches of chicken in the restaurant kitchens of prospective licensees. The taste of the chicken, coupled with Sanders' enthusiasm for the process, convinced many restaurants to adopt the process. Soon Sanders' "finger-lickin-good" Kentucky Fried Chicken was well recognized and commanded a loyal following. By 1963, more than 300 locations were selling Kentucky Fried Chicken. Sanders sold the business in the mid-1960s, but remained active as an advertising spokesperson.

Don't be chicken to try
"I made a resolve... that I was going to amount to something if I could. And no hours, nor amount of labor, nor amount of money would deter me from giving the best that there was in me. And I have done that..." -- Colonel Harland Sanders

September 10, 2018
Monday
Swap Ideas Day

Objectives & reminders

____

____

____

____

Appointments

Early morning

8 a.m.

9 a.m.

10 a.m.

11 a.m.

Noon

1 p.m.

2 p.m.

3 p.m.

4 p.m.

5 p.m.

6 p.m.

Later evening

Drunk-driving's infamous tradition

On September 10, 1897, London police made the first arrest of a drunk automobile driver -- George Smith. Smith's condition caused him to have a traffic accident. He was fined one pound.

Unfortunately, the arrest and fine did not prove to be a particularly effective deterrent for the behavior of the thousands of drunk drivers that followed Smith. Although driving while intoxicated (DWI) is illegal in most countries and punishable by fines and jail sentences, it is still a leading cause of automobile accidents. In the United States alone, alcohol is involved in about one-third of all traffic fatalities -- about 16,000 deaths annually. Another 500,000 people are injured and one billion dollars in property damages are attributed to alcohol-related traffic accidents each year.

Marketing campaigns to curb drinking and driving have yielded mixed results. Simply promoting the idea that one should not drink and drive tends to be less effective than offering specific behavioral alternatives, such as designating a non-drinking driver for the group or using public transportation when intoxicated.

> **Drinking on this road also problematic?**
> "The road to success is always under construction." -- Arnold Palmer, American golfing legend, product spokesman and businessman, born in Latrobe, Pennsylvania on September 10, 1929

Interesting idea

"You must make the product interesting, not just make the ad different. And that's what too many of the copywriters in the U.S. today don't yet understand."
-- Rosser Reeves, American advertising executive who pioneered the concept of the "unique selling proposition," born in Danville, Virginia on September 10, 1910

> **"Unique selling proposition" defined**
> "An advertising strategy that focuses on a product or service attribute that is distinctive to a particular brand and offers an important benefit to the customer."
> -- George E. Belch and Michael A. Belch, *Introduction to Advertising & Promotion*

September 11, 2018
Tuesday
Patriot Day

Objectives & reminders

___

___

___

Appointments

Early morning

8 a.m.

9 a.m.

10 a.m.

11 a.m.

Noon

1 p.m.

2 p.m.

3 p.m.

4 p.m.

5 p.m.

6 p.m.

Later evening

Patriot Day

Also known simply as "9-11," September 11, 2001, is one of the saddest and most horrific days in the history of the United States.

That's the day when Islamic terrorists turned commercial airplanes into flying bombs to attack the World Trade Center Towers in New York City and the Pentagon in Washington, D.C.. It was also the day terrorists caused the crash of Flight 93 near Shanksville, Pennsylvania.

Nearly 3,000 people lost their lives that day and almost 10,000 more were injured. Needless to say, concern for safety and security has climbed sharply as a result of the 9-11 attacks.

Budweiser's 9-11 tribute

Follow the link below to see Budweiser's televised tribute to 9-11. What might have been the objectives of the brand's managers?

https://www.youtube.com/watch?v=A5uEeEWhBCA

It's now a post-9-11 marketplace

"[A]long with everything else, the advertising world -- and what it takes to succeed in that world -- has been fundamentally altered [since September 11, 2001]…

"I'm talking about... [how the] attack itself changed consumers' norms, values, and needs. People now feel somewhat less safe than they did before, and they've made their world a little smaller. Country, church, family, social harmony, and security have become more important while excessive personal gratification, social recognition, and materialism have become less important...

"Interestingly, this kind of thing happens all the time. Not on the same scale as September 11, of course, but every single day there are things that change the ways people see themselves and the ways they arrange their priorities. If you're going to succeed in business, you're going to have to be prepared to identify these changing currents, and more important, react to them appropriately."

> -- Sergio Zyman, former marketing director for The Coca-Cola Company and author of *The End of Advertising As We Know It*, pp. 92-93.

September 12, 2018
Wednesday
National Day of Encouragement

Objectives & reminders

____

____

Appointments

Early morning
8 a.m.
9 a.m.
10 a.m.
11 a.m.
Noon
1 p.m.
2 p.m.
3 p.m.
4 p.m.
5 p.m.
6 p.m.
Later evening

Relationship-building prerequisite

Productivity on the job often depends on co-workers' ability to work together. If working relationships don't exist, not much work is likely to get done. Similarly, productive working relationships between customers and customer-contact employees also enhance company performance.

One of the building blocks of effective working relationships is learning and using other people's names (If you're not convinced, try to count how many great working relationships you have with people whose names you do not know). Business relationships are further enhanced when co-workers' and customers' names are spelled and pronounced correctly.

Former chairman and CEO of General Electric, Jack Welch, had a reputation for productivity. He also knew more than 1,000 GE employees by name, but Welch resigned before Mr…

Rhoshandiatellyneshiaunneveshenk
Koyaanfsquatsiuty Williams

…entered the workforce. According to his birth certificate, R.K.'s birthday falls on September 12, and according to the *Guinness Book of World Records*, R.K.'s birth certificate has on it the longest name on record.

Proper pronunciation matters: Agree or disagree?

Agree	Disagree
"A person's name is to that person the sweetest and most important sound in any language." – Dale Carnegie, author of the 1936 best-seller, *How to Win Friends and Influence People*	"Everybody has a right to pronounce foreign names as he chooses." -- Winston Churchill, former British prime minister (1940-1945, 1951-1955)

What leaders know

"Find the good. It's all around you. Find it, showcase it and you'll start believing it." – James C. "Jesse" Owens, courageous American track star who won four gold medals at the 1936 Olympics in Berlin, Germany. Owens was born in Oakville, Alabama on September 12, 1913.

September 13, 2018
Thursday
Positive Thinking Day

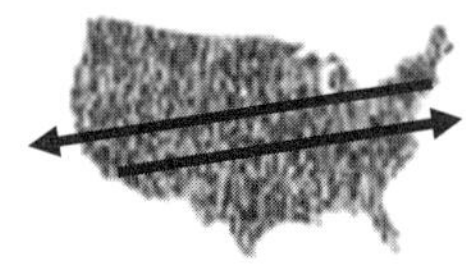

Objectives & reminders

___

___

___

Appointments

Early morning

8 a.m.

9 a.m.

10 a.m.

11 a.m.

Noon

1 p.m.

2 p.m.

3 p.m.

4 p.m.

5 p.m.

6 p.m.

Later evening

"Twice Across America"

The Hudson Motor Car Company's "Twice Across America" publicity campaign began on September 13, 1916, to promote its new engine, nicknamed the "Super Six." Because other automakers had already staged cross-country trips to publicize the durability of their automobiles, Hudson decided to top them with a *round trip* journey – from San Francisco to New York, and back again.

Generating effective media publicity

Hudson's efforts to generate positive media publicity paid off. Note how Hudson followed these guidelines for publicity-seeking events, and how the guidelines remain relevant today.

1. Choose an event that is novel, ambitious and capable of capturing the public's imagination. Few people in 1916 had ever traveled across the country, and even fewer had done so in an automobile.

2. Choose an event that will reflect positively on the company and/or its products. It was easy for observers to believe that Hudson's engine was durable if it could survive the cross-country round trip. In contrast, staging an unrelated event (such as a hot-dog-eating contest) might have had little impact on consumers' perceptions of the Hudson Motor Car Company.

3. Brand the event. Clearly "Twice Across America" sends a more potent (even patriotic) message than simply proclaiming, "we're going to drive a car from San Francisco to New York and then drive back to San Francisco."

4. Announce plans for the event well in advance – to allow time for the media to plan accordingly, and to allow time for public anticipation to build.

5. If possible, involve the media at several levels. Twice Across America was a *national* event, but when the Hudson vehicle rolled down Main Street in hundreds of small towns it became a *local* event as well.

September 14, 2018
Friday
San Jacinto Day (Nicaragua)

Objectives & reminders

___

___

___

Appointments

Early morning

8 a.m.

9 a.m.

10 a.m.

11 a.m.

Noon

1 p.m.

2 p.m.

3 p.m.

4 p.m.

5 p.m.

6 p.m.

Later evening

Good day for a military promotion

Today is one of 24 paydays in 2018 for active duty American military personnel. Typically they're paid on about the 1st and 15th of each month, with paydays moved up a day or two when the 1st or 15th falls on a Saturday, Sunday or federal holiday.

The U.S. armed forces consist of more than 1.4 million active duty personnel, plus 800,000 reserves scattered across the country. Active duty personnel receive an average of $1,900 per pay period (excludes non-cash benefits such as housing, food and health care).

Obviously, military personnel represent an important target market for retail stores and consumer service businesses located near the country's 500+ military bases and coast guard stations. The twice-a-month influx of money can have a significant impact on the local economy, in general, and on individual businesses, in particular.

Consumers' spending patterns tend to coincide with the timing of their receipt of money – such as on paydays. The spending effect is magnified when paydays are followed by weekends, when consumers tend to have more time to shop. So, while any day may be a good one to appeal to military personnel, *today* is a particularly excellent opportunity to do so, because it is both a payday *and* a Friday.

When windows of marketing opportunity tend to be open

1. When buyers have *money* to spend (e.g., paydays, tax refund season).
2. When buyers have *time* to shop (e.g., evenings, weekends and many holidays for most consumers).
3. When buyers have a *need or interest* in the product category (e.g., snow shovels in winter, but not in summer).
4. When buyers are most likely to *access media* and thus can be reached with advertising (e.g., motorists commuting to and from work may be reached with radio advertising during morning and afternoon "drive times").

September 15, 2018
Saturday
International Free Money Day

Objectives & reminders

___

___

___

Appointments

Early morning
8 a.m.
9 a.m.
10 a.m.
11 a.m.
Noon
1 p.m.
2 p.m.
3 p.m.
4 p.m.
5 p.m.
6 p.m.
Later evening

Before e-everything

"E-tailing" (electronic retailing) has attracted the attention of the business world during the last couple of decades as online shopping has gained a foothold as a viable alternative to brick and mortar stores.

But before e-commerce, there were mail-order businesses – the first launched on September 15, 1871: the Army & Navy Co-operative Society Ltd., in London. The following year, the Montgomery Ward mail-order firm was launched in the United States. Hundreds of other mail-order firms followed. Can mail-order firms compete in today's increasingly digital marketplace?

Mail order vs Internet: Pros & cons

Mail order beats Internet retailing

1. Mail order is more inclusive: 16 percent of American adults don't use the Internet, including 42 percent of seniors. Worldwide, 50.4 percent of consumers do not use the Internet.
2. Mail order offers compete with fewer items in consumers' mailboxes than online offers.
3. Some consumers prefer to deal with a paper catalogue than an electronic screen. Some believe it is more difficult to shop online than in a paper catalogue.
4. Many consumers still prefer to send payments through the mail rather than electronically, believing the former method is safer.

Internet retailing beats mail order

1. Reaching consumers electronically is much less expensive on a per-contact basis than direct mail.
2. Product information, prices and other information that's posted online can be changed much quicker and less expensively than revising information in printed catalogues.
3. Many consumers prefer shopping on the Internet because they can compare competing offers more easily before making a purchase decision.
4. Many consumers may discard or can't find a printed catalogue when they need it, but the Internet is always close by.

September 16, 2018
Sunday

Malaysia Day (Malaysia)

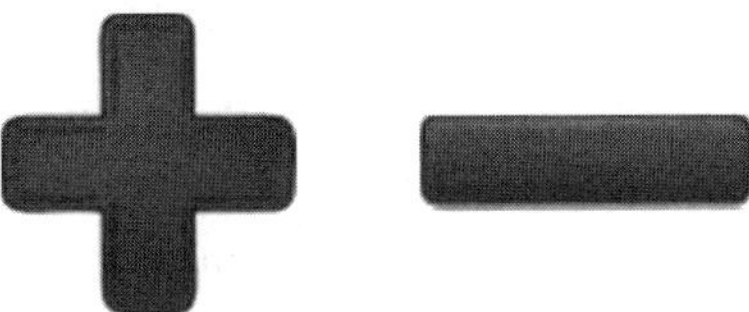

Objectives & reminders

____

____

____

Appointments

Early morning

8 a.m.

9 a.m.

10 a.m.

11 a.m.

Noon

1 p.m.

2 p.m.

3 p.m.

4 p.m.

5 p.m.

6 p.m.

Later evening

Turning points for the United States

On September 16, 1985, the Department of Commerce announced that the U.S. had become a *debtor nation* – meaning that the country owed more money than other countries owed it. Prior to 1985, it had been 71 years since the U.S. had been classified as a debtor nation.

According to another measure, the U.S. also became a *service economy* in 1985. It was that year, for the first time, that consumer households spent more money for services than for manufactured goods.

> **Negative or positive?: Invitation to discuss**
> What are the marketing implications of being a debtor nation and a service economy?

Negative appeals

Most marketers use *positive appeals* by suggesting that good things will happen if you buy or use their brands -- you'll be happier, safer, more attractive, admired, wealthier, and so on.

However, when consumer benefits are not immediate or apparent, *negative appeals* may prompt consumers to act – by saying or implying that something undesirable will happen if the promoted brands are *not* used. For example, a deodorant soap maker points out that other people will be turned-off by your body odor if you don't use their soap. And a producer of auto maintenance supplies suggests that you will have to pay an enormous auto repair bill later if you don't use the right maintenance supplies today.

Interestingly, Albert Szent-Gyorgyi, the Hungarian biochemist who worked extensively with vitamins (e.g., he isolated vitamin C), used a negative appeal to encourage the consumption of vitamins: "A vitamin is a substance that makes you ill if you don't eat it." Szent-Gyorgyi was born in Budapest, Austria-Hungary on September 16, 1893.

Turning a negative into a positive

"I am grateful for all of my problems. After each one was overcome, I became stronger and more able to meet those that were still to come. I grew in all my difficulties." – James Cash Penney, co-founder of the Golden Rule retail stores which evolved into J.C. Penney department stores. Mr. Penney was born in Hamilton, Missouri on September 16, 1875.

September 17, 2018
Monday
Citizenship Day

Objectives & reminders

____

____

____

____

Appointments

Early morning

8 a.m.

9 a.m.

10 a.m.

11 a.m.

Noon

1 p.m.

2 p.m.

3 p.m.

4 p.m.

5 p.m.

6 p.m.

Later evening

Citizenship Day stems from signing of U.S. Constitution

Thirty-eight of 41 delegates at the Constitutional Convention in Philadelphia signed the final draft of the U.S. Constitution on September 17, 1787. Twenty-one months later enough states had ratified the Constitution for it to become the law of the land. The first ten amendments were added to the Constitution in 1791, known as the "Bill of Rights." Since those early days, another 17 amendments have been added (27 total) and the document has been used as a model to draft the Constitutions of several other countries around the globe.

> **Preamble to the U.S. Constitution**
> "We, the people of the United States, in order to form a more perfect union, establish justice, ensure domestic tranquility, provide for the common defence, promote the general welfare, and secure the blessings of liberty to ourselves and our posterity, do ordain and establish this Constitution for the United States of America."

Although not as widely observed in the U.S. as other patriotic holidays such as Independence Day (July 4), Veterans' Day (November 11), Presidents' Day (3rd Monday in February) and Memorial Day (last Monday in May), Citizenship Day is also celebrated with patriotic themes, such as flag waving, parades, speeches, and so on.

Further, Citizenship Day is a great day to celebrate the country's diversity and recognize new citizens. It is a popular day for immigrants to take the oath of citizenship to become U.S. citizens. For example, on September 17, 1984, 10,000 people crowded into Miami, Florida's Orange Bowl to celebrate citizenship and take the oath.

Vision is more than eyesight

"An enterprising person is one who comes across a pile of scrap metal and sees the making of a wonderful sculpture. An enterprising person is one who drives through an old decrepit part of town and sees a new housing development. An enterprising person is one who sees opportunity in all areas of life." – Jim Rohn, American business thinker and motivational consultant, born in Yakima, Washington on September 17, 1930

September 18, 2018
Tuesday
Yom Kippur begins

Objectives & reminders

____

____

____

Appointments

Early morning

8 a.m.

9 a.m.

10 a.m.

11 a.m.

Noon

1 p.m.

2 p.m.

3 p.m.

4 p.m.

5 p.m.

6 p.m.

Later evening

When shortages are worsened

Retailers and consumers have faced shortages several times throughout history. Some are attributed to natural disasters such as droughts, floods and unexpected freezes. Others are blamed on suppliers themselves – for failing to anticipate demand, choosing to restrict supply, labor strikes, or for other reasons. War is sometimes the culprit, and sometimes transportation or other logistical problems are at fault.

Regardless of the reasons, consumers often magnify shortages by hoarding limited supplies. That's what happened in 1939. When war broke out in Europe, *Time* magazine reported (on September 18) that consumers who had normally purchased small day-to-day quantities of sugar, flour, canned goods, and other grocery items, suddenly began buying 50- and 100-pound quantities. Apparently many consumers remembered the shortages of World War I and the fear of shortages caused by another war evoked their squirrel-like instincts – which, of course, compounded the problem of shortages.

How businesses can cope with shortages

1. Minimize supplier-specific shortages by arranging alternative sources of supply *before* shortages occur.
2. Think twice before publicly stating that a shortage exists or is expected. Customers may need time to plan accordingly, but the hoarding phenomenon may magnify the shortages.
3. If the shortage does become well known, offer suggestions to help customers conserve the limited supplies. For example, oil companies advise motorists to slow down and combine shopping trips to save fuel during gasoline shortages.
4. Formulate policies for rationing limited supplies. For example, limit quantities to one or two per customer or arrange to take care of regular customers first. However, carefully consider the policy of simply raising prices to ration supply; customers may view this as unfair price gouging and may remember the practice long after the shortage ends.

September 19, 2018
Wednesday
International Talk Like a Pirate Day

Objectives & reminders

___

___

___

Appointments

Early morning

8 a.m.

9 a.m.

10 a.m.

11 a.m.

Noon

1 p.m.

2 p.m.

3 p.m.

4 p.m.

5 p.m.

6 p.m.

Later evening

Clean marketing on September 19

1849 The first commercial laundry opened for business, in Oakland, California.

1851 William Hesketh Lever was born in Bolton, Lancashire, England. In 1885, Lever teamed with his brother, James, to launch their soap manufacturing business – Lever Brothers Co. – which grew into the multinational conglomerate we know today as Unilever. The company made one of the first packaged soap brands in the world – called Sunlight – which proved to be quite successful.

1876 Melville Reuben Bissell of Grand Rapids, Michigan patented the first practical carpet-sweeper. The Bissell Carpet Sweeper Co. that he and his wife, Anna, founded to capitalize on the invention continues to thrive today.

1887 Graham Edgar was born in Fayetteville, Arkansas. Dr. Edgar developed the octane rating system used to measure a fuel's ability to burn cleanly.

Beauty marketing on September 19

First beauty contest

Beauty contests have worked well as a tool for generating publicity, crowds and sponsorship opportunities.

Credit for the first beauty contest goes to Belgium's "Concours de Beauté," held on September 19, 1888. Three hundred and fifty contestants submitted photographs, from which 21 were chosen to compete personally in the finals. The winner of the 5,000 franc first prize was 18-year-old Bertha Soucaret.

The pencil look

Born in London on September 19, 1949, Lesley Lawson was a British model, actress, and singer better known as "Twiggy" in the late 1960s and early 1970s. Along with Barbie, Twiggy popularized the idealized "thin look" for women -- thus influencing fashion trends and perceptions of beauty.

September 20, 2018
Thursday

Ashura

Objectives & reminders

Appointments

Early morning

---

8 a.m.

---

9 a.m.

---

10 a.m.

---

11 a.m.

Noon

---

1 p.m.

---

2 p.m.

---

3 p.m.

---

4 p.m.

---

5 p.m.

---

6 p.m.

Later evening

Automotive leadership day?

Henry Ford, founder of The Ford Motor Company, handed the presidency of the company to his grandson, Henry Ford II, on September 20, 1945. More than three decades later, the younger Ford fired Lee Iacocca who was then serving as president. Some sources say that Henry II viewed Iacocca as a threat.

Coincidentally(?), also on September 20 (1979), Iacocca was elected as chairman and CEO of one of Ford's chief competitors, Chrysler Corporation. In the years that followed, Iacocca was instrumental in turning around the struggling Chrysler Corporation – apparently proving that he was a threat to Ford.

> **Experience**
> "Don't be afraid... to make mistakes, but for starters try to practice with the small ones, okay? And oh, don't make the same big mistake twice." -- Lee Iacocca

---

Good idea, questionable rationale

In September 1921 a candy and tobacco wholesaler from Dallas, Texas – Jessie G. Kirby – launched a trend in food retailing when he began selling barbeque pork sandwiches to customers who were not particularly interested in dining inside his "Pig Stand" restaurant. That is, he offered what is believed to be the first "drive-thru" or "in car" fast-food service.

Today, fast-food restaurants offer drive-thru service partially for their time-sensitive customers' convenience and partially as a method of expanding their capacity (i.e., the number of seats inside the restaurant may be limited). However, Kirby's rationale was perhaps less customer-friendly; he simply observed, "People are so lazy they don't want to get out of their car to eat."

Leadership communications

"It's through communications that strong leaders have an ability to add value to colleagues. There needs to be a conscious value take-out by the recipient – knowledge should be shared, not hoarded." – Matthew William Barrett, former Chairman and CEO of Barclays Bank, born in County Kerry, Ireland on September 20, 1944

September 21, 2018
Friday
World Gratitude Day

Objectives & reminders

Appointments

Early morning

8 a.m.

9 a.m.

10 a.m.

11 a.m.

Noon

1 p.m.

2 p.m.

3 p.m.

4 p.m.

5 p.m.

6 p.m.

Later evening

Happy birthday: W. Frank Barton

Born in Prague, Oklahoma on September 21, 1917, Barton was a personable and no-nonsense businessman and entrepreneur who corrected people when they addressed him as "Mr. Barton." "Mr. Barton," he would say, "was my father's name; call me 'Frank.'"

Frank began his business career as a teen by selling home-made sausage door-to-door from the trunk of his car. Given the perishable nature of his product, he quickly learned the important calendar-led lesson of having clearance sales on hot summer afternoons. He built upon his sausage experiences by working in other jobs and business ventures for several years, largely in retailing and distribution.

For much of his career, Frank worked for the beleaguered and now defunct retailer Montgomery Ward. When asked what he had learned from working at Montgomery Ward, he simply shook his head and said, "I learned what *not* to do."

In the mid-1970s Frank teamed with Tom Devlin to launch a chain of rent-to-own stores, dubbed Rent-A-Center. By 1978, Rent-A-Center had grown to 10 stores, then to 52 stores by 1982, and to more than 500 by 1987. At that point, the partners sold the business for a reported $594 million – more than a million dollars per store. At last count, there were more than 3,050 Rent-A-Center stores in North America.

Frank thank

How fitting it is for Frank Barton's partner, Tom Devlin, to express his appreciation for Frank's contributions -- not only because today is Frank's birthday, but because today is also World Gratitude Day:

> "Frank Barton became even more valuable to me as we grew to seven and eight stores. As we got bigger, many of the problems associated with growth, like financing and taxes, cropped up. Frank's experience was invaluable. Gratefully, Frank and I got along extremely well. I wouldn't be where I am today if he hadn't supported me in the early stages and mentored me as we grew. I'll never forget his help." -- Tom Devlin

September 22, 2018
Saturday
National Hunting and Fishing Day

Objectives & reminders

___

___

___

Appointments

Early morning

8 a.m.

9 a.m.

10 a.m.

11 a.m.

Noon

1 p.m.

2 p.m.

3 p.m.

4 p.m.

5 p.m.

6 p.m.

Later evening… *Fall Equinox at 9:54 p.m. EDT*

Autumnal Equinox

The season changes from summer to fall in the Northern Hemisphere with the arrival of the Autumnal equinox at 9:54 p.m. (EDT). That is, today the sun is poised directly over the equator which makes the day and night the same length.

Invitation to discuss opportunities

What changes in buyer behaviors and marketing practices are associated with the transition from summer to fall?

National Hunting and Fishing Day

Although the official start of hunting and fishing seasons vary by game and from state to state, the fourth Saturday in September has been designated as National Hunting and Fishing Day since 1972.

The hunting and fishing market in the U.S. is enormous. Almost 14 million hunters spend an annual average of $2,484 on hunting equipment, supplies, travel and other hunting-related expenditures, while fishing enthusiasts total more than 33 million and spend an annual average of $1,262 on fishing-related purchases.

The marketing hunt

The South Carolina Department of Parks, Recreation and Tourism in Columbia, South Carolina offers several tips that marketing-oriented communities can implement to help make their hunting areas more hunter-friendly.

1. "Publicize local licensing requirements as well as any waiting periods on the purchase of guns and ammunition."
2. "Provide checklists and detailed maps on animal hotspots in local areas."
3. "Enlist local hunters as host contacts to visitors."
4. "Publish a list of places that are open early and late, where gas, coffee, box lunches, breakfast, ammunition, sunscreen, bug repellent, hats, water-proof clothing and footgear can be bought and [equipment repairs made]."
5. "Welcome hunters with street signs, banners and festivals."
6. "Encourage motels and restaurants to have early specials and weekend packages." (learn more: www.scprt.com)

September 23, 2018
Sunday

Sukkot (Feast of Tabernacles) begins
First *full* day of autumn

Objectives & reminders

Appointments

Early morning

8 a.m.

9 a.m.

10 a.m.

11 a.m.

Noon

1 p.m.

2 p.m.

3 p.m.

4 p.m.

5 p.m.

6 p.m.

Later evening

Call for gl●bal perspective

"I think we need more professional managers with an understanding of international business. The market is global, so from now on, managers must think of the world as one market." – Fujio Mitarai, former CEO and president of Japan-headquartered Canon, Inc. (manufacturer of camera and office technology), born in Kamae, Oita, Japan on September 23, 1935

Happy birthday: Herbert N. Casson

Born in Odessa, Ontario, Canada on September 23, 1869, Casson was a prolific business writer for more than 40 years. During his career he wrote more than 70 books including a popular guide for marketers called *Ads and Sales* (1911).

In his 1915 book, *The Axioms of Business*, Casson was among the first business writers to articulate the notion that a product's need satisfying potency should represent a more relevant selling point than price, per se. At the time price was the key factor dominating economists' thinking.

Moo marketing

"I once saw a millionaire Pittsburgher buy a painting of a cow for £11,000. He could have bought the cow herself for £15. But the painting had become famous. It was the only one of its kind. Everybody wanted it. And the Pittsburgher wanted it more than he wanted £11,000." – Herbert N. Casson, *The Axioms of Business* (1915, p. 65)

Take two marbles and call me in the morning

"YOUNG MEN and those of middle age who are suffering from the effects of a disease that unfits its victims for business or marriage, permanently cured, at moderate expense... Communications strictly confidential..." – excerpt from an advertisement for "Dr. Butts' Dispensary," published in the *Kansas Free Press* (Topeka, Kansas) on September 23, 1881

September 24, 2018
Monday
Mid-Autumn Festival (China)

Objectives & reminders

___

___

___

Appointments

Early morning

8 a.m.

9 a.m.

10 a.m.

11 a.m.

Noon

1 p.m.

2 p.m.

3 p.m.

4 p.m.

5 p.m.

6 p.m.

Later evening

Happy birthday: James Maury Henson

Puppeteer and creator of the Muppets, Jim Henson was born in Greenville, Mississippi on September 24, 1936. His family of creations including Kermit the Frog, Miss Piggie, Bert, Ernie, and Big Bird, among many others, have entertained and educated both children and adults. Some of his puppets have appeared in sales training videos.

Uncontrollable market force: Agree or disagree?

"Nobody creates a fad. It just happens. People love going along with the idea of a beautiful pig. It's like a conspiracy."
– Jim Henson

A worthwhile sales objective?

"Get out there and sell your socks off!"
– Kermit the Frog

Salute to small businesses

"The heart and soul of our economy is small businesses. They are the people who hire the vast majority of American people. They are the ones with the entrepreneurial dreams and goals who get out and get something done. I don't care if you are a pizza-parlor owner or a doughnut-shop owner or a cobbler." – Joseph P. Kennedy II, former member of the U.S. House of Representatives, from Massachusetts (and nephew of President John F. Kennedy). Joseph P. Kennedy II was born in Boston, Massachusetts on September 24, 1952.

Famous definition

"A corporation is an artificial being, invisible, intangible, and existing only in contemplation of the law." – John Marshall, Chief Justice of the Supreme Court (1801-1835), born in Germantown, Virginia on September 24, 1755

Corporate consideration: Invitation to discuss

If a *corporation* is neither a person nor otherwise tangible, can it act responsibly? Can it be compassionate? Or, is it up to *individuals* within the corporation to act responsibly and with compassion?

September 25, 2018
Tuesday
National Youth Day (Nauru)

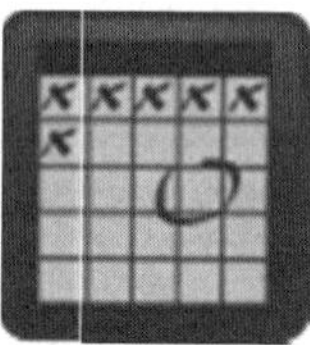

Objectives & reminders

Appointments

Early morning

8 a.m.

9 a.m.

10 a.m.

11 a.m.

Noon

1 p.m.

2 p.m.

3 p.m.

4 p.m.

5 p.m.

6 p.m.

Later evening

Happy birthday: William Faulkner

Born in New Albany, Mississippi on September 25, 1897, Faulkner was one of the most celebrated American novelists. His novels included *The Sound and the Fury* (1929), *Light in August* (1932), and *The Reivers* (1962). Many of his novels involved Southern settings in fictional Yoknapatawpha County, Mississippi. Faulkner forced readers to contemplate important social issues as his characters dealt with conflict, violence, racial tension, and the fallibility of human ideals. In 1950, he won the Nobel Prize for Literature.

Goals and competitors

"Always dream and shoot higher than you know you can do. Don't bother just to be better than your contemporaries or predecessors. Try to be better than yourself."--WF

Decision-making & problem-solving

"[T]he greatest help in meeting any problem with decency and self-respect and whatever courage is demanded, is to know where you yourself stand. That is, to have in words what you believe and are acting from."--WF

Happy birthday: Weekends!

On September 25, 1926, Henry Ford announced the introduction of a relatively new labor concept for The Ford Motor Company employees – the five-day work-week. Mr. Ford reasoned that better-rested employees would be more productive on the job.

However, because Ford was still very interested in what employees did or did not do on their non-working days, he provided guidelines for behavior which he expected employees to follow. He went so far as to establish the company's "Sociological Department." The Department's behavior police visited employees' homes to make sure they were not engaged in any sinful or unsavory practices.

Today, the five-day work-week is commonplace for full-time employees, although about 30 percent of the U.S. workforce works on the weekend. An increasing number of organizations in the U.S. use four-day work-weeks for some employees. The extra day off enables employees to take care of personal business during the week, thus reducing scheduling conflicts and job absenteeism problems.

September 26, 2018 Wednesday

European Day of Languages

Objectives & reminders

Appointments

Early morning

8 a.m.

9 a.m.

10 a.m.

11 a.m.

Noon

1 p.m.

2 p.m.

3 p.m.

4 p.m.

5 p.m.

6 p.m.

Later evening

The Beverly Hillbillies

The CBS sitcom, *The Beverly Hillbillies*, first aired on television on September 26, 1962. The show ran for nine years (followed by decades of reruns) and was the top rated network television show for two of those years.

The Beverly Hillbillies featured a poor and unsophisticated family of "hillbillies" – the Clampetts – who suddenly became wealthy after discovering oil on their Tennessee property. In response to their new-found wealth, the family moved into an affluent neighborhood in Beverly Hills, California but was unable and largely unwilling to shed its previous lifestyle.

Although not intended as a serious show with any particularly profound educational or social value, *The Beverly Hillbillies* did highlight a couple of marketing-relevant lessons, including:

1. the challenges (difficulties?) involved when interacting with others from different social and cultural backgrounds, and

2. the reluctance of some people to completely change their lifestyle (including purchase patterns) as their financial circumstances improve.

Advertisement exposes Clampett myth

Just prior to the 45th anniversary of *The Beverly Hillbillies*, in September 2007, Geico Insurance began running a television ad to promote their inexpensive insurance products. The ad capitalized on the popularity of *The Beverly Hillbillies* by suggesting that the Clampetts did not really get rich by discovering oil, but by switching their insurance to Geico.

Are you a "Clampett"?

Commercial airline personnel refer to inexperienced passengers or those who fear flying as "Clampetts." At JetBlue, flight attendants receive special "soft skills" training to learn how to handle Clampetts and other types of challenging passengers such as drunks, the overly flirtatious, and abusive passengers.

September 27, 2018
Thursday
World Tourism Day

Objectives & reminders

____

____

____

Appointments

Early morning

8 a.m.

9 a.m.

10 a.m.

11 a.m.

Noon

1 p.m.

2 p.m.

3 p.m.

4 p.m.

5 p.m.

6 p.m.

Later evening

World Tourism Day

Launched by the United Nations World Tourism Organization (UNWTO) and first celebrated in 1980, September 27 has become World Tourism Day. The special day's primary objective is to "foster awareness among the international community of the importance of tourism and its social, cultural, political and economic values."

The UNWTO selected September 27 because of the date's potential to garner media attention and business interest around the world – representing the approximate end of the tourism season in the Northern Hemisphere and the beginning of the season in the Southern Hemisphere.

> **Did you know?**
> Tourism is the largest industry in the world -- accounting for about six percent of the world's Gross Domestic Product (GDP).

% % % % % %

World travelers, world marketers

While international tourism is big business, world travel isn't restricted solely to tourists. Merchandise travels too. In a speech delivered on September 27, 2000, FedEx's chairman and CEO, Frederick W. Smith emphasized the trend toward global movement of goods. He noted that about 20 percent of manufactured goods crossed national borders in 2000, but that by the year 2020 more than 80 percent will do so. A "simple reason" drives the trend, according to Smith: "If you are not selling on a global basis, you [simply] will not be able to achieve the [economies] of scale necessary to compete with those who do."

____

Expect more, get more

"No businessman ever attained greater results from his men than did my father [Gustavus F. Swift], largely by the simple expedient of expecting of them greater results than other managers looked for." – Louis F. Swift, president (1903-1931) and chairman (1931-1932) of Swift & Company (meat-processing firm started by his father), born in Sagamore, Massachusetts on September 27, 1861. Today, the company is known as JBS USA Holdings, Inc. (wholly-owned subsidiary of JBS S.A.) and is the second-largest processor of fresh beef and pork in the world.

September 28, 2018
Friday
National Good Neighbor Day

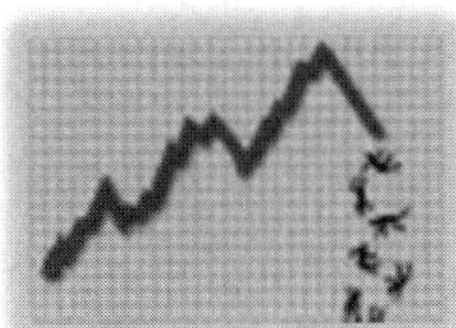

Objectives & reminders

___

___

___

Appointments

Early morning

8 a.m.

9 a.m.

10 a.m.

11 a.m.

Noon

1 p.m.

2 p.m.

3 p.m.

4 p.m.

5 p.m.

6 p.m.

Later evening

A penny for your thoughts?

British entrepreneurs Michael Marks and Tom Spencer signed a partnership agreement on September 28, 1894.

The two went on to launch a retailing empire that began with a "Penny Bazaar" variety store. Within six years the store had become a chain of 12 stores selling household goods, toys, hardware, stationery, earthenware, and other merchandise -- all at the same price, one penny. By 1915 the chain blanketed Great Britain with 140 stores.

A few years after that, in 1922, Marks and Spencer broke away from the penny store concept and launched the chain of department stores that still exists today, Marks & Spencer.

> **Innovative entrepreneurs**
>
> Prior to forming a partnership with Tom Spencer, Michael Marks was already an innovative retailing entrepreneur. For example, as early as 1884 he implemented what was an unusual practice at the time; he arranged store merchandise by price.
>
> As a partnership, Marks and Spencer also were innovative. In the early 1930s, for example, they pioneered a number of consumer research techniques at a time when very few other businesses were formally studying consumers.

"Stunning disconnect": Agree or disagree?

"I'm as mad as hell, and I'm not going to take it anymore!" – Howard Beale, television personality in the Academy Award-winning 1976 movie, *Network*. Beale was played by the British-born Australian actor Peter Finch, born in London on September 28, 1916.

In his book, *What Customers Really Want*, business analyst Scott McKain uses Beale's assertion to summarize many customers' sentiments toward businesses that all too often fail to satisfy customers. According to McKain, "there is simply a stunning disconnect between what customers seek and what organizations deliver" (p. x).

September 29, 2018
Saturday
World Heart Day

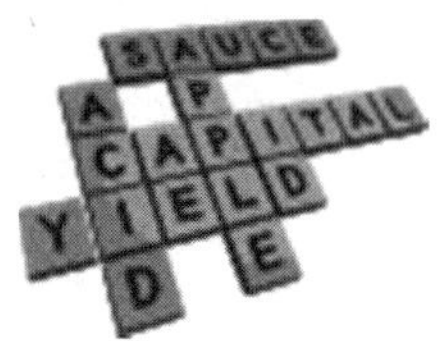

Objectives & reminders

___

___

___

Appointments

Early morning

8 a.m.

9 a.m.

10 a.m.

11 a.m.

Noon

1 p.m.

2 p.m.

3 p.m.

4 p.m.

5 p.m.

6 p.m.

Later evening

What's the Word?

On September 29, 1983, Microsoft introduced Word for MS-DOS 1.00. About six weeks later, the introduction of Microsoft Windows followed. Although media publicity, intermediary relationships and advertising helped promote Word and Windows, word-of-mouth communications were most instrumental.

Today, Microsoft estimates that more than one billion people around the world use Microsoft Office, which includes Word. Interestingly, that's more than all of the people on the planet who speak English as a primary or secondary language.

"Word"- of - mouth

Word-of-mouth is an important factor in the diffusion of most new products, but it seems to be particularly critical when it comes to technology-related products. That is, about two-thirds of consumers who adopt technological innovations (e.g., gadgets, software, apps) credit friends, family members, co-workers or other acquaintances who introduced and oriented them to the new technology.

It follows that technology marketers interested in spreading their products throughout the marketplace would provide incentives and support for the early adopters whose influence is key.

Respect for competitors

"Always assume your opponent to be smarter than you." – Walther Rathenau, German industrialist, CEO of AEG (electrical trust), and Foreign Minister of Germany, born in Berlin on September 29, 1867

Long distance to success

"[N]othing in life that is good and successful is produced overnight, therefore it's a long, long road... I think anybody who loves what they do tends to think of it not as a sacrifice but as a way of life."
-- Sebastian Newbold Coe, President of the International Association of Athletics Federations and former track star (broke 12 world records), born in London on September 29, 1956

September 30, 2018
Sunday
Recovery Day (Canada)

Objectives & reminders

____

____

____

Appointments

Early morning

8 a.m.

9 a.m.

10 a.m.

11 a.m.

Noon

1 p.m.

2 p.m.

3 p.m.

4 p.m.

5 p.m.

6 p.m.

Later evening

Cold weather planning

Seasonal changes in climate are accompanied by numerous changes in consumers' buying behavior and consumption patterns. Of course, the demand for weather-related merchandise such as overcoats, cold remedies and heating oil increases as the temperature drops. Hot food and beverages are substituted for colder alternatives. Consumers' outdoor activities may be moved inside or exchanged for indoor activities. Further, dropping temperatures can play havoc with vehicles and other equipment that operate outdoors. That's why auto repair shops see an upturn in business when cold weather arrives.

Jack Frost's inconsistent cold calls

According to the U.S. National Climatic Data Center, there's a 10 percent chance that one or more freezes (32 degrees or colder) will occur on or before September 30 in Ashland, Kentucky and Kent, Washington, while there's a 50 percent probability in Milford, Iowa and Springfield, Minnesota, and a 90 percent likelihood in Westhope, North Dakota and Corinna, Maine. Cold weather planning is much more effective when organizations know when temperatures are likely to drop.

Shopping behavior is affected by colder weather too. Some frequent shoppers may become infrequent ones as they seek to avoid colder temperatures. They may opt for in-home shopping alternatives or climate controlled shopping environments, such as enclosed malls or large stores that promise "one-stop-shopping" experiences. Other shoppers may prefer to shop only during day-time hours when temperatures may be a few degrees warmer.

The seasonal transition affects business operations too. Farmers, nurseries and other agriculture/horticulture-related businesses are mindful of the effects that colder weather has on plants. For them, the date of the season's first freeze is particularly relevant. Exterior house painters are cognizant of the fact that most paints do not dry properly at lower temperatures. Similarly, construction firms face special materials-related problems when the temperature drops (e.g., concrete doesn't cure properly in freezing temperatures). Transportation companies are challenged too; truck transportation may be delayed by inclement weather and ice may block inland waterway shipping routes altogether.

October 1, 2018
Monday
International Coffee Day

Objectives & reminders

___

___

___

Appointments

Early morning

8 a.m.

9 a.m.

10 a.m.

11 a.m.

Noon

1 p.m.

2 p.m.

3 p.m.

4 p.m.

5 p.m.

6 p.m.

Later evening

Happy New Year!

It may seem premature to be wished a happy New Year on October 1, but only if you're thinking in terms of *calendar years*. If you're thinking in terms of *fiscal years*, a new year could begin today, as it does for the United States federal government -- the largest organizational buyer in the world!

What is a "fiscal year"?
A *fiscal* (or *financial*) *year* is a period of 12 consecutive months used in the preparation of an organization's financial and budgeting reports, including tax returns. A fiscal year is generally referred to in terms of the calendar year on which the *last* day of the fiscal year falls, so a fiscal year beginning on October 1, 2018, and ending on September 30, 2019, for example, might be referred to "FY19."

Although the calendar year is the most frequently chosen fiscal year, U.S. *businesses* may choose the month their fiscal year begins. And their choices are marketing-relevant as both salespeople and the organizational buyers they call on may be influenced by the transition from one fiscal year to the next. Sales reps' quotas or bonuses may coincide with fiscal years; accordingly they may behave differently as the end of the fiscal year approaches -- depending on whether they have reached their quotas already (time for more golf?) or not (more willing to negotiate?).

Because organizational buyers' budgets typically begin anew at the start of the fiscal year, they may be ready to spend when the new funds are allocated. If unspent money from the previous year's budget is not rolled into the new fiscal year, buyers may make advance purchases near the end of the fiscal year or splurge on extra items they'd otherwise avoid. So, organizational marketers could benefit by knowing when their customers' fiscal years begin and end, and how closely buyers' purchase behavior is influenced by budgetary constraints tied to the fiscal year.

International considerations
The U.S. federal government's fiscal year begins on October 1, but fiscal years for the governments of the United Kingdom, Canada, and India begin on April 1. In Australia, the government's new fiscal year begins on July 1.

October 2, 2018
Tuesday
International Day of Non-Violence

Objectives & reminders

Appointments

Early morning

---

8 a.m.

---

9 a.m.

---

10 a.m.

---

11 a.m.

Noon

---

1 p.m.

---

2 p.m.

---

3 p.m.

---

4 p.m.

---

5 p.m.

---

6 p.m.

Later evening

Wealthy businesspeople are dishonest: Agree or disagree?

"It is difficult but not impossible to conduct strictly honest business. What is true is that honesty is incompatible with the amassing of a large fortune." -- Mahatma Gandhi, Indian nationalist leader, born in what is now Gujarat, India on October 2, 1869

Balanced design

"Design is a constant challenge to balance comfort with luxe, the practical with the desirable." -- Donna Karan, American fashion designer and retailer, born in Queens, New York on October 2, 1948

Marketing research does not always speak for itself

"We spend a lot of time trying to read the tea leaves of lifestyle and demographic changes and asking ourselves 'what are the implications of this in shopping patterns and for consumer needs, and what departments do we need to develop and grow?'"

-- Joseph A. Pichler, then CEO and chairman of the Kroger Company (grocery stores), born in St. Louis, Missouri on October 2, 1939

Understanding culture, in part, through language

"Understanding of other languages is almost a necessary, albeit insufficient, condition for the understanding of the phenomenon of culture. One of my criticisms of, especially, American researchers in the field is that, with no knowledge of any foreign language, some believe they can issue statements about foreign cultures; I would doubt the validity of their conclusions." -- Geert Hofstede, Dutch scholar noted for his research of cultural differences summarized in his books which include *Culture's Consequences: International Differences in Work-Related Values* (1980), and *Cultures and Organizations: Software of the Mind* (1991). Dr. Hofstede was born on October 2, 1928.

October 3, 2018
Wednesday
World Cerebral Palsy Day

Objectives & reminders

Appointments

Early morning

8 a.m.

9 a.m.

10 a.m.

11 a.m.

Noon

1 p.m.

2 p.m.

3 p.m.

4 p.m.

5 p.m.

6 p.m.

Later evening

Reaching the children's market on October 3

1924 Harvey Kurtzman was born in Mount Vernon, New York. He was a creative cartoonist who drew with children in mind. In 1952 he founded one of the first publications to target children -- *Mad* magazine.

1955 *The Mickey Mouse Club* premiered on ABC television. Broadcast on weekdays between 5:00 and 6:00 p.m., the show's audience swelled to 20 million children the next season.

1955 Not to be overshadowed by ABC's *Mickey Mouse Club*, CBS television debuted its own children's show on the same day -- *Captain Kangaroo*. The "Captain" entertained both the children of the 1950s and, in subsequent decades, *their* children as well (and even some of their grandchildren).

Multiple children's markets

As also noted on February 5, the potential benefits of appealing to the children's market is enormous, especially when children are viewed as *three* markets:

1. *Immediate buyers*, who have their own money to spend – today.
2. *Purchase influencers*, who sway parents' and others' buying decisions.
3. *Future adult buyers*, who are likely to continue using products and brands they are exposed to as children.

These marbles don't target children

The musical duo of Graham Bonnet and Trevor Gordon made their television debut in the United Kingdom on October 3, 1968, to follow-up their hit song, "Only One Woman." Throughout the world -- except in the United States -- Bonnet and Gordon were known as The Marbles. When asked what he detested most, Bonnet listed hangovers and liars.

October 4, 2018 Thursday

World Animal Day

Objectives & reminders

____

____

____

Appointments

Early morning

8 a.m.

9 a.m.

10 a.m.

11 a.m.

Noon

1 p.m.

2 p.m.

3 p.m.

4 p.m.

5 p.m.

6 p.m.

Later evening

Ohrbach's grand opening promotion precedent

On October 4, 1923, Nathan M. Ohrbach partnered with Max Wiesen to open a retail clothing store in New York City. Originally, the store competed on a price basis and specialized in manufacturers' overstocks and "irregulars." Its slogan touted value: "Ohrbach's, a bonded word for savings… more for less or your money back."

The store's grand opening sale attracted such huge crowds that the store tried to duplicate the opening-day event with a monthly Miracle Day Sale. By the time Wiesen sold his interest in the business to Ohrbach in 1928, Ohrbach had developed a more negative perspective of the monthly Miracle Day Sale, which he promptly discontinued.

> **Promotion addiction**
> "Promotion is like taking dope. You use one dose of it, and you have to have another, and another, and then another. A store advertises a sale of shoes that originally retailed at $24.50, for only $14.95. Actually, they are telling the customer: 'We thought we could get you to pay $24.50 for these things and you wouldn't. So now we are trying to get you to buy them for $14.95.'" -- Nathan M. Ohrbach

Over the years, Ohrbach's grew into a thriving chain of bargain fashion stores with outlets in New York, New Jersey and California. By the early 1960s, the company's annual revenues were about $80 million. The chain was sold to Brenninkmeyers in 1962 and went out of business 25 years later.

No such thing as "risk-free" in business: Agree or disagree?

"If you're not moving forward, you risk getting run over from behind. In advertising – as in all industries and organizations – something that is not risky can, in fact, be *more* risky because it will neither excite an old customer nor attract a new one. You risk everything by risking nothing." – Donny Deutsch, former business talk-show host and head of an advertising agency, in his book (with Peter Knobler), *Often Wrong, Never in Doubt: Unleash the Business Rebel Within* (p. 162), published on October 4, 2005

October 5, 2018
Friday

World Teachers' Day
World Smile Day

Objectives & reminders

___

___

___

Appointments

Early morning

8 a.m.

9 a.m.

10 a.m.

11 a.m.

Noon

1 p.m.

2 p.m.

3 p.m.

4 p.m.

5 p.m.

6 p.m.

Later evening

Statistical precision

Sometimes people are hesitant to trust reports of statistical data and sometimes the reports are not trustworthy. The lack of precision in reporting statistics can lead to gross inaccuracies, confusion and misunderstandings. Often, such lack of precision has nothing to do with intentions to mislead an audience (although that *can* be the case), but it may be due to a faulty memory, sloppy thinking, or an inadequate understanding of statistics. These problems seem to be compounded when statistics are reported verbally, but are also found in written reports as well.

Examples abound. On October 5, 1984, U.S. President Ronald Reagan commented on poverty in the country by saying, "[t]he poverty rate has begun to decline, but it is still going up." Obviously, the poverty rate cannot increase and decrease simultaneously. What Reagan may have meant to say was that the rate of poverty (expressed as a *percentage* of the U.S. population) was on the decline, but because the size of the total population was increasing, the *number* of people at or below the poverty line was continuing to increase.

> # **Statistical reporting: Avoiding confusion** %
>
> Principle: An increase (decrease) in the total *number* of something does not necessarily correspond to an increase (decrease) when the something is expressed as a *percentage* of something else.
>
> Tip: When presenting or discussing data trends, avoid confusion by clarifying whether the trends pertain to the phenomena's frequencies (numbers) or to the frequencies expressed as a percentage of something else.

More than a decade later, U.S. President Bill Clinton was pleased to report a seven percent increase in the nation's GDP (Gross Domestic Product) for the most recent quarter. Unfortunately, he was mistaken. The data did not indicate a seven percent increase in GDP during the quarter; rather the GDP had grown at a rate which would be equivalent to seven percent *if continued throughout an entire year*. In other words, GDP had not grown by seven percent during the quarter, but by *one-fourth* of seven percent.

October 6, 2018
Saturday
German-American Day

Objectives & reminders

___

___

___

Appointments

Early morning

8 a.m.

9 a.m.

10 a.m.

11 a.m.

Noon

1 p.m.

2 p.m.

3 p.m.

4 p.m.

5 p.m.

6 p.m.

Later evening

Comparative advertising in the EC

Comparative advertising is advertising that includes references to one or more specific competitors, such as by naming the competing brand, showing a picture of it, or comparing its attributes to those of your own brand. The practice has become increasingly common in the United States since 1972 when the Federal Trade Commission encouraged comparative advertising as a way of providing buyers with more useful and specific information. Previously used references to "Brand X" or "the leading brand" were thought to be too vague to help consumers make informed purchase decisions.

Elsewhere in the world, comparative advertising may or may not be permitted. Prior to 1997, advertisers in the European Community (EC) were discouraged from the practice because of the maze of laws and regulations across member countries. So, in an effort to integrate the highly diverse laws and regulations regarding comparative advertising, the European Parliament issued a directive on October 6, 1997. Under the 1997 guidelines, comparative advertising is permissible throughout the European Community as long as it is not misleading, doesn't create confusion or discredit or denigrate trademarks, or "take unfair advantage of the reputation of a trade mark, trade name, or other distinguishing marks of a competitor."

Although the guidelines paved the way for comparative advertising in the EC, the wisdom of its use continues to be debated. New entrants in a product category may use comparative advertising to suggest that the new brand compares favorably with the established category leaders or to invite buyers to make their own comparisons. Generally, however, larger or established competitors avoid comparative advertising, believing they have little to gain from giving smaller competitors media exposure.

Stirring cognitive dissonance

"Comparisons can make customers feel uncomfortable, as they are effectively being told that they made the wrong choice when they purchased the competitor's product. To deal with the resulting cognitive dissonance, they are likely to think of reasons for the competitor's product being actually better than yours, despite what your advertising says, and persuade themselves that they did make the right choice." – Frances Brassington & Stephen Pettitt, marketing scholars

October 7, 2018
Sunday
Teachers' Day (Laos)

Objectives & reminders

____

____

____

Appointments

Early morning

8 a.m.

9 a.m.

10 a.m.

11 a.m.

Noon

1 p.m.

2 p.m.

3 p.m.

4 p.m.

5 p.m.

6 p.m.

Later evening

Rosy day!

Rosy promotions ahead

On October 7, 1986, U.S. President Ronald Reagan signed into law a bill that made the rose the country's national flower. Implying that the country's population is diverse, a *New York Times* columnist objected, "No one flower can ever symbolize this nation. America is a bouquet."

Rosy day for the stock market

The Dow Jones Industrial Average (DJIA), a stock index of 30 large U.S. companies broke the 6,000 mark on October 7, 1996 -- exactly one decade after Reagan dubbed the rose as the national flower. From there, the DJIA continued its rosy upward trend for the next few years and almost doubled the 6,000 mark in January 2000. In early July 2007, the DJIA topped 14,000 for the first time, and then 20,000 for the first time in late January 2017.

Finally, roses are red...

Perhaps in anticipation of the future honorary status of the rose, colored advertisements began to appear in newspapers in the 1930s. One of the first was published in Great Britain -- in the *Glasgow Daily Record* -- on October 7, 1936. The ad (or "advert," as the British say) was for Dewar's White Label Whisky.

The contrast effect

When all advertisements in a magazine or newspaper begin to look alike, readers are more likely to ignore them. So, advertisers use contrast as one technique to make their ads stand out and attract attention. For example, they may use larger than standard-size type, use a unique font design, or print an ad upside down or side-ways.

Then came color. With the introduction of color, ads that used color were easily distinguished from black and white ads that still dominated the pages of most publications. Today, because color ads are commonplace, some advertisers revert to the use of black and white ads to achieve contrast.

October 8, 2018
Monday
Columbus Day
Thanksgiving Day (Canada)

Objectives & reminders

Appointments

Early morning

8 a.m.

9 a.m.

10 a.m.

11 a.m.

Noon

1 p.m.

2 p.m.

3 p.m.

4 p.m.

5 p.m.

6 p.m.

Later evening

Columbus Day

Observed on the second Monday in October, Columbus Day is one of the few U.S. federal holidays in 2018. This means that most federal offices and agencies will be closed today, including the U.S. Postal System. State and local government offices, schools, banks, businesses and other organizations often adopt the federal government's list of holidays, but rarely are they required to do so. Can you list 2018's other U.S. federal holidays?

Happy birthday: Harry Gilbert Day

Day was born in Monroe County, Iowa on October 8, 1906. In the 1950s, he was part of the research team at Indiana University that developed and patented the cavity-fighting fluoride additive used in toothpaste. When the Food and Drug Administration approved the additive for toothpaste in 1955, Procter & Gamble (P&G) adopted "fluoristan" as an additive for their new Crest toothpaste which the company introduced in January 1956. Today, Crest is one of P&G's strongest brands.

Extensive advertising by P&G for more than 60 years since Day's innovation has touted the cavity-fighting benefits of the Crest brand -- with one well known and often-repeated advertising assertion that Crest leads to 23 percent fewer cavities.

Did you hear the one about...

The marketing researcher who approached a shopper to inquire about her brand preference for toothpaste? When the consumer mentioned Crest, the interviewer followed-up by asking her to what extent the brand's advertising had affected her preference for Crest.

"None at all," said the independent-minded consumer. "I use my own judgment to decide which brands to purchase. I am not swayed by advertising."

"Why, then," the interviewer asked, "do you purchase Crest?"

"Because," the shopper explained, "as everyone knows, you get 23 percent fewer cavities when you use Crest."

October 9, 2018
Tuesday
Leif Erikson Day
Navaratri

Objectives & reminders

____

____

____

Appointments

Early morning

8 a.m.

9 a.m.

10 a.m.

11 a.m.

Noon

1 p.m.

2 p.m.

3 p.m.

4 p.m.

5 p.m.

6 p.m.

Later evening

Happy birthday: Charles Rudolph Walgreen, Sr.

Born near Galesburg, Illinois on October 9, 1873, Walgreen landed a job in a drug store at the age of 16 – for four dollars a week. Soon after that, he moved to Chicago and gained valuable experience working for several other pharmacists. For eight years he saved his money and noted how he would someday run a drug store differently.

That someday arrived in 1901 when Walgreen agreed to buy the drug store where he worked, for $6,000. Almost immediately, he began implementing marketing-oriented improvements. For example, he installed bright lights and widened store aisles to create a more welcoming and comfortable atmosphere. Further, customers were personally welcomed when they entered the store – either by Walgreen himself, or by his trusted colleague, Arthur Thorsen.

Walgreen also used prompt service to differentiate his drug store further. In particular, one practice amazed customers. When a customer would phone-in an order, Walgreen would repeat the order loudly enough for his assistant to hear. While Walgreen continued to chat with the customer, his assistant delivered the merchandise to the customer's home. Customers were so impressed with the quick service that they told their friends about how Walgreen's could fill and deliver an order before hanging up the telephone.

Advertising with service

"Little extra services are the cheapest kind of advertising that merely takes thought and a few seconds of time."
– Charles R. Walgreen

Needless to say, the positive word-of-mouth generated by Walgreen's merchandising and service innovations helped to grow the business. In 1909, Walgreen opened a second store, then seven others by 1916. By 1926, the chain had grown to 100 stores – by 1994, 2,000 stores, by 2003, 4,000 stores, and by 2017, 8,175 stores.

Marketing smokes and mirrors: Agree or disagree?

Walgreen's should continue to carry mirrors, but follow CVS Pharmacy's lead and stop selling tobacco products.

October 10, 2018
Wednesday
World Mental health Day
Double Tenth Day (China)

10 10

Objectives & reminders

Appointments

Early morning

---

8 a.m.

---

9 a.m.

---

10 a.m. *10:10 on 10-10 !*

---

11 a.m.

Noon

---

1 p.m.

---

2 p.m.

---

3 p.m.

---

4 p.m.

---

5 p.m.

---

6 p.m.

Later evening

Ten ten ten ten

What happens at 10:10 a.m. on October 10 -- the 10th minute of the 10th hour of the 10th day of the 10th month? A company announcement? A deadline? A big meeting? An award ceremony? The blast-off point for a sale, special event or promotion? Or something else? That's up to you, but the ten-fold timing is too memorable to miss.

History of ten ten

It might not have started at 10:10 a.m. (or p.m.), but October 10, 1796, did mark the beginning of the metric system -- measurement that relies on the base 10 numerical system. Today, the metric system is the most frequently used system of measurements in the world.

Refreshing your metric literacy

10 millimeters = 1 centimeter = 0.01 meters
10 centimeters = 1 decimeter = 0.1 meters
10 decimeters = 1 meter
10 meters = 1 decameter
10 decameters = 1 hectometer = 100 meters
10 hectometers = 1 kilometer = 1,000 meters

10-10: Double celebration for China

October 10 is celebrated as a holiday in China to commemorate the anniversary of the outbreak of the Chinese revolution against the Manchu dynasty in 1911. Eighty-nine years later – October 10, 2000 – another reason for celebration occurred; the China Trade Bill was signed, which gave China permanent normal trade relations with the United States. The Bill helped spur economic growth in China.

Daily planning consideration

"True happiness comes to those who do their work well, followed by a refreshing period of rest. True happiness comes from the right amount of work for the day." – Lin Yutang, Chinese philosopher and writer, born in Banzai, China on October 10, 1895

October 11, 2018
Thursday
"You Go, Girl" Day

Objectives & reminders

____

____

____

Appointments

Early morning

8 a.m.

9 a.m.

10 a.m.

11 a.m.

Noon

1 p.m.

2 p.m.

3 p.m.

4 p.m.

5 p.m.

6 p.m.

Later evening

Happy birthday: Anna Eleanor Roosevelt

Born in New York City on October 11, 1884, Roosevelt is often remembered as the First Lady, wife of the 32nd U.S. President, Franklin D. Roosevelt. But Mrs. Roosevelt also enjoyed a successful career apart from her role as First Lady. Most notable were her activities to promote social reforms -- many of which she was deeply committed to prior to her husband's political rise in power. Examples: She worked with the Red Cross during World War I. She fought to improve hospital conditions for the mentally ill. She championed equal rights for women. She challenged business to improve working conditions for female workers.

Maintaining your commitment
"No one can make you feel inferior without your consent."
-- Eleanor Roosevelt, 1937 speech

Later, Eleanor Roosevelt channeled her reform efforts through her roles as a public speaker, newspaper columnist, and delegate to the United Nations General Assembly. In the 1950s she continued her activism, calling for civil and human rights around the world and advocating nuclear disarmament. Mrs. Roosevelt's passionate advocacy for causes she believed in was and continues to be truly inspiring.

Go girls go
As First Lady in the 1930s and 1940s, Eleanor Roosevelt did many things differently than her predecessors. For instance, she held weekly press conferences to discuss primarily women's issues, speaking *solely* to female reporters.

Go boys go: Agree or disagree?
Was it appropriate for Mrs. Roosevelt to ban male reporters from these press conferences?

Would Eleanor agree?

"Accuracy is to a newspaper what virtue is to a lady, but a newspaper can always print a retraction."
– Charles Revson, co-founder of Revlon Cosmetics, born in Manchester, New Hampshire on October 11, 1906

October 12, 2018
Friday
Children's Day (Brazil)

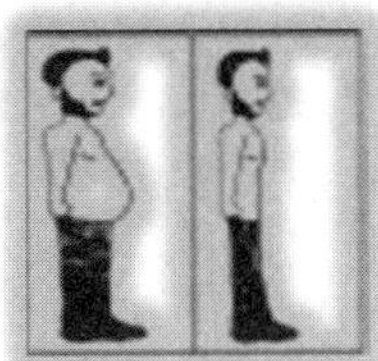

Objectives & reminders

____

____

____

Appointments

Early morning

8 a.m.

9 a.m.

10 a.m.

11 a.m.

Noon

1 p.m.

2 p.m.

3 p.m.

4 p.m.

5 p.m.

6 p.m.

Later evening

Happy birthday: Jean Nidetch

Born in Brooklyn, New York on October 12, 1923, Nidetch grew and grew and grew to become what she described as an "overweight housewife obsessed with eating cookies." In 1961 she weighed 200 pounds.

Determined to lose weight, Nidetch began holding weekly meetings with other women to explore lifestyle changes that could help them to lose weight. Through these meetings, she became convinced that a support system of other people was key to helping people reach their goals. Nidetch personally lost 70 pounds in one year.

Publicly state goals: Agree or disagree?
People tend to be more committed to their goals when they publicly state them. The act of making the goals public helps to define and crystallize what previously might have been vague and fuzzy ideas or wishes. Also, the goal-maker is more likely to feel accountable for attaining goals once they are publicly announced. And, as Nidetch would point out, when other people know about the goals, they can be prepared to offer encouragement and applaud progress -- which further spurs goal-makers' commitment.

However, for an opposing point of view, see this Ted Talk video: https://www.ted.com/talks/derek_sivers_keep_your_goals_to_yourself

Encouraged by the early signs of success for her diet, lifestyle and group support recipe, Nidetch formed Weight Watchers in 1963. The company grew rapidly during the next decade with Nidetch serving as president, head cheerleader and role model. In 1973, she stepped down as president but remained with the company as a consultant until Weight Watchers was sold to the Heinz Company in 1978, for $72 million.

The entrepreneurial spirit
"There will always be new opportunities for those of us who set no limit in our quest to accomplish our goals, and so we will realize our wildest dreams." -- Jean Nidetch

Today, the company operates in 30 countries and employs 25,000 people. Its annual revenues weigh in at $1.7 billion.

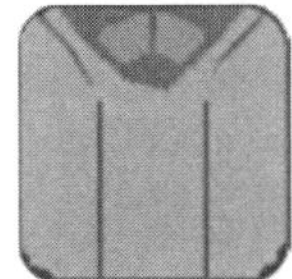

October 13, 2018
Saturday

Astronomy Day *(also observed on April 21)*

Objectives & reminders

Appointments

Early morning

8 a.m.

9 a.m.

10 a.m.

11 a.m.

Noon

1 p.m.

2 p.m.

3 p.m.

4 p.m.

5 p.m.

6 p.m.

Later evening

Customers are Number One

"A customer is the most important visitor on our premises. He is not dependent on us – we are dependent on him. He is not an outsider in our business – he is a part of it. We are not doing him a favor by serving him... he is doing us a favor by giving us the opportunity to do so." – company philosophy of L.L. Bean, the enormously successful clothing and outdoor equipment mail-order firm and online retailer located in Freeport, Maine. The company's founder, Leon Leonwood Bean, who first established the firm's customer-centric culture, was born in Greenwood, Maine on October 13, 1872.

Trade barriers stifle international marketing efforts: Agree or disagree?

"[A]s long as nations are divided by insurmountable trade barriers, as long as national self-sufficiency and self-containment remain political and economic goals, so long shall we witness the phenomena of liquidation and disintegration... But how long will such conditions prevail before humanity will be brought to the realization of the fact that divided against itself it is committing economic and cultural suicide?" – Simon Litman, one of the first scholars to teach marketing and merchandising (at University of California – Berkeley, in 1902-03), and a pioneer in international trade. Born in Odessa, Russia on October 13, 1873, Litman offered this perspective of international trade in 1935 – during the Great Depression.

Further insight 54 years later

"Japan's economic miracle was made possible because the rest of us were ready to keep our markets open to [Japan]." – Margaret Thatcher, former British prime minister (1979-1990), born in Grantham, Lincolnshire, England on October 13, 1925. Ms. Thatcher made this comment in 1989 when encouraging the Japanese to lift trade barriers.

Marketing's momentum

"The thought that life could be better is woven indelibly into our hearts and our brains." – Paul Simon, American singer and songwriter, born in Newark, New Jersey on October 13, 1941

October 14, 2018
Sunday
World Standards Day

Objectives & reminders

____

____

____

Appointments

Early morning

8 a.m.

9 a.m.

10 a.m.

11 a.m.

Noon

1 p.m.

2 p.m.

3 p.m.

4 p.m.

5 p.m.

6 p.m.

Later evening

Newspaper advertising

It was October 14, 1612, when newspaper advertising first emerged -- in the Paris newspaper *Petites Affiches*. Today, advertising has become central to newspapers and magazines. While publishers may think in terms of delivering information to their readers, many also view their job as delivering an audience to their advertisers.

Newspaper advertising today
Also in October, the *Dallas Morning News* was founded, in 1885. Placing a full-page ad in this Texas metropolitan newspaper today costs about $16,840, depending on the day of the week, section of the paper, and other factors. That's about 6 cents per subscriber.

Happy birthday: Winnie-the-Pooh

The fictional character created by author A.A. Milne first appeared in the book "bearing" his name, *Winnie-the-Pooh*, published on October 14, 1926. Pooh also appeared in subsequent books by Milne. In 1929 Milne sold the Pooh merchandising rights, which were eventually acquired by the Walt Disney Corporation in 1961.

Marketing, especially in a bear market
"You can't stay in your corner of the forest waiting for others to come to you. You have to go to them sometimes."
-- Winnie-the-Pooh

Bear essentials of communication

Bearly understood?
"We know what we told him, but we don't know what he heard."
– W. Edwards Deming, quality consultant who pioneered processes such as statistical quality control (SQC) and total quality management (TQM). Deming was born in Sioux City, Iowa on October 14, 1900.

Bear with them
"If the person you are talking to doesn't appear to be listening, be patient. It may simply be that he has a small piece of fluff in his ear."
-- Winnie-the-Pooh

October 15, 2018
Monday
World Students' Day

Objectives & reminders

____

____

____

Appointments

Early morning

8 a.m.

9 a.m.

10 a.m.

11 a.m.

Noon

1 p.m.

2 p.m.

3 p.m.

4 p.m.

5 p.m.

6 p.m.

Later evening

Facilitating product usage across the calendar

Prior to the 1920s, the timing patterns of automobile travel tended to coincide with accommodating seasonal weather patterns. In short, traveling by automobile was primarily a summertime activity. But a couple of season-related trends emerged in the 1920s. For one, state officials in the U.S. increasingly kept roadways open throughout the winter months so motorists could travel year-round.

Another trend was the increase in the number of closed vehicles. To illustrate, in 1919 only 10 percent of automobiles made in America were *closed*; the others were *open* and thus passengers were vulnerable to winter weather. However, on October 15, 1923, *Time* magazine announced that the annual production of closed cars had climbed to 35 percent. By the end of the decade, about 85 percent were closed.

As the 1930s approached, automobile manufacturers were thrilled with the buying public's openness to closed cars, because the trend toward closed cars helped smooth the previously pronounced seasonal peaks-and-valleys patterns in driving and in the purchase of vehicles. The "closed" trend enabled factories to continue to operate productively throughout the year. Industry leaders attributed the increase in winter demand for closed cars to the open highways and to the increased comfort of closed cars in wintry weather.

Other automobile innovations that fight against nature's constraints

Historically, human calendars have followed nature's calendar, e.g., in terms of when to plant, harvest, hunt, venture outside, travel, and so on. But over time humans have enlisted the help of technology to fight against nature's calendrical timing constraints. As for automobile transportation, enclosing cars was only one of many innovations that made motoring more of an anytime activity. Consider some of the others:

- Heating and air conditioning keep motorists more comfortable during extreme seasonal temperatures. Antifreeze/coolants keep engines comfortable.
- Headlights make night-time driving practical.
- Windshield wipers facilitate driving during rainy seasons, while deicers and snow tires minimize the effects of wintry weather.

October 16, 2018
Tuesday
Boss's Day

Objectives & reminders

___

___

___

Appointments

Early morning

8 a.m.

9 a.m.

10 a.m.

11 a.m.

Noon

1 p.m.

2 p.m.

3 p.m.

4 p.m.

5 p.m.

6 p.m.

Later evening

Decision-makers' friends

"Facts are friendly. Facts that tend to reinforce what you are doing and give you a warm glow are nice, because they help in terms of psychic reward. Facts that raise alarms are equally friendly, because they give you clues about how to respond, how to change, how to deal, where to spend the resources." – Henry Schacht, former chairman and CEO of Cummins Engine Company, and chairman and CEO of Lucent Technologies (1995-1998). Schacht was born in Erie, Pennsylvania on October 16, 1934.

Happy birthday: Leon H. Sullivan

Born in Charleston, West Virginia on October 16, 1922, Sullivan was a social reformer and, for 38 years, the entrepreneurial pastor of Zion Baptist Church in Philadelphia. As pastor he formed an investment company called Zion Investment Associates in which he encouraged church members to invest. The company used the invested funds to build an apartment complex, shopping center and garment manufacturing firm, and to launch other business ventures Sullivan believed would be good for investors and good for the community.

In 1977, Sullivan met with a group of business leaders to formulate a code of social responsibility for business, which became known as The Global Sullivan Principles. The principles challenged companies to act responsibly and play a leadership role in the countries and markets in which they operate – to protect human rights, ensure safe working and living conditions for workers, provide schools, and otherwise act responsibly. Sullivan persuaded 184 American companies to commit to The Global Sullivan Principles and submit a report annually documenting their socially responsible behaviors.

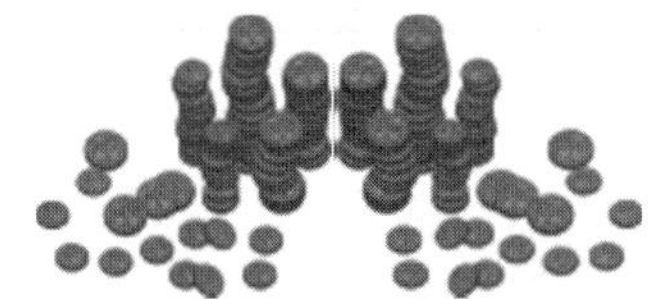

Reminding employees of the importance of customers

"Remember when you get your paycheck, your profit sharing check... every cent of that came from our customers." – David Neeleman, founder of JetBlue Airways, born in Sao Paulo, Brazil on October 16, 1959

October 17, 2018
Wednesday
World Day for Poverty Eradication

Objectives & reminders

___

___

___

Appointments

Early morning

8 a.m.

9 a.m.

10 a.m.

11 a.m.

Noon

1 p.m.

2 p.m.

3 p.m.

4 p.m.

5 p.m.

6 p.m.

Later evening

Happy birthday: Arthur Miller

Born in New York City on October 17, 1915, Miller worked his way through college at the University of Michigan before pursuing a career as a playwright. He wrote several notable plays during his life, including *All My Sons* (1947), *The Crucible* (1953), *A View from the Bridge* (1955), *After the Fall* (1964), and *The Price* (1968).

Perhaps Miller's most celebrated and clearly business-relevant play was *Death of a Salesman* (1949), for which Miller won a Pulitzer Prize. The play's star character was Willy Loman – an older, struggling salesman whose identity was inseparably intertwined with his profession. As Loman saw the world around him changing, Loman coped -- or failed to cope -- by clinging to his pride and longing for the return of the "good ole days" of selling.

Saving your marbles

"Willy was a salesman. And for a salesman, there is no rock bottom to the life. He don't put a bolt to a nut, he don't tell you the law or give you medicine. He's a man way out there in the blue, riding on a smile and a shoeshine. And when they start not smiling back -- that's an earthquake. And then you get yourself a couple of spots on your hat, and you're finished. Nobody dast blame this man. A salesman is got to dream, boy. It comes with the territory." -- Arthur Miller, *Death of a Salesman* (p. 138)

Willy's not alone: The need for business coping skills is timeless

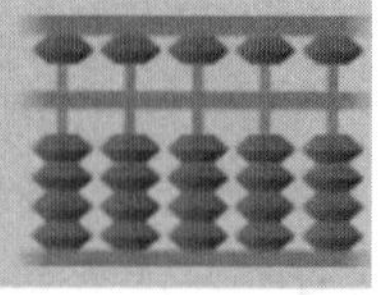

"The global battles in virtually every manufacturing industry are now being won or lost on productivity, on speed, on responsiveness to change. The low-skilled, well-paid work of the postwar era has been designed out, automated, or is done in low-wage areas overseas. Companies can no longer hire people who cannot quickly add the type of value required by an ever more demanding and competitive marketplace."
-- Jack Welch, then chairman and CEO of General Electric, October 17, 1990

October 18, 2018
Thursday
Alaska Day (Alaska)

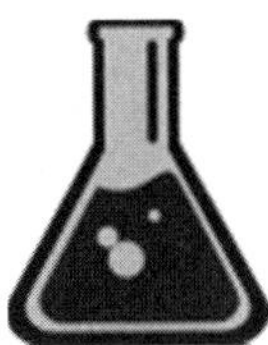

Objectives & reminders

___

___

___

Appointments

Early morning

8 a.m.

9 a.m.

10 a.m.

11 a.m.

Noon

1 p.m.

2 p.m.

3 p.m.

4 p.m.

5 p.m.

6 p.m.

Later evening

The more widely distributed a company's profits, the better: Agree or disagree?

"[W]e want to put the profits of trade into the pockets of the people, not a section of them, but the entire community. Until the people get hold of trade profits they will never be able to undertake the productive business of the world."
– John Thomas Whitehead Mitchell, chairman of the Co-operative Wholesale Society (CWS) in Great Britain from 1869 to 1895, born in Rochdale, Lancashire, England on October 18, 1828

Mitchell certainly not a hypocrite
In sharp contrast to the generous and often controversial compensation packages that top corporate leaders receive today, in the late 1880s Mitchell was paid only £150 of the company's annual £6 million revenues. As the *Rochdale Observer* put it in 1895, "certainly no man ever presided over so vast a concern who took such slender remuneration for so doing."

Happy birthday: Christian Friedrich Schönbein

Born in Metzingen, Germany on October 18, 1799, Schönbein was the German-Swiss chemist and inventor who discovered and named the ozone in 1840.

Five years later, in 1845, Schönbein made a serendipitous discovery when he accidently spilled a mixture of sulfuric and nitric acid on his family's kitchen table during his wife's absence. He quickly grabbed his wife's cotton apron hanging nearby to wipe the spill, which he then hung by the fire to dry before his wife returned home. When the apron exploded, caused by the reaction of the heated nitrate and the cellulose cotton fibers, Schönbein realized the potential value of the "smokeless gunpowder," also known as guncotton or nitrocellulose – which he began producing and marketing around the world.

October 19, 2018
Friday
Mother Teresa Day (Albania)

Objectives & reminders

___

___

___

Appointments

Early morning

8 a.m.

9 a.m.

10 a.m.

11 a.m.

Noon

1 p.m.

2 p.m.

3 p.m.

4 p.m.

5 p.m.

6 p.m.

Later evening

Reaching the teen market

On October 19, 1995, *USA Today* published the findings of a poll that asked teenagers what their favorite activities were. Spending time with friends and watching television tied for first.

> **Invitation to speculate**
> If the same study was repeated today – surveying today's teens -- how might the findings differ from those in 1995? What are the advertising implications of these possible differences?

Capitalizing on these findings, businesses frequently use television advertising to reach teens, and when they do, they often depict teens using their brands in social settings. The peer approval of the brands by the teen actors helps to legitimize the brands.

Business planning 101

Born in Lansdowne, Pennsylvania on October 19, 1909, William H. Newman was a business professor at Columbia University for most of his career. In his 1950 classic, *Administrative Action: The Techniques of Organization and Management*, Dr. Newman offered a broad definition of planning and described the basic nature of planning in business:

> "Speaking generally; planning is deciding in advance what is to be done; that is, a plan is a projected course of action.... Planning in a business enterprise normally involves at least the following steps:
>
> 1. *Recognition of the need for action...* [I]t is recognized that matters cannot be permitted to simply drift with a 'do nothing' attitude...
>
> 2. *Investigation and analysis.* Here the facts of the present situation are studied so that... alternatives may be identified, and information is gathered as to the benefits and the difficulties in applying them.
>
> 3. *Proposal for action.* On the basis of the investigation, the executive develops proposed courses of action; he 'initiates' a plan.
>
> 4. *Decision.* A plan does not really exist until a clear decision is made as to a course of action." (p. 15)

October 20, 2018
Saturday
Mashujaa [Heroes'] Day (Kenya)

Objectives & reminders

Appointments

Early morning

8 a.m.

9 a.m.

10 a.m.

11 a.m.

Noon

1 p.m.

2 p.m.

3 p.m.

4 p.m.

5 p.m.

6 p.m.

Later evening

Marketing Australia

On October 20, 1973, the spectacular Sydney Opera House opened on Bennelong Point in Sydney, Australia. Designed by Danish architect Jøørn Utzon, the US$80 million structure is known for its geometric roof shells comprised of 2,000 panes of glass. The Opera House took 15 years to build. Today, the multi-use building hosts about 3,000 events annually and is routinely featured in advertisements and travel brochures used to market the city and the country.

It has happened before

On October 20, 1980, the U.S. Agriculture Department announced that the year's drought had affected much of the country's crop yields. Peanut production was down by 37 percent for the year, soybeans by 23 percent, and corn by 17 percent. Given the variety of uses for which agricultural products are used (especially peanuts, soybeans and corn), consider how your industry and company could deal with a sudden drop in the supply of your products' key agricultural ingredients.

Big deals on October 20

1803 The U.S. Senate approved the purchase of the Louisiana territory from France for a mere $15 million. In what became known as the Louisiana Purchase, the transaction approximately doubled the geographic size of the U.S. and ensured U.S. control of transportation along the mighty Mississippi River, including the strategic port city of New Orleans where the Mississippi River flowed into the Gulf of Mexico.

1820 Spain sold east Florida to the U.S. for $5 million. For Florida, the deal was a real estate record-breaker at the time, but since then some individual lots have sold for millions of dollars – reinforcing the significance and value of the 1820 sale.

1975 The U.S. announced an agreement to sell six to eight million tons of grain annually to the Soviet Union. The deal not only paved the way for future trade and improved relations between the two super-powers, but the new market proved to be beneficial to American farmers as well.

October 21, 2018
Sunday
Apple Day (United Kingdom)

Objectives & reminders

______

______

______

Appointments

Early morning

8 a.m.

9 a.m.

10 a.m.

11 a.m.

Noon

1 p.m.

2 p.m.

3 p.m.

4 p.m.

5 p.m.

6 p.m.

Later evening

Happy birthday: Leo Burnett

Born in St. Johns, Michigan on October 21, 1891, Burnett attended the University of Michigan where he studied journalism. After college Burnett gained valuable advertising experience working for other people.

In 1935 Burnett created his own advertising agency -- Leo Burnett Co., Inc. -- and soon became a legend by creating an image or aura for the products he promoted -- images that extended beyond mere objective descriptions and rational arguments to justify purchase. That is, Burnett believed, "good advertising does not just circulate information. It penetrates the public mind with desires and beliefs."

The images he created to penetrate the public mind were often embodied in the personalities or demeanor of tangible icons. Four of the icons he created (Jolly Green Giant, Marlboro Man, Pillsbury Doughboy and Tony the Tiger) were rated by *Advertising Age* magazine as among the top ten advertising icons of the 20th century.

✍ Advertising: Hands *on* or hands *off?*
"Any fool can write a bad ad, but it takes a real genius to keep his hands off a good one."
– Leo Burnett

Creativity and fun
"Creative ideas flourish best in a shop which preserves some spirit of fun. Nobody is in business for fun, but that does not mean there cannot be fun in business."
– Leo Burnett

______

It's not how long you work that counts (although it may be easier to find your car in the parking lot)

"[H]ow long the lights are on or your car's in the parking lot really shouldn't be indicative of the quality of the job you're doing." – Anne M. Mulcahy, former CEO of Xerox, born in Rockville Centre, New York on October 21, 1952

Mulcahy is credited with revitalizing Xerox during her tenure as CEO. In October 2006, *Forbes* magazine named her as the fifth most powerful woman in the world.

October 22, 2018
Monday
National Color Day

Objectives & reminders

____

____

____

Appointments

Early morning

8 a.m.

9 a.m.

10 a.m.

11 a.m.

Noon

1 p.m.

2 p.m.

3 p.m.

4 p.m.

5 p.m.

6 p.m.

Later evening

Eggnog sales begin today!

The factors that drive seasonal patterns of purchase and consumption are not always apparent. Buyers' timing may indicate their personal preferences, but could reflect the constraints imposed by sellers, nature, culture, laws or other people or organizations in the buyers' networks. So-called "seasonal" merchandise may not be inherently seasonal. As a result, marketers can be misled by seasonal sales data or the questionable assumptions that accompany the data – which can lead to missed marketing opportunities or other subpar marketing decisions.

Eggnog serves as an excellent example, as it is considered a highly seasonal product in the U.S., Great Britain and elsewhere, but its inherent seasonality is suspect. In some markets, nearly 100 percent of eggnog's annual retail sales will be generated during the 11-week period beginning today, October 22. But, do consumers buy eggnog during the next 11 weeks because that's when they demand it, or do they buy eggnog during that period simply because that's when it's available in stores? Different answers could lead to quite different business decisions – ranging from maintenance of the status quo to year-round distribution. In search of the answer, pouring over a store's sales data for recent years may lead to the assumption of seasonality, but sole reliance on this historical sales data is clearly an insufficient basis for decision-making if eggnog is shelved for only 11 weeks each year.

Of course, eggnog is only one of many categories with seasonal demand patterns that could be challenged. Even for what appears to be highly seasonal items, such as eggnog, there may be a devoted niche of high-involvement buyers willing to pay premium prices and travel out of their local neighborhoods to purchase these products year-round, if available. So, in many instances, serving such niches could be profitable for one or a few sellers in a market where most competitors blindly embrace the assumption of seasonality.

Learn more

This discussion was summarized from "Calendars: Influential and Widely Used Marketing Planning Tools," published in the *Journal of Brand Strategy* (2016, vol. 5, #2, pp. 1-14) and available in its entirety on *Marketing FAME*'s website, www.MarketingMarbles.com. Read the article to learn more.

October 23, 2018
Tuesday
Mole Day

Objectives & reminders

____

____

____

Appointments

Early morning

8 a.m.

9 a.m.

10 a.m.

11 a.m.

Noon

1 p.m.

2 p.m.

3 p.m.

4 p.m.

5 p.m.

6 p.m.

Later evening

Noteworthy descendants born on October 23

1927 W. Barron Hilton, son of Conrad Hilton who founded the Hilton Hotel chain. Barron Hilton followed in his father's footsteps – serving as the company's vice-president beginning in 1954, then as president in 1966, and most recently as co-chair.

1938 Henry John Heinz III, Pennsylvania congressman (1971-1991) whose grandfather founded what became one of the largest food manufacturing companies in the world, H.J. Heinz Company. Before becoming a member of the U.S. House of Representatives and then a senator, Henry III served as the marketing manager for the Heinz Company, from 1965 to 1970.

1942 Michael Crichton, novelist who wrote several best-sellers including *The Andromeda Strain, The Terminal Man, Congo, The Great Train Robbery, Binary, Westworld,* and several others. Crichton's father was the executive editor of *Advertising Age* magazine, the industry's leading publication for news and developments in the field of advertising.

Tip for B2B sales reps
It's not uncommon to send greeting cards to clients or give them small gifts occasionally, but if you want to make a more memorable gesture, do something for clients' children or grandchildren.

1994 Brandon Charles Martin, lifelong percussionist, star bowler, outstanding book rep, and destined for greatness -- and son of marble marketing mania mogul.

Preparation: prerequisite for success

"Talent alone won't make you a success. Neither will being in the right place at the right time, unless you are ready. The most important question is: 'Are you ready?'" – Johnny Carson, 30-year host of *The Tonight Show* (1962-1992), born in Corning, Iowa on October 23, 1925

October 24, 2018
Wednesday
United Nations Day

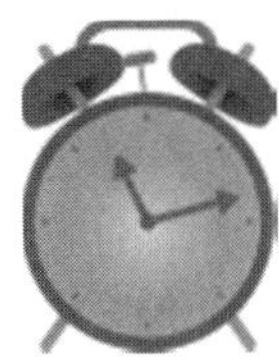

Objectives & reminders

____

____

____

Appointments

Early morning

8 a.m.

9 a.m.

10 a.m.

11 a.m.

Noon

1 p.m.

2 p.m.

3 p.m.

4 p.m.

5 p.m.

6 p.m.

Later evening

Wake up!

Prior to 1876 the few alarm clocks that were made in the United States rang only at 4:00 a.m. (to wake roosters?). They could not be adjusted to ring at a later time. That changed on October 24, 1876, when Seth E. Thomas received a patent for his mechanical wind-up alarm clock that could be adjusted to ring whenever its users desired. The Seth Thomas Clock Company of Thomaston, Connecticut immediately began manufacturing and selling the new alarm clocks.

Thomas' successful innovation should serve as a wake-up call to businesses who fail to recognize that consumers' usage patterns and preferences vary greatly with respect to time. In much the same way that not every consumer wants to awaken at four o'clock in the morning, not every consumer wants (or is able) to shop or conduct personal business during traditional "business hours." Not every consumer is able to enjoy leisure or entertainment services in the evenings or on the weekends.

When prospective buyers' busy schedules conflict with those of the business, the business must decide the extent to which it will insist that buyers bend to its expectations (as alarm clock makers did prior to 1876), versus bending to accommodate buyers' scheduling preferences and constraints (as Seth Thomas did).

> **Alternative perspective of time:**
> **No need for alarm clocks**
> "So far as I know, anything worth hearing is not usually uttered at seven o'clock in the morning; and if it is, it will generally be repeated at a more reasonable hour for a larger and more wakeful audience."
> – Moss Hart, American playwright and songwriter, born in New York City on October 24, 1904

Wake up your priorities!

"The key is not to prioritize what's on your schedule, but to schedule your priorities." – Stephen R. Covey, world-renowned business consultant and author of several influential books including the 1989 best-seller, *The Seven Habits of Highly Effective People.* Covey was born in Salt Lake City, Utah on October 24, 1932.

October 25, 2018
Thursday
Taiwan Retrocession Day

Objectives & reminders

____

____

____

Appointments

Early morning

8 a.m.

9 a.m.

10 a.m.

11 a.m.

Noon

1 p.m.

2 p.m.

3 p.m.

4 p.m.

5 p.m.

6 p.m.

Later evening

It's getting colder!

As the calendar marches further into autumn in the Northern Hemisphere, colder weather grips an increasing number of communities throughout the United States. As discussed on September 30, colder temperatures can affect customers, employees and business operations. Realizing this, astute business-people anticipate the arrival of cold weather and plan accordingly, but the difficulty of their task is compounded by the fact that cold weather tends to arrive on different days in different communities.

Below are a few markets that, in any given year, have a 10 percent probability of experiencing freezing temperatures (32 degrees Fahrenheit or lower) on or before October 25. The dates for which the freeze probability increases to 50 and 90 percent are indicated too. Consider how businesses operating in multiple markets might benefit from this sort of data provided online for more than 3,100 U.S. communities by the National Climatic Data Center.

Community	*10%*	*50%*	*90%*
Carlsbad, NM	Oct 25	Nov 7	Nov 21
Hammond, LA	Oct 25	Nov 10	Nov 25
Macon, GA	Oct 25	Nov 8	Nov 22
Mt Hamilton, CA	Oct 25	Nov 12	Nov 29
Snyder, TX	Oct 25	Nov 6	Nov 19
Tacoma, WA	Oct 25	Nov 13	Dec 1

Integrity is not negotiable

"There is no twilight zone of honesty in business. A thing is right or wrong. It's black or it's white."
– John F. Dodge, American manufacturer who co-founded in 1914, with his brother Horace, Dodge Brothers, Inc. – makers of Dodge vehicles. John was born in Niles, Michigan on October 25, 1864.

____

Why it's called "leadership," not "pullership"

"The very essence of all power to influence lies in getting the other person to participate. The mind that can do that has a powerful leverage on his human world." – Harry Allen Overstreet, philosopher, author and educator (Berkeley, City College of New York), born in San Francisco, California on October 25, 1875

October 26, 2018
Friday
Nevada Day (Nevada)

Objectives & reminders

____

____

____

Appointments

Early morning

8 a.m.

9 a.m.

10 a.m.

11 a.m.

Noon

1 p.m.

2 p.m.

3 p.m.

4 p.m.

5 p.m.

6 p.m.

Later evening

Saving time?

Washing clothes by hand is hard work. That's why a number of inventors in the 19th century scrambled to delegate the task to machines. On October 26, 1858, Hamilton E. Smith of Philadelphia succeeded when he received a patent for a washing machine with a plunger coupled with an ingenious system of cycling reheated water through the machine.

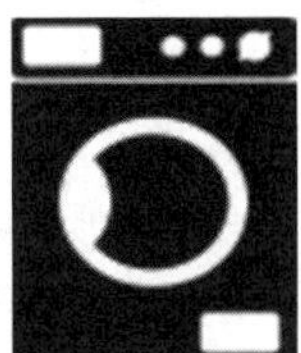

Like many inventions throughout history, washing machines promised to save time for consumers. But when previously laborious chores become easier to accomplish with machines, the tendency is to use all or much of the "saved" time to perform the tasks with greater frequency -- so the net amount of time saved may be negligible. Before washing machines it was common to wear clothes for a week or more before washing them. Today, clothes may be washed after being worn for only a few hours.

Time-saving marketing principle
Making consumption-related tasks easier, quicker or otherwise more convenient for consumers increases buyers' likelihood of engaging in the tasks, which in turn increases the demand for goods and services that facilitate the convenience.

____

Internet too commercial: Agree or disagree?

"We need a format distinction between commercial and noncommercial portals. There is so much commercialization of the Web it's beginning to affect the efficacy of the medium. Without a noncommercial domain, we risk having commercialism affect the architectural efficacy of navigation. For example, look at search. The more paid search listings predominate, the less the quality of information becomes the ranking paradigm. Whether or not it's good for business, it's a bad thing for the intellectual purity and efficacy of the Web... What we are trying to build here is the PBS [Public Broadcasting System] of the Web." – Joe Firmage, born in Salt Lake Ciry, Utah on October 26, 1970. Firmage is an American entrepreneur who has founded or co-founded several Internet businesses, including USWeb and ManyOne Networks.

October 27, 2018
Saturday
Flag Day (Greece)

Objectives & reminders

____

____

____

Appointments

Early morning

8 a.m.

9 a.m.

10 a.m.

11 a.m.

Noon

1 p.m.

2 p.m.

3 p.m.

4 p.m.

5 p.m.

6 p.m.

Later evening

Brought to you by Bristol-Myers

A television show featuring travel films, *Geographically Speaking*, debuted on October 27, 1946. It was the first television show with a designated, identified commercial sponsor -- Bristol-Myers. Presumably when audiences perceive a specific link between a favorite program and an identified sponsor, they feel more indebted to the sponsor and more willing to consider purchasing the sponsor's products. Consider: Do *today's* television audiences perceive such linkages?

Fundamental rule of good etiquette

"Manners are a sensitive awareness of the feelings of others. If you have that awareness, you have good manners, no matter what fork you use." – Emily Post, etiquette expert and author of the 1922 best-seller, *Etiquette in Society, in Business, in Politics, and at Home.* Ms. Post was born in Baltimore, Maryland on October 27, 1872.

Happy birthday: Isaac Merritt Singer

Born near Troy, New York on October 27, 1811, Singer's name is inseparably associated with sewing machines that continue to bear his name. Singer didn't invent the first commercially available sewing machine (Elias Howe did), but he did make numerous improvements to sewing machine designs of the day. He launched his sewing machine manufacturing company in 1850 – I.M. Singer & Company. Initially, he served the professional market of tailors and shirt-makers with his heavy-duty designs. By 1856, however, Singer began reaching the home market with smaller machines.

Singer's success has been attributed to many factors, including user-friendly design innovations, use of interchangeable parts in production, and the strategic location of international production facilities in the U.S., Europe and South America.

Of particular note was Singer's introduction of the "rent-to-own" credit/pricing concept in the late 1850s. Singer's company may have been the first major firm to formally adopt and promote the rent-to-own concept which allowed consumers to rent the $60-machines for a monthly fee of $5. After a year of rental payments, ownership was transferred to the renter. Sales quadrupled during the first year of the rent-to-own innovation.

October 28, 2018
Sunday

National Chocolate Day
Mother-in-Law Day

Objectives & reminders

Appointments

Early morning

8 a.m.

9 a.m.

10 a.m.

11 a.m.

Noon

1 p.m.

2 p.m.

3 p.m.

4 p.m.

5 p.m.

6 p.m.

Later evening

Happy birthday: Patricia Cain Smith

Smith was born in Minneapolis, Minnesota on October 28, 1917. Pursuing an academic career in industrial and organizational psychology, she became the first female granted tenure at Cornell University and later taught at Bowling Green State University.

Among Smith's many contributions to business, she pioneered the development and use of "Behaviorally Anchored Rating Scales" (BARS) to help managers evaluate personnel performance. As its name implies, each BARS scale point describes specific worker behaviors which helps evaluators to be less subjective in the evaluation process. The descriptions provide raters with a basis for a shared understanding of what each rating point means.

Example of the BARS approach

Circle the number below that best corresponds to the sales rep's level of *product knowledge...*

1. He/she is not familiar enough with the product line to recognize the majority of products in the company catalogue.

2. He/she recognizes most products in the product line but usually has to refer to the catalogue or another employee to answer customers' questions about the products.

3. He/she is able to answer most routine questions about most products (such as price, availability, and general applications) without consulting the catalogue or another employee, but often is unable to answer technical product-related questions that customers ask.

4. He/she is able to answer almost all product-related questions that arise.

To illustrate the problem that the BARS approach addresses, consider that a less precise approach, such as simply rating performance on a 1 to 10 scale, leaves one to wonder what an "8" is, for example, and how an "8" differs from a "7" or a "9," or if an "8" is twice as much or twice as good as a "4," and so on. When raters vary in their interpretations of 7s, 8s, 9s, and 4s, biases -- intentional or not -- creep into the evaluation process. The BARS approach helps to eliminate rater-to-rater variation and their accompanying biases.

October 29, 2018
Monday

International Internet Day

Objectives & reminders

____

____

____

Appointments

Early morning

8 a.m.

9 a.m.

10 a.m.

11 a.m.

Noon

1 p.m.

2 p.m.

3 p.m.

4 p.m.

5 p.m.

6 p.m.

Later evening

A few firsts on October 29

1858

First store opened in Denver, Colorado – largely to serve the gold seekers who had begun moving into the area. Within a year, tens of thousands of miners had moved to the booming frontier town named after the Territorial Governor of Kansas at the time, James W. Denver.

1904

First intercity trucking service in the U.S. began hauling goods between the two small Texas towns of Snyder and Colorado City. The concept caught on and entrepreneurs around the country quickly duplicated the concept – especially reaching communities not served by the railroads.

1942

Alaska Highway first opened to traffic. The 1,523-mile transportation artery was built as a supply line to make Alaska more accessible, and thus less vulnerable during World War II. The highway was completed in less than nine months. As incredible as the 1942 construction feat was, also incredible is the fact that today's travelers can drive for hundreds of miles along what is now called the Al-Can Highway without seeing a McDonald's restaurant.

1945

First ballpoint pen sold in the U.S. Branded as the Reynold's Rocket after the entrepreneur who brought the innovation to the U.S., Milton Reynolds, the pen was first available at Gimbel's department store in New York. At $12.50 or $12.95 each (sources disagree), about 8,000 were sold the first day.

October 30, 2018
Tuesday
Doughnut Day

Objectives & reminders

____

____

____

Appointments

Early morning

8 a.m.

9 a.m.

10 a.m.

11 a.m.

Noon

1 p.m.

2 p.m.

3 p.m.

4 p.m.

5 p.m.

6 p.m.

Later evening

From growing to slowing

Results of the 1900 census of the U.S. population were reported on October 30, 1900 (the U.S. Constitution requires that a census be taken every decade). The final tally was 76,295,220, which represented a substantial increase of almost 21 percent over the 1890 census. At the time, New York was the most populous state with 7,268,009 residents. Nevada was the least populous with 42,334 residents.

Today, the United States' population is over 327 million – about 4.3 times what it was in 1900. While the size of the total population continues to grow, the overall growth rate has slowed considerably. The country's annual rate of increase is now about half of what it was in the 1890s.

Not surprisingly, some communities have recently grown much faster than average (most notably Las Vegas, Nevada; Austin, Texas; Mesa, Arizona; Charlotte, North Carolina; Phoenix, Arizona) while the population actually has shrunk in other cities (e.g., St. Louis, Missouri; Baltimore, Maryland; Buffalo, New York; Pittsburgh, Pennsylvania; Cincinnati, Ohio; Detroit, Michigan).

When the rate of population growth slows and there are fewer "new" consumers entering the market, marketers may feel they can't afford to lose valued customers, so they may shift some emphasis from customer acquisition to customer retention. To grow the business, they may look for ways to increase buyers' rate of consumption, e.g., by offering quantity discounts, using larger packages, and promoting new uses for existing products.

Five ways to keep valued customers

1. Improve product and service quality.
2. Personalize service (learn and use customers' names, smile).
3. Customize products and services to meet customers' precise requirements.
4. Offer incentives to encourage customer loyalty (e.g., "a better price for a better customer").
5. Say "thank you" often.

October 31, 2018
Wednesday
Halloween

Objectives & reminders

____

____

____

Appointments

Early morning

8 a.m.

9 a.m.

10 a.m.

11 a.m.

Noon

1 p.m.

2 p.m.

3 p.m.

4 p.m.

5 p.m.

6 p.m.

Later evening

Happy Halloween!

What to feed the competition on Halloween

"Eye of newt, and toe of frog,
Wool of bat, and tongue of dog,
Adder's fork, and blink-worm's sting,
Lizard's leg, and owlet's wing,
For a charm of powerful trouble,
Like a hell-broth boil and bubble."
-- William Shakespeare

Halloween spending

Americans now spend about $8.4 billion annually on Halloween-related candy, decorations, costumes and greeting cards -- an average of $82.93 per consumer, according to the National Retail Federation's 2016 data. An estimated 71 percent of households distribute candy to trick-or-treaters. Collectively, American consumers buy more candy for Halloween than they do for any other holiday.

Not surprisingly, Wal-Mart is among the sales leaders in most Halloween-related merchandise categories. Less known is the fact that "Wal-Mart Stores" was incorporated on Halloween Day in 1969. For about seven years prior to that, Sam Walton's retail stores were known as Discount City.

Slow sales day?

Despite the huge amount of money consumers spend on Halloween candy, decorations, costumes, and greeting cards, Halloween night can be an especially slow sales night for stores selling non-Halloween items.

To counter this phenomenon, some retailers build customer traffic by promoting trick-or-treating inside their stores, malls, or shopping centers. Trick-or-treaters visit each store or department to receive treats in a safe environment. As they do, accompanying parents are exposed to merchandise displayed along the way.

The superstitious on Halloween

Twenty-five percent of Americans participating in a Gallup poll said they were "somewhat" or "very" superstitious. Thirteen percent claimed they are disturbed when black cats cross their paths.

November 1, 2018
Thursday
All Saints Day

Objectives & reminders

Appointments

Early morning

---

8 a.m.

---

9 a.m.

---

10 a.m.

---

11 a.m.

Noon

---

1 p.m.

---

2 p.m.

---

3 p.m.

---

4 p.m.

---

5 p.m.

---

6 p.m.

Later evening

November symbols

Topaz is November's birthstone. The flower of the month is the chrysanthemum.

Invitation to discuss
Which types of businesses could benefit from the variation in birthstones and flowers from month to month? Suggest how marketers of these and other businesses might capitalize on these monthly symbols.

●●●●●●●●●●

A sporting month

November is probably the busiest sports-related month of the year in the U.S. With so many sports activities competing for media coverage during November, businesses hoping to receive publicity for new product announcements or grand openings might consider timing these events in other months instead -- months in which the media are less likely to be inundated with sports-related stories.

Having a ball
"Just about every sport on every level except… soccer, among a few others – is playing [in November]. Local schools [are] involved in the playoffs in different sports, and the NBA [begins]; the NFL [hits] full stride; the college football picture [begins] to shape up; college basketball [starts]…; and so on."
-- Shane Stark, then Staff Writer for the *Tyler* [Texas] *Morning Telegraph*

●●●●●●●●●●

To get busy, perfection is not required

"If you do a lot of things to build business, you'll build business. They don't have to be done perfectly to work, although the better you do them, the better they'll work. But the main point is that you have to do them – a lot." – Joe Girard, legendary sales professional who once held the retail record for selling the most automobiles – an average of 18 a week for 14 years. Girard was born in Detroit, Michigan on November 1, 1928.

November 2, 2018
Friday
All Souls Day

Objectives & reminders

Appointments

Early morning

8 a.m.

9 a.m.

10 a.m.

11 a.m.

Noon

1 p.m.

2 p.m.

3 p.m.

4 p.m.

5 p.m.

6 p.m.

Later evening

Programming ➔ radios ➔ audiences ➔ advertisers

Only a few years after radio was invented and still in its infancy, Frank Conrad conceived the idea of broadcasting music from his Westinghouse Company lab in Pittsburgh, Pennsylvania.

The company picked up the idea and began regular broadcasts on Pittsburgh's KDKA on November 2, 1920. KDKA broadcast the news on that day, including the results of the Presidential election between Warren G. Harding and James M. Cox.

At the time, Westinghouse's primary objective was not the promotion of music or news, per se; but the company realized that appealing programming would stimulate the sale of radios, which it did. The next year Americans paid $10 million for radios. By the year after that (1922), about 500 radio stations were broadcasting programs to attract audiences.

Today, news and music are central to the programming of most radio stations. Without appealing content, audiences won't tune in. Without audiences, advertisers won't follow.

For your marketing consideration
Consider how radio audiences vary across programming formats. How could marketers' knowledge of audience differences be used to increase the effectiveness of ad campaigns and marketing programs?

Societies create choices, while the study of economics helps guide us through the selection process

"A well-coordinated and smoothly functioning society gives individuals more opportunity to choose; it does not guarantee that they will choose well. The economic way of thinking, especially in a democracy, is an important preliminary. But it is no more than that." – Paul T. Heyne, former American economics professor (Valparaiso University, Southern Methodist University, and University of Washington in Seattle), born on November 2, 1931. This quotation is from the 7th edition of his widely read textbook, *The Economic Way of Thinking* (p. 607).

November 3, 2018
Saturday
National Sandwich Day

Objectives & reminders

___

___

___

Appointments

Early morning

8 a.m.

9 a.m.

10 a.m.

11 a.m.

Noon

1 p.m.

2 p.m.

3 p.m.

4 p.m.

5 p.m.

6 p.m.

Later evening

Happy birthday: John Montague & Stephen F. Austin

Montague was born on November 3, 1718, and became the Fourth Earl of Sandwich. Among his many accomplishments, Montague served as England's Secretary of State, Postmaster General and the First Lord of the Admiralty. Outside of Great Britain, however, Montague may be best known for inventing what we now call the *sandwich*.

One day in 1762 while playing a marathon game of cards Montague felt too preoccupied to stop for a traditional meal, so he asked a servant to bring him a piece of meat inserted between two slices of bread. The sandwich concept soon caught on among other convenience-oriented consumers.

Montague's birthday has not gone unnoticed by modern-day businesses. DowBrands, for example, maker of Ziploc Sandwich Bags has designated Montague's birthday as "Ziploc National Sandwich Day," for which both Montague and Ziploc have received more than a sandwich's worth of publicity. Although it is doubtful that the Earl used Ziploc Sandwich Bags in the 18th century, that didn't stop DowBrands from promoting the occasion.

The larger point is that there are numerous birthdays and events scattered throughout history that are potentially marketing-relevant. At some point in time, someone, somewhere invented something, launched a business, started a trend, or otherwise did or said something noteworthy -- something that did or could impact the future of the business, industry, brand, or product category. Identifying and promoting these dates -- as DowBrands did – makes marketing sense.

Alternatively, birthdays and historical events tied to the local community could be celebrated. For example, a western-wear clothing store in Austin, Texas might sponsor a western dance contest or civic parade (both featuring authentic early-19th-century clothing) to celebrate the life and vision of Austin's founder -- Stephen F. Austin -- who was born on November 3, 1793.

Mr. Austin was a prominent figure in the history of Texas. He fought for Texas' independence from Mexico, ran for the Presidency of Texas (losing to Sam Houston), and served as Texas' Secretary of State.

November 4, 2018
Sunday

Daylight Saving Time ends
Unity Day (Russia)

Objectives & reminders

Adjust clocks for DST

Appointments

Early morning

8 a.m.

9 a.m.

10 a.m.

11 a.m.

Noon

1 p.m.

2 p.m.

3 p.m.

4 p.m.

5 p.m.

6 p.m.

Later evening

Daylight cut

Daylight Saving Time (DST) in most of the U.S. ends today. 2:00 a.m. suddenly becomes 1:00 a.m.

Employee theft cut

According to some estimates, employees steal more from businesses than shoplifters. One of the first innovations to battle the problem -- the cash register -- was patented on November 4, 1879 (some sources say 1880).

Apparently Dayton, Ohio bar owner James J. Ritty had grown tired of his bartenders pilfering money from the business so he developed a device that resembled a clock, but instead of showing hours and minutes, the hands displayed dollars and cents for everyone nearby to see. The belief was that if cashiers knew that other people could visibly verify the amount recorded, the likelihood of recording the correct amount would increase.

The invention's internal mechanisms kept track of a grand total by adding each transaction recorded. Although initial sales of cash registers were sluggish, the National Cash Register Company was formed in 1884 to develop the market.

Making change

Although Ritty's original cash register was simply a recording device, later models included money drawers that would open with each transaction. Unfortunately, dishonest employees would sometimes beat the technology by bypassing the cash register altogether and pocketing the money collected without ringing-up the sales on the cash register.

In an attempt to counter this form of employee theft, ingenious retailers began charging odd amounts for merchandise. This *odd pricing* practice decreased the chances that customers would offer the exact amount in payment. If the sale amount was $4.95, for example, the customer could be expected offer a five-dollar bill for payment. Unless the transaction was rung-up on the cash register, the money drawer would not open for the employee to retrieve the customer's change.

November 5, 2018
Monday
Guy Fawkes Day (U.K)

Objectives & reminders

___

___

___

Appointments

Early morning

8 a.m.

9 a.m.

10 a.m.

11 a.m.

Noon

1 p.m.

2 p.m.

3 p.m.

4 p.m.

5 p.m.

6 p.m.

Later evening

Fantasy wealth?

Still struggling to get through the Great Depression, most American consumers in the mid-1930s were ready for some form of economic relief or reason to be encouraged. On November 5, 1935, they found it when Parker Brothers released the board game called Monopoly. The game afforded consumers with a temporary distraction, a brief period during which players could acquire property, accumulate wealth and spend money -- albeit play money. Since its 1935 debut, 250+ million sets of Monopoly have been sold and 500+ million people have played the game.

Bad day for guys named "Guy"

November 5 is "Guy Fawkes Day" in the United Kingdom, in recognition and, yes, celebration of the 1605 gunpowder plot to blow up King James I and Parliament.

On November 4, 1605 -- the night before the planned explosions -- 20 barrels of gunpowder were found secretly positioned in the cellar of the Parliament building. The conspirators were tracked down, arrested, and beheaded. Among the conspirators was the group's mastermind, Guy Fawkes.

The next year Parliament enacted a law to make November 5 an annual day of public thanksgiving and celebration. Fireworks and bonfires featuring "Guy" roastings are part of the celebration.

The changing Face(book) of advertising

"Once every [one] hundred years media changes. The last hundred years have been defined by the mass media. The way to advertise was to get into the mass media and push out your content. That was the last hundred years. In the next hundred years information won't be just pushed out to people, it will be shared among the millions of connections people have. Advertising will change. You will need to get into these connections." – Mark Zuckerberg, CEO of Facebook (social network website). Zuckerberg shared this observation on November 5, 2007, when he announced that Facebook was launching a new advertising platform that would allow advertisers to target Facebook's users and tap into users' online social networks. Users soon began to "like" the ads.

November 6, 2018
Tuesday
Election Day

Objectives & reminders

____

____

____

Appointments

Early morning

8 a.m.

9 a.m.

10 a.m.

11 a.m.

Noon

1 p.m.

2 p.m.

3 p.m.

4 p.m.

5 p.m.

6 p.m.

Later evening

Election Day

Although state and local elections occur throughout the year, the first Tuesday after the first Monday in November is set aside for national elections in the U.S. As such, today is a state holiday in 14 U.S. states. Most major national elections occur in even-numbered years (e.g., 2016, 2018, 2020.). Presidential elections occur on alternating even-numbered years (e.g., 2012, 2016, 2020).

Happy birthday: Gail Borden

Born in Norwich, New York on November 6, 1801, Borden moved south with his parents in 1814, eventually finding himself in Texas in 1829 where he founded a newspaper with his brother in 1835.

In the late 1840s Borden identified a need to supply settlers with economical and portable food products as they migrated westward. First, he developed a concentrated "meat biscuit" but manufacturing problems blocked its success. As a result, Borden lost most of his life's savings.

Undaunted, Borden tried again -- the second time with a condensed milk product (patented in 1856), and later with condensed tea, coffee, cocoa, and fruit juices. Borden's perseverance paid off as the Borden Milk Company prospered. Today, we associate Borden with a variety of food products as well as chemicals.

What do you get when you mix milk with glue?

Elsie has been the spokescow for Borden's condensed milk and other dairy products since the 1930s. Her popularity prompted the company to introduce Elmer the spokesbull a few years later to represent some of Borden's chemical products, such as Elmer's Glue.

Consider the extent to which the use of Elsie and Elmer may confuse consumers or mix the images of the respective product categories they represent. Is there a danger of positioning milk too closely to glue in consumers' minds? Should either Elsie or Elmer moooove aside?

November 7, 2018
Wednesday
Opera Day (Hungary)

Objectives & reminders

___

___

___

Appointments

Early morning

8 a.m.

9 a.m.

10 a.m.

11 a.m.

Noon

1 p.m.

2 p.m.

3 p.m.

4 p.m.

5 p.m.

6 p.m.

Later evening

Happy birthday: Tom Peters

Born in Baltimore, Maryland on November 7, 1942, Peters was one of the most widely read American management gurus of the 1980s and 1990s. Early in his career, Peters served in the military and in the federal government's Office of Management and Budget. He gained considerable business experience as a consultant for Peate Marwick Mitchell and then for McKinsey & Company before forming his own consulting and seminar firm in the early 1980s, the Tom Peters Group.

Peters has authored or co-authored numerous business books, including his million-selling 1982 book, *In Search of Excellence,* co-authored with Robert H. Waterman, Jr. In it, several successful companies were analyzed to identify common characteristics that made them "excellent." Among other characteristics, Peters and Waterman found that excellent companies:

1. Have a bias for action. They'd rather act immediately with a *good* idea than to wait too long for a *perfect* idea to come along.

2. Are close to their customers. They know what their customers like and don't like. They communicate frequently with customers, and they view listening as a central part of the communication process.

3. Stress autonomy and entrepreneurship. Employees are encouraged to be innovative and take initiative. But when unforeseen mishaps or mistakes are encountered along the way employees are not unfairly reprimanded for their initiative.

4. Achieve productivity through people. Management attributes its present success and future potential to the capabilities of people throughout the organization.

5. Practice hands-on, value-driven leadership. Managers are not afraid to "get their hands dirty," but they don't micro-manage either.

6. Stick to their knitting. That is, they avoid straying very far from the businesses they know best unless compelling reasons prompt them to do so.

November 8, 2018
Thursday
National Cappuccino Day

Objectives & reminders

____

____

____

Appointments

Early morning

8 a.m.

9 a.m.

10 a.m.

11 a.m.

Noon

1 p.m.

2 p.m.

3 p.m.

4 p.m.

5 p.m.

6 p.m.

Later evening

Consumers and technology

On November 8, 2005, Harris Interactive reported the findings of a survey of 1,174 adult consumers in the United States. The survey probed consumers' attitudes toward new technologies. When reminded that "new technologies and products are hitting the market all the time," the following percentages of respondents said these statements best reflected their "attitude toward new technology in general":

- 54% "As long as it works and the price is right – I'll consider it."
- 31% "I need to know a lot more detail before considering new technology products or services."
- 14% "I believe new technology is usually better. I'm interested already."
- 1% "I don't trust it."

More specifically, when asked how much various factors impacted their purchase decisions for new electronic equipment such as cell phones, televisions and home computers, 61 percent of the surveyed consumers rated "ease of use" as a 9 or 10 (on a ten-point scale where 1 = "no impact" and 10 = "major impact") followed by "customer service" (58%), "no hassle installation" (57%), "getting a thorough understanding on how it works" (53%), "warranty" (50%), "easy to switch back if I don't like the new product/service" (50%), and "contract length or other commitment" (50%). Interestingly, only 23 percent rated the "brand of the company offering the product or service" as a 9 or 10.

Research methodology to consider
Sometimes the findings of a study can vary considerably, depending on a number of methodological factors – including the method of administration. The Harris Interactive survey was conducted *online*. Consider how the results of the survey might have differed if the same survey were conducted with a paper-and-pencil instrument *mailed* to prospective respondents, or if the same survey questions were asked in a *telephone* survey.

November 9, 2018
Friday
World Freedom Day

Hey! Who turned out the lights in here?

Objectives & reminders

______

______

______

Appointments

Early morning

8 a.m.

9 a.m.

10 a.m.

11 a.m.

Noon

1 p.m.

2 p.m.

3 p.m.

4 p.m.

5 p.m.

6 p.m.

Later evening

Anticipating the unanticipated

At the time, the Great Blackout in the Northeast on November 9, 1965, was the biggest electrical grid failure ever experienced in the United States. It began about 5:15 p.m. when a transmission line relay failed which caused interconnected power operators throughout the grid to shut down their generators in an effort to prevent overloading their equipment. The bottom line: Power was out for 13 hours, affecting 25 million people.

Although the 13-hour blackout was less-than-illuminating in a literal sense, the event reminds us that the balance between supply and demand is often a precarious one that can be disrupted for a variety of reasons. The best advice is to anticipate the unanticipated. That is, supply-demand imbalances may not be expected on any given day, but over time they're inevitable. Anticipating their eventuality and planning accordingly not only serves customers, but in some cases -- such as electrical power outages -- can save lives.

Positive thinking
"The element of the unexpected and the unforeseeable is what gives some of its relish to life and saves us from falling into the mechanical thralldom of the logicians."
– Winston Churchill, British Prime Minister (1940-1945, 1951-1955)

Sometimes the factors that potentially disrupt the balance between supply and demand are easily identified -- e.g., equipment failure, severe weather, and regional growth patterns in the case of electrical utilities. To the extent that these and other causal factors can be identified and anticipated or prevented, planning is enhanced and crises are avoided.

More difficult to anticipate are the causal factors that create a ripple-like effect to disrupt the supply-demand balance in *other* businesses and industries. For example, during the Great Blackout, the power failure caused the subway system to shut down abruptly, leaving 800,000 people trapped or stranded. The downed subway system, in turn, crippled demand for businesses located in shopping districts. On the demand upside, the Great Blackout caused a sharp spike in demand for telephone services. That is, 62 million phone calls were placed in New York City during the blackout -- a single-day record that wasn't broken until the tragic day of September 11, 2001.

November 10, 2018
Saturday
World Science Day

Objectives & reminders

____

____

____

Appointments

Early morning

8 a.m.

9 a.m.

10 a.m.

11 a.m.

Noon

1 p.m.

2 p.m.

3 p.m.

4 p.m.

5 p.m.

6 p.m.

Later evening

Happy birthday: Julie K. Martin

Born in Wichita, Kansas on November 10, 2000, Julie Martin weighed only one pound and 12 ounces. Because she was not "supposed" to be born for another three months, Julie joined the ranks of an ever-increasing number of premature babies or "preemies" (less than 37 weeks gestation). Further attesting to her premature status, Miss Martin arrived a full seven days before World Prematurity Day, observed annually on November 17.

Annually, preemies account for about 10 percent of all newborns in the United States. Collectively, these tiny babies account for $26.2 billion in annual spending – mostly for health care, but also for specially-designed (extra small) products such as diapers, clothing, bedding and so on. As in most growing markets, opportunities abound for businesses that notice the trend and take steps to serve the market.

Premature business decisions

When decision-makers grow tired of considering new information or additional alternatives, many simply reach for a conclusion, however premature, observed Martin Fischer who was born in Kiel, Germany on November 10, 1879. The implication, of course, is that business leaders should guard against using fatigue as a criterion or excuse for making premature business decisions. Like premature babies, premature business decisions can prove to be expensive.

Happy birthday: *Sesame Street*

Today is the anniversary of the broadcast debut of the most widely viewed television program for children in the world – *Sesame Street.* First aired on November 10, 1969, the show uses a combination of animation, "muppets" and live actors to entertain and educate preschoolers in 140 countries.

Beyond its appeal to children, *Sesame Street* has not escaped the attention of marketing professionals who look to replicate the show's success elements on their own streets. For example, Jill Tooley, creative marketer director at Quality Logo Products in Aurora, Illinois points to the masterful orchestration of the show's endless stream of details as an important take-away for marketers. Although varied, the songs, dances and skits all contribute to conveying and reinforcing the main points of the day without distracting the audience. In other words, the big ideas are never lost in a Sesame Sea of details.

November 11, 2018
Sunday

Veterans' Day

(known as Remembrance Day in some countries)

Objectives & reminders

____

____

____

Appointments

Early morning

8 a.m.

9 a.m.

10 a.m.

11 a.m.

Noon

1 p.m.

2 p.m.

3 p.m.

4 p.m.

5 p.m.

6 p.m.

Later evening

100-year anniversary

Germany signed the armistice agreement on November 11, 1918 – ending the "Great War" (now known as World War I) and paving the way for the annual salute to veterans beginning on November 11, 1919. Today, the U.S. recognizes the service and sacrifice of veterans of all wars. Accordingly, Veterans' Day represents a great opportunity for marketers to honor veterans.

Today's living U.S. veterans…

1. Comprise almost nine percent of the adult population, 21.4 million.
2. Represent a wide age spectrum. One-third have not yet reached their 55th birthday.
3. Are mostly males, but 7.3 percent are females.
4. Were more likely to have served during the Vietnam era (7.1 million) than any other war.
5. Enjoy an above-average median household income of about $62,000 (19% higher than U.S. median).
6. Own 2.5 million businesses.
7. Are reasonably well-educated. Twenty-six percent have a Bachelor's degree (vs. 30.4% of general U.S. adult population).

Remembering the Great Depression

The effects of the Great Depression were so severe that the experience remained etched on the minds of most people who lived through that 1930s era. Many consumers still fear repeating the experience and their frugal consumption habits, preference for secure jobs, negative attitudes toward debt, and reluctance to invest in the stock market reflect their fear.

Writer and critic Gertrude Stein revisited the Great Depression when she expressed her concerns on November 11, 1945: "Too many Americans are dependent for everything on a 'job'... Americans don't own their high standard of living, they only rent it, which means that they are likely to lose it suddenly as so many did in the depression."

November 12, 2018
Monday
Veterans' Day (observed)

Objectives & reminders

____

____

____

Appointments

Early morning

8 a.m.

9 a.m.

10 a.m.

11 a.m.

Noon

1 p.m.

2 p.m.

3 p.m.

4 p.m.

5 p.m.

6 p.m.

Later evening

Dollars and sense

Although the *Holy Bible* warns that "...the love of money is the root of all evil..." (I Timothy, 6:10), Washington Irving's concern that the message wasn't fully embraced prompted him to coin the phrase "the Almighty Dollar." The phrase was part of a story by Irving ("The Creole Village") published in *The Knickerbocker Magazine* on November 12, 1836. The full phrase was: "The Almighty Dollar, that great object of universal devotion throughout the land."

The now-familiar phrase has prodded generations of people to reconsider the role of money in their lives.

Since Irving's first reference to the Almighty Dollar, several industrialists have warned businesses against the pursuit of money as an end in itself. For example, when steel magnate Andrew Carnegie was a young man in 1868 he reminded himself in a personal memo that, "No idol [is] more debasing than the worship of money." A few decades later automaker Henry Ford observed that "a company in business only for money is a poor kind of business."

More recently and more vividly, oil tycoon and financier Clint Murchison, Jr., used metaphor to suggest that money should be thought of as a tool to invest and to help others, but not to hoard: "Money is like manure. If you spread it around it does a lot of good. But if you pile it up in one place it stinks."

Marketing, business & money: Five invitations to discuss

1. To what extent does money motivate sales reps and other marketing employees?
2. Is it in the best interest of customers for salespeople to be paid sales commissions?
3. Is the goal of "making money" too broad to provide marketers with sufficient guidance when developing marketing plans?
4. Is "profit" a dirty word?
5. Is it wrong for a company to make "too much" money? If so, how much is "too much"?

November 13, 2018
Tuesday
World Kindness Day

Objectives & reminders

____

____

____

Appointments

Early morning

8 a.m.

9 a.m.

10 a.m.

11 a.m.

Noon

1 p.m.

2 p.m.

3 p.m.

4 p.m.

5 p.m.

6 p.m.

Later evening

Vietnam Veterans Memorial

An estimated 150,000 Vietnam veterans and their families marched to the site of the Vietnam Veterans Memorial in Washington, D.C. on November 13, 1982. There, the memorial was officially dedicated.

The memorial is a v-shaped wall made of black granite, upon which the names of 57,939 Americans are engraved -- the names of those who lost their lives in the Vietnam War during the 1960s and early 1970s.

During the two years after the dedication ceremony more than five million people visited the memorial. More than seven million American veterans from the Vietnam War are still alive today.

Green as a marketing "must": Agree or disagree?

What do marketing and public relations professionals think of the green movement? Released on November 13, 2006, the findings of an independent study commissioned by Green Portfolio (division of Portfolio Communications) helped to answer this question. The study involved interviews with marketing and PR professionals in 125 firms. Among other findings, the study revealed the following:

- 58 percent of the respondents claimed that being green provides companies with a competitive advantage, but 72 percent of the companies had no green marketing plans in place.

- 50 percent of the respondents said that an organization's green credentials are important to customers. Further, 48 percent asserted that customers are prepared to pay more for environmentally friendly products and services.

> **Green sincerity is critical**
> "The marketing and communications profession sees clear competitive advantage in being green but the survey also shows that organizations can't 'greenwash' their credentials. A surface veneer isn't enough when it comes to the environment; companies have to be doing it." – Rebecca Dunstan, environmental PR consultant at Green Portfolio, November 13, 2006

November 14, 2018
Wednesday
World Diabetes Day

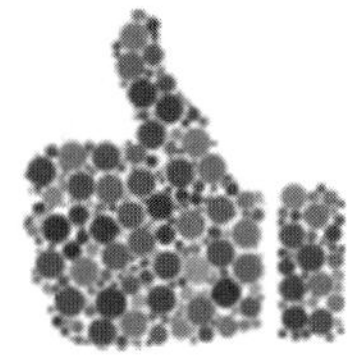

Objectives & reminders

____

____

____

Appointments

Early morning

8 a.m.

9 a.m.

10 a.m.

11 a.m.

Noon

1 p.m.

2 p.m.

3 p.m.

4 p.m.

5 p.m.

6 p.m.

Later evening

Pygmalion pricing?

"I gave a little courage to the company. We were discounting our products. We were always ten percent to fifteen percent lower than the competition, not because we were more clever [about cutting costs] but because we were more shy."

"Normally, when you lose money, you cut prices. But then you have a losing attitude. I increased the prices, without looking at the products, by 15 percent. The market reacted the way I was convinced it would: Immediately the volume increased. The Olivetti people began to believe in themselves when they stopped discounting."

> – Carlo De Benedetti, then CEO of Olivetti & Company (1978-1996), the Italian office equipment firm that was losing money at the rate of about $10 million monthly when De Benedetti took the helm of the company. De Benedetti is credited with reversing the downward trend. Not surprisingly, he was born on November 14 – in 1934, in Turin, Italy.

Relevant principles

Consider how the following principles help to explain the wisdom of De Benedetti's decision to raise prices, especially with regard to Olivetti employees and customers.

- *Pygmalion effect:* The tendency for people to behave in the way respected others expect them to behave. Expect a lot, get a lot. Expect a little, get a little.

$$P \overset{?}{=} Q$$

- *Principle of the price-quality relationship:* In the absence of expertise or relevant information upon which to evaluate product quality, price is often used as a surrogate measure of quality, i.e., the higher the price, the higher the quality. Or, as the old adage goes, "You get what you pay for."

November 15, 2018
Thursday
America Recycles Day

Objectives & reminders

____

____

____

Appointments

Early morning

8 a.m.

9 a.m.

10 a.m.

11 a.m.

Noon

1 p.m.

2 p.m.

3 p.m.

4 p.m.

5 p.m.

6 p.m.

Later evening

Living with inflation

In an effort to deal with Germany's problem of rampant inflation, the German government introduced a new piece of currency on November 15, 1923 -- worth one *trillion* of the old marks. That sounds like quite a bit of money, but the new bill was worth only about five loaves of bread. Not surprisingly, wages had spiraled out of control as well; in Berlin, construction workers earned almost three trillion marks per day.

In 1914, prior to the start of World War I, it took about 4.2 German marks to buy one U.S. dollar. By November 1923 (five years after the war), the same dollar cost 4.2 trillion marks.

____

Managing inflation

Seventy-one years after Germany's introduction of the new mark, the U.S. Federal Reserve Board grappled with America's less serious inflation problems caused by rapid economic growth. On November 15, 1994, the "Fed" attempted to slow the pace of economic growth by raising short-term interest rates by 75 basis points (i.e., three-fourths of a percentage point), from 4.75% to 5.50%. This move caused several banks to raise their lending rates as well, which made borrowing money more expensive for both businesses and consumers. Ordinarily, the Fed adjusts short-term interest rates only 25 basis points at a time -- sometimes 50 basis points, but very rarely 75.

____

Living with children by managing the environment

"Don't say 'Hands off'
Don't say 'Don't touch'
Cause no one here forbids
So put your paws on anything
We built this place for kids"

This was a poem written by Arto Monaco and placed on a sign posted at the Land of Makebelieve, a children's amusement park opened in Upper Jay, New York in 1954. As the sign implies, Monaco had a reputation for being children-oriented.

Monaco was not only a poet, but an artisan, toy-maker and amusement park visionary too -- born in Elizabethtown, New York on November 15, 1913.

November 16, 2018
Friday
International Day for Tolerance

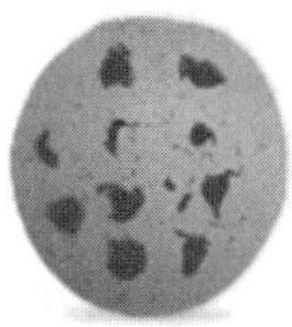

Objectives & reminders

___

___

___

Appointments

Early morning

8 a.m.

9 a.m.

10 a.m.

11 a.m.

Noon

1 p.m.

2 p.m.

3 p.m.

4 p.m.

5 p.m.

6 p.m.

Later evening

Old product, new form

The Nestlé Company launched a new product form on November 16, 1939 – chocolate chips. The innovation expanded the market for chocolate as cooks found chocolate chips convenient for baking chocolate chip cookies and other desserts. Not surprisingly, recipes calling for chocolate chips proliferated.

Old product form, new market

When business faculty from the U.S. arrived in Bratislava, Slovakia (central Europe) in 1993 to help Comenius University launch a new American-style business school, the hosts were presented with gifts they had never seen before -- bags of chocolate chips.

Slovaks were not familiar with the product form prior to receiving the chocolate chips, but the chips were so enthusiastically appreciated that the Americans brought additional bags of chocolate chips on return trips.

Chocolate chip principles

Because not every product or product form is universally available, it pays to search for "new" product ideas in other markets. Marketers may find them in other countries or regions. Further, introducing a proven product to a new geographic market is often less risky than developing and introducing a completely new item.

Marshall on innovation

"I believe that the root of most innovation comes from the supplier-customer interface, not the lab. The most innovative companies are the ones that listen and that don't feel threatened or defensive about criticism… Do not be overly reliant on internal processes and systems. There is no substitute for direct, face-to-face interaction with customers." – Sir Colin Marshall, 1998. At the time, Marshall was chairman and CEO of British Airways. He was born in London on November 16, 1933.

November 17, 2018
Saturday
World Prematurity Day

Objectives & reminders

Appointments

Early morning

8 a.m.

9 a.m.

10 a.m.

11 a.m.

Noon

1 p.m.

2 p.m.

3 p.m.

4 p.m.

5 p.m.

6 p.m.

Later evening

Happy birthday: Nancy Green

Born as a slave in Montgomery County, Kentucky on November 17, 1834, Green was probably the first African-American model used in U.S. national advertising and packaging. At the age of 56, Green's picture as "Aunt Jemima" became part of the Aunt Jemima Pancake Mix trademark.

Within three years, Green's role as Aunt Jemima had expanded to that of the brand's spokesperson. At the World's Columbian Exposition in Chicago, Aunt Jemima demonstrated the pancake mix and served thousands of sample pancakes, which helped generate a flood of more than 50,000 orders.

For the next 30 years, Green continued to play the role of Aunt Jemima as she toured the country promoting "her" pancake mix and using free samples to coax people to try the brand. Her friendly personality, coupled with her storytelling skills and reputation as a good cook made Green particularly effective as Aunt Jemima. Sales soared.

Shortly after Green's death in 1923, the company was sold to the Quaker Oats Company. Since then, other women have promoted the brand by playing the role of Aunt Jemima.

Marketing lessons from Aunt Jemima

First, Aunt Jemima Pancake Mix was one of the first convenience food products. Its success helped pave the way for hundreds of convenience foods that followed.

> Today, marketers know there's usually a market for brands that are easy to use and promise to save busy consumers' time.

Second, the makers of Aunt Jemima Pancake Mix were among the first to recognize and capitalize upon the marketing potential of free samples.

> Today, marketers know that samples can be extremely effective in raising awareness and enticing consumers to experience the brand. Samples can be particularly effective when the brand experience is difficult to convey fully in advertising communications – such as the *taste* of a food item.

November 18, 2018
Sunday

National Day of Mourning (Germany)

Objectives & reminders

____

____

____

Appointments

Early morning

8 a.m.

9 a.m.

10 a.m.

11 a.m.

Noon

1 p.m.

2 p.m.

3 p.m.

4 p.m.

5 p.m.

6 p.m.

Later evening

Common sense marketing management

"I just used common sense... in running my business. But from the first I was determined to run it in what I called a woman's way, because... after all, it was women who purchased gelatine." – Rose Markward Knox, born in Mansfield, Ohio on November 18, 1857. Rose Knox co-founded the Knox Gelatine Company in 1889 with her husband Charles. She successfully ran the company herself, and tripled its size, after Charles died in 1908.

Opportunities in failure

"May every young scientist remember... and not fail to keep his eyes open for the possibility that an irritating failure of his apparatus to give consistent results may once or twice in a lifetime conceal an important discovery." – Patrick Maynard Stuart Blackett, the "father of operational research," born in London on November 18, 1897

Avoid corporate complacency by defining competition broadly

Although The Coca-Cola Company may enjoy 42 percent of the total carbonated soft drink market (vs. Pepsi's 30%), Roberto C. Goizueta, the company's former CEO from 1981 until his death in 1997, was quick to point out that its share of the total "beverage" market was closer to three percent. According to Goizueta, "The enemy is coffee, milk, tea, water." Goizueta was born in Havana, Cuba on November 18, 1931.

Just because consumers believe something doesn't mean it's true

"Polling is merely an instrument for gauging public opinion. When a... leader pays attention to poll results, he is, in effect, paying attention to the views of the people. Any other interpretation is nonsense."
– George H. Gallup, pioneer in advertising research and public opinion polling techniques who founded the American Institute of Public Opinion in 1936 (renamed the Gallup Organization, Inc. in 1958). Gallup was born in Jefferson, Iowa on November 18, 1901.

November 19, 2018
Monday
International Men's Day

Objectives & reminders

Appointments

Early morning

8 a.m.

9 a.m.

10 a.m.

11 a.m.

Noon

1 p.m.

2 p.m.

3 p.m.

4 p.m.

5 p.m.

6 p.m.

Later evening

Happy birthday: John Francis "Jack" Welch, Jr.

Born in Peabody, Massachusetts on November 19, 1935, Welch earned a doctorate in chemical engineering from the University of Illinois in 1960. After graduating, Welch began working as an engineer at General Electric. By the late 1960s, Welch had moved into management at GE and was named CEO and chairman in 1981.

Proactive leadership
"Change before you have to."
– Jack Welch

For the next twenty years (1981-2001) under Welch's leadership, GE's financial performance was extraordinary -- so much so that some analysts dubbed Welch as one of the two most effective managers of the twentieth century, along with Alfred P. Sloan, Jr. of General Motors. When asked if he agreed with this distinction, Welch replied that he had not known Alfred Sloan.

Encouraging "boundaryless" behavior
"In large, old institutions like ours [General Electric], people tend to build layers and walls between themselves and others. These walls cramp people, inhibit creativity, waste time, restrict vision, smother dreams, and slow things down. The challenge is to break down these walls and barriers... In a boundaryless atmosphere, a good idea sprouts and blossoms and is nurtured by all. No one cares where the seed came from. Ideas are judged on the basis of their quality rather than the altitude of their origin." – Jack Welch

Naïve listening: Agree or disagree?
"When you are a leader, your job is to have all the questions. You have to be incredibly comfortable looking like the dumbest person in the room. Every conversation you have about a decision, a proposal, or a piece of market information has to be filled with you saying, 'What if?' and 'Why not?' and 'How come?'" – Jack Welch

November 20, 2018
Tuesday
African Industrialization Day

Objectives & reminders

____

____

____

Appointments

Early morning

8 a.m.

9 a.m.

10 a.m.

11 a.m.

Noon

1 p.m.

2 p.m.

3 p.m.

4 p.m.

5 p.m.

6 p.m.

Later evening

The Road Ahead

Microsoft's co-founder, and at the time, chairman and CEO, Bill Gates, had his first book published on November 20, 1995. Titled *The Road Ahead*, the book examined the likely roles technology would play in the way people live, learn and work in the future.

Education and information technology on the road ahead: Are we there yet?

"I believe that information technology will empower people of all ages, both inside and outside the classroom, to learn more easily, enjoyably, and successfully than ever before... The people who resist change will be confronted by the growing number of people who see that better ways of learning are available thanks to technology." – Bill Gates, *The Road Ahead*

The road home

A sizeable step was taken to shrink the British Empire on November 20, 1926. On that day at the Imperial Conference in London, long-standing British colonies were granted self-governing status. Canada, Australia, New Zealand, South Africa, and Newfoundland were to become independent nations and "masters of their own destiny." India would have to wait until World War II passed before gaining its independence from Britain.

The road to free enterprise

"Our enemies assert that capitalism enslaves the worker and will destroy itself. It is our national faith that the system of competitive enterprise offers the best hope for individual freedom, social development, and economic growth. Thus, every businessman who cheats on his taxes, fixes prices, or underpays his labor, every union official who makes a collusive deal, misuses union funds, damages the free enterprise system in the eyes of the world and does a disservice to the millions of honest Americans in all walks of life." – Robert F. Kennedy, former U.S. Attorney General and New York Senator (and brother of President John F. Kennedy), born in Brookline, Massachusetts on November 20, 1925

November 21, 2018
Wednesday
World Television Day

Objectives & reminders

____

____

____

Appointments

Early morning

8 a.m.

9 a.m.

10 a.m.

11 a.m.

Noon

1 p.m.

2 p.m.

3 p.m.

4 p.m.

5 p.m.

6 p.m.

Later evening

One way to stifle customer complaints

There are many reasons why dissatisfied customers may not voice their complaints to offending companies. Often customers believe that voicing their dissatisfaction is a waste of time or too much hassle. Employees or managers may not be responsive, or front-line workers may stifle customer complaints by failing to relay them to management for action.

Service businesses too frequently insincere: Agree or disagree?
"[L]ip services are the most frequent services rendered by private firms."
– Evert Gummesson, world renowned service scholar

At least one disgruntled passenger was discouraged from complaining to United Airlines on November 21, 2004, when he telephoned United Airlines' lost-baggage representative Maria Taylor to complain about the company's failure to honor a promise to deliver lost luggage.

When the customer specifically asked Ms. Taylor to pass along the complaint to management so that steps could be taken to avoid similar service mishaps in the future, Taylor refused, claiming that any customer comments she forwarded would simply be "hearsay."

Unfortunately, handling the complaint in this way not only kept management from receiving the feedback and improving service, but it left the customer with the impression that United Airlines wasn't interested in honoring its commitment or hearing customers' concerns.

Dissatisfaction multiplied
Frequently customer dissatisfaction has as much or more to do with the way a complaint is addressed than with the mishap that ignited the original dissatisfaction. In the United Airlines example, the customer's original dissatisfaction associated with the lost luggage was magnified twice – by the company's failure to deliver the lost luggage as promised and then by the service reps' refusal to forward the complaint to management.

November 22, 2018
Thursday
Thanksgiving Day

Objectives & reminders

____

____

____

Appointments

Early morning

8 a.m.

9 a.m.

10 a.m.

11 a.m.

Noon

1 p.m.

2 p.m.

3 p.m.

4 p.m.

5 p.m.

6 p.m.

Later evening

Brief history of Thanksgiving

Thanksgiving in the United States dates back to the Pilgrim period of 1621 when the governor of Massachusetts, William Bradford, orchestrated a three-day festival to celebrate and show gratitude for the season's bountiful harvest. Bradford invited local Native Americans or "Indians."

For several decades after the original Thanksgiving festival, the celebration was repeated annually, primarily as a New England custom. In 1789, President George Washington attempted to expand the meaning of Thanksgiving to include an appreciation of the U.S. Constitution. In 1863 President Abraham Lincoln proclaimed that the *last* Thursday in November should be set aside for Thanksgiving. That's when the celebration was widely adopted on a national basis.

By 1941, Thanksgiving weekend had become the unofficial start of the Christmas shopping season, so President Franklin D. Roosevelt made a slight adjustment in the scheduling of the holiday to allow retailers a little more time to move merchandise. That's when the *fourth* Thursday in November was designated as Thanksgiving.

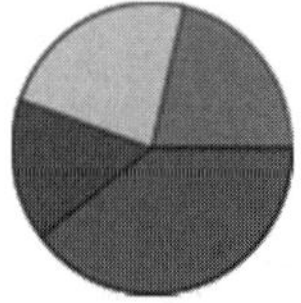

Thanksgiving for businesses

Depending on the context, between 14 and 34 percent of store shoppers are not thanked for their purchases. For many consumers, especially older ones, the failure of a sales rep, cashier or other employee to say "thank you" makes quite a negative impression.

One study found that an insurance company's customers were more likely to renew their policies if they first received a letter thanking them for being a customer. Another study found that a jewelry store's customers were more likely to make *additional* purchases within the next twelve months if they received a "thank you" phone call on the day following a purchase.

Especially given the shopping season that follows, Thanksgiving may be the best single day of the year for businesses to make a special effort to thank their customers, employees and other constituencies.

November 23, 2018
Friday
Black Friday

Objectives & reminders

______

______

______

Appointments

Early morning

8 a.m.

9 a.m.

10 a.m.

11 a.m.

Noon

1 p.m.

2 p.m.

3 p.m.

4 p.m.

5 p.m.

6 p.m.

Later evening

Black Friday: The day after Thanksgiving

Also known as "Black Friday," the day after Thanksgiving – today – is a holiday in 24 of 50 U.S. states. Workers who don't have to report to their jobs today may seize the opportunity to shop for Christmas gifts.

Exercising retail caution

Although the day after Thanksgiving is often thought of as the unofficial start of the holiday shopping season, retailers who wait until today to launch their holiday merchandising programs are likely to miss *many* sales opportunities.

Accordingly, the day after Thanksgiving is always a big day for U.S. retailers – rivaled in recent years only by the Saturday before Christmas. About one of every four U.S. consumers shops for holiday gifts on Black Friday. Further reinforcing the wisdom of reaching and serving high-volume purchasers, five percent of Black Friday shoppers in 2016 accounted for 35 percent of the day's revenues.

Characteristics of consumers who begin shopping *later* in the season

Although about half of U.S. shoppers already have begun holiday shopping for the season, few have finished. Yet as Christmas approaches, retailers are mindful of the distinctions between early vs. late holiday shoppers. Those more likely to procrastinate tend to be:

1. Male. Men are more likely than women to wait until the last few days before Christmas to begin or finish their holiday shopping.

2. Price-conscious. In contrast, a good selection of merchandise is relatively more important to those who shop early. Still, intense competition tends to lead to heavy discounting on Black Friday.

3. Less likely to splurge on gifts for themselves. But there are plenty of exceptions.

November 24, 2018
Saturday
Small Business Saturday

Objectives & reminders

______

______

______

Appointments

Early morning

8 a.m.

9 a.m.

10 a.m.

11 a.m.

Noon

1 p.m.

2 p.m.

3 p.m.

4 p.m.

5 p.m.

6 p.m.

Later evening

Small Business Saturday

Launched and first promoted by American Express in 2010 to encourage American holiday shoppers to patronize small and local businesses on the Saturday following Thanksgiving, Small Business Saturday has grown steadily in terms of public awareness, publicity and shoppers' spending behavior.

Winning customers

"No one likes to feel that he or she is being sold something... We much prefer to feel that we are buying of our own accord or acting on our own ideas. We like to be consulted about our wishes, our wants, our thoughts." – Dale Carnegie, interpersonal relations guru and author of the best-selling book first published in 1936, *How to Win Friends and Influence People*, born in Maryville, Missouri on November 24, 1888

Happy birthday: Tom C. Fouts

Born in Carroll County, Indiana on November 24, 1918, Fouts was the lead singer for the musical group Captain Stubby and the Buccaneers. In 1954 the group recorded their biggest hit – a radio jingle for Roto-Rooter, the plumbing firm. Since then, the jingle has been used, and continues to be used, in countless advertisements for Roto-Rooter and its network of 500+ franchises – making it one of history's longest-running musical jingles.

♪♫ Plumb(er) hit ♫ ♪
"Roto-Rooter, that's the name,
and away go troubles down the drain."
Listen… https://youtu.be/9avf_U8h3_M

Anatomy of a successful jingle

1. Catchy tune – invites consumers to sing along.
2. Includes company name. Top-of-mind awareness makes it easy for consumers to remember the name to Google or look up in a telephone directory when the service is needed.
3. Alludes to company's problem-solving capability – i.e., the jingle gives prospective customers an idea of what the company does.
4. Evokes effective visual imagery of problems flushed away.

November 25, 2018
Sunday
Teachers' Day (Indonesia)

Objectives & reminders

___

___

___

Appointments

Early morning

8 a.m.

9 a.m.

10 a.m.

11 a.m.

Noon

1 p.m.

2 p.m.

3 p.m.

4 p.m.

5 p.m.

6 p.m.

Later evening

Promotion firsts on November 25

1876

First advertisement for a premium gift scheme: "H. Smith begs respectfully to inform his customers that he continues to give discount Tea Tickets to every purchaser of a ¼-lb of Tea and upwards, quality very superior. A large number of useful and Ornamental Articles kept in stock, which are given in exchange for Tea Tickets."

1905

The first advertisement in the U.S. for a radio system (actually a telegraph used for sending and receiving only dots and dashes) appeared in *Scientific American*: "WIRELESS TELEGRAPH The 'Telimco' Complete Outfit, comprising 1 inch Spark Coil, Strap Key, Sender, Sensitive Relay, Coherer, with Automatic Decoherer and Sounder, 4 Ex. Strong Dry Cells, all necessary wiring, including send and catch wires, with full instructions and diagrams, $8.50. Guaranteed to work up to one mile. Send for Illust. Pamphlet & 64-page catalogue. ELECTRO IMPORTING CO., 32 Park Place, New York"

1966

Ronald McDonald, McDonald's spokes-clown, first appeared in Macy's department store's Thanksgiving Day Parade, in New York City. Ronald has appeared in the parade in almost every year since then. By the early 1990s, marketing research indicated that 96 percent of surveyed consumers were aware of Ronald McDonald – a slightly lower percentage than that garnered by Santa Claus. Further attesting to McDonald's market presence and the power of advertising, another study revealed that 70 percent of surveyed Canadian school children believed that John Macdonald founded a chain of hamburger restaurants – presumably McDonald's. In fact, John Macdonald served as the first prime minister of Canada (1867-1873, 1878-1891).

November 26, 2018
Monday
Cyber Monday

Objectives & reminders

____

____

Appointments

____
Early morning
____
8 a.m.
____
9 a.m.
____
10 a.m.
____
11 a.m.
____
Noon
____
1 p.m.
____
2 p.m.
____
3 p.m.
____
4 p.m.
____
5 p.m.
____
6 p.m.
____
Later evening
____

Cyber Monday

The rise of online shopping over the last couple of decades has prompted many consumers to shop online upon returning to work on the Monday after Thanksgiving. Known as Cyber Monday, today is a particularly popular online shopping day for millenials. Beyond Cyber Monday, per se, all Mondays between Thanksgiving and Christmas tend to be high sales volume days for online retailers.

Happy birthday: Walter L. Anderson

Anderson was born in St. Mary's, Kansas on November 26, 1880. In 1916 he converted a street car into a retail hamburger stand, in Wichita, Kansas. A few years and three burger business concepts later, Anderson partnered with Edgar Waldo "Billy" Ingram to form White Castle restaurants – the first hamburger fast-food chain in the United States.

The first White Castle opened in 1921 and was positioned as a clean and economical dining establishment for the entire family. Anderson remained active in the company through the 1920s and into the 1930s.

> **Marketing salute to Mom**
> Among other innovations in the early days of White Castle, the fast-food chain recruited families and stressed convenience with a promotional appeal that was difficult to deny:
>
> **"Give Mother a Night Off."**

Discontent is the mother of business ideas: Agree or disagree?

"Most business ideas come from being dissatisfied with a product or service and thinking, 'I can do this better and I can do this differently, and ideally I can change the marketplace I am going into forever.' Another way of putting it is that you feel passionately about something on the one hand, and really hate something on the other." – Lord Karan Bilimoria, founder and chairman of Cobra Beer, born in Hyderabad, Telangana, India on November 26, 1961

November 27, 2018
Tuesday
Teachers' Day (Spain)

Objectives & reminders

Appointments

Early morning

8 a.m.

9 a.m.

10 a.m.

11 a.m.

Noon

1 p.m.

2 p.m.

3 p.m.

4 p.m.

5 p.m.

6 p.m.

Later evening

Motivation insights

As pioneers in the study of human motivation, David C. McClelland and his colleagues had their seminal book published on November 27, 1953: *The Achievement Motive.* The book, along with other publications by McClelland's research teams, suggests that people are motivated by a mix of needs for achievement, power, and social affiliation. For most of us, one of the three categories tends to be more motivational than the other two.

Achievement-oriented people like to get things done. They tend to be action-oriented, take pride in their accomplishments and value tangible results. Many times they are goal-oriented and are likely to respond positively to challenges and record-breaking attempts. Accordingly, they are frequently "score-keepers"; one might expect achievement-oriented sales reps to know how many units they've sold and how many more units they need to sell to break the company record.

Power-oriented people like to exert influence. They value a sense of control, want to participate in decisions (especially those likely to affect them) and like to be "in the know." Managers often keep power-oriented people motivated by granting them latitude or "empowering" them to pursue their jobs as they see fit, keeping them abreast of company plans and upcoming initiatives, soliciting their opinions and recommendations, or by putting them "in charge" of something.

People with a high need for *social affiliation* may be described as "people persons." They enjoy being around others, enjoy chit-chat, and are likely to prefer face-to-face contact over email exchanges. Building a consensus is important to them and maintaining the harmony in a group can take precedent over other decision-making criteria, i.e., to avoid conflict they may not disagree with colleagues even when they think they are wrong. Not surprisingly, people with strong social affiliation needs are likely to be very effective in customer-contact positions such as sales or customer service.

Ask !

Not sure what motivates members of the marketing team? McClelland recommends simply asking them. They may not know, but often they do.

November 28, 2018
Wednesday
Independence Day (Panama)

Objectives & reminders

____

____

____

Appointments

Early morning

8 a.m.

9 a.m.

10 a.m.

11 a.m.

Noon

1 p.m.

2 p.m.

3 p.m.

4 p.m.

5 p.m.

6 p.m.

Later evening

Happy birthday: Berry Gordy, Jr.

Born in Detroit, Michigan on November 28, 1929, Gordy's extensive business career was inseparably intertwined with music as early as 1953 when he opened a record store. As a hobby, he also wrote songs that began to sell in 1957. Soon, he began producing singles for recording artists which led to his founding of Motown Records in 1959.

By 1963 Motown recordings were frequently hits, featuring groups like the Supremes, Temptations, Marvelettes, Four Tops, Martha and the Vandellas, and others. The success continued throughout the 1960s and well into the 1970s. In 1970 alone, 14 Motown singles topped the pop charts. Since then, Motown Industries has diversified into other forms of entertainment including motion pictures, television and publishing.

Creating a vision

Business visionaries often see and understand what others fail to see or cannot understand. Berry Gordy clearly saw the music business as something more than simply cutting and distributing records. For example, he once explained the Motown sound: "[It] is not just climbing up out of poverty, escaping from it -- it's being young, creating, doing things with dignity. It's pride."

Employees (not customers) are #1: Agree or disagree?

"You can't take care of your customers unless you take care of your people. Everyone has good machines. Our co-workers are the only tie-breakers for us."
– Paul Orfalea, founder of Kinko's (1970), born in Los Angeles on November 28, 1947

What are you thinking?

"All that a man achieves and all that he fails to achieve is the direct result of his own thoughts.... As he thinks, so he is; as he continues to think, so he remains."
– James Allen, British philosopher and author of *As a Man Thinketh* (1902), from which this quotation was taken. Allen was born in Leicester, England on November 28, 1864.

November 29, 2018
Thursday
Electronic Greetings Day

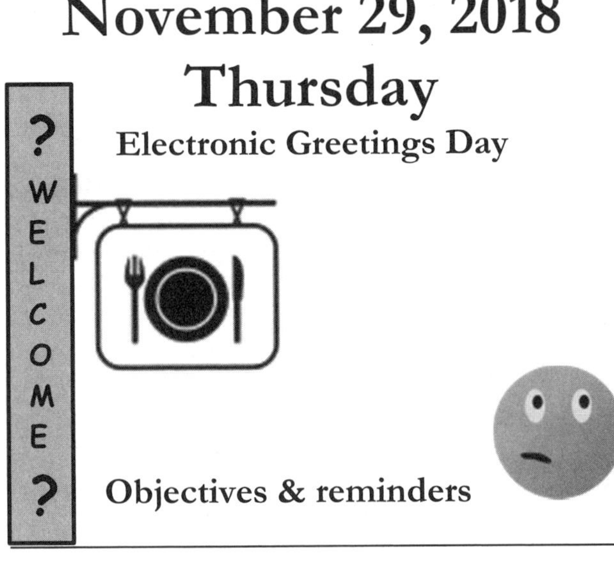

Objectives & reminders

Appointments

Early morning

8 a.m.

9 a.m.

10 a.m.

11 a.m.

Noon

1 p.m.

2 p.m.

3 p.m.

4 p.m.

5 p.m.

6 p.m.

Later evening

Happy birthday: Jayceon T. Taylor

Also known by his rapper name – The Game – Taylor was born in Los Angeles on November 29, 1979. Since 2001, he's recorded multiple albums and received several accolades, including two Grammy Award nominations and *The New York Times*' recognition for the best hip hop album of 2006.

Game expresses himself through his music, but also with the multiple tattoos covering much of his body -- including his face, neck, head, arms and chest. Although 14-20 percent of the U.S. population owns at least one tattoo, few people have as many as Game.

Sporting a tank-top shirt in 2013, Game entered Pasadena, California's upscale "Houston's" restaurant with the expectation of a first-class meal. Instead, he allegedly was denied service by the restaurant's manager who objected to the collection of tattoos that were reportedly viewed as a threat to other customers. Expressing his outrage, Game appealed to his Twitter followers to boycott the restaurant.

Since Game was ejected from Houston's, the media has reported cases of restaurant personnel elsewhere who have insisted that tattooed guests cover their tattoos or, in the case of tattoos on the face or neck, leave the premises. Some managers have pointed to dress code policies in defense of their anti-tattoo practices, while others have noted the disturbing nature of visible tattoos that may be gang-related.

Although the legal waters are a bit muddy, U.S. laws generally do not protect tattoo wearers, per se, from discriminatory practices in the same way that they are intolerant of differential treatment based on gender, marital status, race and ethnicity. Still, tattooed customers – like The Game – who feel unfairly treated, may stir negative publicity by calling for boycotts, complaining to the mass media or spreading negative word-of-mouth through social media.

Your turn to address the issue

If you were in charge of marketing and customer service for a local restaurant near campus and the manager asked you to formulate a policy or guidelines for the treatment of tattooed customers, **what would you recommend?** For helpful information and insights, see the 2016 article by Chris Baumann and his colleagues, "Taboo tattoos?..." published in the *Journal of Retailing and Consumer Services*, volume 29, pp. 31-39.

November 30, 2018
Friday
Computer Security Day

Objectives & reminders

____

____

____

Appointments

Early morning

8 a.m.

9 a.m.

10 a.m.

11 a.m.

Noon

1 p.m.

2 p.m.

3 p.m.

4 p.m.

5 p.m.

6 p.m.

Later evening

Another 5th Friday marketing opportunity

Today is one of only four Fridays in 2018 that's also the 5th Friday of the month. As discussed on March 30, 5th Fridays often correspond to financial windfalls for workers who are paid on Fridays. And, extra money in consumers' pockets often corresponds to an increased willingness to spend. Plan accordingly.

Sticker shock

On November 30, 1927, automobile buyers were hit with "sticker shock," i.e., the unpleasant surprise of realizing the price is much higher than expected. The price of a new Ford jumped from $385 to $570 -- a 48 percent increase.

Today, marketers of consumer durables and other big-ticket items try to save buyers from experiencing sticker shock, because sticker shock discourages buyers and becomes a purchase obstacle. One way they do this is by raising prices in smaller increments (although perhaps more frequently), realizing that smaller price hikes are usually more palatable and may go unnoticed.

Another approach is to mention price frequently in advertising and sales materials. When buyers don't purchase the items frequently, the publicized pricing information helps them to re-gauge their expectations so they won't be shocked by the price when ready to buy.

A third approach is to stress the product's improved performance characteristics or less-than-obvious features that promise additional benefits. Buyers are less likely to resist price increases when they perceive an increase in value.

Nonparametric pricing principle

$P ☞ ☺☺☺ =?= $P < V

where:

$P = price (what customers pay)
☞ = leads to
☺☺☺ = satisfied customers
=?= = if
$P = price (what customers pay)
< = is less than
V = value (worth customers perceive)

December 1, 2018
Saturday
World AIDS Day

Objectives & reminders

____

____

____

Appointments

Early morning

8 a.m.

9 a.m.

10 a.m. – *Dr. Pepper time*

11 a.m.

Noon

1 p.m.

2 p.m. – *Dr. Pepper time*

3 p.m.

4 p.m. – *Dr. Pepper time*

5 p.m.

6 p.m.

Later evening

Marketing to influencers

Charles C. Alderton was a young pharmacist working at the Old Corner Drug Store in Waco, Texas in 1885. In addition to pharmacy it seems that one of Alderton's interests was the daughter of a local physician. As a ploy to win the support of the young lady's father, Charles Pepper, Alderton concocted a uniquely flavored beverage which he named after Dr. Pepper. The first of billions of glasses of Dr. Pepper was served on December 1, 1885.

Happy hours

The Dr. Pepper Company launched the "10, 2, and 4" advertising campaign in 1927 that would run for 50-plus years. According to the campaign's prescription, people could revive their energy throughout the workday by drinking Dr. Peppers at 10:00 a.m., 2:00 p.m., and 4:00 p.m.

A sitting ovation!

December 1, 1913, was a landmark day in the history of convenience. That's when the first customer-centric drive-in automobile service station – Good Gulf Gasoline – began pumping gasoline in Pittsburgh, Pennsylvania. The station featured a covered area to shield vehicles and customers from the rain, as well as free air, water, and restrooms. Further, it stayed open 24 hours a day, which was a rare business practice in those days.

The owners of Good Gulf Gasoline -- Gulf Refining Company -- had the foresight to locate the station on the corner of a high-traffic intersection. Seventy years later the wisdom of the decision was reinforced when a study found that sales for gasoline retailers located at intersections were 40 percent higher, on average, than those not located at intersections.

When customers say "no"

"Look at misfortune the same way you look at success: Don't panic. Do your best and forget the consequences." – Walter Alston, American baseball player and manager, born in Venice, Ohio on December 1, 1911

December 2, 2018
Sunday
Hanukkah begins

Objectives & reminders

____

____

____

Appointments

Early morning

8 a.m.

9 a.m.

10 a.m.

11 a.m.

Noon

1 p.m.

2 p.m.

3 p.m.

4 p.m.

5 p.m.

6 p.m.

Later evening

Happy Hanukkah

Beginning at sundown today, Hanukkah is celebrated as one of the most joyous periods on the Jewish calendar. Celebrations often include the exchange of gifts or the donation of gifts to charity. The eight-day festival is scheduled according to the Jewish calendar, so the dates vary from year to year on the Gregorian calendar. Still Hanukkah typically occurs near the time of the Northern Hemisphere's winter solstice.

Hanukkah is also known as the Feast of Lights to signify the relighting of the perpetual lamp in the Temple. Accordingly, the lighting of the eight-branched candlestick -- the Hanukkah Menorah -- remains a custom in synagogues and Jewish homes.

Hanukkah, also known as...
- Festival of Hanukkah
- Feast of Dedication
- Feast of Lights
- Holiday of Lights

Giving, refocused

Retailers are well aware of the popularity of gift-giving across many religions and cultures at this time of year, yet some (many?) consumers share a concern that perhaps the holiday season has become over-commercialized. Those concerned urge us not to lose sight of the true meaning of gift-giving during the holiday season. Such a concern is certainly not a recent phenomenon, as the following excerpt from the December 1892 issue of *The Ladies World* demonstrates.

> "If you have money to spend on presents, do not waste it on people richer than yourself, but on those poorer. Above all, in sending presents do not send articles that cost money and are vulgar and tawdry. A piece of music, a note written on Christmas Day, wishing many happy returns, or a few flowers, entail no obligation, require no work, and do their own work of love as well as costly gifts…"

Invitation to debate

To what extent can the commercial aspects of the holiday season coexist with the original religious meanings attributed to this period?

December 3, 2018
Monday

World Day for Persons with Disabilities
Illinois Statehood Day

Objectives & reminders

____

____

____

Appointments

Early morning

8 a.m.

9 a.m.

10 a.m.

11 a.m.

Noon

1 p.m.

2 p.m.

3 p.m.

4 p.m.

5 p.m.

6 p.m.

Later evening

Illinois' 200th birthday

Two hundred years ago today, Illinois became the 21st state. With a population of only 34,620 on December 3, 1818, the state has grown to more than 12.8 million people today – making it the fifth most populous state in the country (behind California, New York, Texas and Florida). Almost three of every four Illinois consumers live in "Chicagoland" – the third largest metropolitan area in the U.S.

Here are a few additional Illinois facts. Consider the possible marketing implications of each one.

1. The state flower is the purple violet; the state tree is the white oak and the state bird is the northern cardinal.
2. Only three states (California, Texas and Ohio) manufacture more goods than Illinois.
3. Chemicals, machinery and food are the top-three manufacturing categories for Illinois.
4. Hispanics are the fastest growing minority segment in the state. Fifteen percent of the state's population speaks Spanish.

The IBM prerequisite?

With an original capitalization of $100,000, Herman Hollerith organized the Tabulating Machine Company (TMC) on December 3, 1886. Twenty-five years later, Hollerith sold the company to the newly formed Computing-Tabulating-Recording Company (CTR) for about $1,000,000. In addition to TMC, CTR purchased a few other small companies.

Three years later, in 1914, Thomas J. Watson, Sr. joined CTR as general manager. His vision for the company extended beyond the "tabulating" technology of the day, and it also extended beyond the U.S. So, in 1924, CTR's name was changed to the now familiar "International Business Machines Corporation," IBM. Under Watson's leadership, IBM experienced more than a 100-fold increase in sales.

Did you know?

IBM's nickname, "Big Blue," has nothing to do with the color of the company's products. Rather, the nickname stems from the dark blue suits the IBM sales force once wore. Traditionally, IBM's sales force was regarded among the best trained and most competent sales forces in the world.

December 4, 2018
Tuesday
National Cookie Day

Objectives & reminders

Appointments

Early morning

---

8 a.m.

---

9 a.m.

---

10 a.m.

---

11 a.m.

Noon

---

1 p.m.

---

2 p.m.

---

3 p.m.

---

4 p.m.

---

5 p.m.

---

6 p.m.

Later evening

A shoe-in for marketing opportunity

On December 4, 1922, the U.S. Department of Commerce announced that American women wear 1.6 million different styles of shoes. While this statistic might have shocked the marketplace in 1922, today it is common for consumers in industrialized countries to find an infinite number of purchase alternatives in many product categories.

Although such a staggering number of choices may seem to represent an overwhelming amount of competition, optimistic marketers can look to several related principles that reinforce the marketplace reality that opportunity accompanies choice. Here are three such principles:

P1 As long as buyers' needs, tastes and requirements vary, the array of products available in a category will vary as well. If buyers agreed as to what constitutes the "ideal" product solution, only one brand would be necessary.

P2 Because buyers' needs, perceptions, and attitudes change over time, the mix of available products also evolves over time. Where there is change, business opportunities abound.

P3 There are no limits to creativity. There is always one more way to do something -- another design, another size, another color, another feature or ingredient to add (or delete), another message to communicate, another point of distribution, and so on.

Leadership insight

"No pressure, no diamonds." – Thomas Carlyle, Scottish philosopher, historian and writer, born in Ecclefechan, Scotland on December 4, 1795

No pressure, no aluminum

"[W]e need to be careful that we don't become self-satisfied. We can't become complacent. We need to keep pressing ourselves to improve to reach levels that other people can't imagine." – Paul O'Neill, then chairman and CEO of Alcoa, Inc. (world's largest producer of aluminum), born in St. Louis, Missouri on December 4, 1935

December 5, 2018
Wednesday
International Volunteer Day

Objectives & reminders

___

___

___

Appointments

Early morning
8 a.m.
9 a.m.
10 a.m.
11 a.m.
Noon
1 p.m.
2 p.m.
3 p.m.
4 p.m.
5 p.m.
6 p.m.
Later evening

Arkansas socks-it-to-em

Students at the University of Central Arkansas (Conway) broke a Guinness World Record in early December 2005 for the largest Christmas stocking. According to Guinness, the stocking was almost 54 feet long and more than 26 feet wide. The stocking was filled with toys for children.

As students at UCA learned, one great way to generate publicity is to challenge a world record. If the effort is tied to a seasonal interest (e.g., Christmas) and promises to benefit a worthwhile charitable cause (e.g., toys for children), an even greater potential for publicity exists. Indeed, *USA Today* publicized the record with an article on December 5, 2005.

Followed by the past

Philip Musica lost his job on December 5, 1938. He had been the CEO of a pharmaceuticals company, but also had a criminal past and had served time in prison. It seems that Musica's picture was printed in a newspaper and a company employee recognized Musica as an ex-convict. Apparently, when the company's board learned of Musica's past, they decided that being a criminal was not the ideal experience for a CEO. So, Musica was fired.

Bouncing back or falling flat?
Although it is possible to overcome one's past and start anew, often people are followed by -- haunted by -- their past. Our daily decisions shape our future and the future of those who depend on us. While it may take years to build a strong reputation, it takes only a moment to destroy one.

More than a Mickey Mouse organization

"I saw very early in this business one thing – that organization was where you had to put the emphasis. You have to break things down, specialize." – Walt Disney, founder of the Disney business empire, born in Chicago, Illinois on December 5, 1901

December 6, 2018
Thursday
St. Nicholas Day
Independence Day (Finland)

Objectives & reminders

Appointments

Early morning

8 a.m.

9 a.m.

10 a.m.

11 a.m.

Noon

1 p.m.

2 p.m.

3 p.m.

4 p.m.

5 p.m.

6 p.m.

Later evening

It's a doozy!

Automobile designer and manufacturer Fred Duesenberg was born in Lippe, Germany on December 6, 1876.

In 1885 Duesenberg and his family moved to the United States where they soon began building racing bicycles. That business evolved into the production of motorcycles and high-performance engines, which then led Fred and his brother, Augie, to launch the Duesenberg Automobile & Motors Company in St. Paul, Minnesota in 1913. Seven years later, the Duesenbergs moved the company to Indianapolis, Indiana where they introduced the Model A.

Like other automakers of the day, the Duesenbergs promoted their automobiles by competing in races. In the early 1920s their race cars won the Indianapolis 500 three times as well as the Grand Prix in Le Mans, France.

Despite the brothers' impressive racing record and reputation as world-class automobile engineers, their passenger cars failed to sell well and the company struggled to stay in business. However, the company's fate began to change late in 1926 when the brand was repositioned by the Cord Corporation who had acquired the automaker earlier that year. The repositioning involved a new and highly differentiated model, not-so-creatively dubbed the "Model J," which was bigger and more luxurious than existing models in the Cord line. E.L. Cord himself described the Model J as, "the finest thing on four wheels."

The luxurious Model Js were promoted as upscale and prestigious vehicles. Prices of up to $25,000 reinforced the upscale dimension, while print ads reinforced the prestige of owning a Model J by associating the automobile with successful or successful-looking men – accompanied by headlines that read simply, "He drives a Duesenberg." It wasn't long before the reputation of the Model J infiltrated pop culture; anything that was luxurious, prestigious, big, high-performance, or otherwise clearly differentiated in a positive way was regarded as a "doozy."

Unfortunately, the Great Depression of the 1930s was not a kind period for the Model J or most other luxury brands in the United States. The last Duesenberg was made in 1937 when the Cord Corporation folded.

December 7, 2018
Friday
Pearl Harbor Remembrance Day

Objectives & reminders

____

____

____

Appointments

Early morning

8 a.m.

9 a.m.

10 a.m.

11 a.m.

Noon

1 p.m.

2 p.m.

3 p.m.

4 p.m.

5 p.m.

6 p.m.

Later evening

Remembering Pearl Harbor

December 7, 1941, was a day of infamy that propelled the U.S. into World War II. On that day 2,403 Americans were killed and 1,178 wounded by the Japanese attack on the U.S. naval base in Pearl Harbor, Hawaii. Nineteen ships and 150 to 200 planes were destroyed. Today, December 7 is set aside as Pearl Harbor Remembrance Day to commemorate the event and pay tribute to those who died and survived on that day in 1941.

The ripple effect

Events around the world often trigger unanticipated effects on businesses. For example, when the Japanese bombed Pearl Harbor on December 7, 1941, movie theaters across the United States reported a 50 percent drop in attendance that day.

Perhaps more predictable was the effect on the stock market. The day after the attack many traders dumped their investments causing the Dow Jones Industrial Average to drop almost four percent.

Today, the business world is even more closely interconnected than it was in 1941, so staying abreast of world affairs is a good investment of one's time.

Happy birthday: Victor Kermit Kiam, II

Born in New Orleans, Louisiana on December 7, 1926, Victor Kiam's positive personal experience with Remington electric razors prompted him to buy controlling interest in their manufacturer, Remington Products Company. Perceiving an open window of marketing opportunity, Kiam promoted his ownership of the company when he starred in his own testimonial ads in which he proclaimed, "I liked them so much, I bought the company!" Later, Kiam loved football so much that he bought the New England Patriots.

> **Quality counts**
> "You can hype a questionable product for a little while, but you'll never build an enduring business." – Victor Kiam, II

December 8, 2018
Saturday
Feast of the Immaculate Conception

Objectives & reminders

____

____

____

Appointments

Early morning

8 a.m.

9 a.m.

10 a.m.

11 a.m.

Noon

1 p.m.

2 p.m.

3 p.m.

4 p.m.

5 p.m.

6 p.m.

Later evening

Get Well Soon, Happy Birthday, & Merry Christmas!

The first greeting card was printed on December 8, 1843 – a Christmas card by Henry Cole. Today, greeting cards are used not only by consumers to maintain their relationships with other consumers, but by marketers as well. Often marketers want to keep in touch with customers, express their interest and concern for customers, and otherwise stay "top-of-mind," but don't want every customer contact to be characterized by an overt sales pitch. Greeting cards serve that purpose well.

> **The Flip side of greeting cards ☺**
> American comedian Flip Wilson was born on the 90th anniversary of greeting cards, December 8, 1933. Accordingly, he noted: "Get well cards have become so humorous that if you don't get sick you're missing half the fun."

____

Christmas erupts?

Upscale retailer Neiman-Marcus has featured at least one unusual or outrageous gift in its annual Christmas catalogue -- not with the expectation of selling the off-beat items, but in order to generate publicity and stimulate word-of-mouth for their stores and catalogue. On December 8, 1976, for example, the company offered "his" and "hers" volcanic craters. Presumably imported from Greece, the craters were priced at $5,000 per set.

____

Happy birthday: William C. Durant

Born in Boston, Massachusetts on December 8, 1861, Durant was a high school dropout. After gaining some business experience in his grandfather's lumberyard he organized a horse-drawn carriage manufacturing company in 1885. Although his carriage company prospered, it became apparent to Durant that advances in transportation technology would eventually threaten the supremacy of horse-drawn carriages. So, in 1904 he seized the opportunity to invest in the Buick Motor Company. The company quickly expanded by acquiring Cadillac, Oldsmobile, and about 20 other companies. By 1911, Durant had gained control of the company that we now know as General Motors.

December 9, 2018
Sunday
International Anti-Corruption Day

Objectives & reminders

____

____

____

Appointments

Early morning

8 a.m.

9 a.m.

10 a.m.

11 a.m.

Noon

1 p.m.

2 p.m.

3 p.m.

4 p.m.

5 p.m.

6 p.m.

Later evening

Happy birthday: Joel Chandler Harris

Born in Eatonton, Georgia on December 9, 1848, Harris was both a journalist for the *Atlanta Constitution* newspaper and a fiction writer. Harris' fables of Uncle Remus, Brer Rabbit, Tar Baby and other fictional characters have entertained and instructed generations of children.

In one story of Brer Rabbit, budding businesspeople learn an important lesson about decision-making. That is, *people don't want to be told or sold. They want to reach their own conclusions and make their own decisions.*

Apparently Brer Rabbit understood this principle. After being caught by Mr. Fox, Rabbit pretended to pressure Fox to do anything *except* throw him into the briar patch. Because Fox resented a decision being imposed on him, he acted in the opposite manner -- by tossing Rabbit into the briar patch. Of course, that's what Rabbit really wanted, so he was able to escape. Rabbit outfoxed Fox.

Climbing out of the rut

"Humans are allergic to change. They love to say, 'We've always done it this way.' I try to fight that. That's why I have a clock on my wall that runs counter-clockwise." – Grace Murray Hopper, computer scientist and Rear Admiral in the U.S. Navy, born in New York City on December 9, 1906

Happy birthday: Lorraine C. Petersen

Born in Fresno, California on December 9, 1892, Petersen's name is not widely recognized, but her likeness is. In the early 1900s, she posed as the model for the Sun-Maid Raisin logo.

Thawed curiosity freezes vegetables

"Go around asking a lot of damn fool questions and taking chances. Only through curiosity can we discover opportunities, and only by gambling can we take advantage of them." – Clarence Birdseye, whose questions, curiosity and willingness to roll his marbles led him to discover the process for freezing vegetables and then launch the frozen-food company that bears his name. Birdseye was born in Brooklyn, New York on December 9, 1886.

December 10, 2018
Monday

Green Monday

(2nd biggest day of the year for online holiday shopping)

Human Rights Day

Objectives & reminders

Appointments

Early morning
8 a.m.
9 a.m.
10 a.m.
11 a.m.
Noon
1 p.m.
2 p.m.
3 p.m.
4 p.m.
5 p.m.
6 p.m.
Later evening

From Model T to Model I

The Ford Motor Company reached a milestone on December 10, 1915, when the 1,000,000th Model T rolled off the assembly line. Ford's assembly line innovations and other production efficiencies helped lower costs and thus prices so owning an automobile became a realistic aspiration for most middle-income families in the United States.

Fast forward to December 10, 1970, when Ford announced another innovative milestone -- the hiring of Lee Iacocca as president (later Iacocca also ran other companies, such as Ford's competitor, Chrysler Corporation). Iacocca prided himself on his straightforward, no-nonsense management style. For example, rather than getting bogged down in detailed planning exercises, he simply kept a single page with ten priorities listed on it -- his "hot list" of issues that he addressed personally. According to Iacocca, "I've never seen a long-range business plan that couldn't be boiled down to a single page of priorities."

Iacocca on management style

"When all is said and done, management is a code of values and judgments. And that's why, in the end, you have to be yourself... Pick a style that you're comfortable with and stick with it. You can have role models, but don't try to be somebody else. Be yourself, stay natural and... smile once in a while!" -- Lee Iacocca

---

Happy birthday: Carl Groos

Born in Heidelberg, Germany on December 10, 1861, Groos was a psychologist interested in children's cognitive development. He was one of the first professionals to recognize the important role of play in children's development and preparation for adulthood.

Today, toy-makers often stress the educational and skill-building value of their products -- often not even referring to them as "toys." By doing so, parents, grandparents and other buyers are less likely to think of toys as discretionary items, but as *essential* tools for children's development.

Child's play is serious business.

December 11, 2018
Tuesday
International Mountain Day

Objectives & reminders

Appointments

Early morning

8 a.m.

9 a.m.

10 a.m.

11 a.m.

Noon

1 p.m.

2 p.m.

3 p.m.

4 p.m.

5 p.m.

6 p.m.

Later evening

Macy's advertising glossary ☺

Early in December 1944, advertising copywriters from Manhattan's R.H. Macy & Co. department store shared a little Christmas advertising humor with readers of *The New York Times.* Poking fun at their profession and both genders, they advertised *The Man's Glossary of Unfamiliar Words & Phrases -- As Used by Advertising Writers to Describe Female Apparel and Appurtenances.* Here are a few examples for budding copywriters who are vocabulary-challenged:

- *Gossamer*: "the nearest thing to nothing -- and better in black."
- *Mink*: "when a woman turns around to look at another woman -- that's mink!"
- *Sable*: "when a woman in mink turns around to look at another woman."
- *Lush*: "anything softer than stone."
- *Glamorous*: "anything plus a sequin."
- *Fabulous*: "we haven't seen anything like it for an hour."

Copywriting principle

The less precise a word, the greater the number of images likely to be evoked by its use. Although people tend to assign their own meanings to words, some words are much more ambiguous than others. Choosing between a precise word and an ambiguous substitute depends on the role the copywriter wants the audience's imagination to play.

Thank you Jell-O!

On December 11, 1953, the makers of Jell-O brand gelatin launched a new product -- chocolate pudding. The brand extension was an ideal fit for Jell-O. The dessert category was comparable to the company's existing gelatin category; pudding could be sold in the same distribution outlets, utilized comparable production technology, could be priced and promoted similarly to gelatin, and its adoption didn't require consumers to radically alter their purchase or usage behavior. Yet, pudding was different enough from gelatin to appeal to consumers' need for variety. For the undecided, some of today's 700-plus Jell-O recipes call for both gelatin *and* pudding.

December 12, 2018
Wednesday
Our Lady of Guadalupe Day (Mexico)

Objectives & reminders

Appointments

Early morning

8 a.m.

9 a.m.

10 a.m.

11 a.m.

Noon

1 p.m.

2 p.m.

3 p.m.

4 p.m.

5 p.m.

6 p.m.

Later evening

Bonus challenge: Ansoff-flavored Jell-O?
Using Ansoff's Matrix, categorize Jell-O's brand extension strategy described on December 11. Then evaluate the appropriateness of the strategy using Ansoff's guidelines.

Happy 100th birthday: Igor Ansoff

Born in Vladivostok, Russia on December 12, 1918, Ansoff enjoyed a career as an engineer, mathematician and military strategist. In 1965 he established himself as a pioneer in business strategy with the publication of his first of six strategic management books, *Corporate Strategy*. Perhaps the most well-known contribution of *Corporate Strategy* is known as Ansoff's Matrix (or Ansoff's Grid) – his conceptualization of business development options, consisting of four strategic alternatives.

Market development (existing products, new customers)	***Diversification*** (new products, new customers)
Market penetration (existing products, existing customers)	***Product development*** (new products, existing customers)

Market penetration. In the short run, the least risky approach to business development is pitching existing products to existing customers. Tactics such as increasing advertising expenditures or the size of the sales force, or offering quantity discounts are typical of marketing efforts encountered here.

Product development involves new products developed for existing customers. This strategy works well for firms skilled at developing and introducing new products -- if they have loyal customers willing to try the new items. But, new product flops can jeopardize a firm's reputation and dilute the potency of the original brand.

Selling existing products to new markets – *market development* – makes sense when markets are fairly homogeneous and have similar product requirements, when few entrenched competitors exist, or if marketing economies of scale are likely.

Finally, *diversification* involves new products for new markets and is the most risky strategic option. The company's lack of experience with either the new products or the new markets are enormous risks when neither the products nor markets are new to entrenched competitors. However, diversification might make sense if competition is weak, if the new markets are similar in important ways to markets currently served, or if the new products capitalize on the firm's existing competencies.

December 13, 2018
Thursday
National Guard Birthday

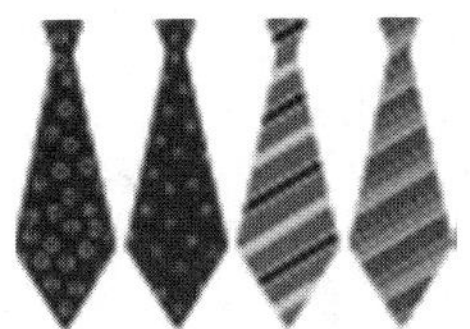

Objectives & reminders

____

____

____

Appointments

Early morning

8 a.m.

9 a.m.

10 a.m.

11 a.m.

Noon

1 p.m.

2 p.m.

3 p.m.

4 p.m.

5 p.m.

6 p.m.

Later evening

Convenience trend continues

The consumer convenience cause scored another victory on December 13, 1928, when the clip-on tie was designed. Although the innovation was never universally embraced, it did find a viable market segment.

Today, competitive businesses routinely seek ways to build convenience into their products and services as a means of differentiating their offerings and giving buyers more value. Convenience may involve the actual *use* of products (e.g., clip-on ties), their *preparation* (e.g., instant pudding), their *maintenance* (e.g., self-cleaning ovens), their *acquisition* (e.g., drive-thru windows), or their *disposal* (e.g., conveniently-located trash cans).

As consumers' lifestyles become increasingly harried, many consumers are willing to spend more money for products that promise and deliver additional convenience – in effect, trading money for time.

Tips for aspiring executives

Born near Dayton, Ohio on December 13, 1844, John Henry Patterson was a noteworthy businessperson. He founded the National Cash Register Company (NCR) where he continually trained, coached and otherwise influenced thousands of executives. Here's a small sampling of Patterson's professional development insights for executives:

1. *What's the objective?:* "You must make a habit of thinking in terms of a defined objective."

2. *Be prepared to make a decision:* "An executive is a man who decides; sometimes he decides right, but always he decides."

3. *Don't be stubborn:* "Only fools and dead men don't change their minds. Fools won't. Dead men can't."

4. *Management is a full time job:* "Leaving business at the office sounds like a good rule, but it is one that can easily be carried too far... Dismissing business after office hours has a nice sound, but I have found that often the business does not come back after the recess!"

December 14, 2018
Friday
Alabama Day (Alabama)

Objectives & reminders

Appointments

Early morning

---

8 a.m.

---

9 a.m.

---

10 a.m.

---

11 a.m.

Noon

---

1 p.m.

---

2 p.m.

---

3 p.m.

---

4 p.m.

---

5 p.m.

---

6 p.m.

Later evening

Ann & Andy for Christmas

Toy shoppers on December 14, 1914, were the first to buy what would become one of the most popular toys of all time -- Raggedy Ann dolls, first trademarked by Johnny Gruelle.

Within four years, Gruelle wrote and illustrated a book of children's stories about the yarn-haired, button-eyed dolls to help spur sales. Other books followed. Today, both the dolls and copies of the original book, *Raggedy Ann Stories* (1918) are collectors' items.

Learn more about it

Today, Raggedy Ann and Raggedy Andy collectors can learn more about the dolls, books, and related merchandise by visiting the Raggedy Ann & Andy Museum in Arcola, Illinois – the birthplace of Johnny Gruelle (1880). Further capitalizing on the popularity of the dolls, the small town hosts an annual Raggedy Ann & Andy Festival in mid-May.

Raggedy Ann's little brother – Raggedy Andy – wasn't "born" until 1920, and unfortunately for Raggedy Andy marketers, Raggedy Ann dolls sold circles around Raggedy Andy dolls. In fact, very few male dolls targeted to boys sold well until 1964 when Hasbro introduced G.I. Joe – the 12-inch military-themed doll line.

Perhaps the key to G.I. Joe's success was the fact that Hasbro did not refer to him as a "doll." Instead, G.I. Joe was the beginning of a new category for boys – aptly dubbed "action figures."

Imitation pearls of wisdom?

Recognizing the shortage of natural pearls, a French rosary-bead maker named Jacquin first made imitation pearls on December 14, 1656, by coating the inside of hollow glass beads with a substance made from fish scales.

Today, as shortages of the "real thing" in numerous product categories (pearls, diamonds, furs, precious metals, artwork) drive prices up, innovative yet imitative businesses frequently find markets for less expensive imitations or substitutes among less-than-affluent consumers.

December 15, 2018
Saturday

Bill of Rights Day

(read the presidential proclamation at www.presidency.ucsb.edu/ws/?pid=16046)

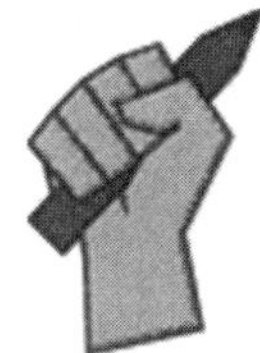

Objectives & reminders

____

____

Appointments

Early morning

8 a.m.

9 a.m.

10 a.m.

11 a.m.

Noon

1 p.m.

2 p.m.

3 p.m.

4 p.m.

5 p.m.

6 p.m.

Later evening

First Amendment to the U.S. Constitution

Ratified on December 15, 1791, the First Amendment prohibits Congress from enacting laws that infringe on a series of individual liberties – such as the freedom of religion, the freedom of the press, the right to peaceably assemble, the right to complain to the government and the freedom of speech.

Among these civil liberties, perhaps free speech has stirred the most debate during the last 80 years. Interestingly, "free speech" issues were not particularly challenged until the 20th century when multiple interpretations and applications of the concept surfaced with regard to war protests, arguably unpatriotic remarks, obscenity and pornography, libel and slander, memoirs of serial killers, and even flag-burning.

Perhaps the most recent interpretation of "free speech" is the marketing perspective offered by sales consultant, speaker and writer Jeffrey Gitomer. That is, in his book, *Little Red Book of Selling*, Gitomer suggests that salespeople should use free speeches to market themselves. He advises:

> "The best way to market yourself is give yourself to the market. Expose yourself to your prospects. My advice: Free speech. Or to put it a clearer way – speak for free. Free speech pays. Big pay. And free speech has rewards. Big rewards. NOTE WELL: I said 'speech' not 'sales pitch.'" (p. 68)

Gitomer goes on to list what he believes to be the key benefits of delivering free 15-20 minute speeches to civic organizations: e.g., the opportunity for sales reps to sell themselves, build their networks, help their communities, build their speaking and presentation skills, gain exposure to potential new customers, and establish or reestablish their presence, among other benefits.

Free speech tip

"Hang around after the meeting. That's when you find out what your impact was and who your best prospects are." – Jeffrey Gitomer, *Little Red Book of Selling* (p. 70)

December 16, 2018
Sunday
National Day (Bahrain)

Objectives & reminders

____

____

____

Appointments

Early morning

8 a.m.

9 a.m.

10 a.m.

11 a.m.

Noon

1 p.m.

2 p.m.

3 p.m.

4 p.m.

5 p.m.

6 p.m.

Later evening

Happy birthday: Margaret Mead

Born in Philadelphia, Pennsylvania on December 16, 1901, Mead was a cultural anthropologist whose research on a variety of issues such as gender roles, adolescence, personality, and child rearing, among others, demonstrated the profound effect that one's culture has on behavior.

Mead's work, along with that of other cultural anthropologists, has helped marketers to realize that a full understanding of a buyer's behavior requires an understanding of the cultural context from which the buyer emerged.

We are what we learn

"Our humanity rests upon a series of learned behaviors, woven together into patterns that are infinitely fragile and never directly inherited." -- Margaret Mead

Time travel

To understand consumers, study the period during which they came of age. "All of us who grew up before World War II are immigrants in time, immigrants from an earlier world, living in an age essentially different from anything we knew before." -- Margaret Mead

---

APA ban lifted

A much-debated ruling was made by the U.S. Federal Trade Commission (FTC) on December 16, 1992. The FTC ordered the American Psychological Association (APA) to stop enforcing parts of its Ethical Principles of Psychologists dealing with advertising. Previously, the APA's code of ethics had prohibited advertising (even if truthful) that compared or differentiated services, appealed to fears or other emotions, or included personal testimonials. The FTC order was finalized later that month.

Invitation to debate

- Was the APA's ban defensible?
- Was the FTC's order to lift the ban justifiable?

December 17, 2018
Monday
Wright Brothers Day

Objectives & reminders

Appointments

Early morning

8 a.m.

9 a.m.

10 a.m.

11 a.m.

Noon

1 p.m.

2 p.m.

3 p.m.

4 p.m.

5 p.m.

6 p.m.

Later evening

Christmas lights

Hanging lights on Christmas trees has been a tradition for a number of years. Today, electric lights have replaced candles in most homes. Electric lights for Christmas trees were first advertised in December 1901, in the *Ladies' Home Journal.* Not surprisingly, they were produced by inventor Thomas A. Edison's company, the Edison General Electric Co. of Harrison, New Jersey.

Happy birthday: Kerry F.B. Packer

Born in Sydney, Australia on December 17, 1937, Packer was a major shareholder in the Australian conglomerate Publishing and Broadcasting Ltd., which owns newspapers, magazines, television stations, Internet interests, and other businesses. Packer also had interests in casinos and a ski resort. With a net worth once estimated at US$4.2 billion, Packer was believed to be the richest person in Australia and one of the wealthiest people in the world. In addition to his wealth and media influence, Packer's sometimes "volcanic temper" and poor health (including eight heart attacks and a kidney transplant) are also noteworthy.

Change happens
"The fact that I have entered into IT-related business is proof that businesses have to evolve and keep with time. One has to re-invent continuously." -- Kerry Packer

---

19th century Fear Factor

Poet and newspaper editor John Greenleaf Whittier was born in Haverhill, Massachusetts on December 17, 1807. He observed that some degree of risk-taking always accompanies success -- in business and in life -- yet he frequently observed people's reluctance to set aside their fears and risk failure. "Who never climbs..." he observed, "rarely falls."

Why wait?
"For all sad words of tongue and pen, the saddest are those, 'It might have been.'" -- John Greenleaf Whittier

December 18, 2018
Tuesday
Free Shipping Day

Objectives & reminders

____

____

____

Appointments

Early morning

8 a.m.

9 a.m.

10 a.m.

11 a.m.

Noon

1 p.m.

2 p.m.

3 p.m.

4 p.m.

5 p.m.

6 p.m.

Later evening

General Motors struggles

Coupled with the trend toward increasingly smaller and well-defined market segments, GM also faced an economic recession and increased global competition in 1991. Accordingly, on December 18 of that year GM announced plans to shut down 21 plants over a four-year period -- a move that would cost 74,000 workers their jobs. In January 2006, General Motors announced another round of plant closings and layoffs.

Too general: Agree or disagree?
In an age of market segmentation, *General* Motors' targeted market segments are too "*general*."

Recognizing that General Motors wasn't the only American company to experience a significant erosion of competitiveness over the previous two decades, early in 2006 President George W. Bush unveiled his vision for strengthening the competitiveness of American businesses. His proposal called for billions of additional dollars to be invested in science and technology initiatives.

Turning point in American history

The 13th Amendment was formally added to the U.S. Constitution on December 18, 1865, after the last of the required three-fourths of the states had ratified the amendment earlier in the month. The amendment abolished slavery in the United States, 246 years after the first ship with slaves imported from Africa landed at Jamestown, Virginia.

13th Amendment
"Neither slavery nor involuntary servitude, save as a punishment for crime whereof the party shall have been duly convicted, shall exist within the United States, or any place subject to their jurisdiction."

Almost three years before the 13th Amendment was adopted, President Abraham Lincoln had issued the Emancipation Proclamation during the Civil War, but concerns that the Proclamation might not be enforceable after the war prompted Congress to propose the 13th Amendment.

December 19, 2018
Wednesday
National Hard Candy Day

Objectives & reminders

____

____

____

Appointments

Early morning

8 a.m.

9 a.m.

10 a.m.

11 a.m.

Noon

1 p.m.

2 p.m.

3 p.m.

4 p.m.

5 p.m.

6 p.m.

Later evening

Advertising spills and spillovers

Of the millions of slogans and campaign lines that advertisers generate annually, only a small percentage are remembered after the campaign ends. Even fewer spill into the culture's popular usage. However, if "we try harder" (Avis rental cars) we can "absolutely, positively" (Federal Express) recall some examples from the latter category. If not, "just do it" (Nike) anyway, but "don't leave home without it" (American Express). If "they're GREAT" (Kellogg's Frosted Flakes) we may remember and use them for years; otherwise we may find ourselves asking, "Where's the beef?" (Wendy's hamburgers).

Unfortunately, not all well-known advertising slogans and lines that spill into everyday conversations are clearly associated with the sponsoring company, product or brand.

Memorable line,
but who's the sponsor?

This famous advertising line was first broadcast on December 19, 1985, and continues to be used: "I've fallen and I can't get up."

Happy birthday: Alan N. Cohen

Born in Passaic, New Jersey on December 19, 1930, Cohen is a familiar name to sports enthusiasts in the northeastern United States. His illustrious career included the roles he played as the chairman and CEO of the Madison Square Garden Corporation, owner of the New York Knicks and New York Rangers. Also, he was co-owner of the New Jersey Nets and the Boston Celtics.

One of Cohen's marketing innovations was to increase the number of advertisements that could be prominently displayed during NBA basketball games. He did this with revolving court-side ads that could be displayed for a few moments before transitioning to other ads. The technique increased the number of ads that could be displayed during a game, thus substantially enhancing ad revenues. Today, the technique is associated with a variety of spectator sporting events in a number of sports stadiums and arenas around the world.

December 20, 2018
Thursday
International Human Solidarity Day

Objectives & reminders

Appointments

Early morning

8 a.m.

9 a.m.

10 a.m.

11 a.m.

Noon

1 p.m.

2 p.m.

3 p.m.

4 p.m.

5 p.m.

6 p.m.

Later evening

It's a Wonderful Life

The Christmas-time classic produced and directed by Frank Capra was released on December 20, 1946. The inspirational film tells of George Bailey (played by James Stewart) who responded to a personal financial crisis by contemplating suicide on Christmas Eve. In Bailey's hour of need, his guardian angel interceded and showed him the positive impact his life has had on others. The angel showed Bailey the negative direction the community would have taken and how many people would have suffered if it had not been for Bailey's good works. Until then Bailey had failed to recognize the contributions he had made.

In his book, *Hardwiring Excellence*, Quint Studer suggests that business leaders can benefit from the lessons derived from *It's a Wonderful Life*. That is, workers may not understand the impact of their contributions on the job – how valuable and important their work is, and how it directly or indirectly affects the lives of customers and co-workers. They may feel discouraged, or even despondent. But all of this can change when someone (and not necessarily a guardian angel) takes the time to point out that their work is worthwhile and has purpose.

What employees want

"They want to believe the organization has the right purpose… that their job is worthwhile, [and] they want to make a difference."
– Quint Studer, *Hardwiring Excellence* (p. 141)

It's *another* wonderful life

Although George Bailey was a fictional character, Morrie Schwartz wasn't. Born in New York City on December 20, 1916, Schwartz was a beloved sociology professor at Brandeis University who touched the lives of thousands of students, including author Mitch Albom whose inspirational conversations with Dr. Schwartz formed the basis of his 1997 best-seller, *Tuesdays With Morrie*. Schwartz understood what Bailey eventually realized:

> "The way you get meaning into your life is to devote yourself to loving others… to your community around you, and… to creating something that gives you purpose and meaning." – Morrie Schwartz

December 21, 2018
Friday

December Solstice
Blue Christmas

Objectives & reminders

Appointments

Early morning

8 a.m.

9 a.m.

10 a.m.

11 a.m.

Noon

1 p.m.

2 p.m.

3 p.m.

4 p.m.

5 p.m. *Solstice: 5:23 p.m. EST*

6 p.m.

Later evening

Winter solstice

Fall gives way to winter today in the Northern Hemisphere, marked by the winter solstice -- a point during the year when the sun is farthest south from the Equator, making today the shortest day of the year in terms of the number of daylight hours. Although winter officially begins with the solstice, the occasion is generally recognized on the following day – tomorrow – the first *full* day of winter. But, note that in the Southern Hemisphere, the seasons are reversed; summer begins.

Flash(light) of marketing insight
James Morgan, of Cuyahoga Falls, Ohio has declared today to be National Flashlight Day. His rationale: People are more likely to need flashlights on the longest night of the year than at any other time. With free publicity generated for the beginning of winter, why not piggyback on the winter solstice to promote the sale and use of flashlights? What other products, services or organizations could capitalize on the seasonal change?

Arrival of winter accompanied by arrival of counter-seasonal marketing

We know that marketing efforts tend to be most effective when consumers are in the mood to buy – and those moods are often seasonal. Understandably, that's when demand tends to be high. Still, businesses try a variety of product modifications, advertising appeals, price discounts and other efforts to boost sluggish demand during the off season.

For soft drinks, not surprisingly, demand is high when people are most likely to be thirsty – during warm weather. The Coca-Cola Company realized this in the early 1920s, prior to launching an ad campaign to increase wintertime consumption. The print campaign (also discussed on June 28) showed snow skiers carrying bottles of Coke while skiing – implying that Coke-drinking is a natural wintertime behavior. More recently, the company's winter advertising has taught us that polar bears enjoy drinking Coke during the winter -- implying that *people* should do the same.

Attempts to lift lagging off-season sales can be dangerously expensive. Quite often there are compelling reasons for low demand during the off season, so limited marketing resources may be better spent boosting demand for in-season items instead.

December 22, 2018
Saturday

First *full* day of winter in the Northern Hemisphere
Final Saturday before Christmas
Mother's Day (Indonesia)

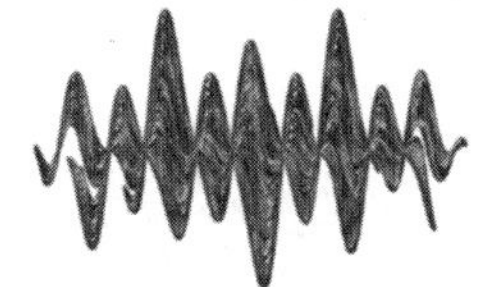

Objectives & reminders

____

____

____

Appointments

Early morning

8 a.m.

9 a.m.

10 a.m.

11 a.m.

Noon

1 p.m.

2 p.m.

3 p.m.

4 p.m.

5 p.m.

6 p.m.

Later evening

Is unplanned variability of services always undesirable? What's your opinion?

Unlike most modern-day manufactured goods, services often involve a human element in their production and delivery that introduces extra variability in the outputs. Accordingly, service outputs are likely to vary from location to location within a service organization, from employee to employee, and even from minute to minute for the same employee in the same location. In other words, customers who order the same service from the same company may not necessarily receive the same service.

Conventional wisdom suggests that variable service outputs play havoc with customers' expectations, and if customers don't know what to expect, they are more likely to be dissatisfied with the service they receive. That's why most service businesses try to eliminate as much unplanned variation as possible by training employees to follow detailed operation procedures and in many instances replacing variability-prone service workers with more consistent technology.

McDonald's is a prime example of a service firm whose success has been built, in part, on its consistency of service. A McDonald's Big Mac purchased in one location is pretty much identical to those purchased elsewhere.

It may be argued, however, that some degree of unplanned inconsistency is desirable, i.e., that the uncertainty of not knowing quite what to expect makes the service experience more exciting or more interesting for customers.

Spectator sporting events are prime examples; who wants to watch a perfectly scripted and choreographed game in which the outcome of every play and the final score are known in advance?

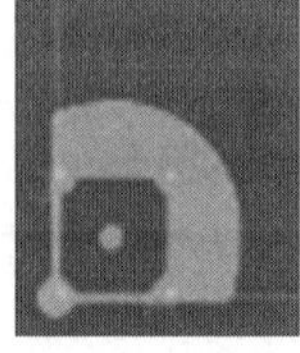

Perhaps Connie Mack, the legendary American baseball player, manager and owner, said it best when he commented on the appeal of baseball: "Any minute, any day, some players may break a long-standing record. That's one of the fascinations about the game – the unexpected surprises." Mack was born in Brookfield, Massachusetts on December 22, 1862.

December 23, 2018
Sunday
Festivus

Objectives & reminders

____

____

____

Appointments

Early morning

8 a.m.

9 a.m.

10 a.m.

11 a.m.

Noon

1 p.m.

2 p.m.

3 p.m.

4 p.m.

5 p.m.

6 p.m.

Later evening

Published one night too early?

On December 23, 1823, the *Troy Sentinel* first published Clement Clarke Moore's classic poem, *A Visit From St. Nicolas.*

Today, the poem and its theme is frequently reprinted on promotional literature and other items. For example, restaurants include the poem on disposable holiday placemats and in children's activity booklets. The poem is now in the *public domain*, meaning that the copyright has expired, so the poem can be reprinted without seeking the copyright-holder's permission.

Excerpts from
A Visit From St. Nicolas
"Twas the night before Christmas,
when all through the house
Not a creature was stirring,
not even a mouse:
The stockings were hung by
the chimney with care,
In hopes that St. Nicholas
soon would be there."
-- Clement C. Moore

Commercial version?
"Twas two days before Christmas
and all through the mall.
Not a retailer was sleeping,
not one at all.
The leotards were hung by the
chimney display,
With hopes that shoppers
would grab them and pay."
-- Cal Marbleous

Success keys:
Apply yourself and be persistent

"I have succeeded in business not because I have more natural ability than those who have not succeeded, but because I have applied myself harder and stuck to it longer. I know plenty of people who have failed to succeed in anything who have more brains than I had, but they lacked application and determination."– James Buchanan Duke, pioneer in the cigarette market and founder of the American Tobacco Company, born in New York City on December 23, 1856

December 24, 2018
Monday
Christmas Eve

Objectives & reminders

____

____

____

Appointments

Early morning

8 a.m.

9 a.m.

10 a.m.

11 a.m.

Noon

1 p.m.

2 p.m.

3 p.m.

4 p.m.

5 p.m.

6 p.m.

Later evening

Santa mystery solved

What child hasn't contemplated the logistical problems that Santa faces on Christmas Eve? They ask, "How is it that Santa has enough time in a single night to visit the homes of all the children in the world?" One parental response, of course, is that there are several Santas or several helpers, each assigned to their own territory.

On December 24, 1978, the "how many Santas" mystery was solved when 3,000 Santas were identified. The Santas worked for Polaroid as part of a consumer promotion – delivering Polaroid's instant-movie systems to the homes of purchasers.

Non-Santa mysteries

Speaking of mysteries, best-selling mystery writer Mary Higgins Clark, who was born in Bronx, New York on December 24, 1927, began her career in advertising. Before finishing her studies at Fordham University, she worked as an advertising assistant at Remington Rand (later Sperry Rand).

Happy birthday: Howard Robard Hughes, Jr.

Born in Humble, Texas on December 24, 1905, Hughes was goal-oriented throughout his life. As a teen, he aspired someday to be the world's best golfer, best movie producer and best pilot. Although he did not realize all of his goals, he wasted little time pursuing them, especially those involving business. The entrepreneur began making movies, formed the Caddo Rock Drill Bit Company, and launched Hughes Aircraft -- all while still in his 20s. By his mid-30s, Howard Hughes had become the majority shareholder in Transcontinental & West Airline (TWA). He went on to amass a net worth in excess of one billion dollars.

Hughes the deal-maker

Howard Hughes had the reputation of being a shrewd negotiator. He usually got what he wanted. According to Hughes, "Once you consent to some concession, you can never cancel it and put things back the way they are."

December 25, 2018
Tuesday
Christmas Day

Have a marbleous holiday?

Objectives & reminders

Appointments

Early morning

8 a.m.

9 a.m.

10 a.m.

11 a.m.

Noon

1 p.m.

2 p.m.

3 p.m.

4 p.m.

5 p.m.

6 p.m.

Later evening

Political correctness run amok?

"Merry Christmas" was once an integral part of American retailers' December communications -- expressed verbally by cashiers and sales clerks as well as printed on promotional literature, shopping bags, store signage, displays and even product packages.

Today, many retailers fear offending the four percent of consumers who choose not to celebrate Christmas, so they substitute more ambiguous gestures for "Merry Christmas," such as "Season's greetings," "Happy holidays," and "Merry winter." In some instances, company policies go so far (too far?) as to *prohibit* employees from wishing customers a "Merry Christmas."

Seasonal tolerance: Agree or disagree?

"[N]one of us is entitled to be wished a 'happy' or 'merry' anything by anybody. We should appreciate that people are kind enough to wish us well. Hearing 'Happy Holidays' from someone does not infringe on one's ability to have a 'Merry Christmas.' Nor does it negate, deny or oppress one's personal religious beliefs. I can't understand why some individuals are so vehemently opposed to the issue of a generic holiday greeting..."

"We Americans [should be more tolerant]. This tolerance includes not becoming irate when someone wishes you a 'Happy Holiday' and not insisting everyone wish you a 'Merry Christmas.' It also includes not becoming irate when someone wishes you a 'Merry Christmas' and not insisting everyone wish you a 'Happy Holiday.' The sentiment behind the words is more important than the words themselves." -- Jennifer Markle, York, Pennsylvania

In terms of shopping bags, product packages, store signage and displays, there is some logic for using a wintery gesture or theme (such as snowflakes, a horse-drawn sleigh, or a snow-covered cabin in the woods) instead of those more clearly associated with Christmas (e.g., Christmas trees or Santas). That is, winter themes may be used after the Christmas holiday passes, but "Christmas merchandise" is likely to lose its sales appeal immediately after Christmas. Likewise, Christmas-themed shopping bags, store signage and displays quickly become obsolete after Christmas.

December 26, 2018
Wednesday

Kwanzaa begins

Boxing Day

Objectives & reminders

____

____

____

Appointments

Early morning

8 a.m.

9 a.m.

10 a.m.

11 a.m.

Noon

1 p.m.

2 p.m.

3 p.m.

4 p.m.

5 p.m.

6 p.m.

Later evening

"Second" Christmas season begins

Retailers aren't allowed to rest just because Christmas is behind them. After-Christmas sales, gift returns and exchanges, and redemption of gift cards earmark the next several days. In fact, about 10-15 percent of total holiday retail sales are generated the week following Christmas.

In particular, retailers will be extra busy today in the six states that observe the day as a state holiday -- Kansas, Kentucky, North Carolina, New Hampshire, South Carolina and Texas.

Kwanzaa begins

Held for the first time in Los Angeles on December 26, 1966, Kwanzaa was inspired by African harvest festivals. Today, the seven-day non-religious observance still begins on December 26 and celebrates the African-American family, culture and community.

Boxing Day

Boxing Day is celebrated throughout Great Britain, Canada, Australia, and New Zealand on December 26 each year, except when December 26 falls on a Saturday or Sunday, in which case the holiday is observed on the following Monday or Tuesday.

Why not?

Regardless of whether Boxing Day is traditionally recognized in your community, why not express your appreciation for the service providers that serve you, your company, or your community? Go boxing today!

The holiday is used to recognize and thank public service workers who have made our life easier throughout the year -- mail carriers, garbage collectors, school crossing guards, package delivery personnel, and so on. According to the tradition which began more than 800 years ago, small gifts are "boxed" and given to these people as post-Christmas gifts.

Today, gifts may include money as well as small gifts. Government offices, banks and many businesses may be closed for Boxing Day in the countries that celebrate the holiday.

December 27, 2018
Thursday
Third Day of the 12 Days of Christmas

Objectives & reminders

Appointments

Early morning

8 a.m.

9 a.m.

10 a.m.

11 a.m.

Noon

1 p.m.

2 p.m.

3 p.m.

4 p.m.

5 p.m.

6 p.m.

Later evening

Gift card season

Although gift cards may not expire for five years, many gift card recipients flock to the stores to redeem their cards immediately after Christmas. So retailers must be prepared for a post-Christmas gift card rush.

Gift card statistics

- Gift cards account for as much as 25 percent of some retailers' holiday sales.
- 56 percent of surveyed U.S. adults said they had purchased one or more gift cards in the previous year. Almost half reported redeeming one themselves.
- 87 percent of respondents redeeming gift cards asserted that gift cards were easy to use.
- 59 percent of surveyed consumers said they would appreciate receiving a gift card (most requested holiday gift item).

An estimated $25.9 billion worth of gift cards were sold by U.S. retailers during the 2015 holiday season, but gift cards' true value to retailers is much greater than their face values imply.

First, because the cards are purchased in advance, they represent -- in effect -- interest-free loans to the retailers.

Second, 72 percent of gift card recipients spend more than the face value of the cards they redeem – an average of 20-38 percent more (estimates vary).

Third, because gift card recipients view the cards as "free money," they tend to be less price-sensitive when redeeming the cards. In other words, they are more willing to pay full price for merchandise, which means higher profit margins for retailers.

Fourth, card recipients who have not previously shopped in the store may be so positively impressed when they visit the store to redeem their cards that they become regular customers, which represents a future stream of revenue for the retailer.

Fifth, because gift cards allow recipients to do their own shopping, the merchandise they select is less likely to be returned, so the extra costs associated with returns are minimized.

December 28, 2018
Friday
Pledge of Allegiance Day

100%

Objectives & reminders

Appointments

Early morning

8 a.m.

9 a.m.

10 a.m.

11 a.m.

Noon

1 p.m.

2 p.m.

3 p.m.

4 p.m.

5 p.m.

6 p.m.

Later evening

Happy birthday: Adam Vinatieri

Born in Yankton, South Dakota on December 28, 1972, Vinatieri is a professional football player – formerly with the New England Patriots (1996-2005) and currently with the Indianapolis Colts.

Vinatieri has contributed to his teams' appearance in five Super Bowl games, leading to four Super Bowl victories. In his role as kicker, he has a reputation as a clutch performer who fails to let the pressure of a big game or play negatively affect him.

Every day is the Super Bowl

"You can't go out and expect to do well when the pressure is on if you don't put the pressure on yourself. That means in practice, in the off-season, or when nobody else is there.... In training, I always kick with my helmet on – and buckled... And every training kick matters, just like it's a game. There should be no difference in intensity."
– Adam Vinatieri

Fortune magazine studied Vinatieri's enviable record of success and grace under pressure with an eye toward providing insights to help businesspeople elevate their performance to Super Bowl caliber. While few of us can expect to be great kickers, per se, we can benefit by applying Vinatieri's insights (in the accompanying boxes) to our chosen careers.

Metrics matter

"I chart kicks all throughout the season. I may do 75 kicks a day in training, a lot of which are filmed and charted. The coach sits there with a stop watch to measure the 'get-off time,' which is from the time the ball is snapped to the time you kick it. If you're too fast, you're out of control. Too slow, the ball gets blocked.... If you're less than perfect, there's a reason for it. Your job is to find it." – Adam Vinatieri

Think "continuous improvement"

"Unless you go 100 percent on all your field goals... there's room for improvement." – Adam Vinatieri

December 29, 2018
Saturday

International Cello Day

Objectives & reminders

____

____

____

Appointments

Early morning

8 a.m.

9 a.m.

10 a.m.

11 a.m.

Noon

1 p.m.

2 p.m.

3 p.m.

4 p.m.

5 p.m.

6 p.m.

Later evening

December 29 in U.S. business legislative/legal history

1950

The Celler-Kefauver Anti-Merger Act was passed to strengthen and expand the previously passed landmark Clayton Anti-Trust Act. The new Act attempted to restrict the formation of monopolistic mergers and acquisitions that would threaten competition. Part of the Act banned corporations from monopolizing the equipment and property (including land) of other firms.

1970

The Williams-Steiger Occupational Safety and Health Act was passed, to go into effect the following April. The Act applied to businesses engaged in interstate commerce-related activities. The Act established within the Department of Labor the Occupational Safety and Health Administration (OSHA) – charged with the responsibility of developing and enforcing industrial safety standards to ensure a healthful work environment for workers. OSHA makes job-site inspections, requires detailed records of work-related deaths, injuries and illnesses, and can levy fines against employers for up to $1,000 per day for failure to correct safety violations in a timely manner.

1976

The Federal Reserve Board (FRB) ruled that firms granting credit to consumers could not use age, race/ethnicity, or religion as a basis for granting or withholding credit. Similarly, the FRB also banned firms from discriminating against credit applicants that were welfare recipients (Note: The FRB had previously ruled against the use of gender and marital status when making credit-granting decisions).

December 30, 2018
Sunday
Rizal Day (Philippines)

Objectives & reminders

____

____

____

Appointments

Early morning

8 a.m.

9 a.m.

10 a.m.

11 a.m.

Noon

1 p.m.

2 p.m.

3 p.m.

4 p.m.

5 p.m.

6 p.m.

Later evening

Happy birthday: Asa Griggs Candler

Born in Villa Rica, Georgia on December 30, 1851, Candler owned a drugstore early in his career, but his career changed rapidly after buying the coveted Coca-Cola formula from its inventor, John Pemberton, in the late 1880s. That initial $2,300 investment, followed by substantial investments in advertising at a rate of $50,000 per year, helped Coca-Cola to become a *national* beverage within a few years. After earning millions of dollars, and giving away millions to nonprofit organizations, Candler sold the business in 1919 for $25 million.

More than money
"I don't know a single day in my life when I have been moved by a desire to make money."
– Asa G. Candler, age 64

High cost of safety innovation

December 30, 1903, was a tragic day in the history of Chicago. That's when a fire raged through the Iroquois Theater and killed 571 people. Fewer people would have died, but the panicked crowd pushed against the inside-opening doors to prevent them from opening. A review of the tragedy led to the design of safer doors that open to the outside, a design concept still used today.

"Creative work" is an oxymoron: Agree or disagree?

"What we call creative work, ought not to be called work at all, because it isn't. I imagine that Thomas Edison [inventor with 1,093 patents] never did a day's work in his last fifty years." – Stephen B. Leacock, Canadian economist, humorist and writer, born in Swanmoor, England on December 30, 1869

Good company for decision-making

"I keep six honest serving men. They taught me all I know. Their names are What and Why and When and How and Where and Who." – Rudyard Kipling, novelist, poet, journalist, and Nobel Prize winner, born in Bombay, India on December 30, 1865

December 31, 2018
Monday
New Year's Eve

Objectives & reminders

____

____

____

Appointments

Early morning

8 a.m.

9 a.m.

10 a.m.

11 a.m.

Noon

1 p.m.

2 p.m.

3 p.m.

4 p.m.

5 p.m.

6 p.m.

Later evening

New Year's Eve: One last holiday in three states

Although widely celebrated, New Year's Eve is not a holiday everywhere. But it is a state holiday in Louisiana, Michigan and Wisconsin.

Year-end celebrations

December 31 is usually associated with parties and celebrations to usher in the New Year, but why not celebrate the organization's achievements for the year, especially record-breaking achievements. That's what General Motors did on the last day of 1955 when they announced earnings for the year of almost $1.2 billion -- making it the first U.S. firm to surpass the billion-dollar mark in a single year.

Are you looking?

If you can't find something to celebrate, you're not looking hard enough. Consider: Company performance for the year (revenues, earnings, number of new customers, number of new locations, technological innovations, etc.), or milestones in the company's history (e.g., one-millionth customer served, one-billionth item shipped).

Alternatively, consider celebrating milestones attained by star stores or departments. Or, what about individual performers -- sales reps who sold record amounts or heroic customer service reps that saved accounts by going beyond the call of duty? Still other possibilities are awards or recognition for the best cost-saving suggestions offered by employees this year. *Remember, there's always something to celebrate.*

Last chance deductions

Tax-payers in the United States who itemize their tax deductions may be able to reduce their taxes for the year by donating money or goods to qualifying nonprofit organizations -- but only if they make their donations before the year ends. So, nonprofits that depend on charitable donations should think about reminding donors of the impending deadline. For those that accept donated goods, the time between Christmas Day and New Year's Day is a particularly good period to remain open a few extra hours to accept them.

Make sure to use the **super-detailed INDEX** that begins on the next page. With more than 11,000 entries there's a good chance that it will lead you to the pages within this year's edition of *Marketing FAME* that talk about the concept, topic, organization, brand, product category, industry, person, holiday, occasion, event, city, state or country that you're interested in.

Index

Numbers after each entry refer to the corresponding month and day of month on which information about the entry may be found. Examples: 1-23 refers to January 23, while 10-6 refers to October 6.

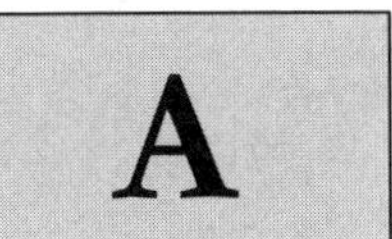

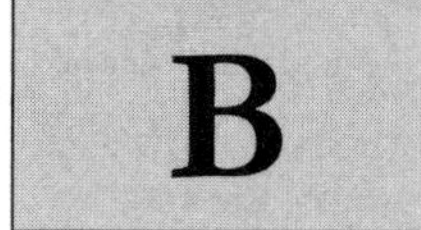

B

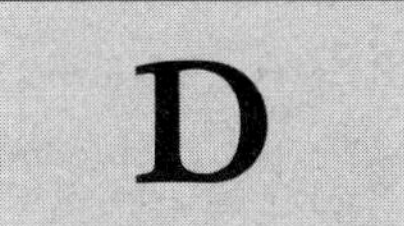
D

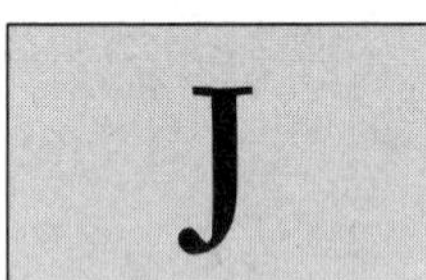

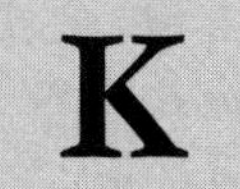

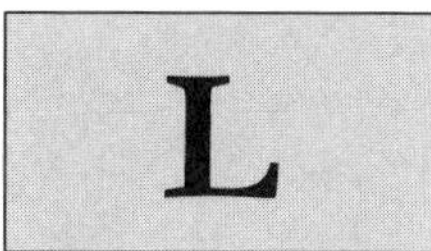

The "Big Apple"

O

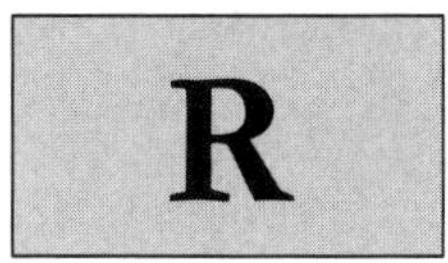

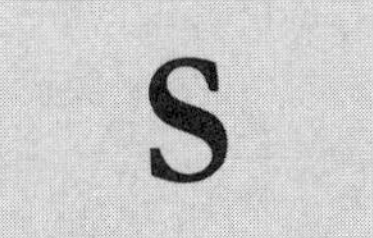

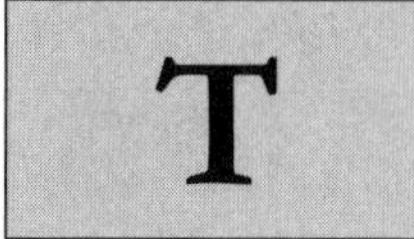
T

U

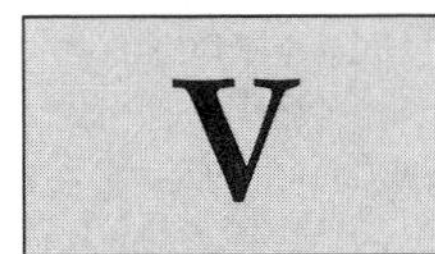

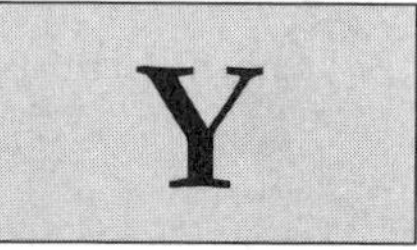

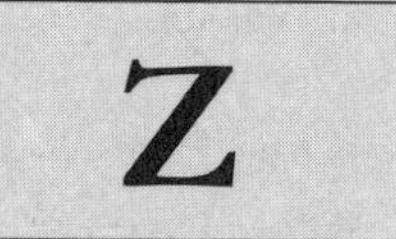

We gotta roll away for now, but thanks for a marbleous year. We're headed for 2019... hope to see you there !

We'll miss you !

As we say in marketing, buy now !

About the author: Charles L. Martin

Dr. Martin spent his youth in the northern suburbs of Atlanta, Georgia where he developed a love of tenpin bowling and began his business career in the bowling business before venturing to college as a collegiate bowler at Vincennes University (Vincennes, Indiana) and then to West Texas State University (now West Texas A&M, Canyon) where he earned a BBA in Marketing (1981) and an MBA (1982). He went on to earn a Ph.D. in Marketing at Texas A&M University (College Station).

In 1985, Dr. Martin joined the faculty at Wichita State University (WSU) in south central Kansas where he's taught a variety of both undergraduate and graduate courses. Today, Dr. Martin is the Full Professor of Marketing in WSU's W. Frank Barton School of Business.

Dr. Martin also served as the Marketing Editor of the world's leading trade and consumer publication for tenpin bowling, *Bowlers Journal International* (1990-2000), and as the Editor of an academic journal that focuses on the marketing-related challenges faced in the service sector, *The Journal of Services Marketing* (1990-2014). As a consultant, he's worked with numerous organizations such as the National Bowling Council, Bowling Proprietors' Association of America, American Bowling Congress, and several bowling-related companies.

Outside of the U.S., Dr. Martin gained valuable international experience as a visiting scholar and/or visiting editor at several universities throughout the world, including Comenius University (Bratislava, Slovakia), Sogang University (Seoul, Korea), University of Westminster (U.K.), University of Liverpool (U.K.), Manchester Business School (U.K.), Queensland University of Technology (Brisbane, Australia), and Bond and Griffith Universities (Gold Coast, Australia). Further, he has spoken as a keynote speaker at several international conferences in recent years, e.g., Lahore (Pakistan), Macau (China), Hong Kong (China), Kyrenia (Cyprus), Manchester (U.K.), and Calgary (Canada).

In addition to teaching, consulting, editing journals and visiting faraway lands, Dr. Martin is an active researcher and business writer as well. He's had more than 300 sole- or co-authored manuscripts published including dozens of professional journal articles and several books. His publications address a wide variety of topics pertaining to marketing management, services, consumer behavior, retailing, sports marketing and teamwork, among others.

Most recently, Professor Martin has pioneered research in the role that calendars play in shaping marketing practices and influencing buyer behavior – what he has dubbed as "calendar-led marketing" and "calendar-led buyer behavior." This research has contributed greatly to the development of the *Marketing FAME* book series and to several published and forthcoming journal articles regarding the interplay of calendars, marketing, and buyer behavior. If you'd like to learn more about these topics, see the discussion and the list of student-friendly articles on the sixth page of the "Welcome Students!" section, near the beginning of *Marketing FAME*. Some of these papers are posted in their entirety at www.MarketingMarbles.com -- *Marketing FAME*'s official website.

Dr. Martin expects to continue the *Marketing FAME* series with new editions published annually. Each year's content differs greatly from that of the previous year, so you'll never be bored reading the latest edition. So, in the spirit of improving future editions, please relay your questions and comments to Professor Martin. For example, tell him about your most or least favorite stories in this year's edition or suggest new stories for future editions. He may be reached through the series' website, www.MarketingMarbles.com or directly at WSU, Charles.Martin@wichita.edu

This page says "thank you for reading the 2018 edition of *Marketing FAME*" and that if you remember the promotion code "2019MARBLES" you could save a bundle on the 2019 edition.